D1032930

BATMAN: WHITE KNIGHT
PRESENTS

HARLEY QUINN

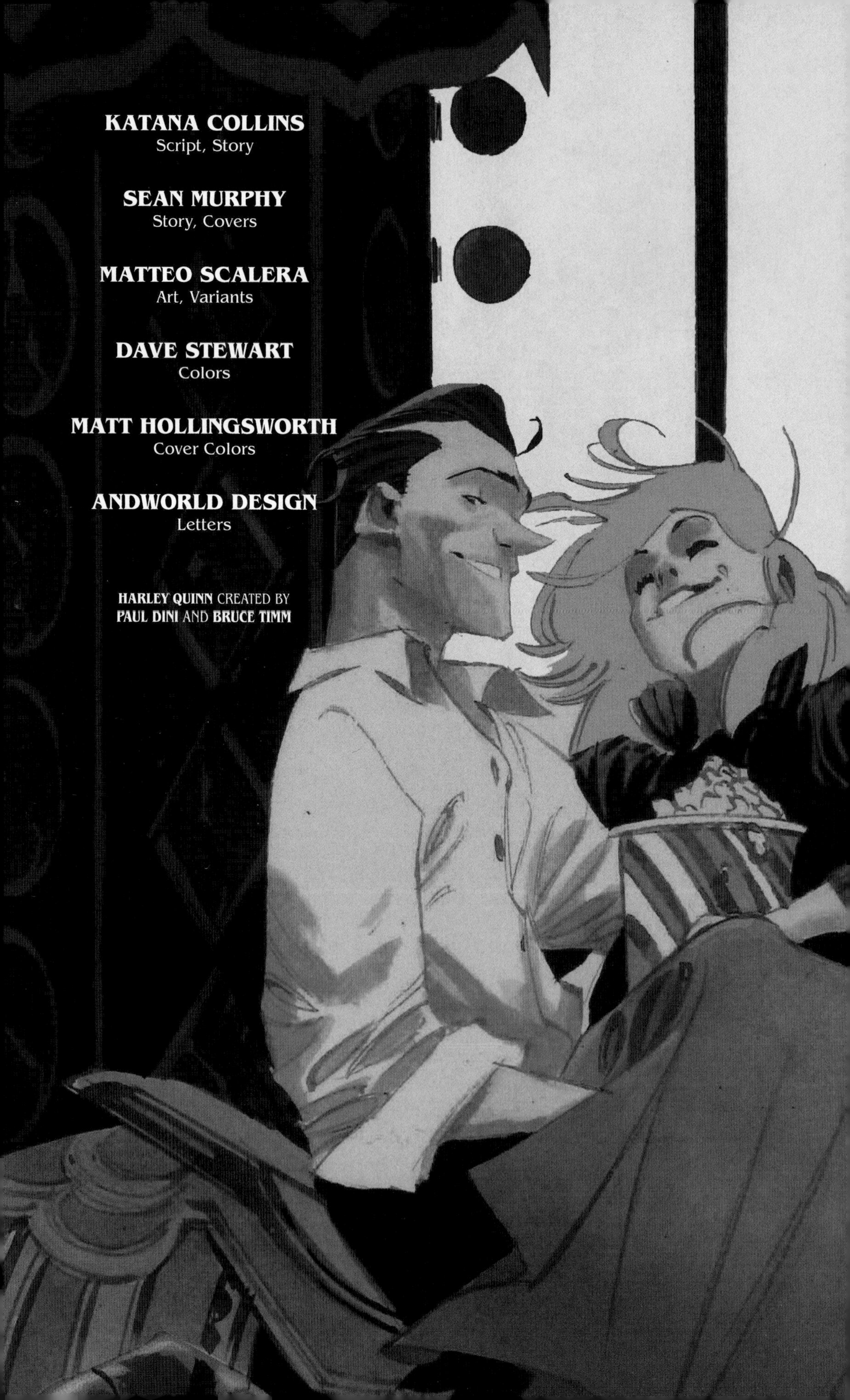

KATANA COLLINS
Script, Story

SEAN MURPHY
Story, Covers

MATTEO SCALERA
Art, Variants

DAVE STEWART
Colors

MATT HOLLINGSWORTH
Cover Colors

ANDWORLD DESIGN
Letters

HARLEY QUINN CREATED BY
PAUL DINI AND **BRUCE TIMM**

BATMAN: WHITE KNIGHT PRESENTS HARLEY QUINN

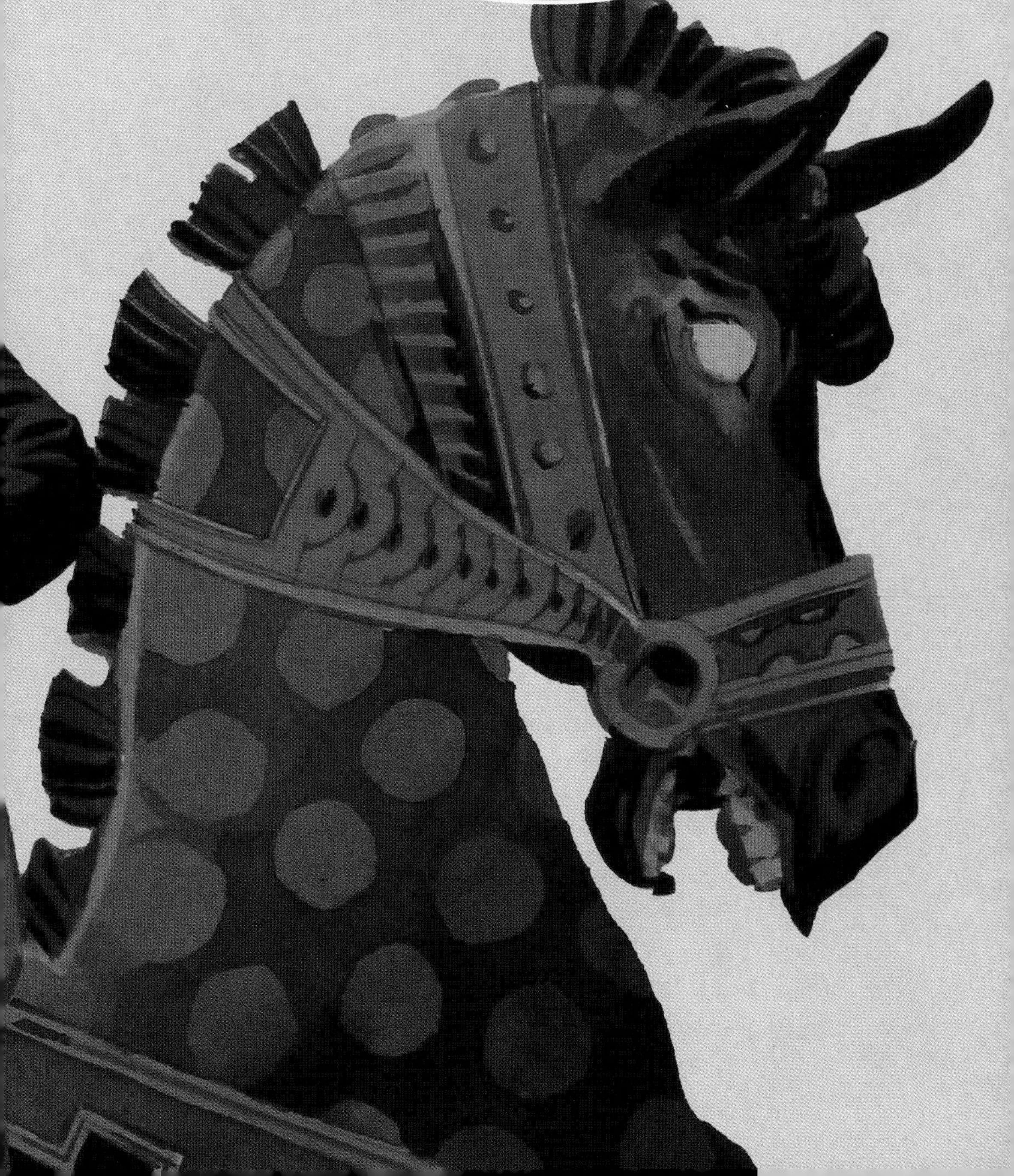

MAGGIE HOWELL
Editor – Original Series & Collected Edition

STEVE COOK
Design Director – Books

MEGEN BELLERSEN
Publication Design

CHRISTY SAWYER
Publication Production

MARIE JAVINS
Editor-in-Chief, DC Comics

DANIEL CHERRY III
Senior VP – General Manager

JIM LEE
Publisher & Chief Creative Officer

JOEN CHOE
VP – Global Brand & Creative Services

DON FALLETTI
VP – Manufacturing Operations & Workflow Management

LAWRENCE GANEM
VP – Talent Services

ALISON GILL
Senior VP – Manufacturing & Operations

NICK J. NAPOLITANO
VP – Manufacturing Administration & Design

NANCY SPEARS
VP – Revenue

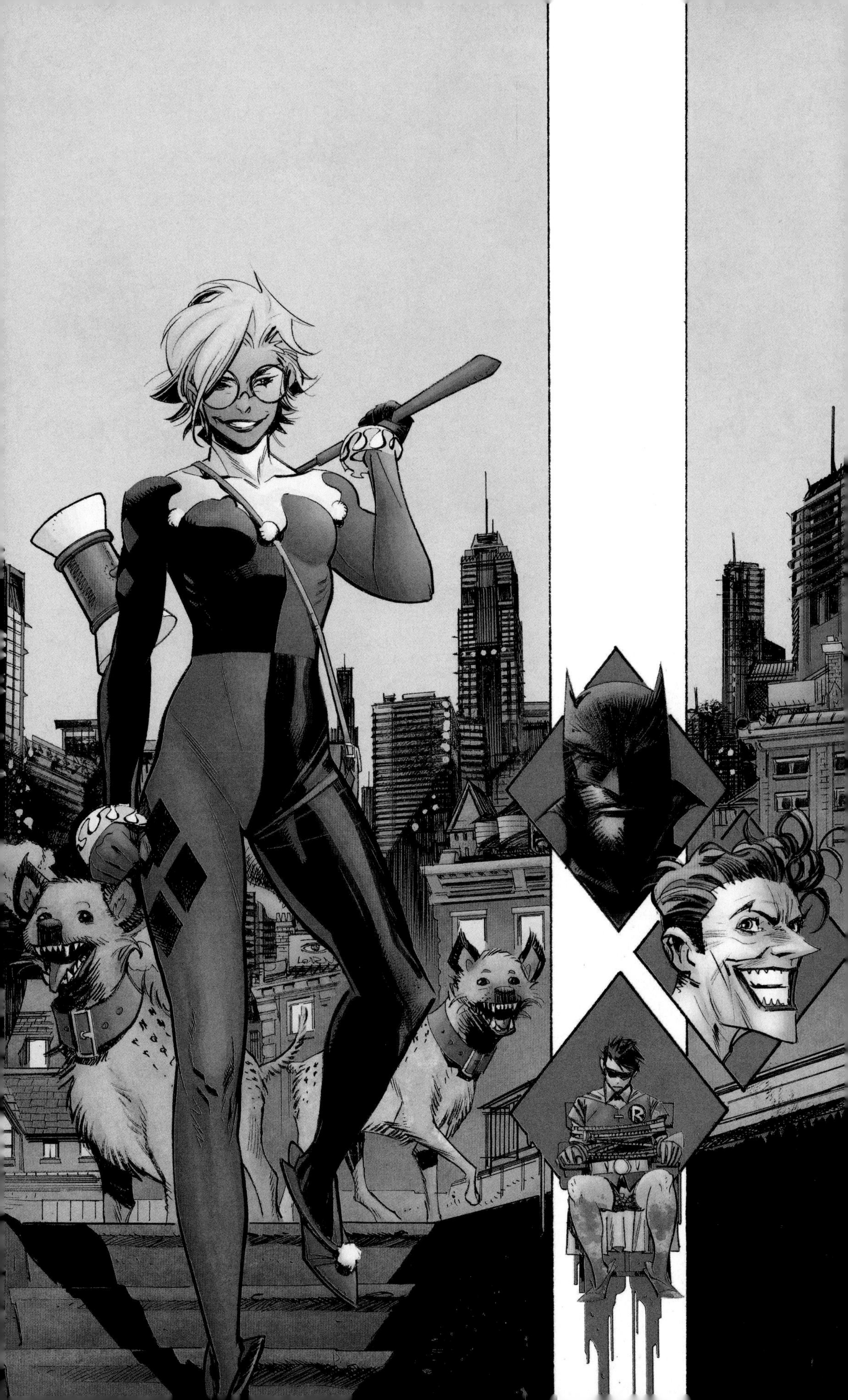

EVERYONE ALWAYS SAYS THAT THE JOKER RUINED ME.
THAT HE TURNED ME INTO A MONSTER.
THE TRUTH IS, I DIDN'T MEET HIM IN ARKHAM, LIKE EVERYONE THINKS. WE MET LONG BEFORE THEN, WHEN HE WAS JUST JACK NAPIER.
IT WAS JACK I MET. JACK I FELL IN LOVE WITH.
AND HE DIDN'T RUIN ME...
I RUINED HIM.
WITHOUT ME, THE JOKER WE KNOW MAY NEVER HAVE EXISTED.

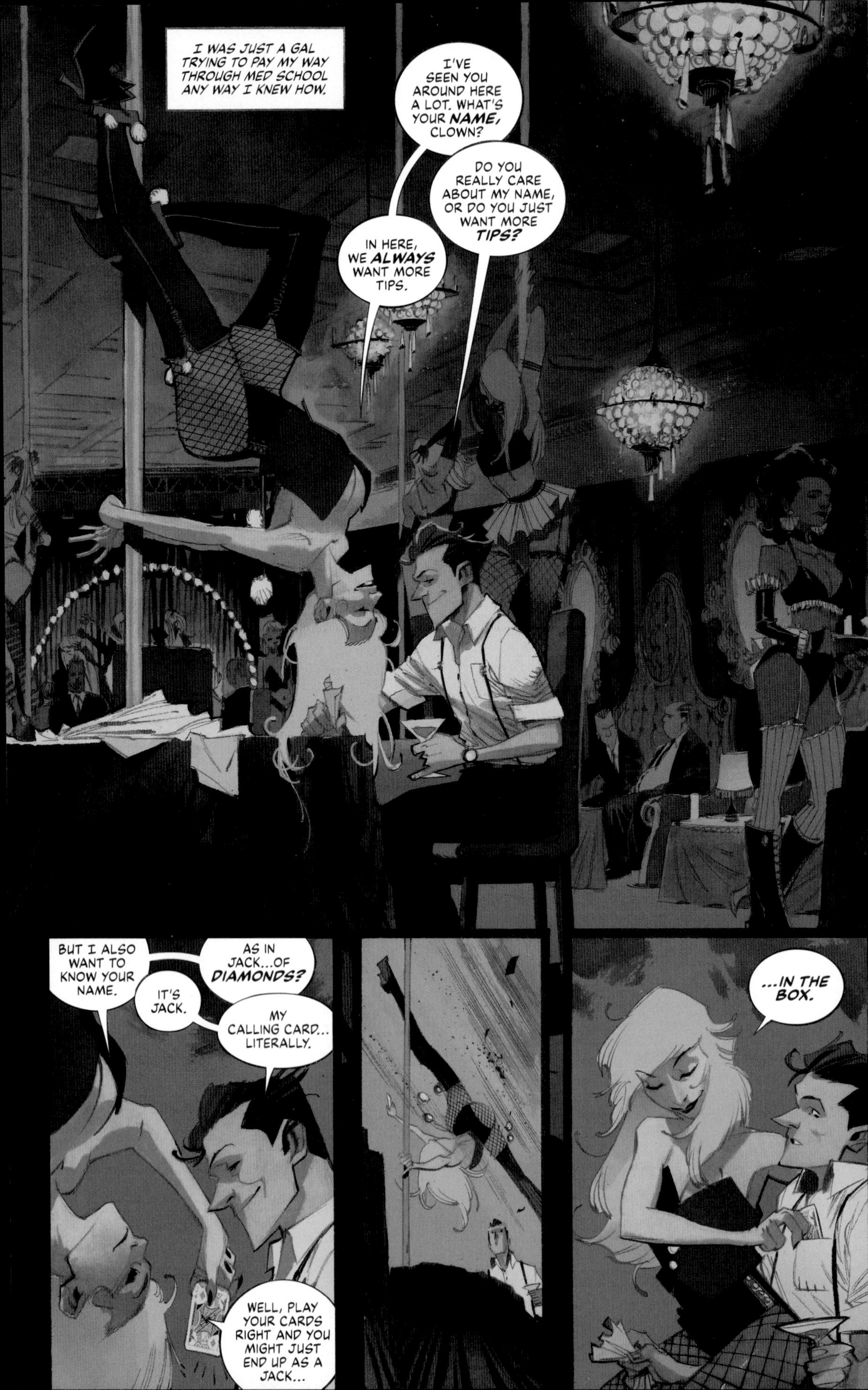

I WAS JUST A GAL TRYING TO PAY MY WAY THROUGH MED SCHOOL ANY WAY I KNEW HOW.
I'VE SEEN YOU AROUND HERE A LOT. WHAT'S YOUR **NAME,** CLOWN?
DO YOU REALLY CARE ABOUT MY NAME, OR DO YOU JUST WANT MORE **TIPS?**
IN HERE, WE **ALWAYS** WANT MORE TIPS.
BUT I ALSO WANT TO KNOW YOUR NAME.
IT'S JACK.
AS IN JACK...OF **DIAMONDS?**
MY CALLING CARD... LITERALLY.
WELL, PLAY YOUR CARDS RIGHT AND YOU MIGHT JUST END UP AS A JACK...
...IN THE BOX.

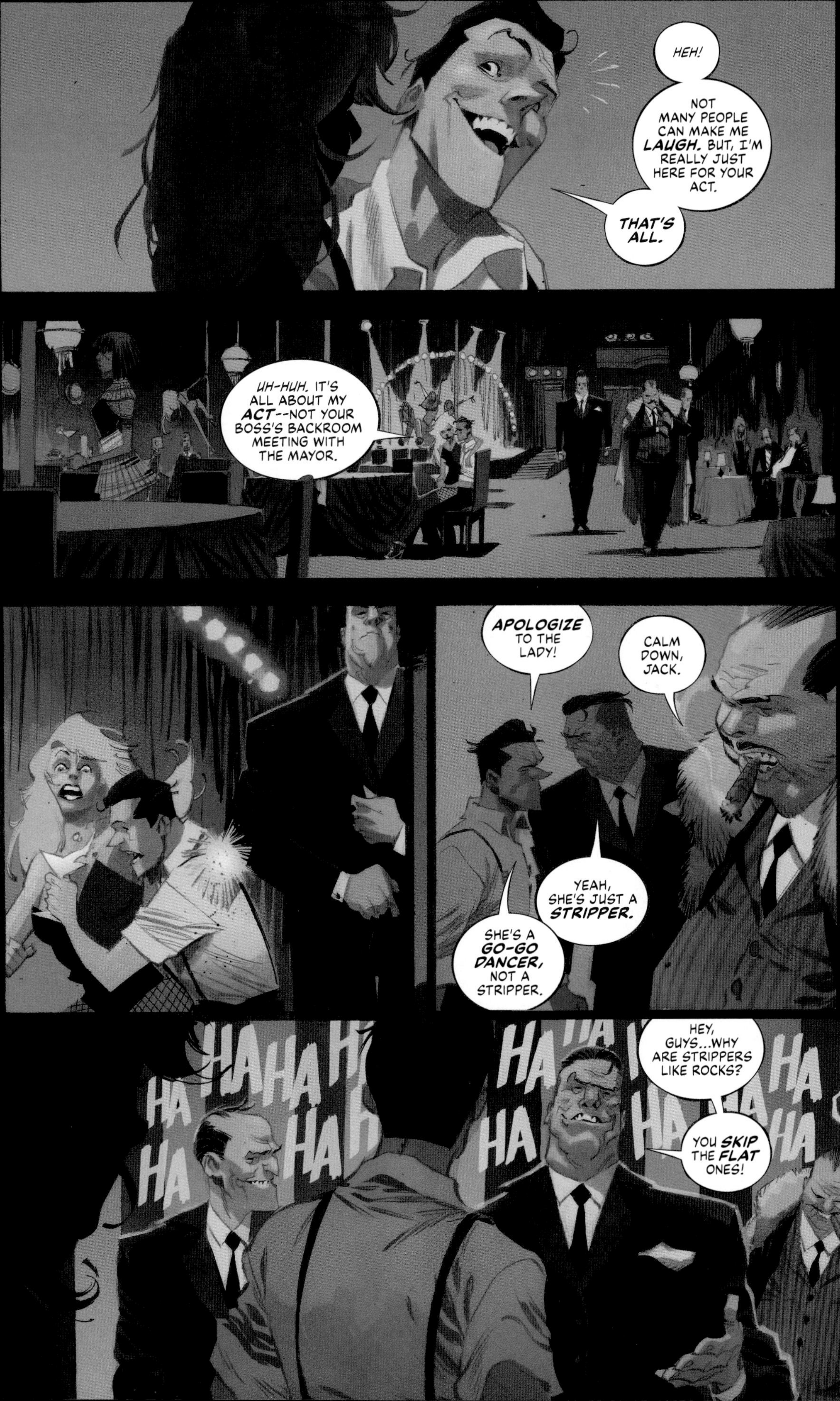
HEH!
NOT MANY PEOPLE CAN MAKE ME LAUGH. BUT, I'M REALLY JUST HERE FOR YOUR ACT.
THAT'S ALL.
UH-HUH. IT'S ALL ABOUT MY ACT--NOT YOUR BOSS'S BACKROOM MEETING WITH THE MAYOR.
APOLOGIZE TO THE LADY!
CALM DOWN, JACK.
YEAH, SHE'S JUST A STRIPPER.
SHE'S A GO-GO DANCER, NOT A STRIPPER.
HEY, GUYS...WHY ARE STRIPPERS LIKE ROCKS?
YOU SKIP THE FLAT ONES!
HA HA HA HA HA HA HA HA HA HA HA HA

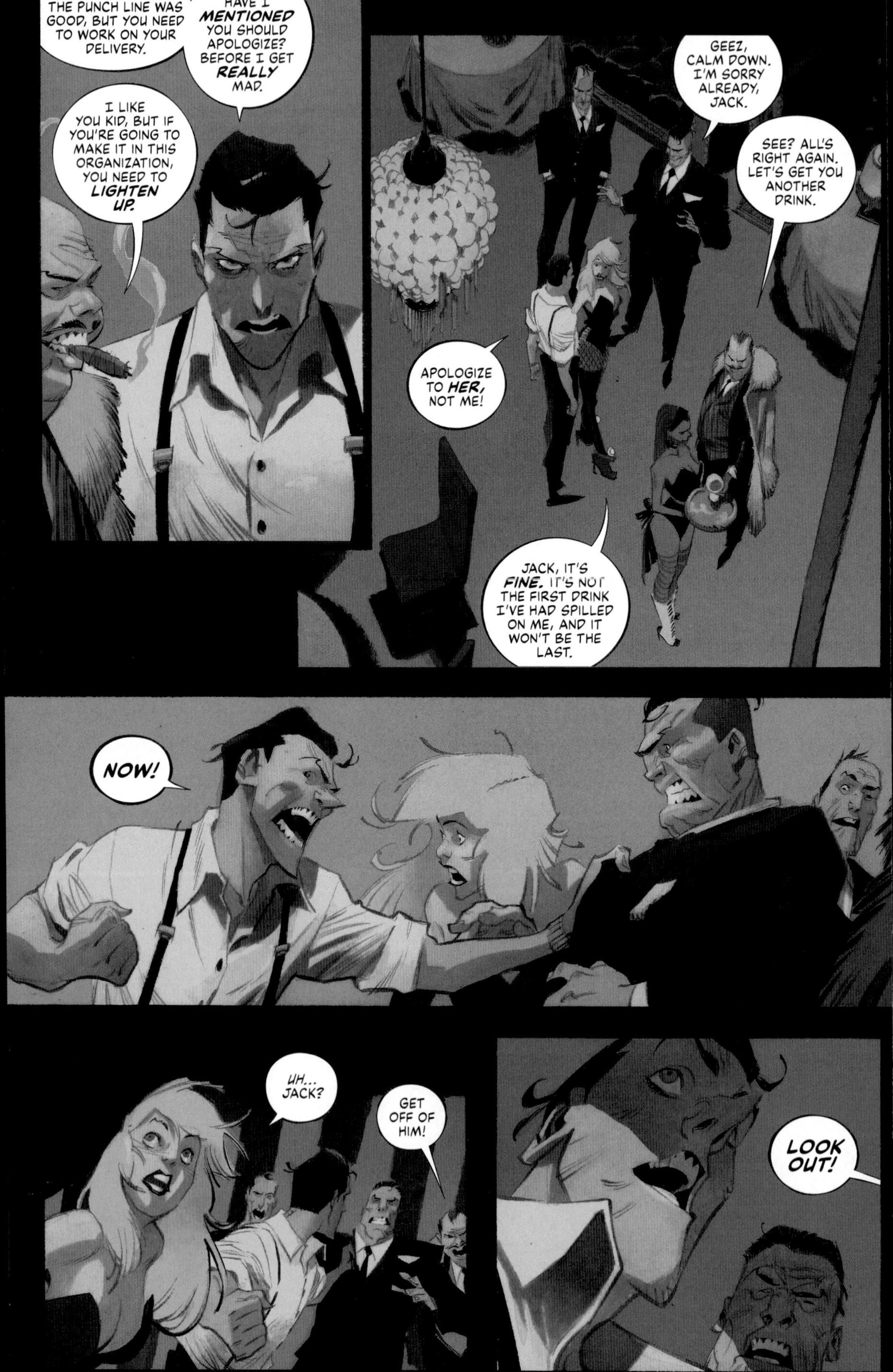

THE PUNCH LINE WAS GOOD, BUT YOU NEED TO WORK ON YOUR DELIVERY.
HAVE I MENTIONED YOU SHOULD APOLOGIZE? BEFORE I GET REALLY MAD.
I LIKE YOU KID, BUT IF YOU'RE GOING TO MAKE IT IN THIS ORGANIZATION, YOU NEED TO LIGHTEN UP.
GEEZ, CALM DOWN. I'M SORRY ALREADY, JACK.
SEE? ALL'S RIGHT AGAIN. LET'S GET YOU ANOTHER DRINK.
APOLOGIZE TO HER, NOT ME!
JACK, IT'S FINE. IT'S NOT THE FIRST DRINK I'VE HAD SPILLED ON ME, AND IT WON'T BE THE LAST.
NOW!
UH... JACK?
GET OFF OF HIM!
LOOK OUT!

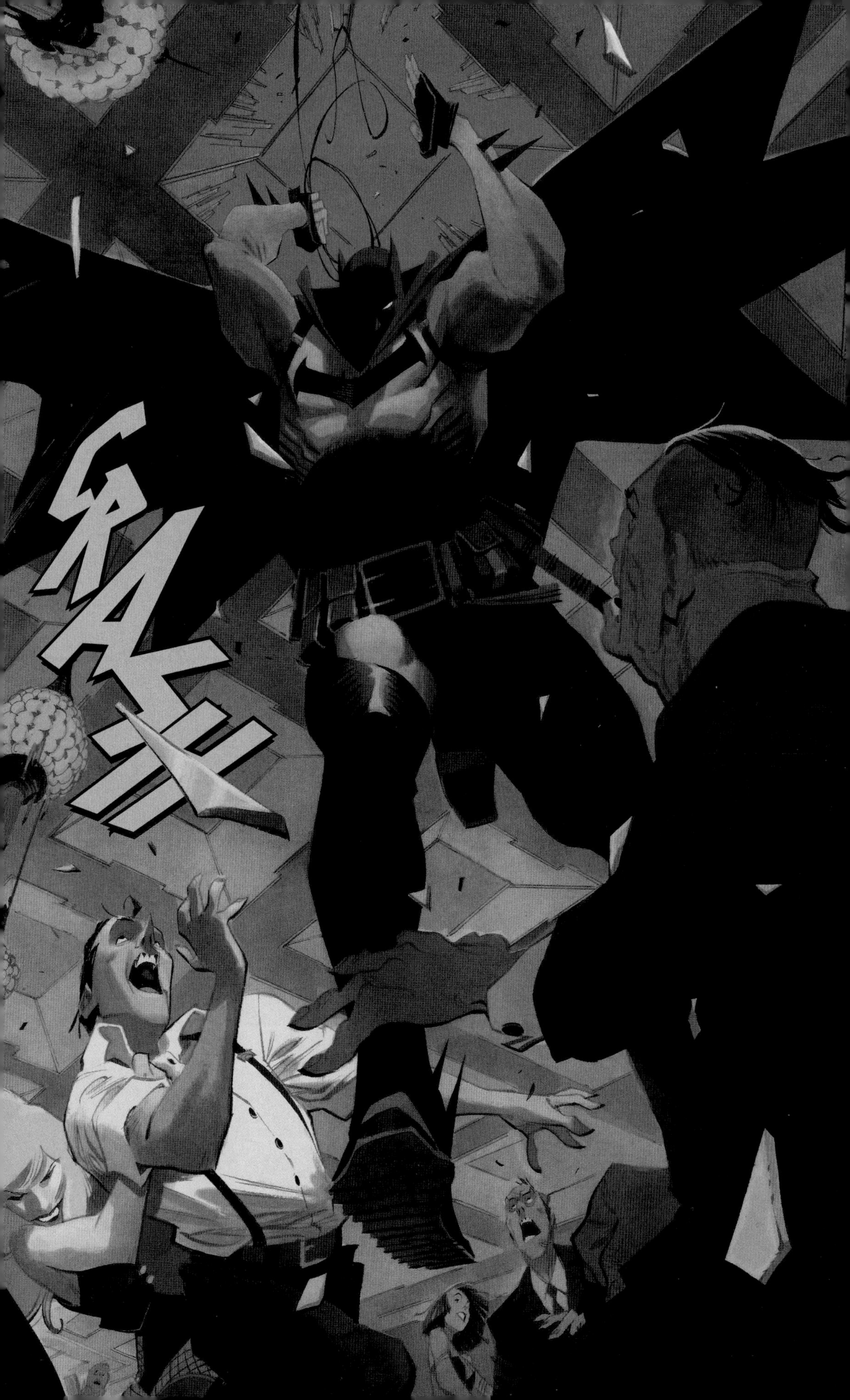
CRASH

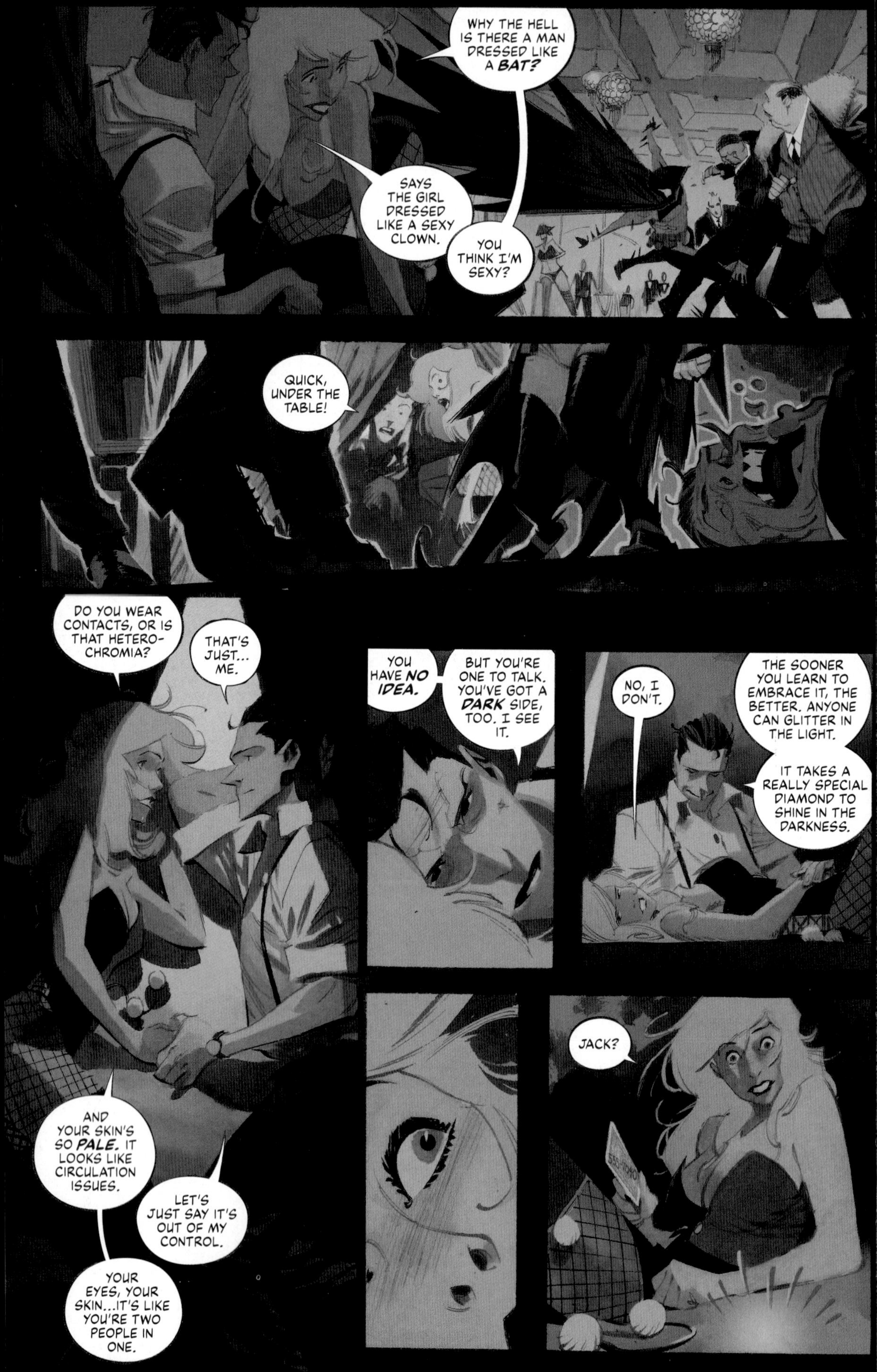

WHY THE HELL IS THERE A MAN DRESSED LIKE A **BAT?**
SAYS THE GIRL DRESSED LIKE A SEXY CLOWN.
YOU THINK I'M SEXY?
QUICK, UNDER THE TABLE!
DO YOU WEAR CONTACTS, OR IS THAT HETERO-CHROMIA?
THAT'S JUST... ME.
AND YOUR SKIN'S SO **PALE.** IT LOOKS LIKE CIRCULATION ISSUES.
LET'S JUST SAY IT'S OUT OF MY CONTROL.
YOUR EYES, YOUR SKIN...IT'S LIKE YOU'RE TWO PEOPLE IN ONE.
YOU HAVE **NO IDEA.**
BUT YOU'RE ONE TO TALK. YOU'VE GOT A **DARK** SIDE, TOO. I SEE IT.
NO, I DON'T.
THE SOONER YOU LEARN TO EMBRACE IT, THE BETTER. ANYONE CAN GLITTER IN THE LIGHT.
IT TAKES A REALLY SPECIAL DIAMOND TO SHINE IN THE DARKNESS.
JACK?

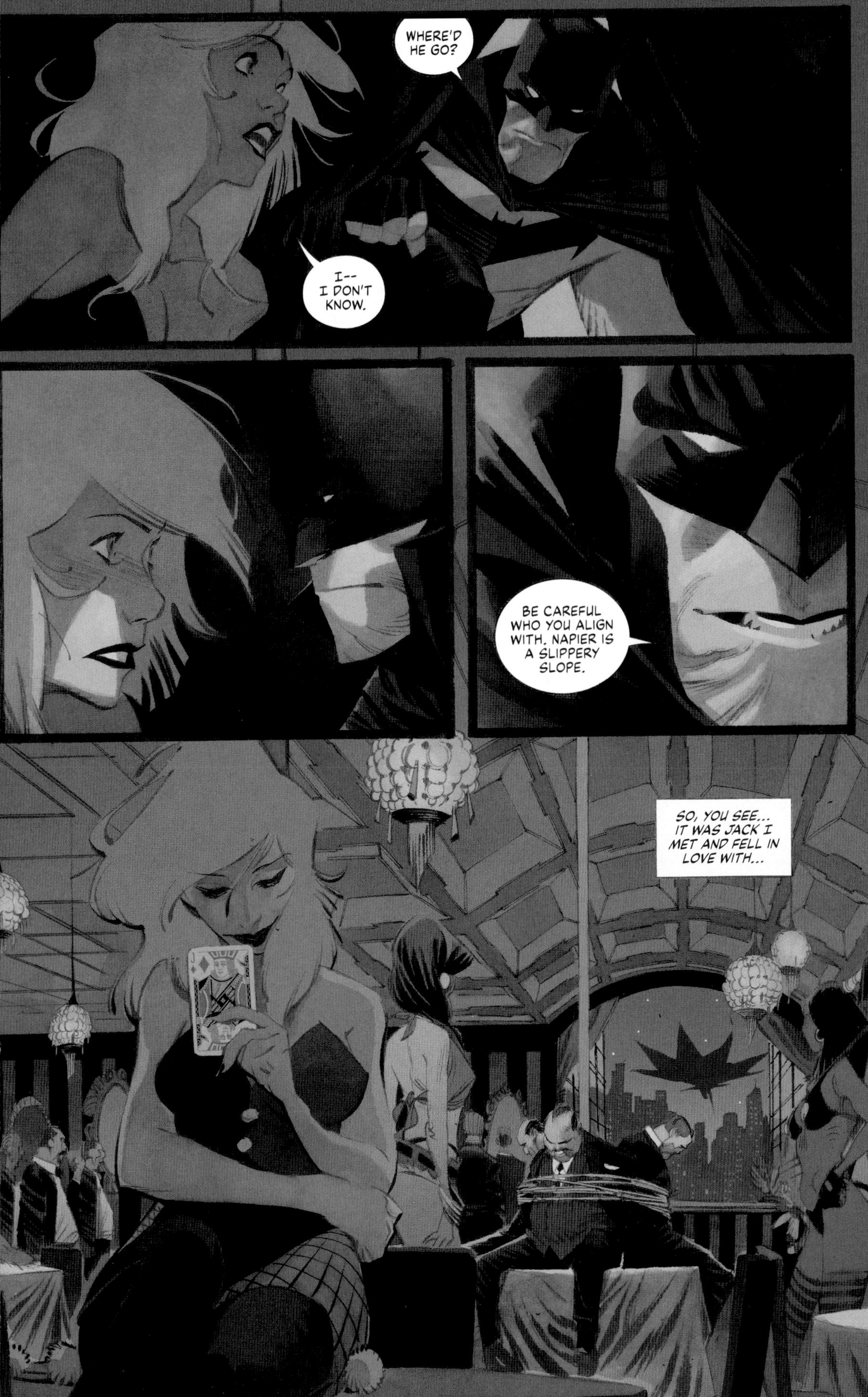
WHERE'D HE GO?
I-- I DON'T KNOW.
BE CAREFUL WHO YOU ALIGN WITH. NAPIER IS A SLIPPERY SLOPE.
SO, YOU SEE... IT WAS JACK I MET AND FELL IN LOVE WITH...

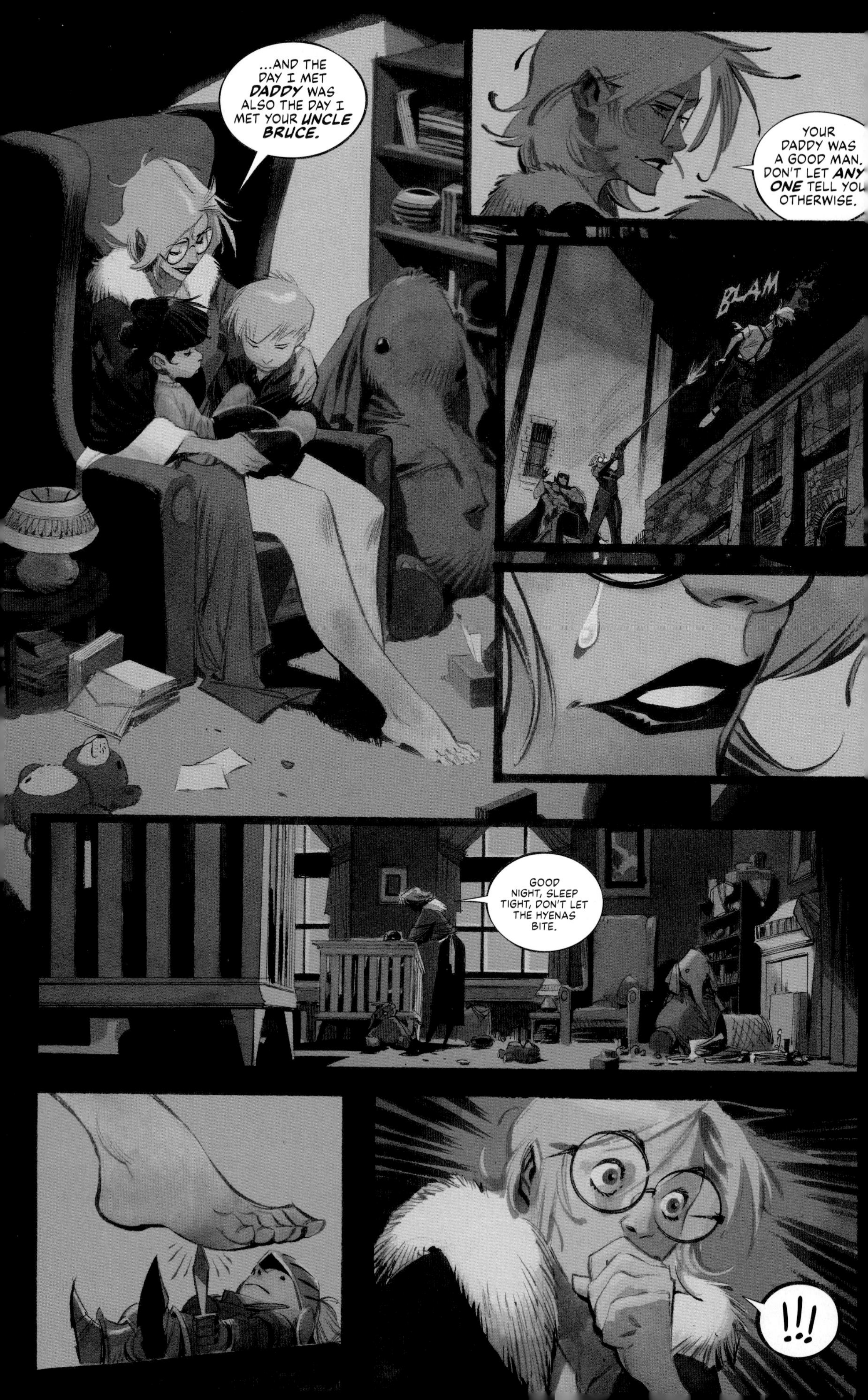
...AND THE DAY I MET DADDY WAS ALSO THE DAY I MET YOUR UNCLE BRUCE.
YOUR DADDY WAS A GOOD MAN. DON'T LET ANY ONE TELL YOU OTHERWISE.
BLAM
GOOD NIGHT, SLEEP TIGHT, DON'T LET THE HYENAS BITE.
!!!

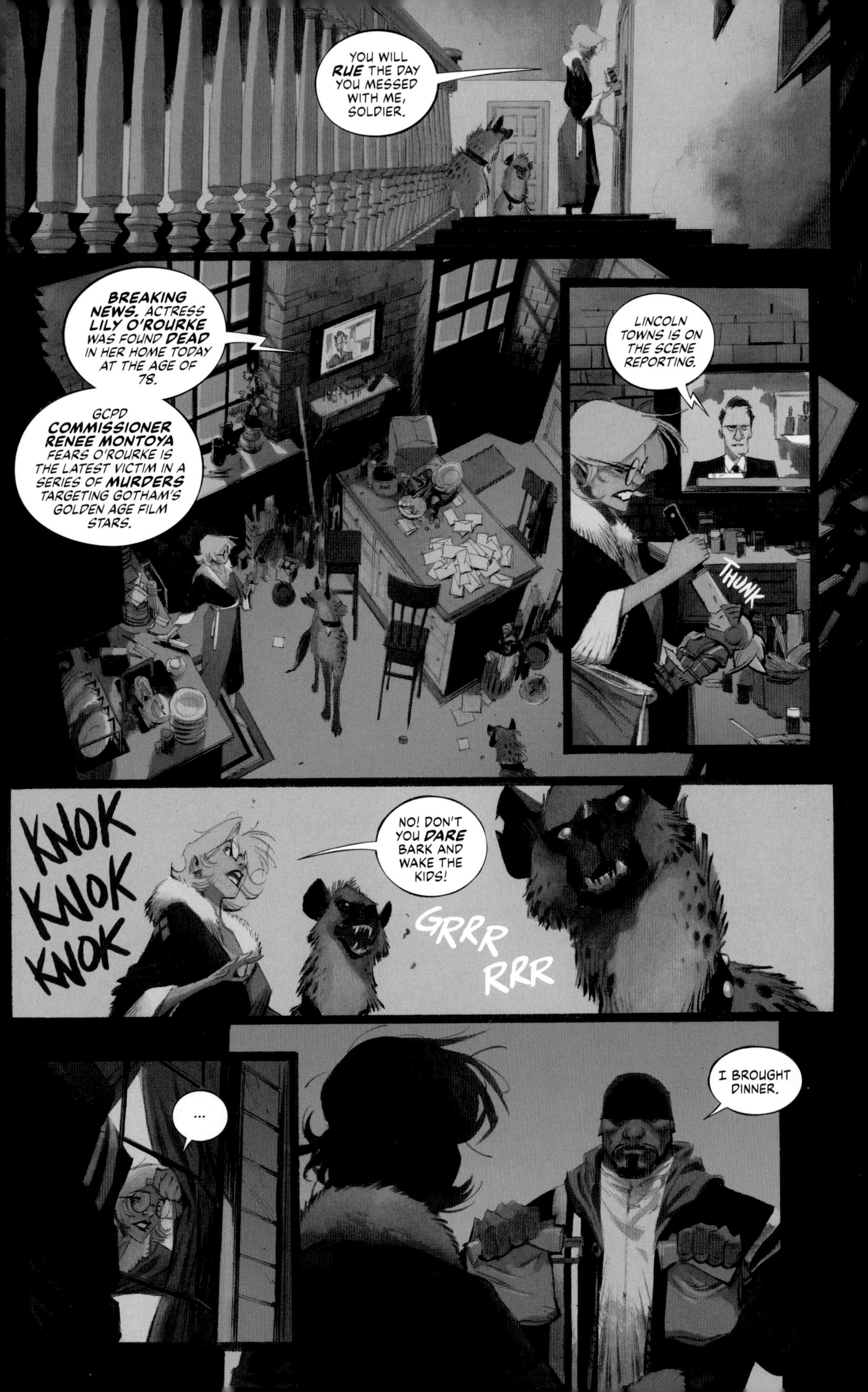
YOU WILL RUE THE DAY YOU MESSED WITH ME, SOLDIER.
BREAKING NEWS. ACTRESS LILY O'ROURKE WAS FOUND DEAD IN HER HOME TODAY AT THE AGE OF 78.
GCPD COMMISSIONER RENEE MONTOYA FEARS O'ROURKE IS THE LATEST VICTIM IN A SERIES OF MURDERS TARGETING GOTHAM'S GOLDEN AGE FILM STARS.
LINCOLN TOWNS IS ON THE SCENE REPORTING.
THUNK
KNOK KNOK KNOK
NO! DON'T YOU DARE BARK AND WAKE THE KIDS!
GRRR RRR
...
I BROUGHT DINNER.

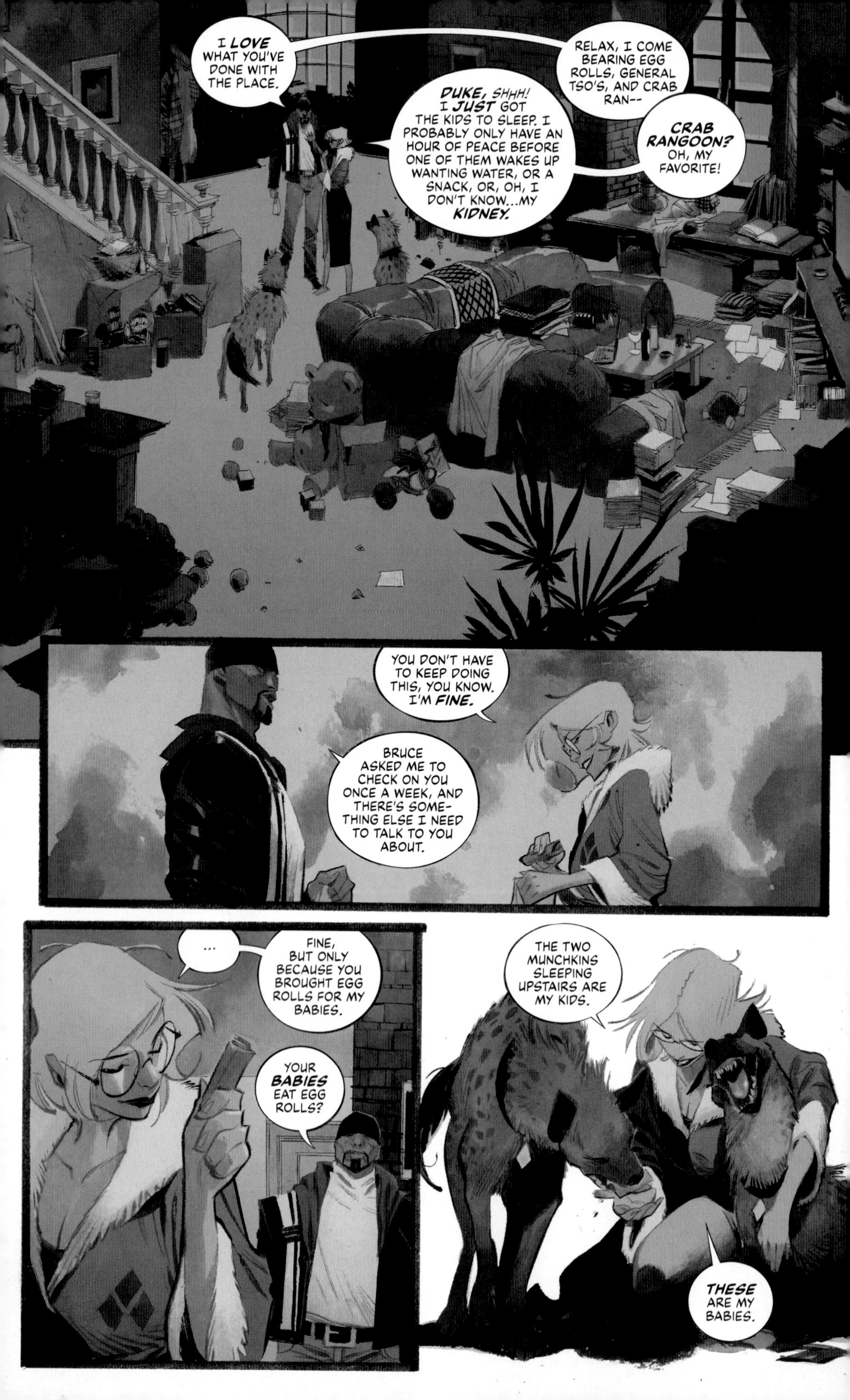
I LOVE WHAT YOU'VE DONE WITH THE PLACE.
RELAX, I COME BEARING EGG ROLLS, GENERAL TSO'S, AND CRAB RAN--
DUKE, SHHH! I JUST GOT THE KIDS TO SLEEP. I PROBABLY ONLY HAVE AN HOUR OF PEACE BEFORE ONE OF THEM WAKES UP WANTING WATER, OR A SNACK, OR, OH, I DON'T KNOW...MY KIDNEY.
CRAB RANGOON? OH, MY FAVORITE!
YOU DON'T HAVE TO KEEP DOING THIS, YOU KNOW. I'M FINE.
BRUCE ASKED ME TO CHECK ON YOU ONCE A WEEK, AND THERE'S SOME-THING ELSE I NEED TO TALK TO YOU ABOUT.
...
FINE, BUT ONLY BECAUSE YOU BROUGHT EGG ROLLS FOR MY BABIES.
YOUR BABIES EAT EGG ROLLS?
THE TWO MUNCHKINS SLEEPING UPSTAIRS ARE MY KIDS.
THESE ARE MY BABIES.

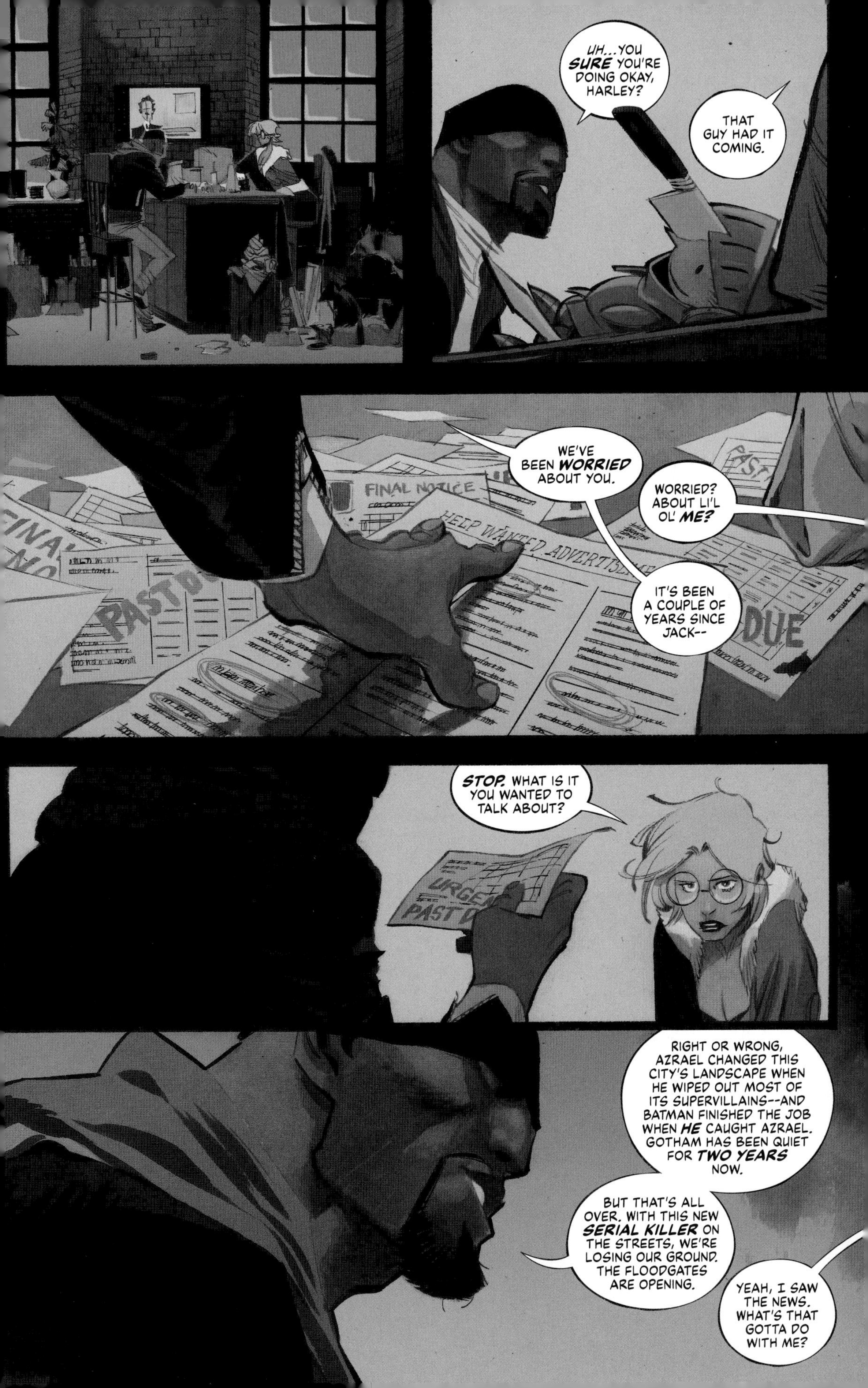
UH...YOU SURE YOU'RE DOING OKAY, HARLEY?
THAT GUY HAD IT COMING.
FINAL NOTICE
HELP WANTED ADVERTISEMENT
PAST DUE
WE'VE BEEN WORRIED ABOUT YOU.
WORRIED? ABOUT LI'L OL' ME?
IT'S BEEN A COUPLE OF YEARS SINCE JACK--
DUE
STOP. WHAT IS IT YOU WANTED TO TALK ABOUT?
RIGHT OR WRONG, AZRAEL CHANGED THIS CITY'S LANDSCAPE WHEN HE WIPED OUT MOST OF ITS SUPERVILLAINS--AND BATMAN FINISHED THE JOB WHEN HE CAUGHT AZRAEL. GOTHAM HAS BEEN QUIET FOR TWO YEARS NOW.
BUT THAT'S ALL OVER. WITH THIS NEW SERIAL KILLER ON THE STREETS, WE'RE LOSING OUR GROUND. THE FLOODGATES ARE OPENING.
YEAH, I SAW THE NEWS. WHAT'S THAT GOTTA DO WITH ME?

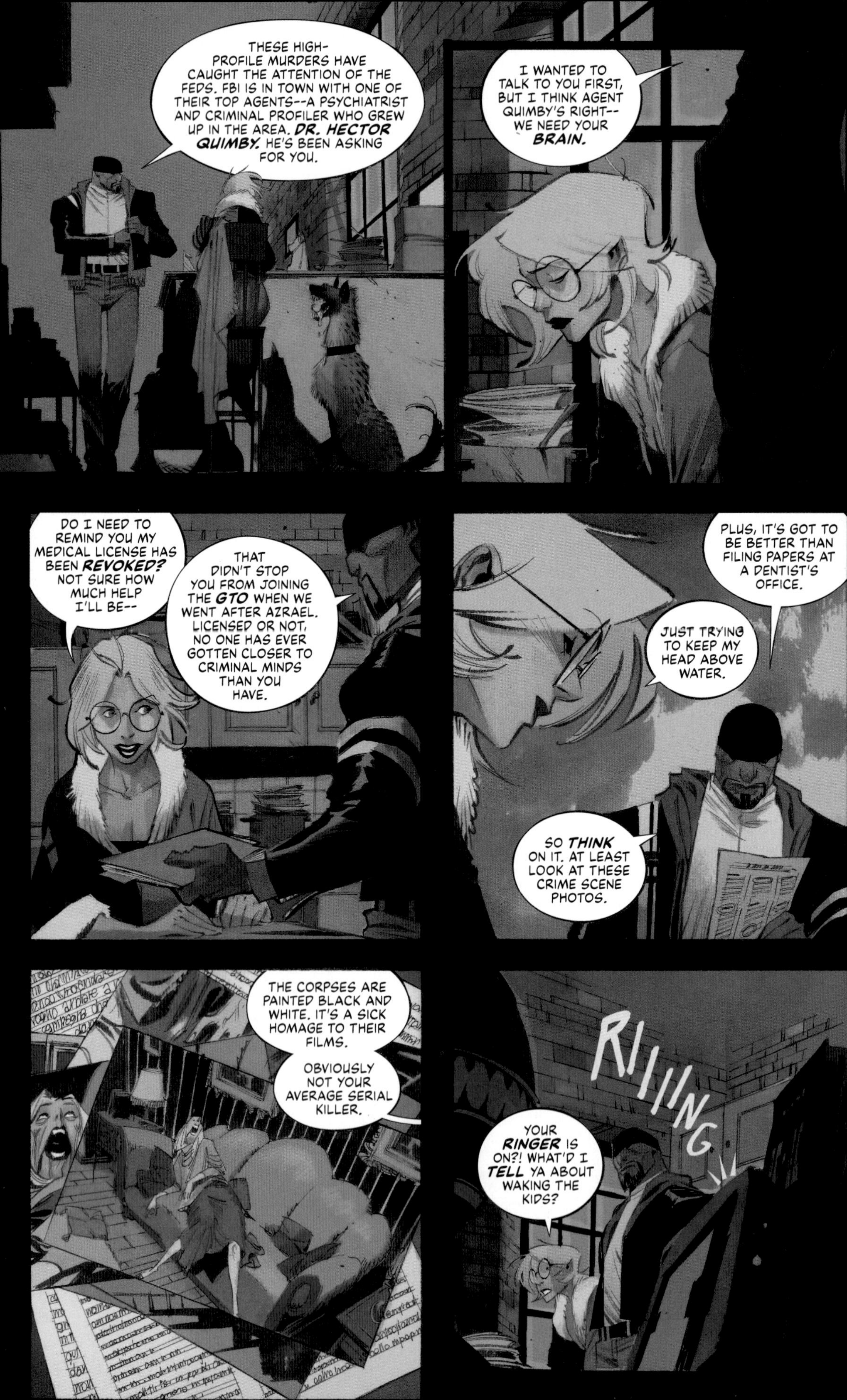
THESE HIGH-PROFILE MURDERS HAVE CAUGHT THE ATTENTION OF THE FEDS. FBI IS IN TOWN WITH ONE OF THEIR TOP AGENTS--A PSYCHIATRIST AND CRIMINAL PROFILER WHO GREW UP IN THE AREA. DR. HECTOR QUIMBY. HE'S BEEN ASKING FOR YOU.
I WANTED TO TALK TO YOU FIRST, BUT I THINK AGENT QUIMBY'S RIGHT-- WE NEED YOUR BRAIN.
DO I NEED TO REMIND YOU MY MEDICAL LICENSE HAS BEEN REVOKED? NOT SURE HOW MUCH HELP I'LL BE--
THAT DIDN'T STOP YOU FROM JOINING THE GTO WHEN WE WENT AFTER AZRAEL. LICENSED OR NOT, NO ONE HAS EVER GOTTEN CLOSER TO CRIMINAL MINDS THAN YOU HAVE.
PLUS, IT'S GOT TO BE BETTER THAN FILING PAPERS AT A DENTIST'S OFFICE.
JUST TRYING TO KEEP MY HEAD ABOVE WATER.
SO THINK ON IT. AT LEAST LOOK AT THESE CRIME SCENE PHOTOS.
THE CORPSES ARE PAINTED BLACK AND WHITE. IT'S A SICK HOMAGE TO THEIR FILMS.
OBVIOUSLY NOT YOUR AVERAGE SERIAL KILLER.
RIIING
YOUR RINGER IS ON?! WHAT'D I TELL YA ABOUT WAKING THE KIDS?

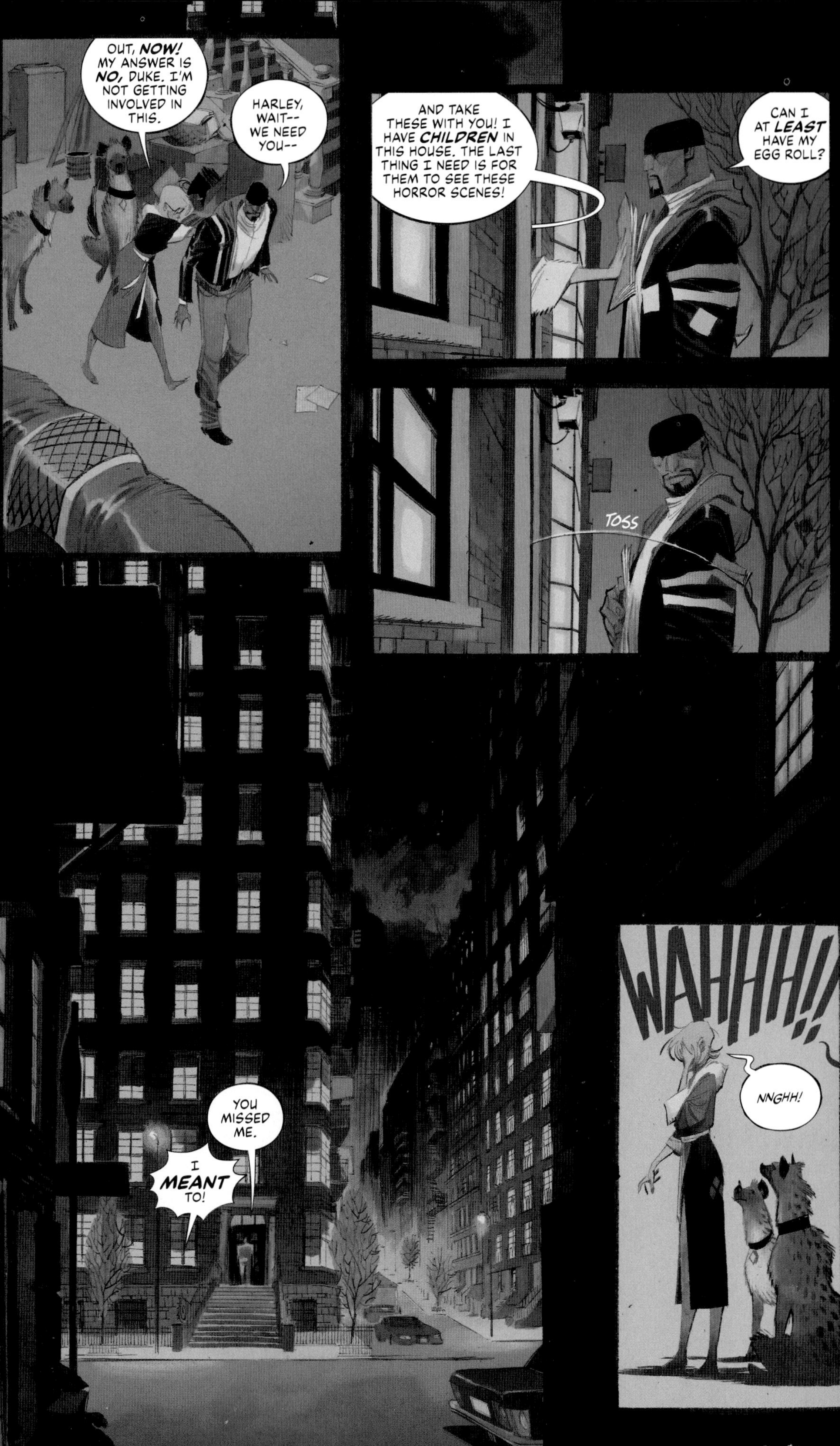
OUT, NOW! MY ANSWER IS NO, DUKE. I'M NOT GETTING INVOLVED IN THIS.
HARLEY, WAIT-- WE NEED YOU--
AND TAKE THESE WITH YOU! I HAVE CHILDREN IN THIS HOUSE. THE LAST THING I NEED IS FOR THEM TO SEE THESE HORROR SCENES!
CAN I AT LEAST HAVE MY EGG ROLL?
TOSS
YOU MISSED ME.
I MEANT TO!
WAHHH!!
NNGHH!

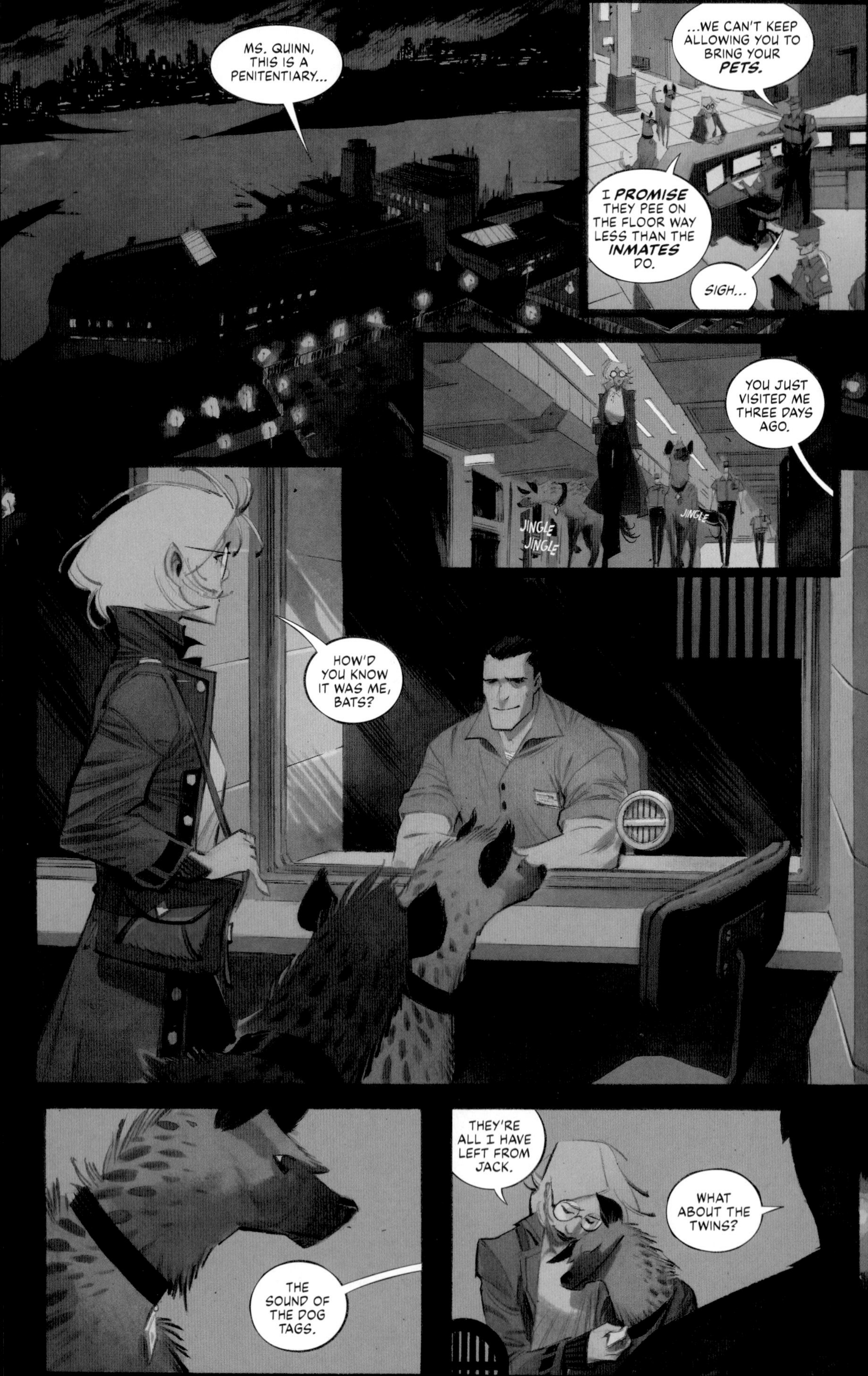
MS. QUINN, THIS IS A PENITENTIARY...
...WE CAN'T KEEP ALLOWING YOU TO BRING YOUR PETS.
I PROMISE THEY PEE ON THE FLOOR WAY LESS THAN THE INMATES DO.
SIGH...
YOU JUST VISITED ME THREE DAYS AGO.
JINGLE
JINGLE
JINGLE
HOW'D YOU KNOW IT WAS ME, BATS?
THE SOUND OF THE DOG TAGS.
THEY'RE ALL I HAVE LEFT FROM JACK.
WHAT ABOUT THE TWINS?

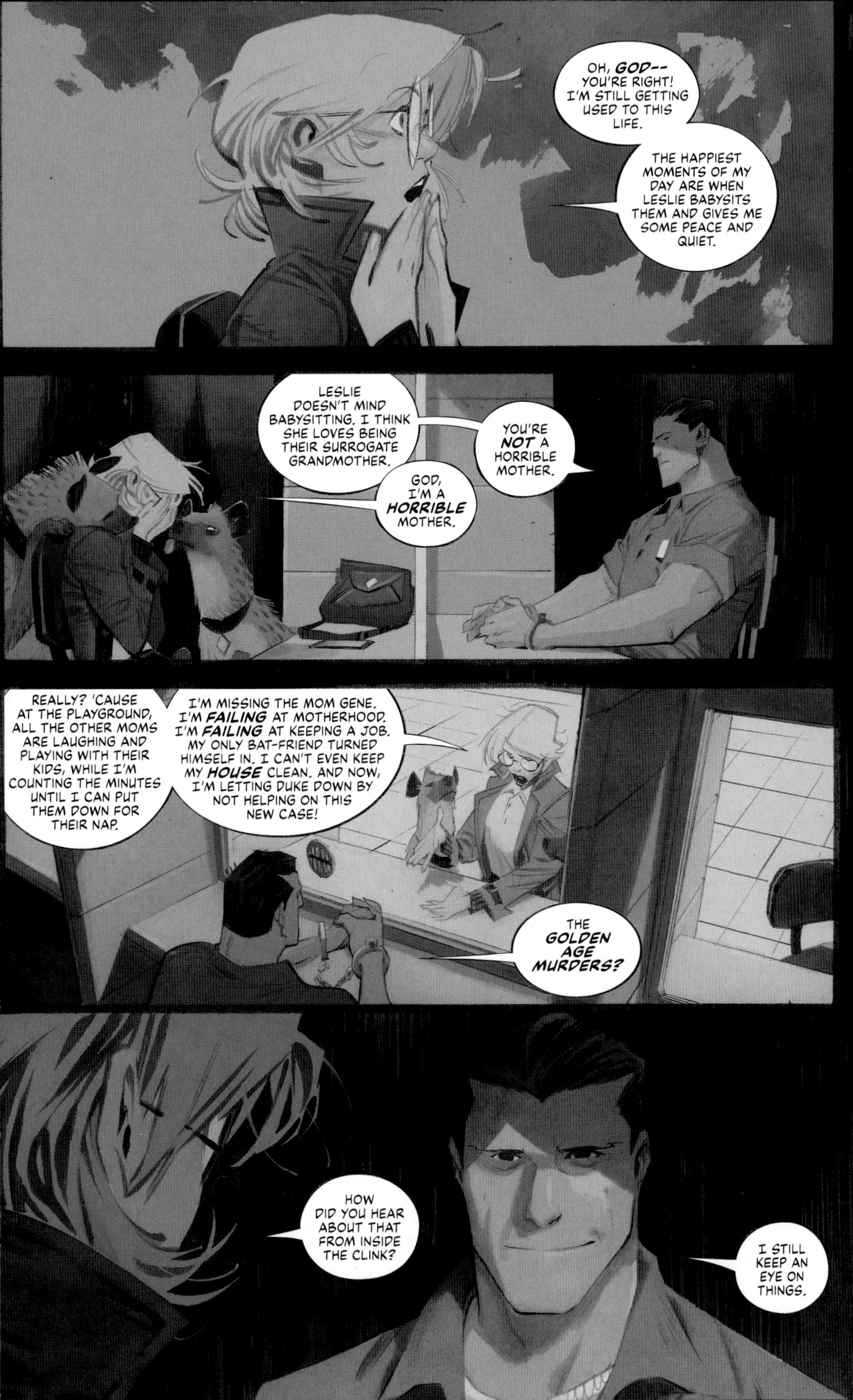
OH, GOD-- YOU'RE RIGHT! I'M STILL GETTING USED TO THIS LIFE.
THE HAPPIEST MOMENTS OF MY DAY ARE WHEN LESLIE BABYSITS THEM AND GIVES ME SOME PEACE AND QUIET.
LESLIE DOESN'T MIND BABYSITTING. I THINK SHE LOVES BEING THEIR SURROGATE GRANDMOTHER.
GOD, I'M A HORRIBLE MOTHER.
YOU'RE NOT A HORRIBLE MOTHER.
REALLY? 'CAUSE AT THE PLAYGROUND, ALL THE OTHER MOMS ARE LAUGHING AND PLAYING WITH THEIR KIDS, WHILE I'M COUNTING THE MINUTES UNTIL I CAN PUT THEM DOWN FOR THEIR NAP.
I'M MISSING THE MOM GENE. I'M FAILING AT MOTHERHOOD. I'M FAILING AT KEEPING A JOB. MY ONLY BAT-FRIEND TURNED HIMSELF IN. I CAN'T EVEN KEEP MY HOUSE CLEAN. AND NOW, I'M LETTING DUKE DOWN BY NOT HELPING ON THIS NEW CASE!
THE GOLDEN AGE MURDERS?
HOW DID YOU HEAR ABOUT THAT FROM INSIDE THE CLINK?
I STILL KEEP AN EYE ON THINGS.

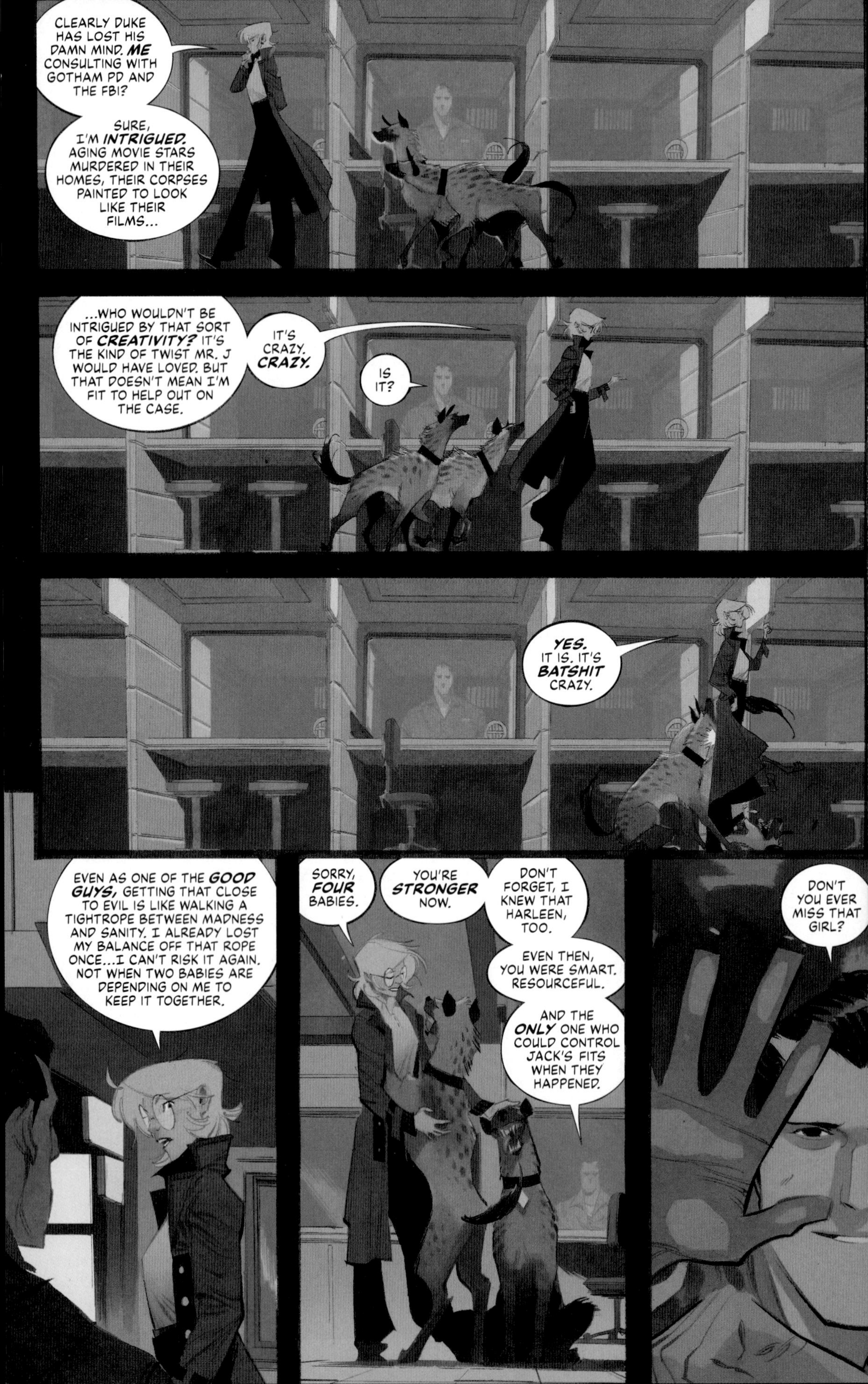
CLEARLY DUKE HAS LOST HIS DAMN MIND. ME CONSULTING WITH GOTHAM PD AND THE FBI?
SURE, I'M INTRIGUED. AGING MOVIE STARS MURDERED IN THEIR HOMES, THEIR CORPSES PAINTED TO LOOK LIKE THEIR FILMS...
...WHO WOULDN'T BE INTRIGUED BY THAT SORT OF CREATIVITY? IT'S THE KIND OF TWIST MR. J WOULD HAVE LOVED. BUT THAT DOESN'T MEAN I'M FIT TO HELP OUT ON THE CASE.
IT'S CRAZY. CRAZY.
IS IT?
YES. IT IS. IT'S BATSHIT CRAZY.
EVEN AS ONE OF THE GOOD GUYS, GETTING THAT CLOSE TO EVIL IS LIKE WALKING A TIGHTROPE BETWEEN MADNESS AND SANITY. I ALREADY LOST MY BALANCE OFF THAT ROPE ONCE...I CAN'T RISK IT AGAIN. NOT WHEN TWO BABIES ARE DEPENDING ON ME TO KEEP IT TOGETHER.
SORRY, FOUR BABIES.
YOU'RE STRONGER NOW.
DON'T FORGET, I KNEW THAT HARLEEN, TOO.
EVEN THEN, YOU WERE SMART. RESOURCEFUL.
AND THE ONLY ONE WHO COULD CONTROL JACK'S FITS WHEN THEY HAPPENED.
DON'T YOU EVER MISS THAT GIRL?

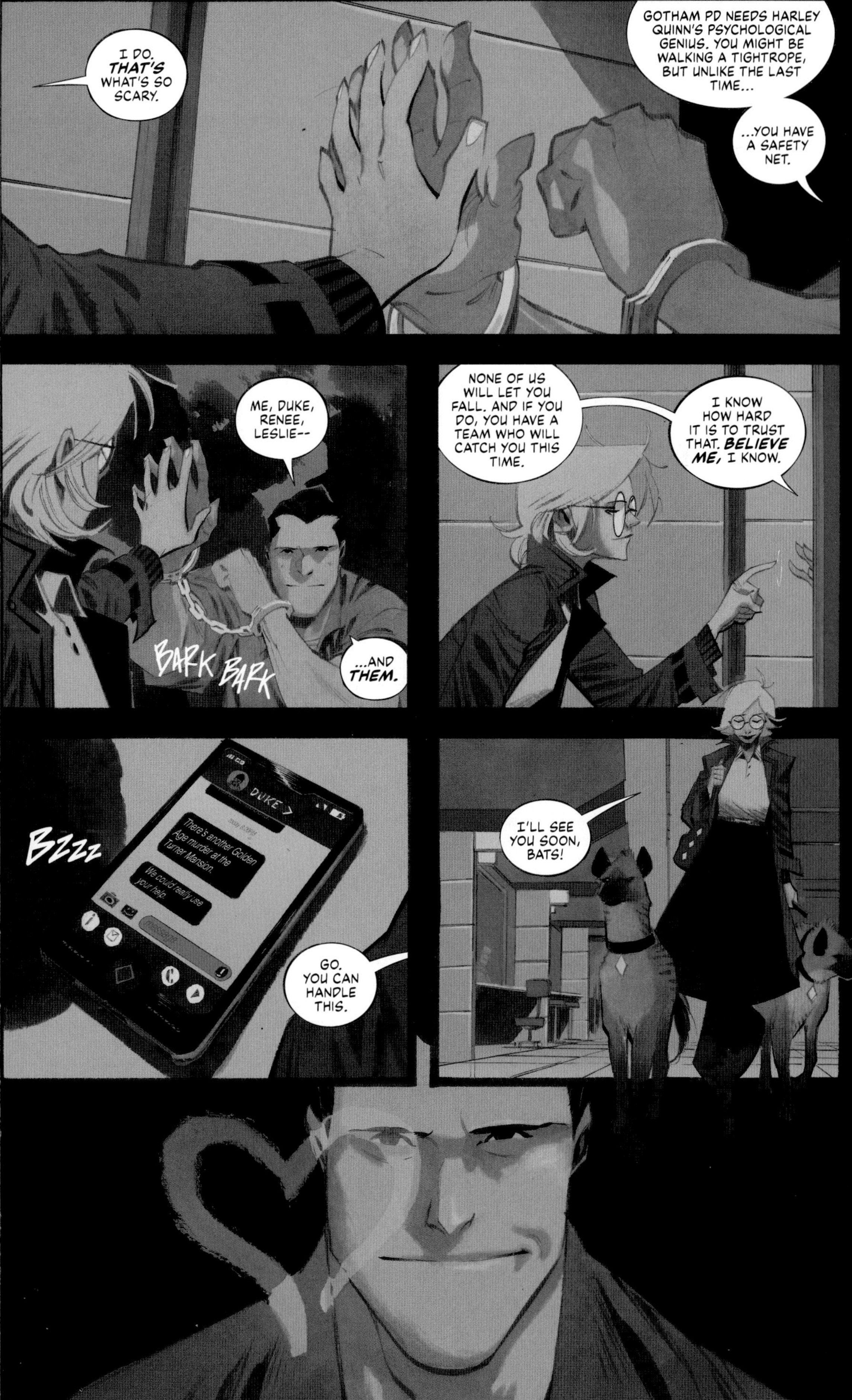
I DO. THAT'S WHAT'S SO SCARY.
GOTHAM PD NEEDS HARLEY QUINN'S PSYCHOLOGICAL GENIUS. YOU MIGHT BE WALKING A TIGHTROPE, BUT UNLIKE THE LAST TIME...
...YOU HAVE A SAFETY NET.
ME, DUKE, RENEE, LESLIE--
BARK BARK
...AND THEM.
NONE OF US WILL LET YOU FALL. AND IF YOU DO, YOU HAVE A TEAM WHO WILL CATCH YOU THIS TIME.
I KNOW HOW HARD IT IS TO TRUST THAT. BELIEVE ME, I KNOW.
BZZZ
DUKE >
There's another Golden Age murder at the Turner Mansion.
We could really use your help.
GO. YOU CAN HANDLE THIS.
I'LL SEE YOU SOON, BATS!

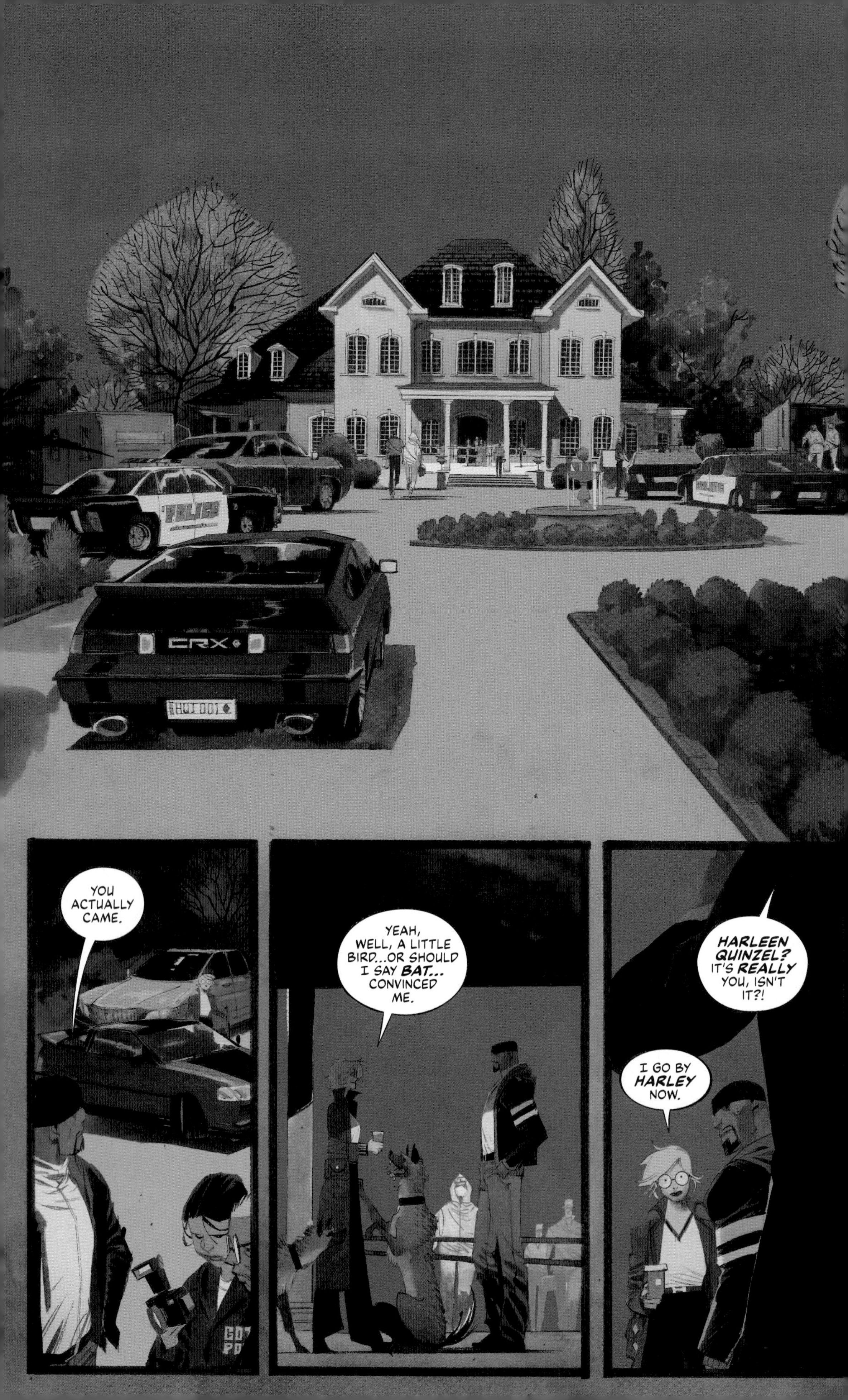
CRX
HQI 001
YOU ACTUALLY CAME.
YEAH, WELL, A LITTLE BIRD...OR SHOULD I SAY BAT... CONVINCED ME.
HARLEEN QUINZEL? IT'S REALLY YOU, ISN'T IT?!
I GO BY HARLEY NOW.

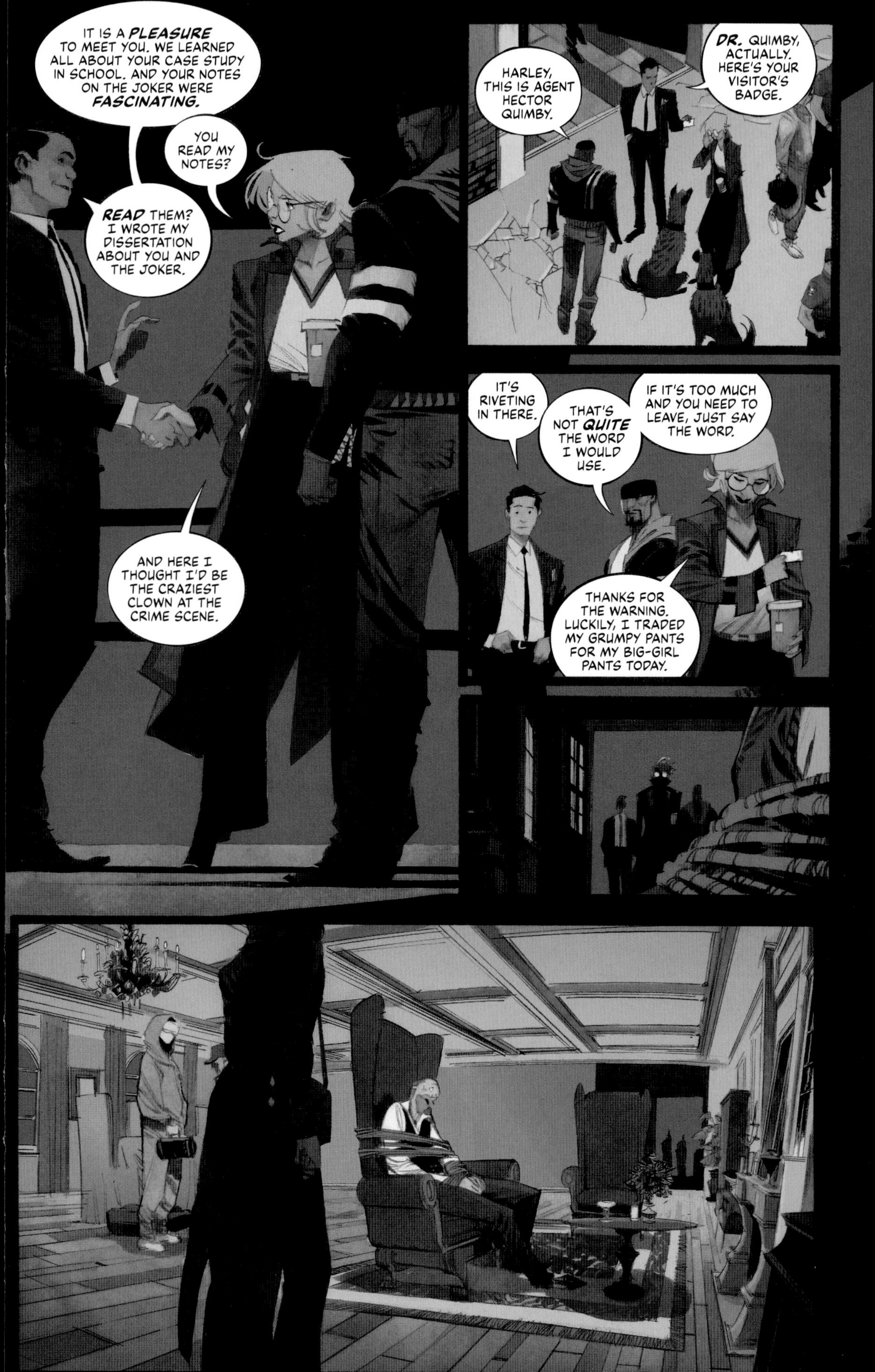
IT IS A PLEASURE TO MEET YOU. WE LEARNED ALL ABOUT YOUR CASE STUDY IN SCHOOL. AND YOUR NOTES ON THE JOKER WERE FASCINATING.
YOU READ MY NOTES?
READ THEM? I WROTE MY DISSERTATION ABOUT YOU AND THE JOKER.
AND HERE I THOUGHT I'D BE THE CRAZIEST CLOWN AT THE CRIME SCENE.
HARLEY, THIS IS AGENT HECTOR QUIMBY.
DR. QUIMBY, ACTUALLY. HERE'S YOUR VISITOR'S BADGE.
IT'S RIVETING IN THERE.
THAT'S NOT QUITE THE WORD I WOULD USE.
IF IT'S TOO MUCH AND YOU NEED TO LEAVE, JUST SAY THE WORD.
THANKS FOR THE WARNING. LUCKILY, I TRADED MY GRUMPY PANTS FOR MY BIG-GIRL PANTS TODAY.

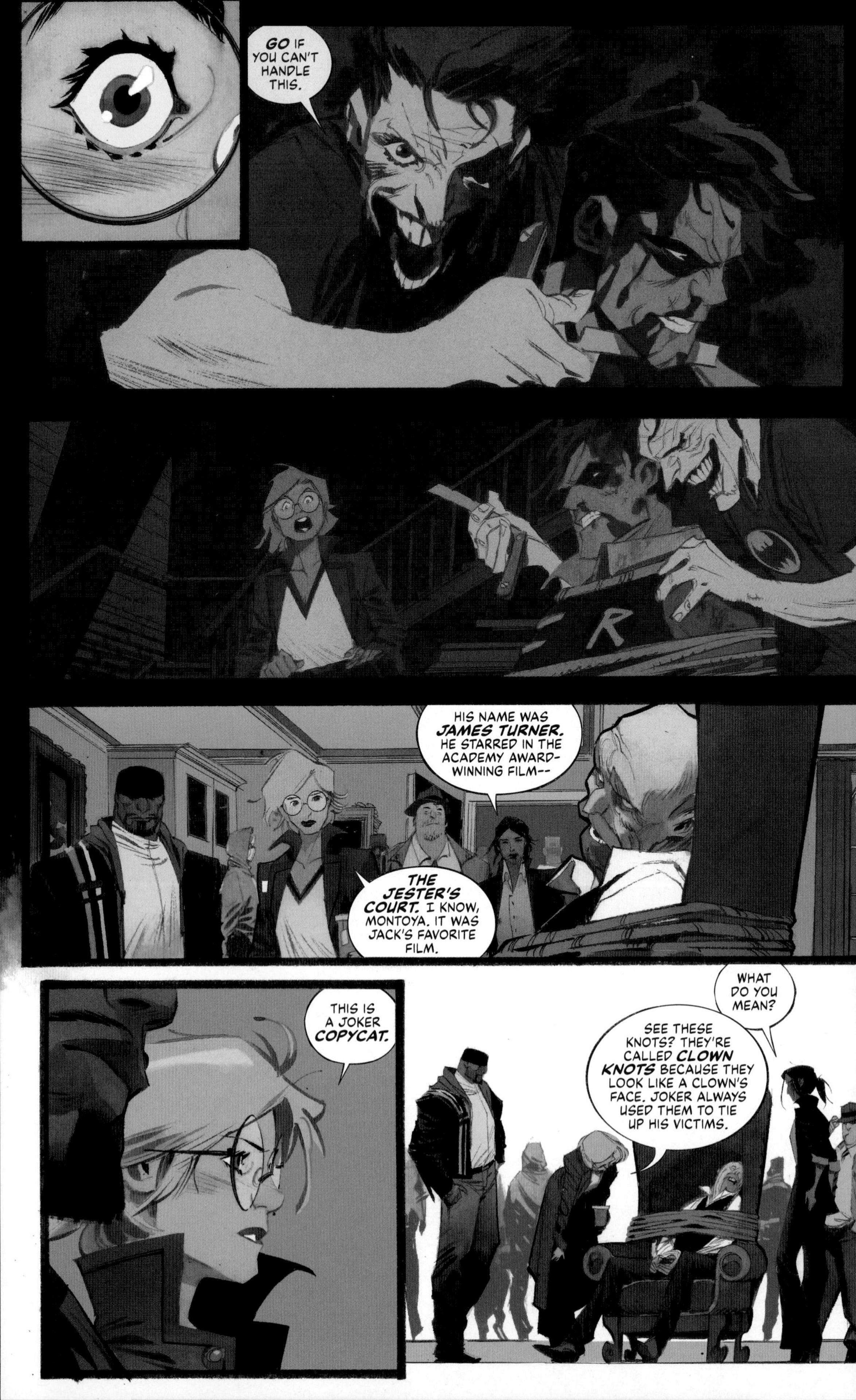
GO IF YOU CAN'T HANDLE THIS.
HIS NAME WAS JAMES TURNER. HE STARRED IN THE ACADEMY AWARD-WINNING FILM--
THE JESTER'S COURT. I KNOW, MONTOYA. IT WAS JACK'S FAVORITE FILM.
THIS IS A JOKER COPYCAT.
WHAT DO YOU MEAN?
SEE THESE KNOTS? THEY'RE CALLED CLOWN KNOTS BECAUSE THEY LOOK LIKE A CLOWN'S FACE. JOKER ALWAYS USED THEM TO TIE UP HIS VICTIMS.

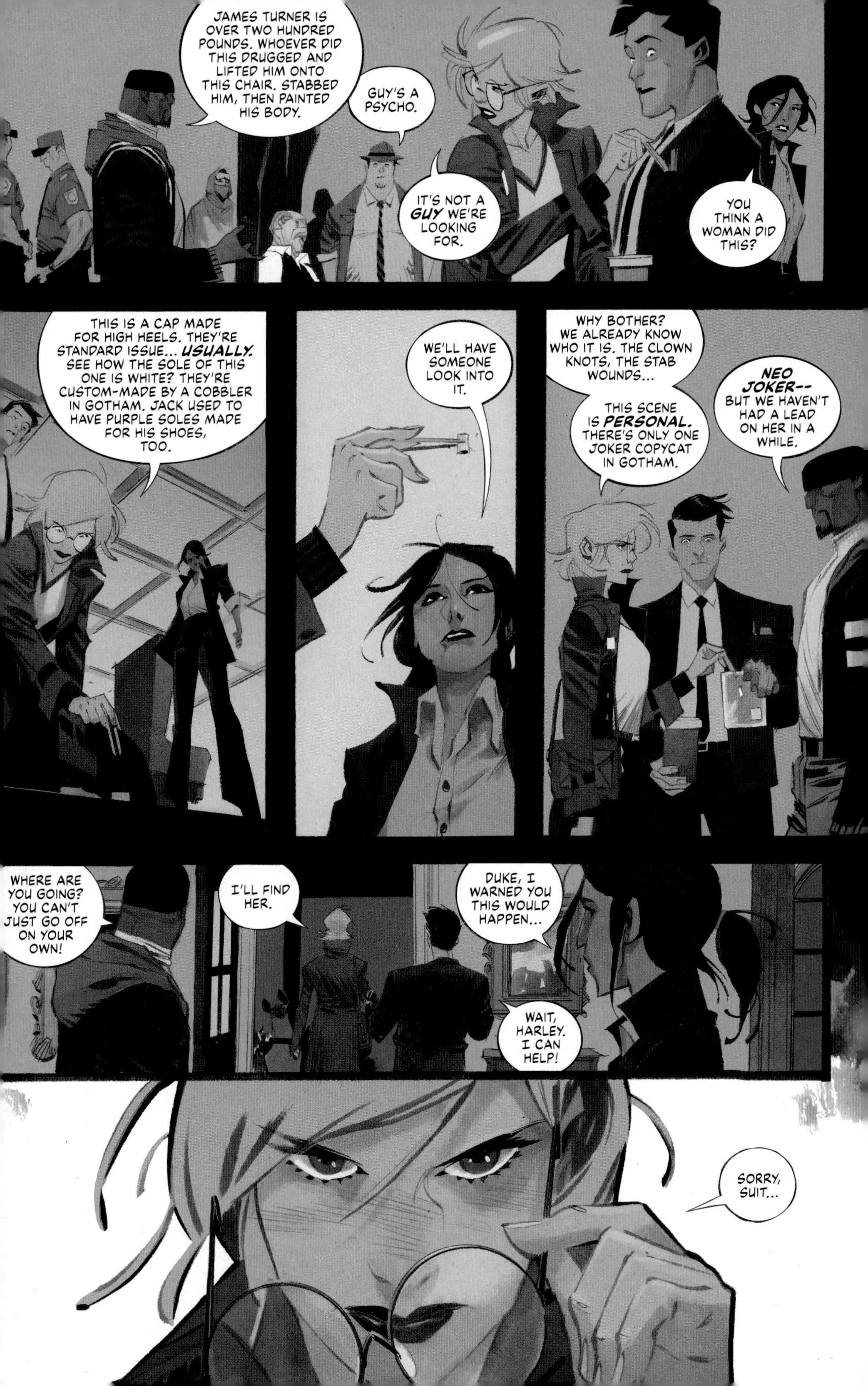

JAMES TURNER IS OVER TWO HUNDRED POUNDS. WHOEVER DID THIS DRUGGED AND LIFTED HIM ONTO THIS CHAIR. STABBED HIM, THEN PAINTED HIS BODY.
GUY'S A PSYCHO.
IT'S NOT A GUY WE'RE LOOKING FOR.
YOU THINK A WOMAN DID THIS?
THIS IS A CAP MADE FOR HIGH HEELS. THEY'RE STANDARD ISSUE... USUALLY. SEE HOW THE SOLE OF THIS ONE IS WHITE? THEY'RE CUSTOM-MADE BY A COBBLER IN GOTHAM. JACK USED TO HAVE PURPLE SOLES MADE FOR HIS SHOES, TOO.
WE'LL HAVE SOMEONE LOOK INTO IT.
WHY BOTHER? WE ALREADY KNOW WHO IT IS. THE CLOWN KNOTS, THE STAB WOUNDS...
THIS SCENE IS PERSONAL. THERE'S ONLY ONE JOKER COPYCAT IN GOTHAM.
NEO JOKER-- BUT WE HAVEN'T HAD A LEAD ON HER IN A WHILE.
WHERE ARE YOU GOING? YOU CAN'T JUST GO OFF ON YOUR OWN!
I'LL FIND HER.
DUKE, I WARNED YOU THIS WOULD HAPPEN...
WAIT, HARLEY. I CAN HELP!
SORRY, SUIT...

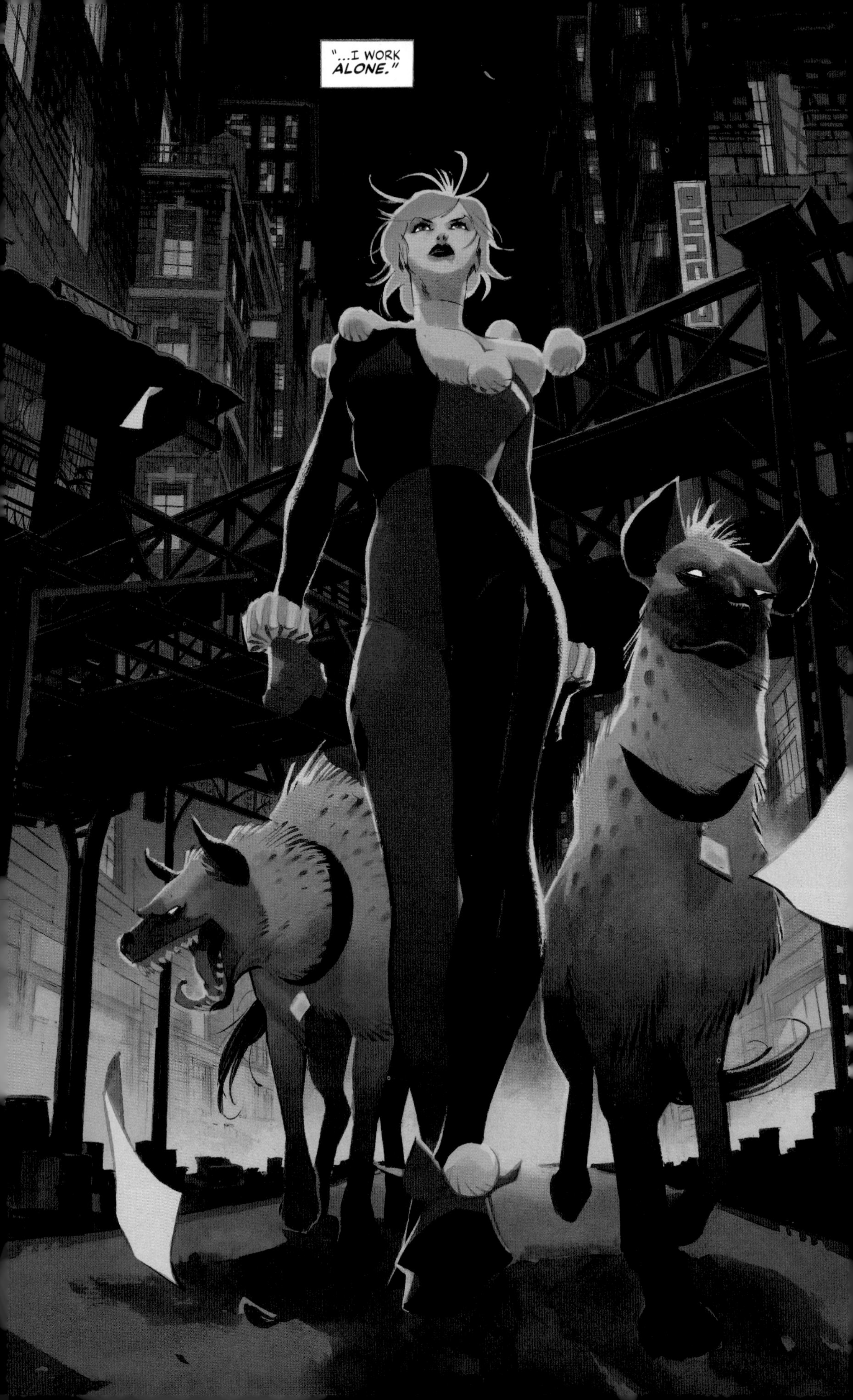
"...I WORK ALONE."

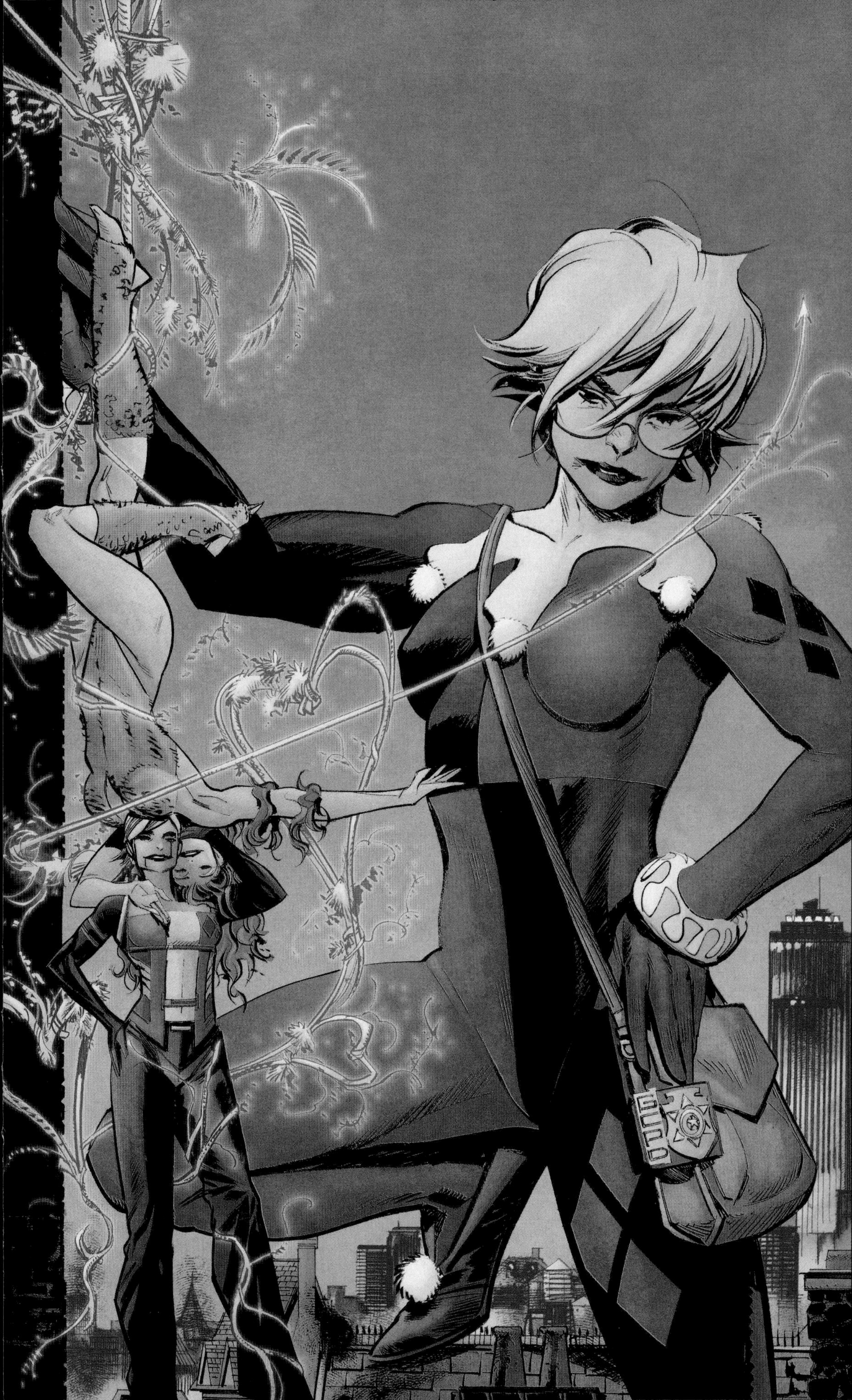

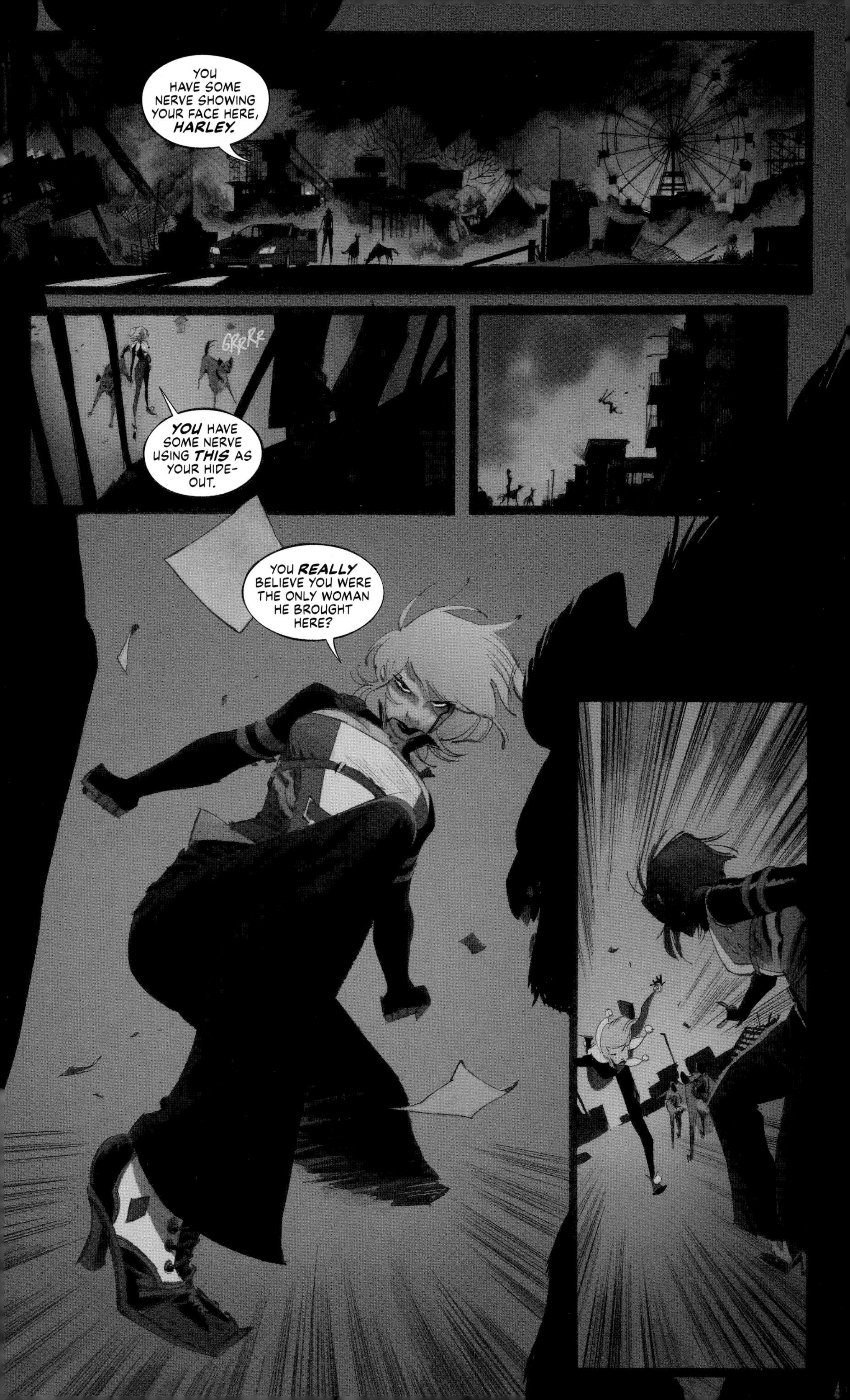
YOU HAVE SOME NERVE SHOWING YOUR FACE HERE, HARLEY.
GRRRR
YOU HAVE SOME NERVE USING THIS AS YOUR HIDE-OUT.
YOU REALLY BELIEVE YOU WERE THE ONLY WOMAN HE BROUGHT HERE?

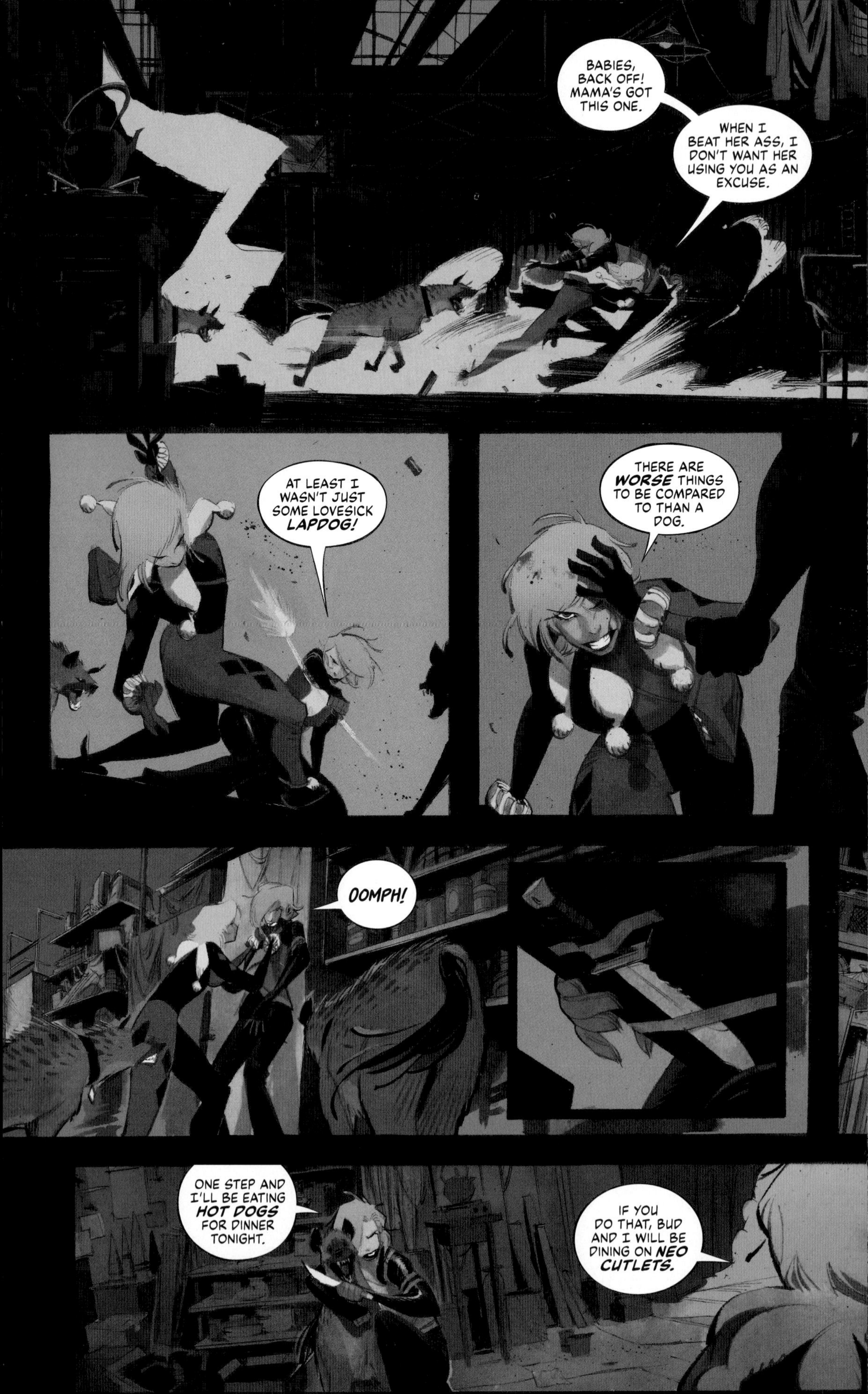

BABIES, BACK OFF! MAMA'S GOT THIS ONE.
WHEN I BEAT HER ASS, I DON'T WANT HER USING YOU AS AN EXCUSE.
AT LEAST I WASN'T JUST SOME LOVESICK **LAPDOG!**
THERE ARE **WORSE** THINGS TO BE COMPARED TO THAN A DOG.
OOMPH!
ONE STEP AND I'LL BE EATING **HOT DOGS** FOR DINNER TONIGHT.
IF YOU DO THAT, BUD AND I WILL BE DINING ON **NEO CUTLETS.**

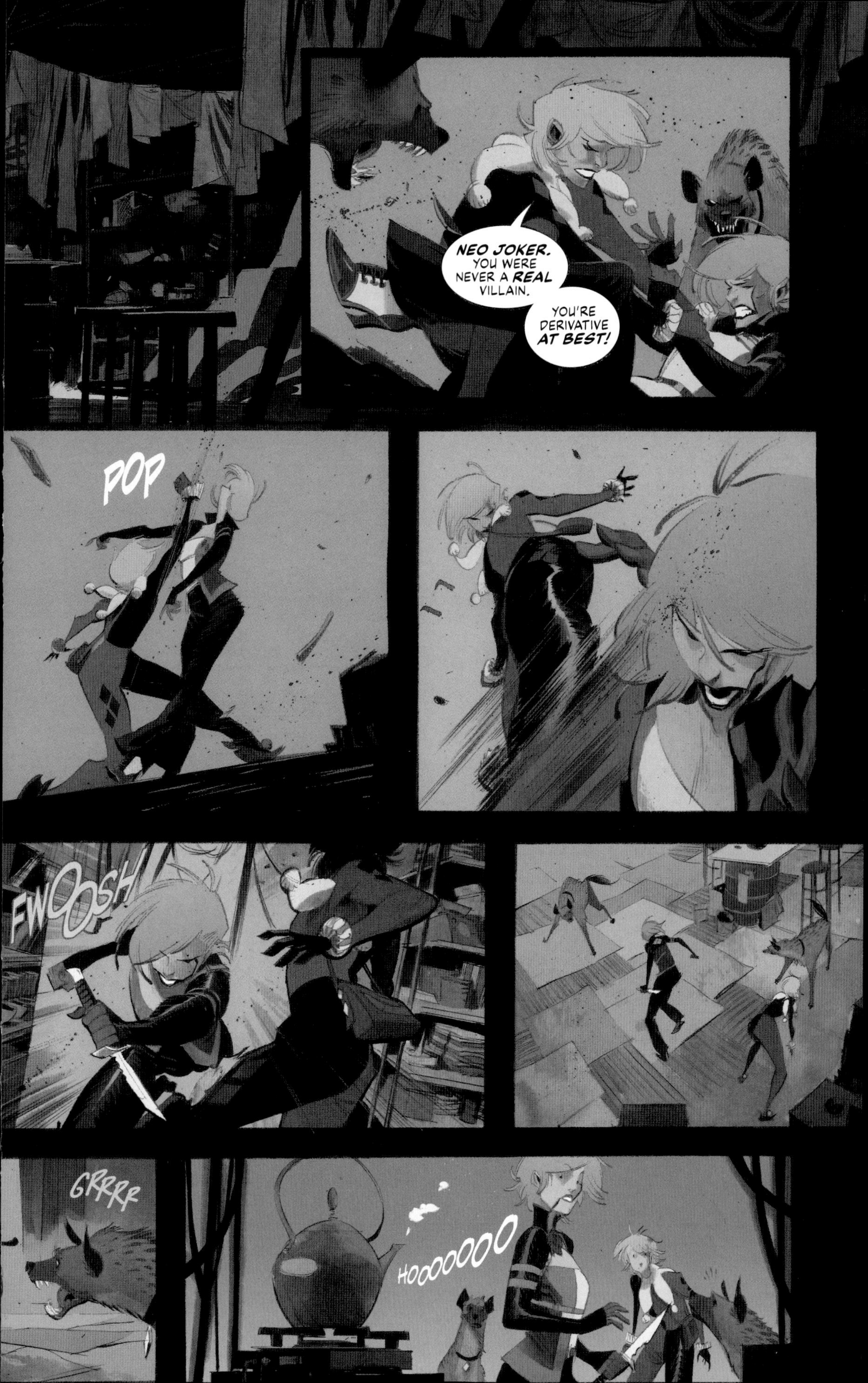
NEO JOKER. YOU WERE NEVER A REAL VILLAIN.
YOU'RE DERIVATIVE AT BEST!
POP
FWOOSH
GRRRR
HOOOOOOO

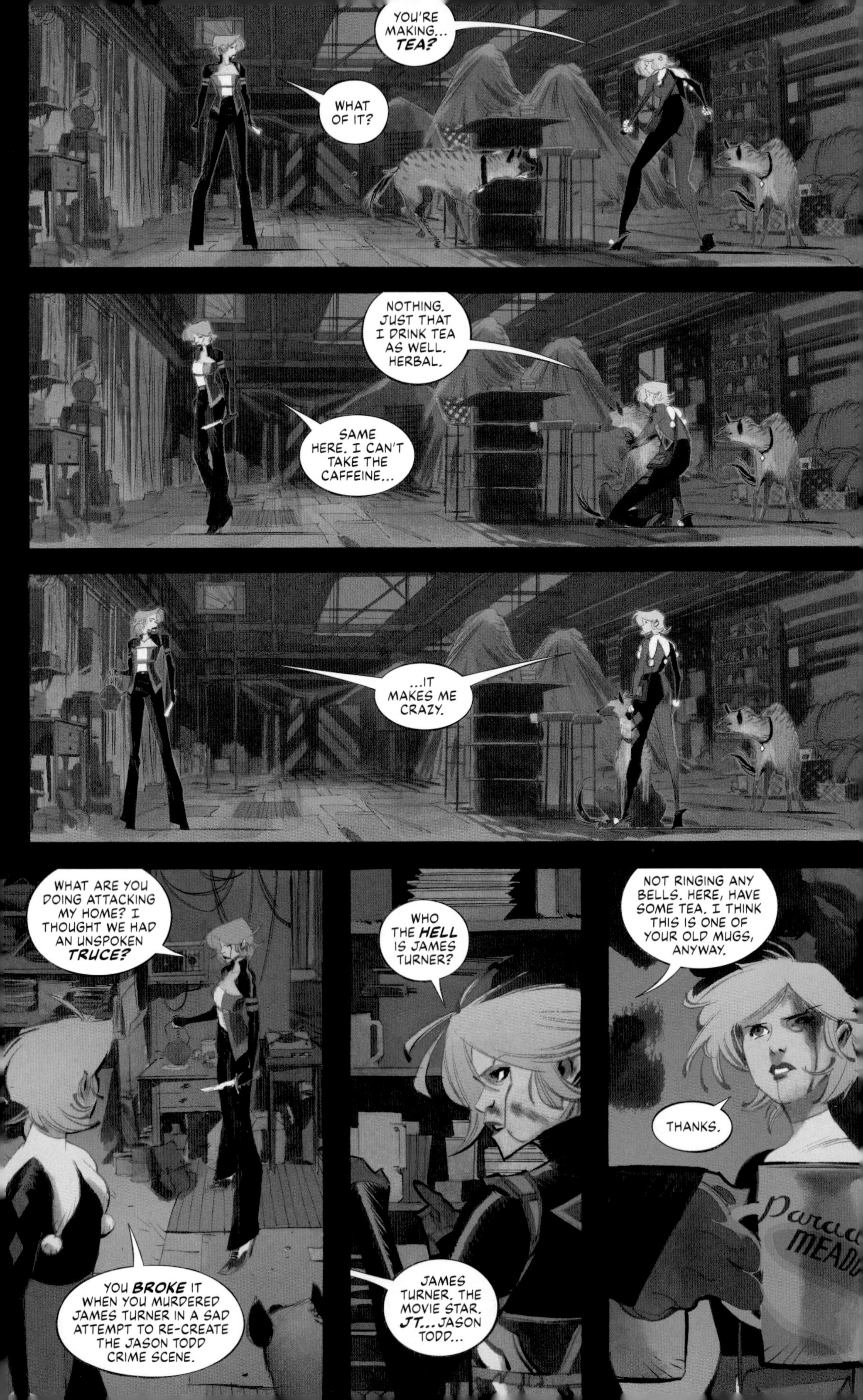
YOU'RE MAKING... TEA?
WHAT OF IT?
NOTHING. JUST THAT I DRINK TEA AS WELL. HERBAL.
SAME HERE. I CAN'T TAKE THE CAFFEINE...
...IT MAKES ME CRAZY.
WHAT ARE YOU DOING ATTACKING MY HOME? I THOUGHT WE HAD AN UNSPOKEN TRUCE?
YOU BROKE IT WHEN YOU MURDERED JAMES TURNER IN A SAD ATTEMPT TO RE-CREATE THE JASON TODD CRIME SCENE.
WHO THE HELL IS JAMES TURNER?
JAMES TURNER. THE MOVIE STAR. JT... JASON TODD...
NOT RINGING ANY BELLS. HERE, HAVE SOME TEA. I THINK THIS IS ONE OF YOUR OLD MUGS, ANYWAY.
THANKS.

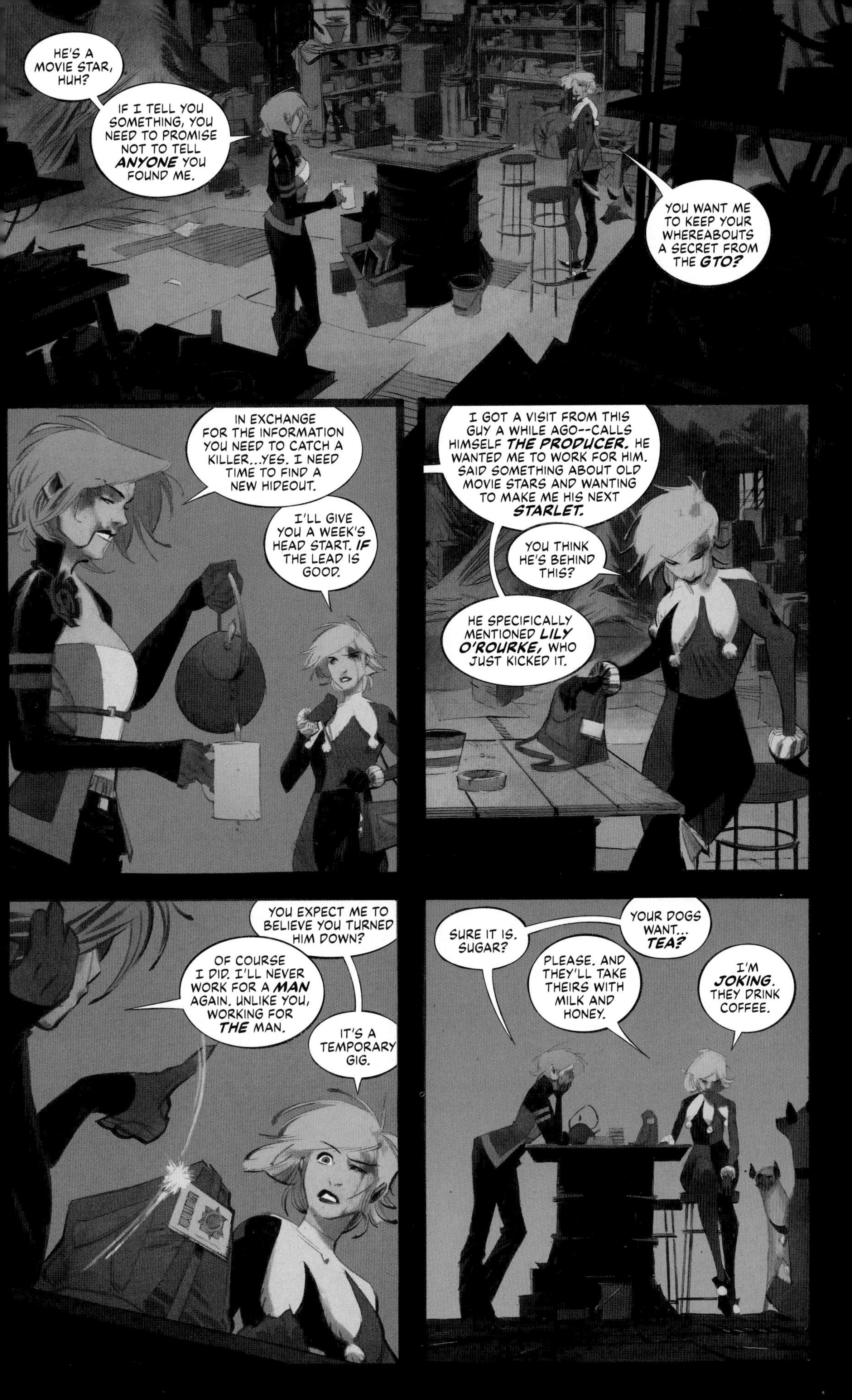
HE'S A MOVIE STAR, HUH?
IF I TELL YOU SOMETHING, YOU NEED TO PROMISE NOT TO TELL ANYONE YOU FOUND ME.
YOU WANT ME TO KEEP YOUR WHEREABOUTS A SECRET FROM THE GTO?
IN EXCHANGE FOR THE INFORMATION YOU NEED TO CATCH A KILLER...YES. I NEED TIME TO FIND A NEW HIDEOUT.
I'LL GIVE YOU A WEEK'S HEAD START. IF THE LEAD IS GOOD.
I GOT A VISIT FROM THIS GUY A WHILE AGO--CALLS HIMSELF THE PRODUCER. HE WANTED ME TO WORK FOR HIM. SAID SOMETHING ABOUT OLD MOVIE STARS AND WANTING TO MAKE ME HIS NEXT STARLET.
YOU THINK HE'S BEHIND THIS?
HE SPECIFICALLY MENTIONED LILY O'ROURKE, WHO JUST KICKED IT.
YOU EXPECT ME TO BELIEVE YOU TURNED HIM DOWN?
OF COURSE I DID. I'LL NEVER WORK FOR A MAN AGAIN. UNLIKE YOU, WORKING FOR THE MAN.
IT'S A TEMPORARY GIG.
SURE IT IS. SUGAR?
YOUR DOGS WANT... TEA?
PLEASE. AND THEY'LL TAKE THEIRS WITH MILK AND HONEY.
I'M JOKING. THEY DRINK COFFEE.

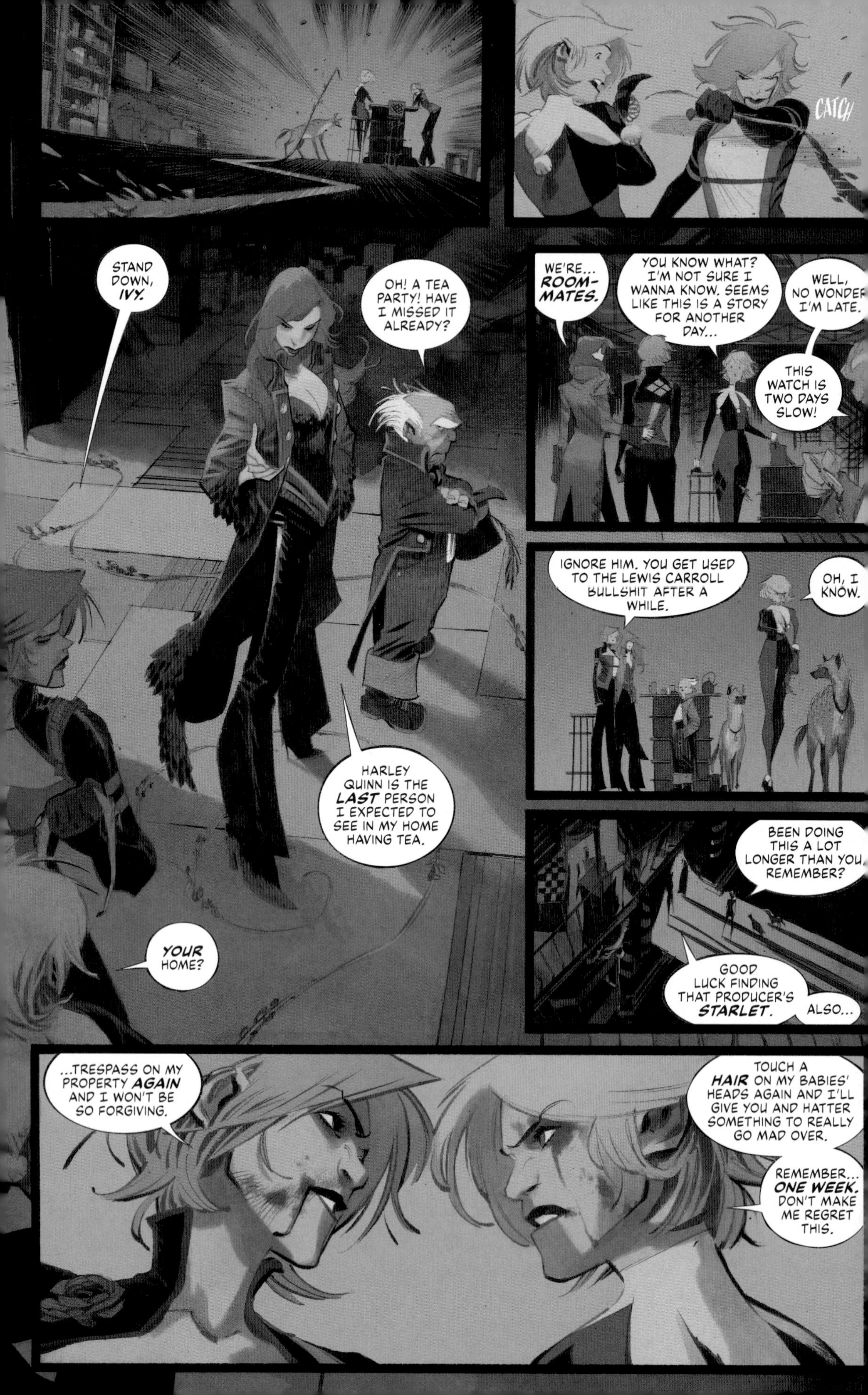
CATCH
STAND DOWN, IVY.
OH! A TEA PARTY! HAVE I MISSED IT ALREADY?
HARLEY QUINN IS THE LAST PERSON I EXPECTED TO SEE IN MY HOME HAVING TEA.
YOUR HOME?
WE'RE... ROOM-MATES.
YOU KNOW WHAT? I'M NOT SURE I WANNA KNOW. SEEMS LIKE THIS IS A STORY FOR ANOTHER DAY...
WELL, NO WONDER I'M LATE.
THIS WATCH IS TWO DAYS SLOW!
IGNORE HIM. YOU GET USED TO THE LEWIS CARROLL BULLSHIT AFTER A WHILE.
OH, I KNOW.
BEEN DOING THIS A LOT LONGER THAN YOU, REMEMBER?
GOOD LUCK FINDING THAT PRODUCER'S STARLET.
ALSO...
...TRESPASS ON MY PROPERTY AGAIN AND I WON'T BE SO FORGIVING.
TOUCH A HAIR ON MY BABIES' HEADS AGAIN AND I'LL GIVE YOU AND HATTER SOMETHING TO REALLY GO MAD OVER.
REMEMBER... ONE WEEK. DON'T MAKE ME REGRET THIS.

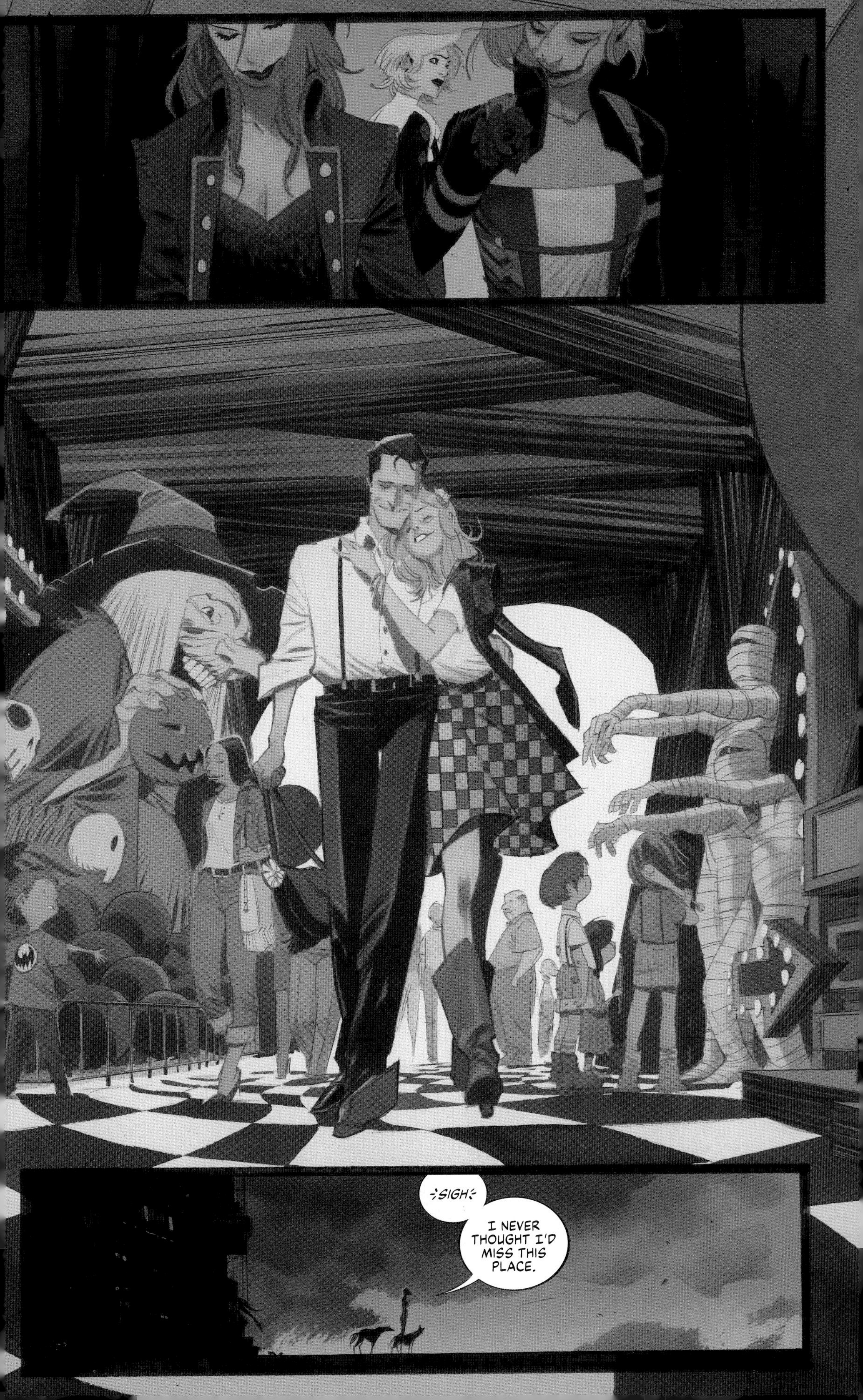
SIGH
I NEVER THOUGHT I'D MISS THIS PLACE.

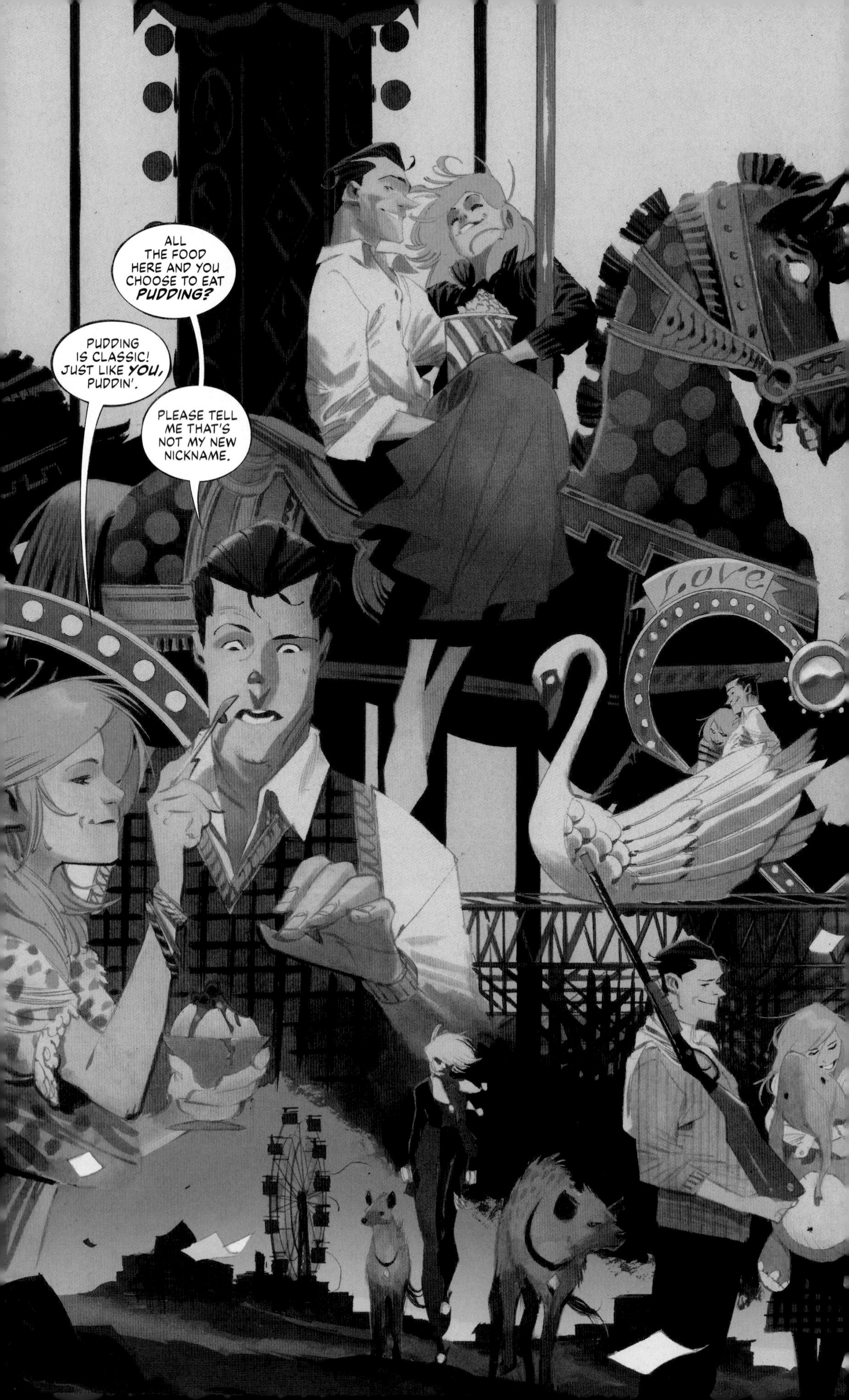
ALL THE FOOD HERE AND YOU CHOOSE TO EAT PUDDING?
PUDDING IS CLASSIC! JUST LIKE YOU, PUDDIN'.
PLEASE TELL ME THAT'S NOT MY NEW NICKNAME.
Love

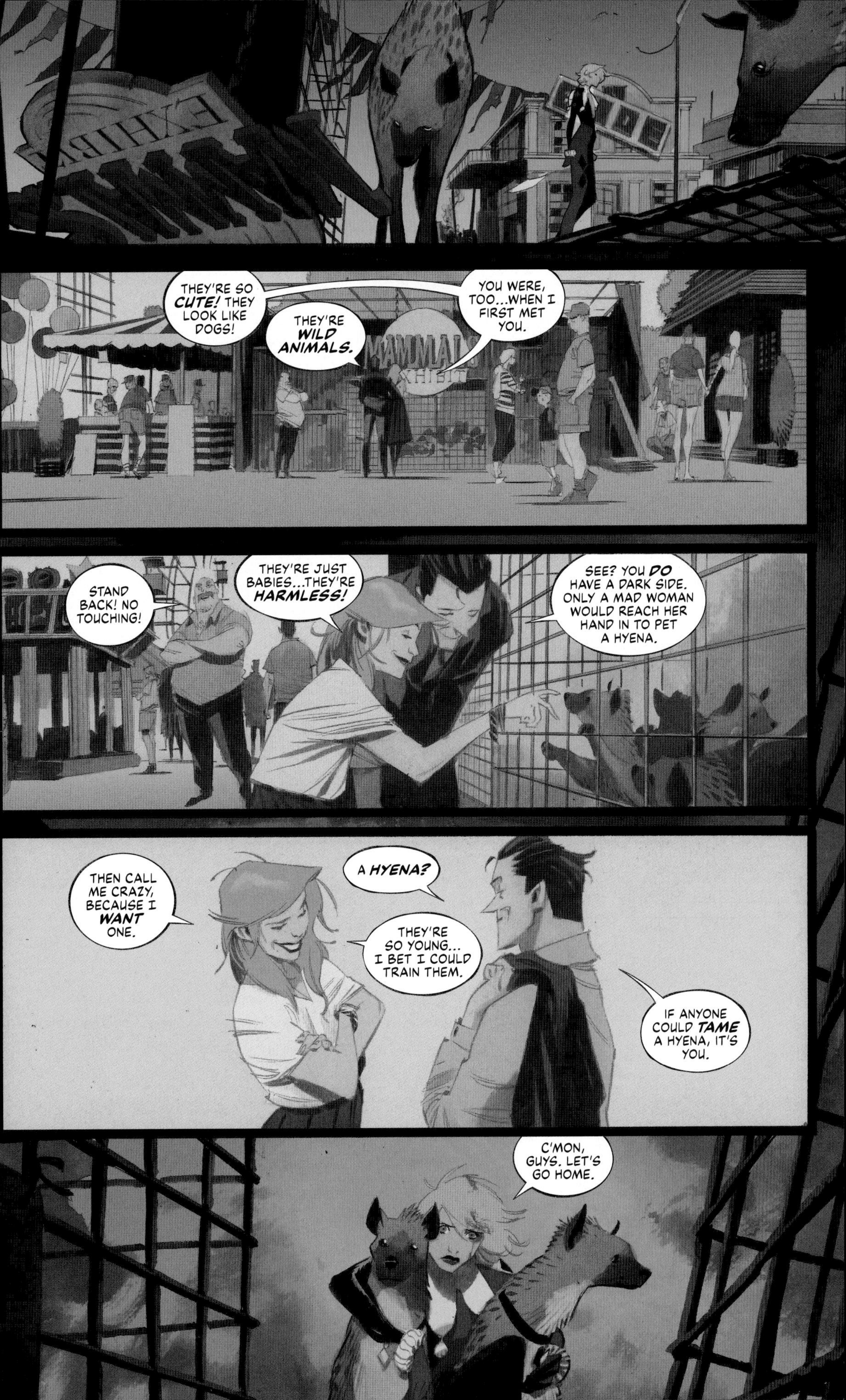
EXHIBIT
THEY'RE SO CUTE! THEY LOOK LIKE DOGS!
THEY'RE WILD ANIMALS.
YOU WERE, TOO...WHEN I FIRST MET YOU.
MAMMAL EXHIBIT
STAND BACK! NO TOUCHING!
THEY'RE JUST BABIES...THEY'RE HARMLESS!
SEE? YOU DO HAVE A DARK SIDE. ONLY A MAD WOMAN WOULD REACH HER HAND IN TO PET A HYENA.
THEN CALL ME CRAZY, BECAUSE I WANT ONE.
A HYENA?
THEY'RE SO YOUNG... I BET I COULD TRAIN THEM.
IF ANYONE COULD TAME A HYENA, IT'S YOU.
C'MON, GUYS. LET'S GO HOME.

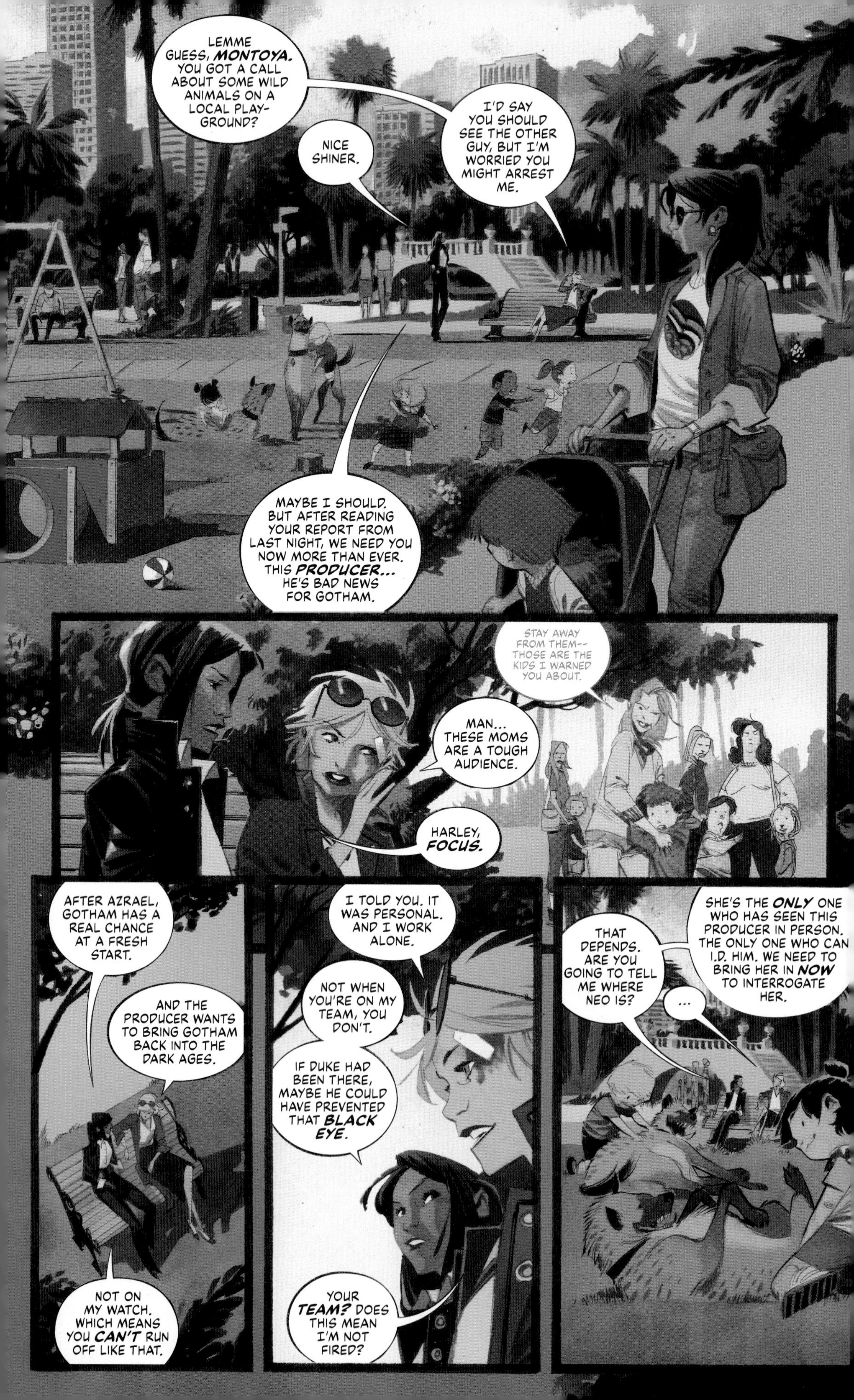
LEMME GUESS, MONTOYA. YOU GOT A CALL ABOUT SOME WILD ANIMALS ON A LOCAL PLAY-GROUND?
I'D SAY YOU SHOULD SEE THE OTHER GUY, BUT I'M WORRIED YOU MIGHT ARREST ME.
NICE SHINER.
MAYBE I SHOULD. BUT AFTER READING YOUR REPORT FROM LAST NIGHT, WE NEED YOU NOW MORE THAN EVER. THIS PRODUCER... HE'S BAD NEWS FOR GOTHAM.
STAY AWAY FROM THEM-- THOSE ARE THE KIDS I WARNED YOU ABOUT.
MAN... THESE MOMS ARE A TOUGH AUDIENCE.
HARLEY, FOCUS.
AFTER AZRAEL, GOTHAM HAS A REAL CHANCE AT A FRESH START.
AND THE PRODUCER WANTS TO BRING GOTHAM BACK INTO THE DARK AGES.
NOT ON MY WATCH. WHICH MEANS YOU CAN'T RUN OFF LIKE THAT.
I TOLD YOU. IT WAS PERSONAL. AND I WORK ALONE.
NOT WHEN YOU'RE ON MY TEAM, YOU DON'T.
IF DUKE HAD BEEN THERE, MAYBE HE COULD HAVE PREVENTED THAT BLACK EYE.
YOUR TEAM? DOES THIS MEAN I'M NOT FIRED?
SHE'S THE ONLY ONE WHO HAS SEEN THIS PRODUCER IN PERSON. THE ONLY ONE WHO CAN I.D. HIM. WE NEED TO BRING HER IN NOW TO INTERROGATE HER.
THAT DEPENDS. ARE YOU GOING TO TELL ME WHERE NEO IS?
...

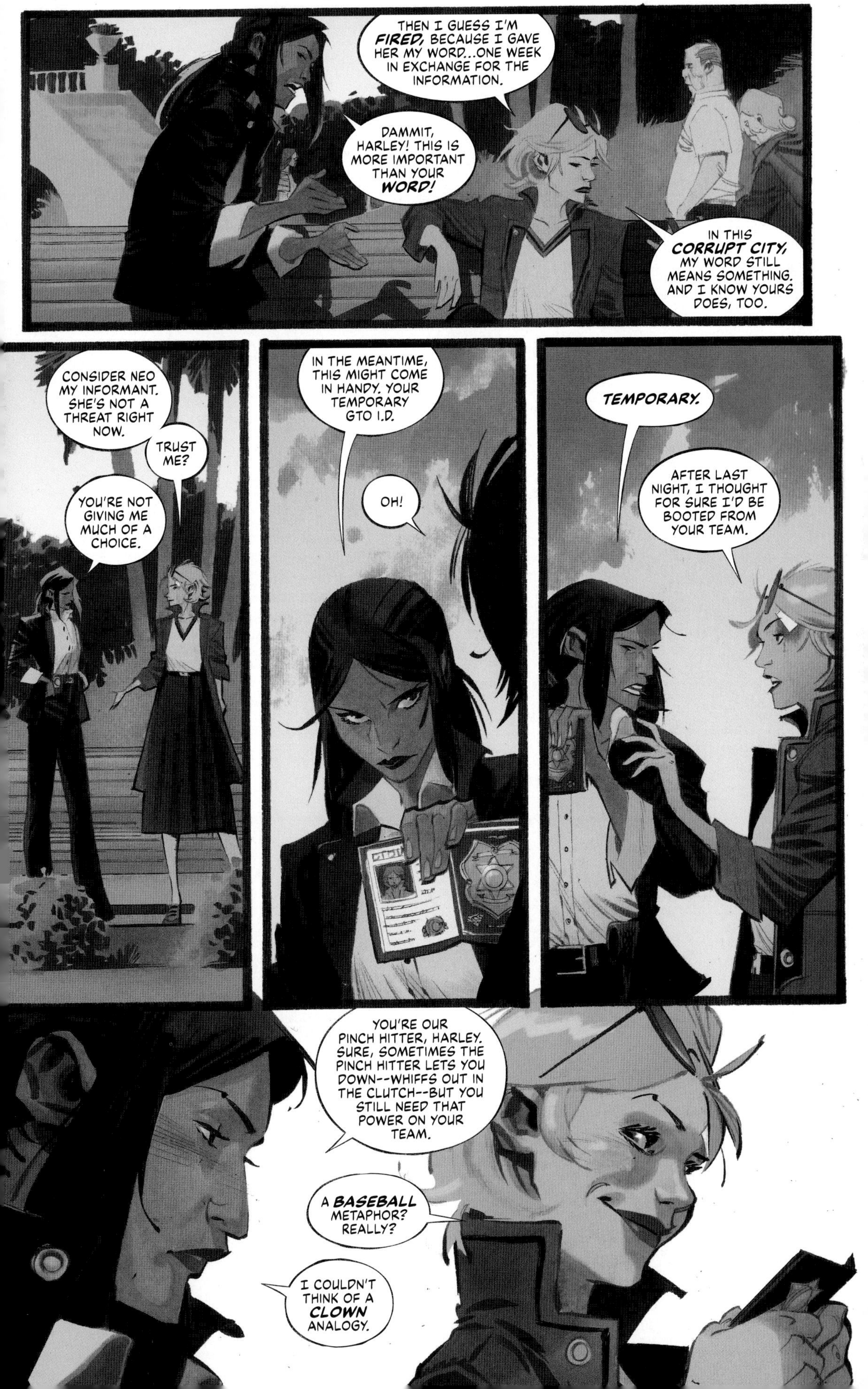
THEN I GUESS I'M FIRED, BECAUSE I GAVE HER MY WORD...ONE WEEK IN EXCHANGE FOR THE INFORMATION.
DAMMIT, HARLEY! THIS IS MORE IMPORTANT THAN YOUR WORD!
IN THIS CORRUPT CITY, MY WORD STILL MEANS SOMETHING. AND I KNOW YOURS DOES, TOO.
CONSIDER NEO MY INFORMANT. SHE'S NOT A THREAT RIGHT NOW.
TRUST ME?
YOU'RE NOT GIVING ME MUCH OF A CHOICE.
IN THE MEANTIME, THIS MIGHT COME IN HANDY. YOUR TEMPORARY GTO I.D.
OH!
TEMPORARY.
AFTER LAST NIGHT, I THOUGHT FOR SURE I'D BE BOOTED FROM YOUR TEAM.
YOU'RE OUR PINCH HITTER, HARLEY. SURE, SOMETIMES THE PINCH HITTER LETS YOU DOWN--WHIFFS OUT IN THE CLUTCH--BUT YOU STILL NEED THAT POWER ON YOUR TEAM.
A BASEBALL METAPHOR? REALLY?
I COULDN'T THINK OF A CLOWN ANALOGY.

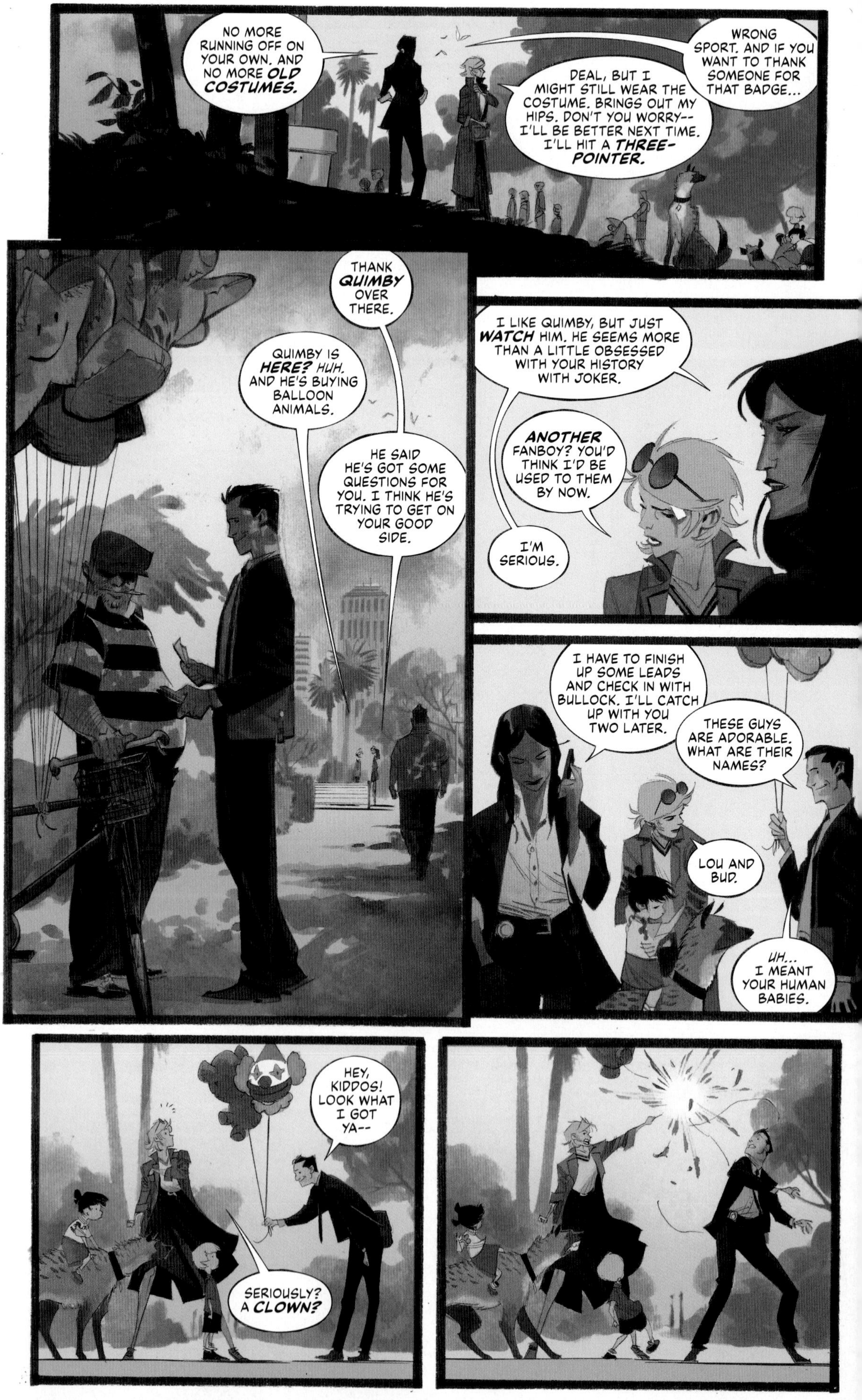
NO MORE RUNNING OFF ON YOUR OWN. AND NO MORE OLD COSTUMES.
DEAL, BUT I MIGHT STILL WEAR THE COSTUME. BRINGS OUT MY HIPS. DON'T YOU WORRY-- I'LL BE BETTER NEXT TIME. I'LL HIT A THREE-POINTER.
WRONG SPORT. AND IF YOU WANT TO THANK SOMEONE FOR THAT BADGE...
THANK QUIMBY OVER THERE.
QUIMBY IS HERE? HUH. AND HE'S BUYING BALLOON ANIMALS.
HE SAID HE'S GOT SOME QUESTIONS FOR YOU. I THINK HE'S TRYING TO GET ON YOUR GOOD SIDE.
I LIKE QUIMBY, BUT JUST WATCH HIM. HE SEEMS MORE THAN A LITTLE OBSESSED WITH YOUR HISTORY WITH JOKER.
ANOTHER FANBOY? YOU'D THINK I'D BE USED TO THEM BY NOW.
I'M SERIOUS.
I HAVE TO FINISH UP SOME LEADS AND CHECK IN WITH BULLOCK. I'LL CATCH UP WITH YOU TWO LATER.
THESE GUYS ARE ADORABLE. WHAT ARE THEIR NAMES?
LOU AND BUD.
UH... I MEANT YOUR HUMAN BABIES.
HEY, KIDDOS! LOOK WHAT I GOT YA--
SERIOUSLY? A CLOWN?

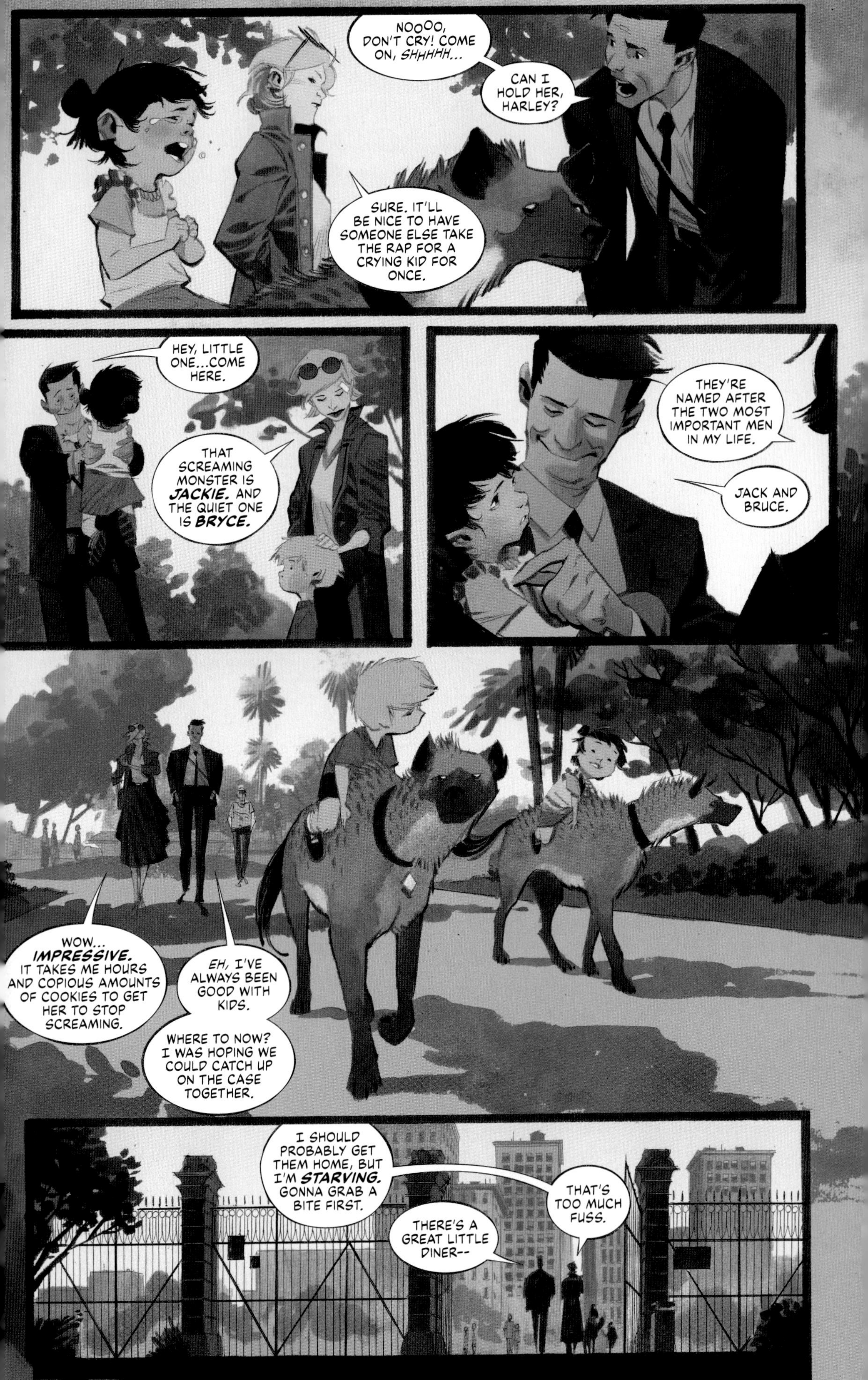
NOOOO, DON'T CRY! COME ON, *SHHHHH...*
CAN I HOLD HER, HARLEY?
SURE. IT'LL BE NICE TO HAVE SOMEONE ELSE TAKE THE RAP FOR A CRYING KID FOR ONCE.
HEY, LITTLE ONE...COME HERE.
THAT SCREAMING MONSTER IS ***JACKIE.*** AND THE QUIET ONE IS ***BRYCE.***
THEY'RE NAMED AFTER THE TWO MOST IMPORTANT MEN IN MY LIFE.
JACK AND BRUCE.
WOW... ***IMPRESSIVE.*** IT TAKES ME HOURS AND COPIOUS AMOUNTS OF COOKIES TO GET HER TO STOP SCREAMING.
EH, I'VE ALWAYS BEEN GOOD WITH KIDS.
WHERE TO NOW? I WAS HOPING WE COULD CATCH UP ON THE CASE TOGETHER.
I SHOULD PROBABLY GET THEM HOME, BUT I'M ***STARVING.*** GONNA GRAB A BITE FIRST.
THAT'S TOO MUCH FUSS.
THERE'S A GREAT LITTLE DINER--

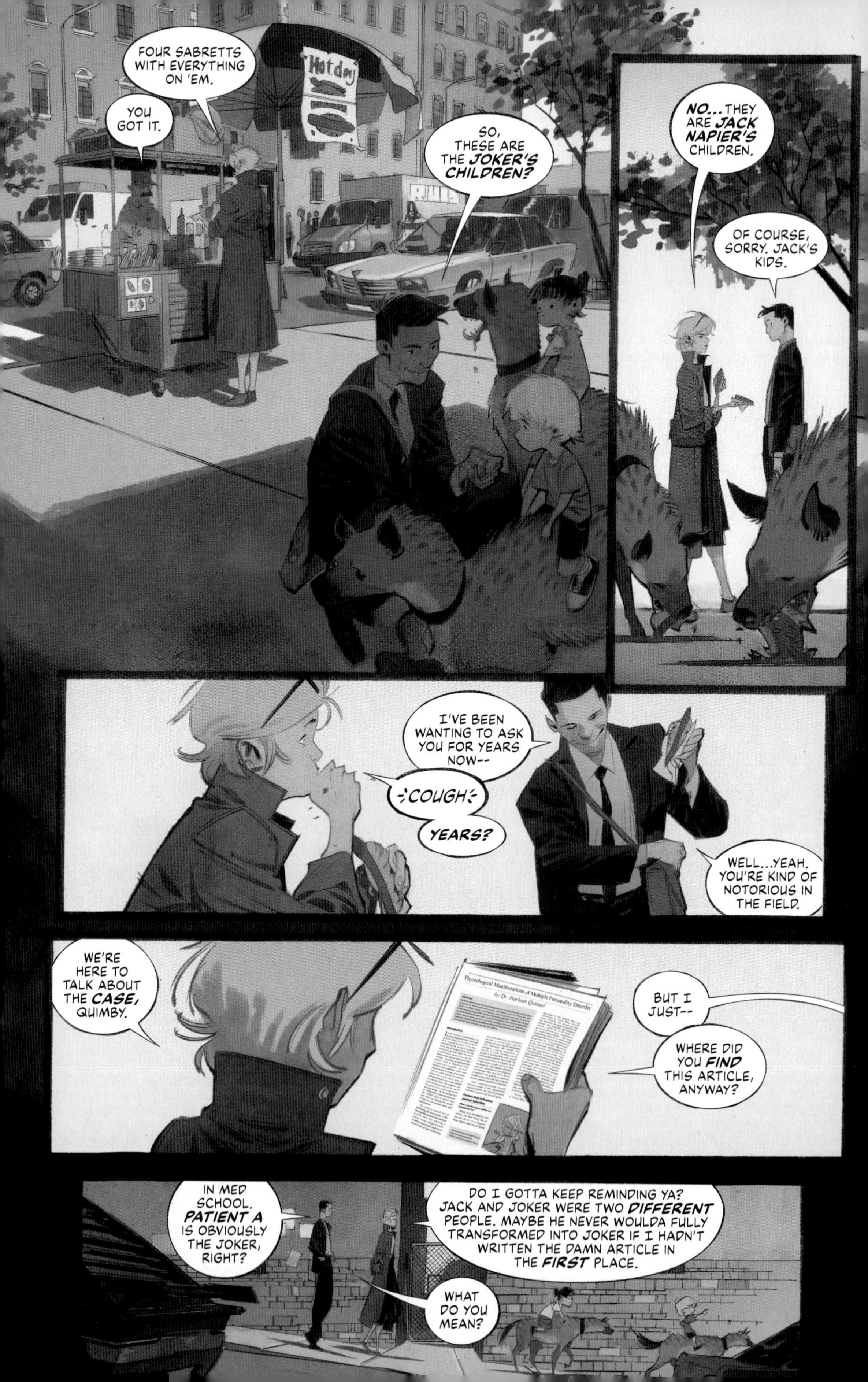
FOUR SABRETTS WITH EVERYTHING ON 'EM.
YOU GOT IT.
SO, THESE ARE THE *JOKER'S CHILDREN?*
NO... THEY ARE *JACK NAPIER'S* CHILDREN.
OF COURSE, SORRY. JACK'S KIDS.
I'VE BEEN WANTING TO ASK YOU FOR YEARS NOW--
COUGH
YEARS?
WELL...YEAH. YOU'RE KIND OF NOTORIOUS IN THE FIELD.
WE'RE HERE TO TALK ABOUT THE *CASE,* QUIMBY.
Physiological Manifestations of Multiple Personality Disorder
by Dr. Harleen Quinzel
BUT I JUST--
WHERE DID YOU *FIND* THIS ARTICLE, ANYWAY?
IN MED SCHOOL. *PATIENT A* IS OBVIOUSLY THE JOKER, RIGHT?
DO I GOTTA KEEP REMINDING YA? JACK AND JOKER WERE TWO *DIFFERENT* PEOPLE. MAYBE HE NEVER WOULDA FULLY TRANSFORMED INTO JOKER IF I HADN'T WRITTEN THE DAMN ARTICLE IN THE *FIRST* PLACE.
WHAT DO YOU MEAN?

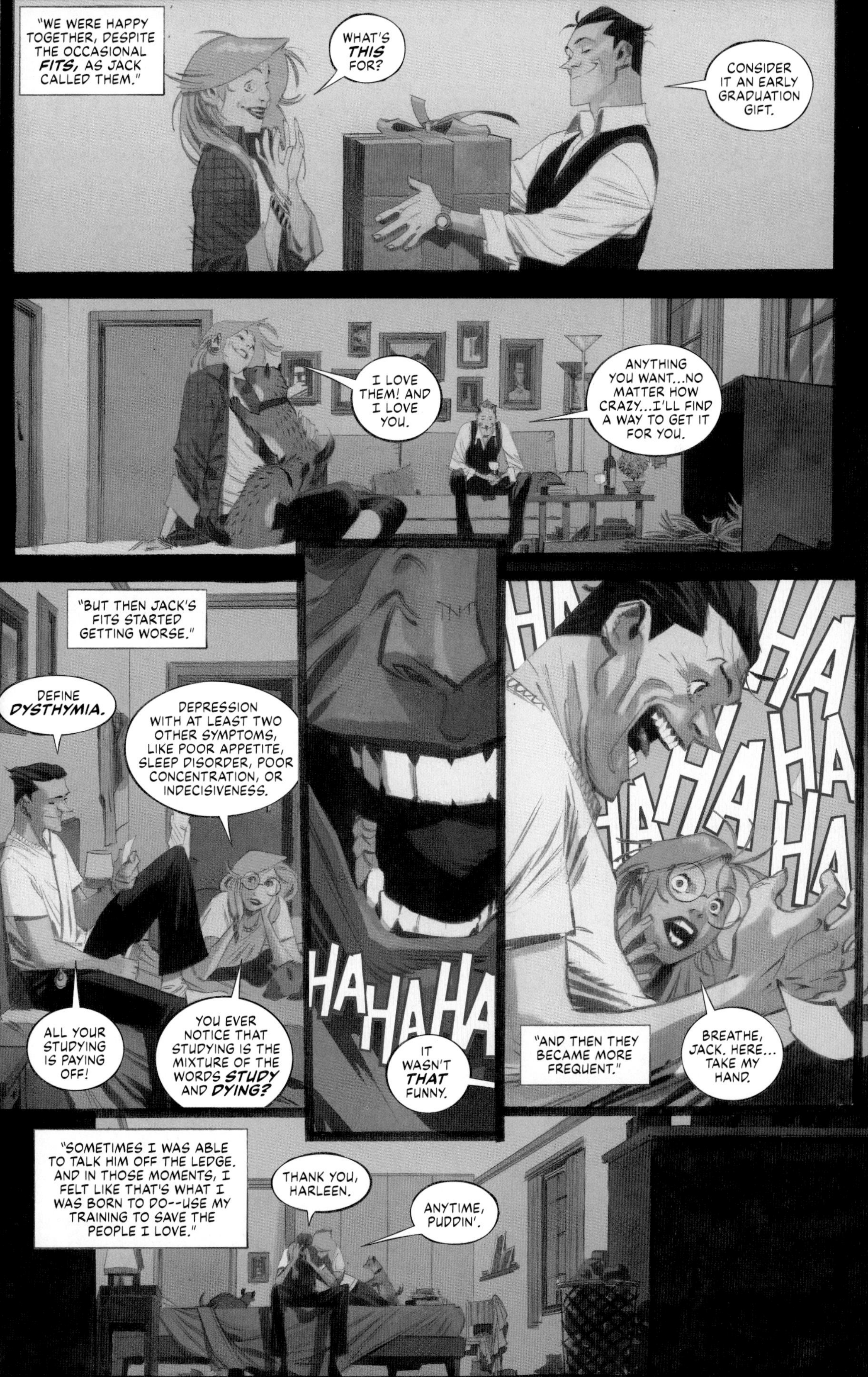
"WE WERE HAPPY TOGETHER, DESPITE THE OCCASIONAL FITS, AS JACK CALLED THEM."
WHAT'S THIS FOR?
CONSIDER IT AN EARLY GRADUATION GIFT.
I LOVE THEM! AND I LOVE YOU.
ANYTHING YOU WANT...NO MATTER HOW CRAZY...I'LL FIND A WAY TO GET IT FOR YOU.
"BUT THEN JACK'S FITS STARTED GETTING WORSE."
DEFINE DYSTHYMIA.
DEPRESSION WITH AT LEAST TWO OTHER SYMPTOMS, LIKE POOR APPETITE, SLEEP DISORDER, POOR CONCENTRATION, OR INDECISIVENESS.
ALL YOUR STUDYING IS PAYING OFF!
YOU EVER NOTICE THAT STUDYING IS THE MIXTURE OF THE WORDS STUDY AND DYING?
HAHAHA
IT WASN'T THAT FUNNY.
HAHAHAHAHAHAHAHA
"AND THEN THEY BECAME MORE FREQUENT."
BREATHE, JACK. HERE... TAKE MY HAND.
"SOMETIMES I WAS ABLE TO TALK HIM OFF THE LEDGE. AND IN THOSE MOMENTS, I FELT LIKE THAT'S WHAT I WAS BORN TO DO--USE MY TRAINING TO SAVE THE PEOPLE I LOVE."
THANK YOU, HARLEEN.
ANYTIME, PUDDIN'.

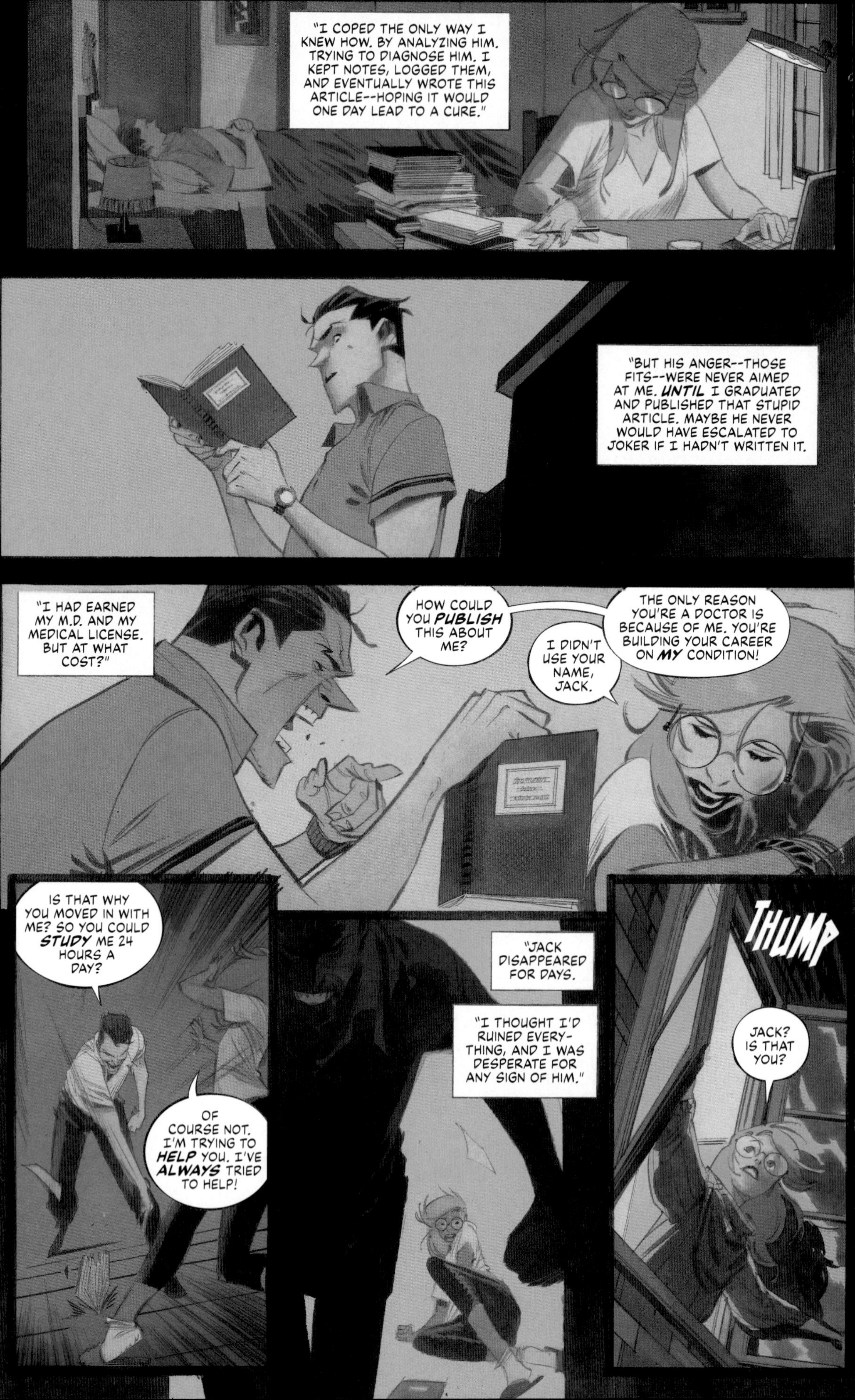
"I COPED THE ONLY WAY I KNEW HOW. BY ANALYZING HIM. TRYING TO DIAGNOSE HIM. I KEPT NOTES, LOGGED THEM, AND EVENTUALLY WROTE THIS ARTICLE--HOPING IT WOULD ONE DAY LEAD TO A CURE."
"BUT HIS ANGER--THOSE FITS--WERE NEVER AIMED AT ME. UNTIL I GRADUATED AND PUBLISHED THAT STUPID ARTICLE. MAYBE HE NEVER WOULD HAVE ESCALATED TO JOKER IF I HADN'T WRITTEN IT.
"I HAD EARNED MY M.D. AND MY MEDICAL LICENSE. BUT AT WHAT COST?"
HOW COULD YOU PUBLISH THIS ABOUT ME?
I DIDN'T USE YOUR NAME, JACK.
THE ONLY REASON YOU'RE A DOCTOR IS BECAUSE OF ME. YOU'RE BUILDING YOUR CAREER ON MY CONDITION!
IS THAT WHY YOU MOVED IN WITH ME? SO YOU COULD STUDY ME 24 HOURS A DAY?
OF COURSE NOT. I'M TRYING TO HELP YOU. I'VE ALWAYS TRIED TO HELP!
"JACK DISAPPEARED FOR DAYS.
"I THOUGHT I'D RUINED EVERYTHING, AND I WAS DESPERATE FOR ANY SIGN OF HIM."
THUMP
JACK? IS THAT YOU?

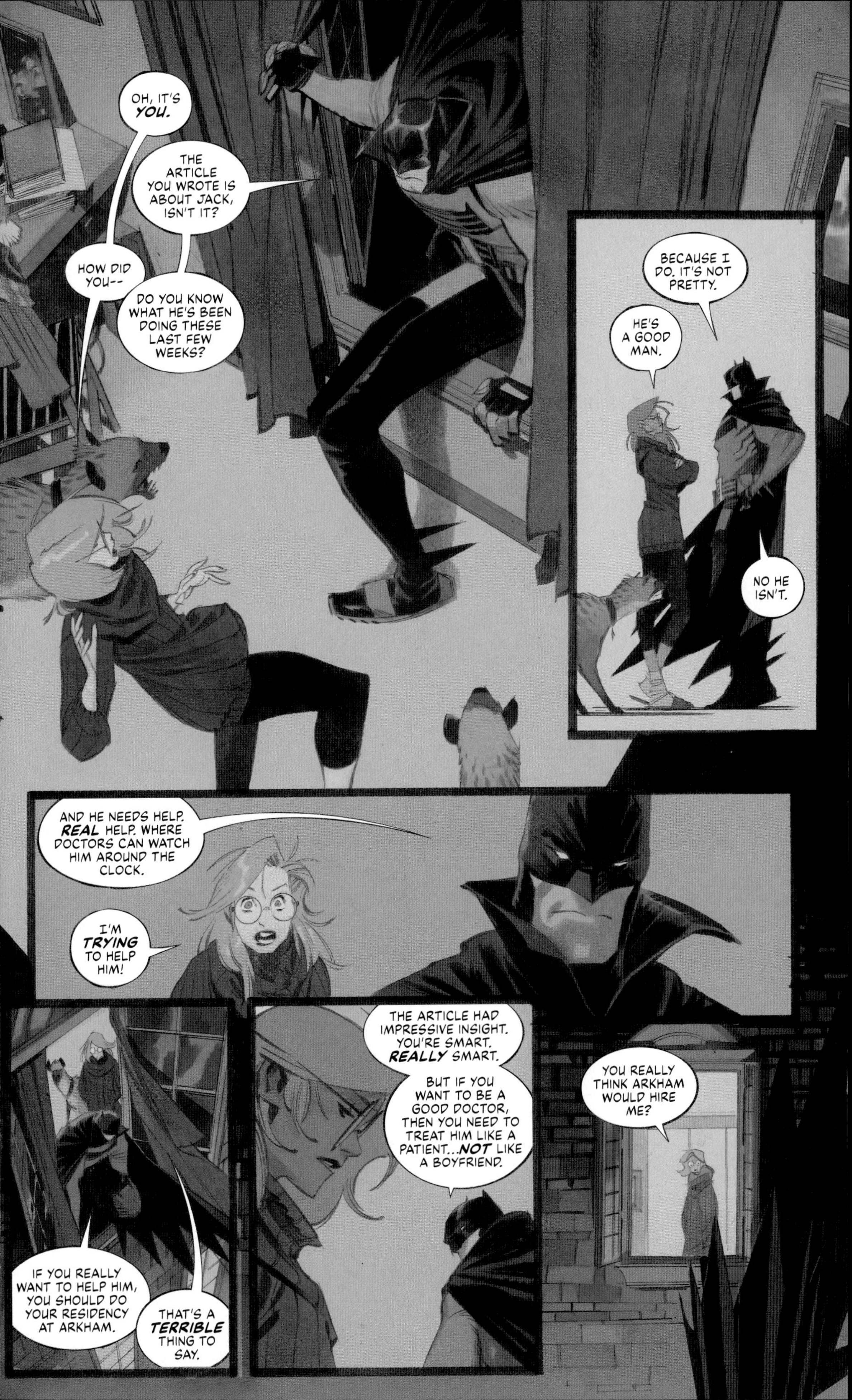
OH, IT'S YOU.
THE ARTICLE YOU WROTE IS ABOUT JACK, ISN'T IT?
HOW DID YOU--
DO YOU KNOW WHAT HE'S BEEN DOING THESE LAST FEW WEEKS?
HE'S A GOOD MAN.
BECAUSE I DO. IT'S NOT PRETTY.
NO HE ISN'T.
AND HE NEEDS HELP. REAL HELP. WHERE DOCTORS CAN WATCH HIM AROUND THE CLOCK.
I'M TRYING TO HELP HIM!
IF YOU REALLY WANT TO HELP HIM, YOU SHOULD DO YOUR RESIDENCY AT ARKHAM.
THAT'S A TERRIBLE THING TO SAY.
THE ARTICLE HAD IMPRESSIVE INSIGHT. YOU'RE SMART. REALLY SMART.
BUT IF YOU WANT TO BE A GOOD DOCTOR, THEN YOU NEED TO TREAT HIM LIKE A PATIENT...NOT LIKE A BOYFRIEND.
YOU REALLY THINK ARKHAM WOULD HIRE ME?

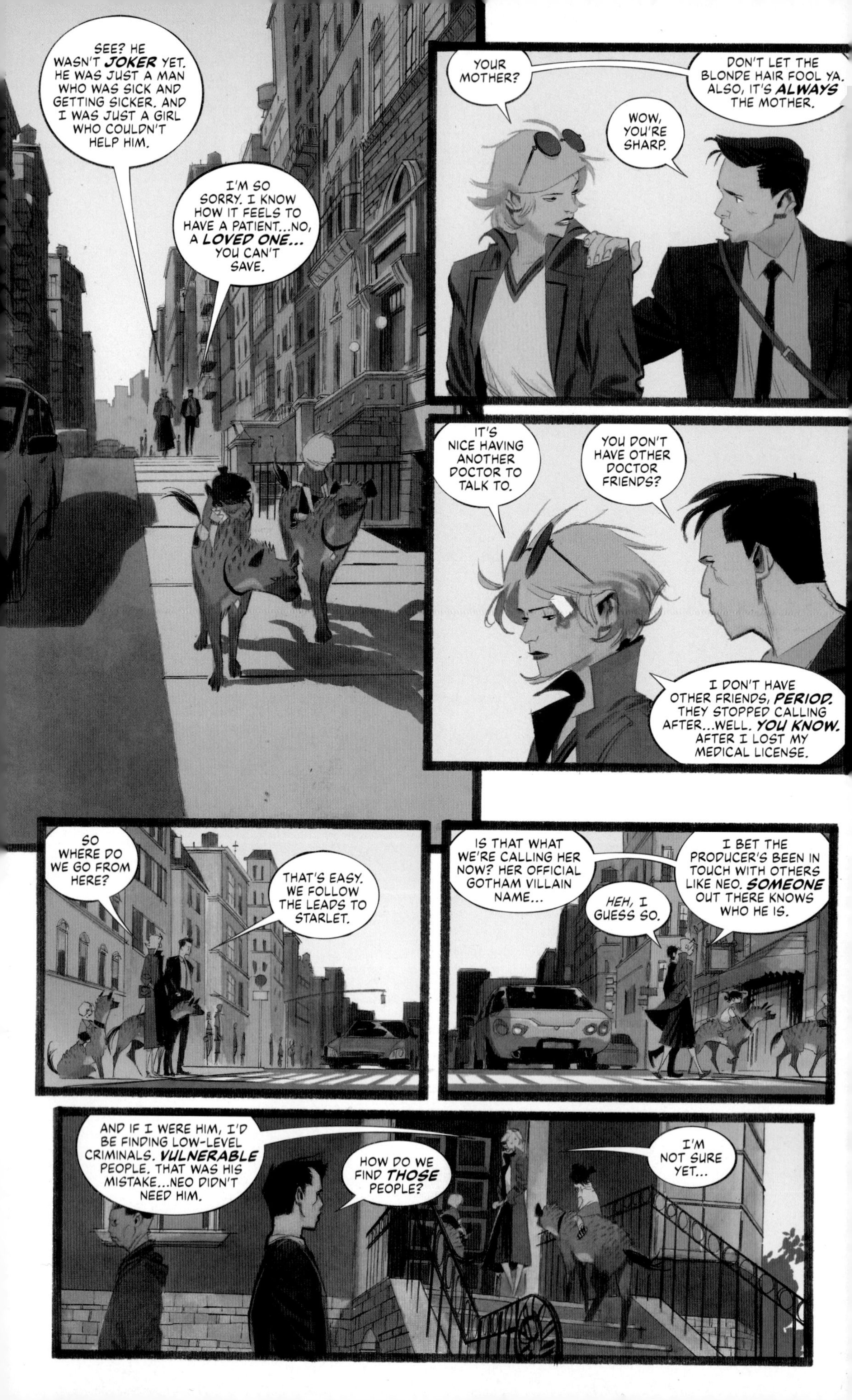
SEE? HE WASN'T JOKER YET. HE WAS JUST A MAN WHO WAS SICK AND GETTING SICKER. AND I WAS JUST A GIRL WHO COULDN'T HELP HIM.
I'M SO SORRY. I KNOW HOW IT FEELS TO HAVE A PATIENT...NO, A LOVED ONE... YOU CAN'T SAVE.
YOUR MOTHER?
DON'T LET THE BLONDE HAIR FOOL YA. ALSO, IT'S ALWAYS THE MOTHER.
WOW, YOU'RE SHARP.
IT'S NICE HAVING ANOTHER DOCTOR TO TALK TO.
YOU DON'T HAVE OTHER DOCTOR FRIENDS?
I DON'T HAVE OTHER FRIENDS, PERIOD. THEY STOPPED CALLING AFTER...WELL. YOU KNOW. AFTER I LOST MY MEDICAL LICENSE.
SO WHERE DO WE GO FROM HERE?
THAT'S EASY. WE FOLLOW THE LEADS TO STARLET.
IS THAT WHAT WE'RE CALLING HER NOW? HER OFFICIAL GOTHAM VILLAIN NAME...
HEH, I GUESS SO.
I BET THE PRODUCER'S BEEN IN TOUCH WITH OTHERS LIKE NEO. SOMEONE OUT THERE KNOWS WHO HE IS.
AND IF I WERE HIM, I'D BE FINDING LOW-LEVEL CRIMINALS. VULNERABLE PEOPLE. THAT WAS HIS MISTAKE...NEO DIDN'T NEED HIM.
HOW DO WE FIND THOSE PEOPLE?
I'M NOT SURE YET...

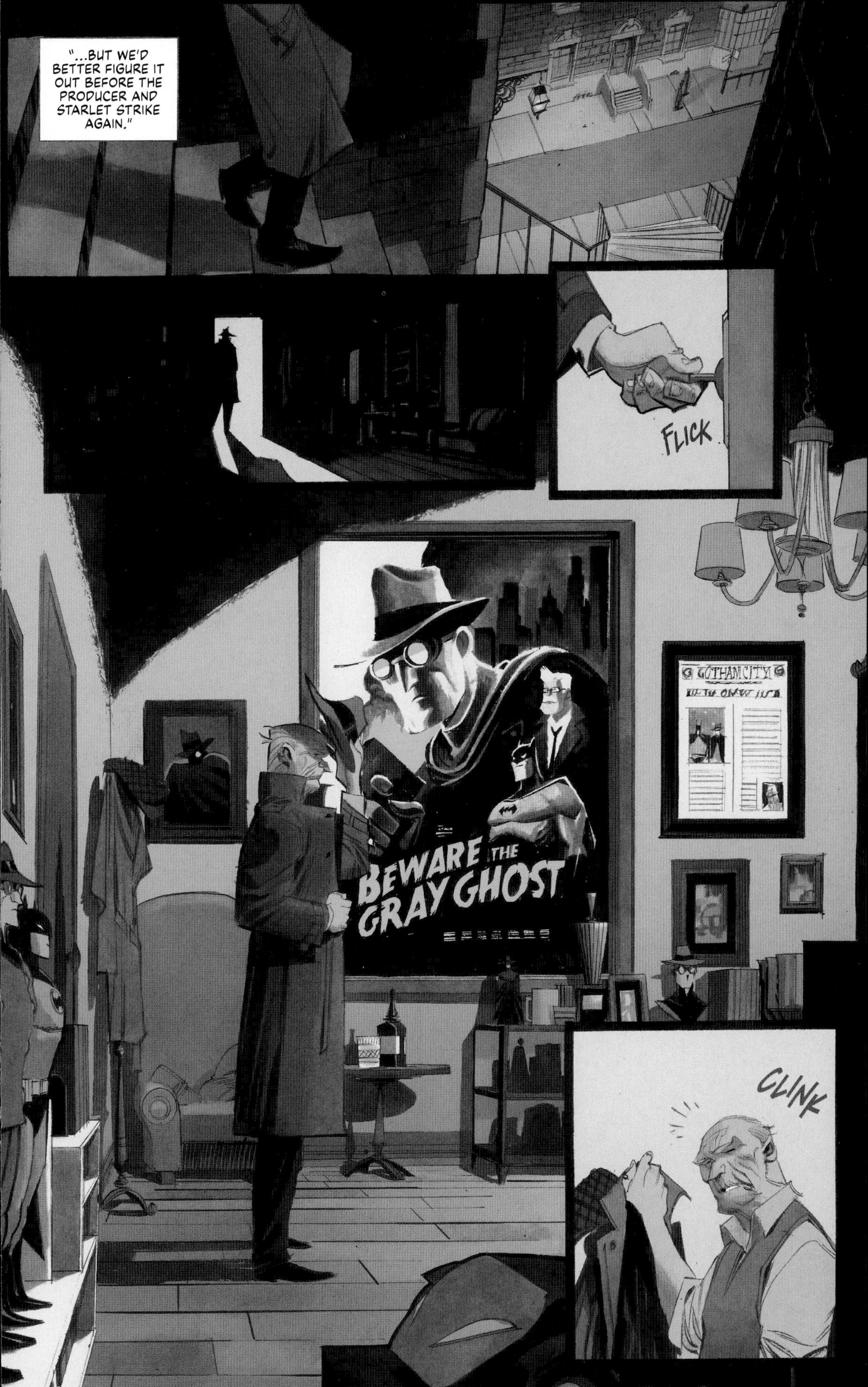
"...BUT WE'D BETTER FIGURE IT OUT BEFORE THE PRODUCER AND STARLET STRIKE AGAIN."
FLICK
BEWARE THE GRAY GHOST
CLINK

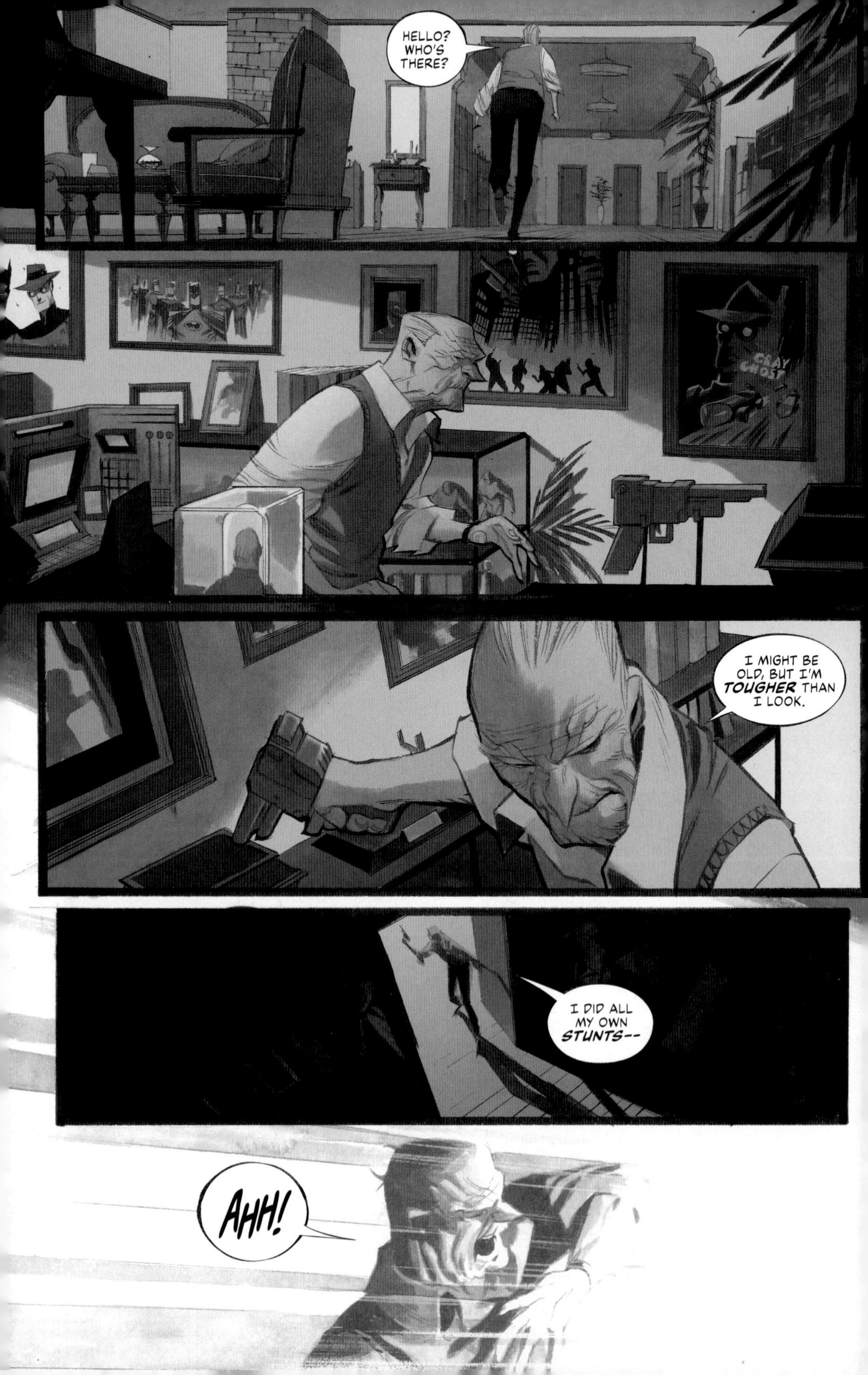
HELLO? WHO'S THERE?
GRAY GHOST
I MIGHT BE OLD, BUT I'M TOUGHER THAN I LOOK.
I DID ALL MY OWN STUNTS--
AHH!

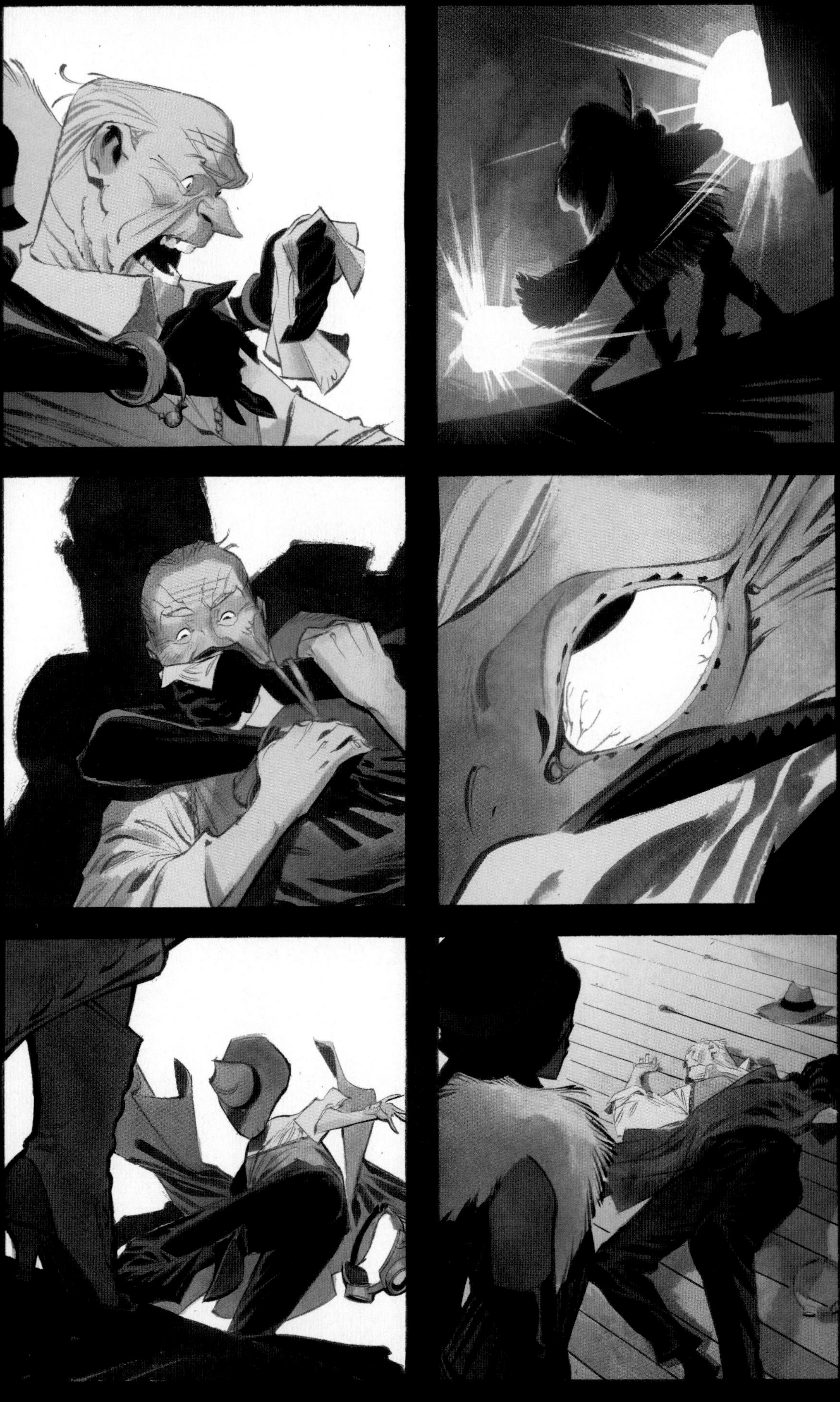

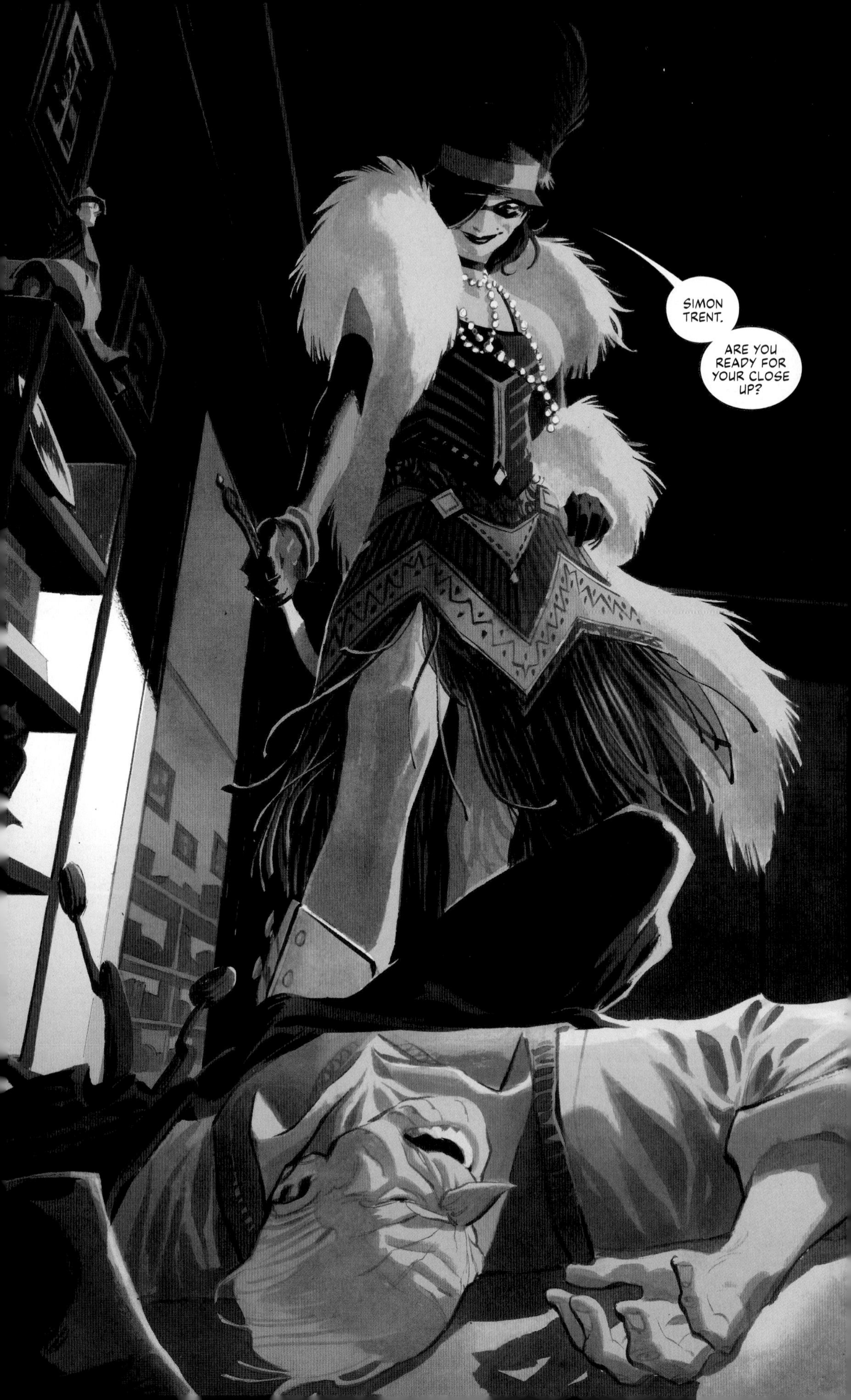
SIMON TRENT.
ARE YOU READY FOR YOUR CLOSE UP?

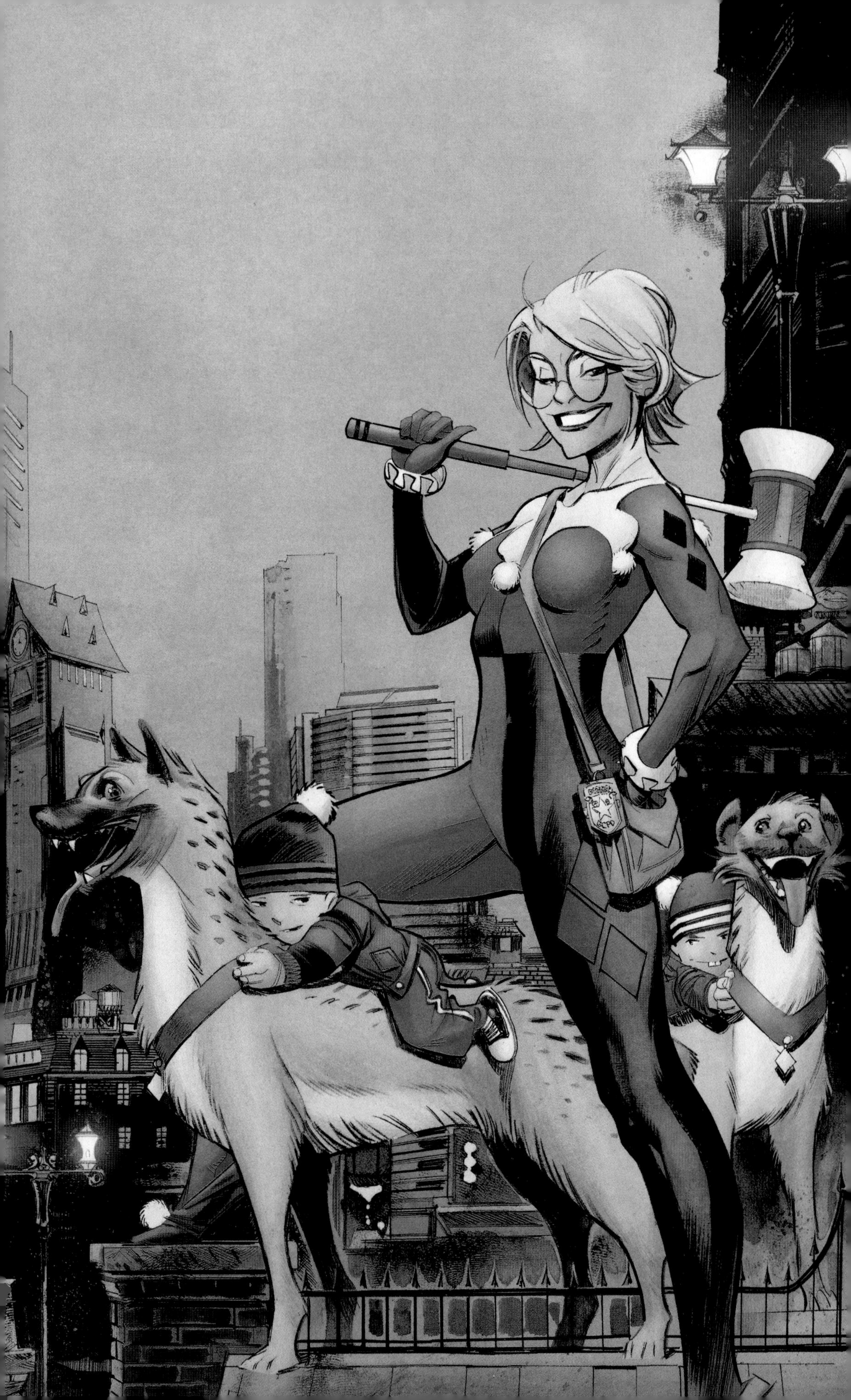
GCPD

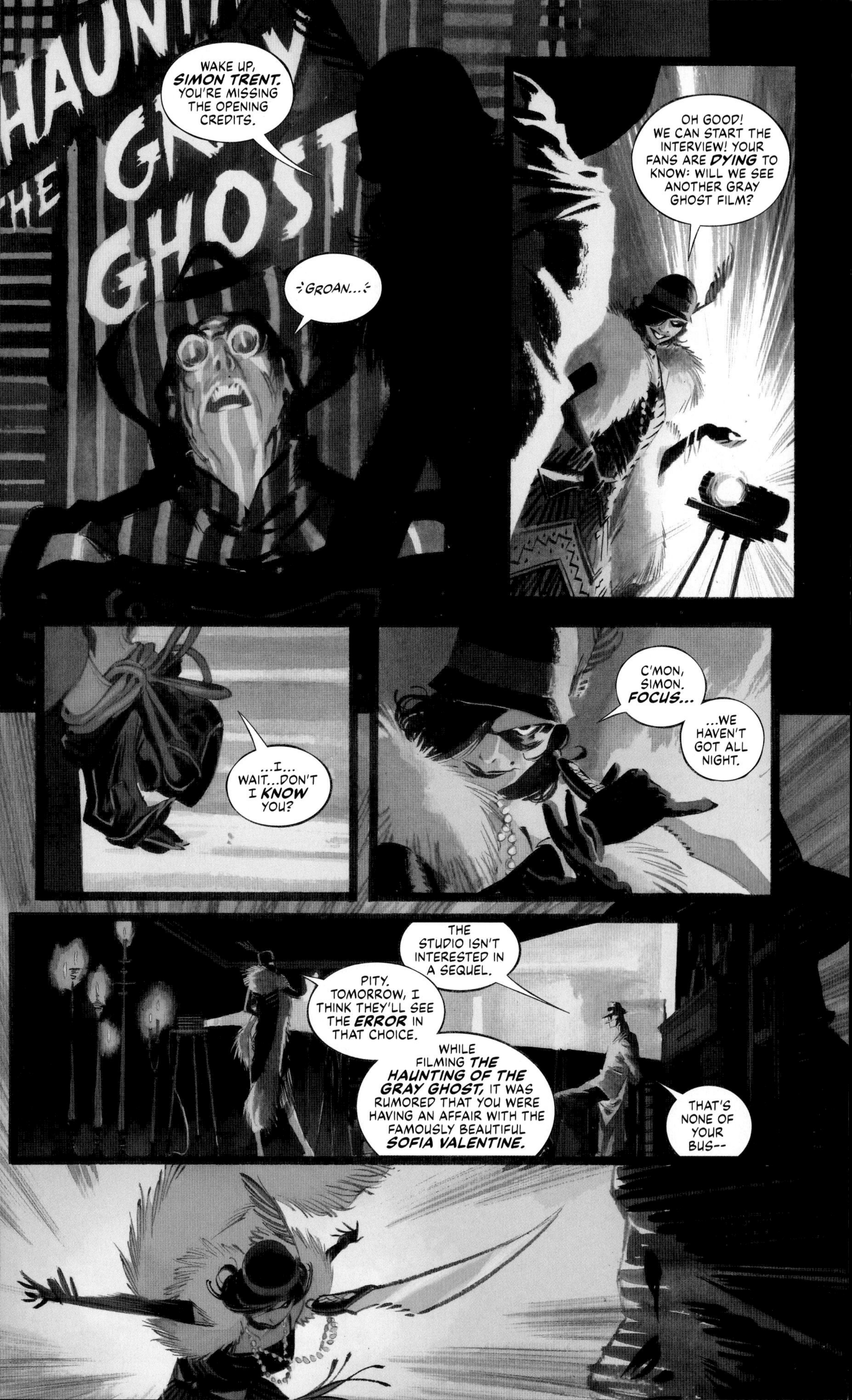

THE HAUNTING OF THE GRAY GHOST
WAKE UP, SIMON TRENT. YOU'RE MISSING THE OPENING CREDITS.
GROAN...
OH GOOD! WE CAN START THE INTERVIEW! YOUR FANS ARE DYING TO KNOW: WILL WE SEE ANOTHER GRAY GHOST FILM?
...I... WAIT...DON'T I KNOW YOU?
C'MON, SIMON. FOCUS...
...WE HAVEN'T GOT ALL NIGHT.
THE STUDIO ISN'T INTERESTED IN A SEQUEL.
PITY. TOMORROW, I THINK THEY'LL SEE THE ERROR IN THAT CHOICE.
WHILE FILMING THE HAUNTING OF THE GRAY GHOST, IT WAS RUMORED THAT YOU WERE HAVING AN AFFAIR WITH THE FAMOUSLY BEAUTIFUL SOFIA VALENTINE.
THAT'S NONE OF YOUR BUS--

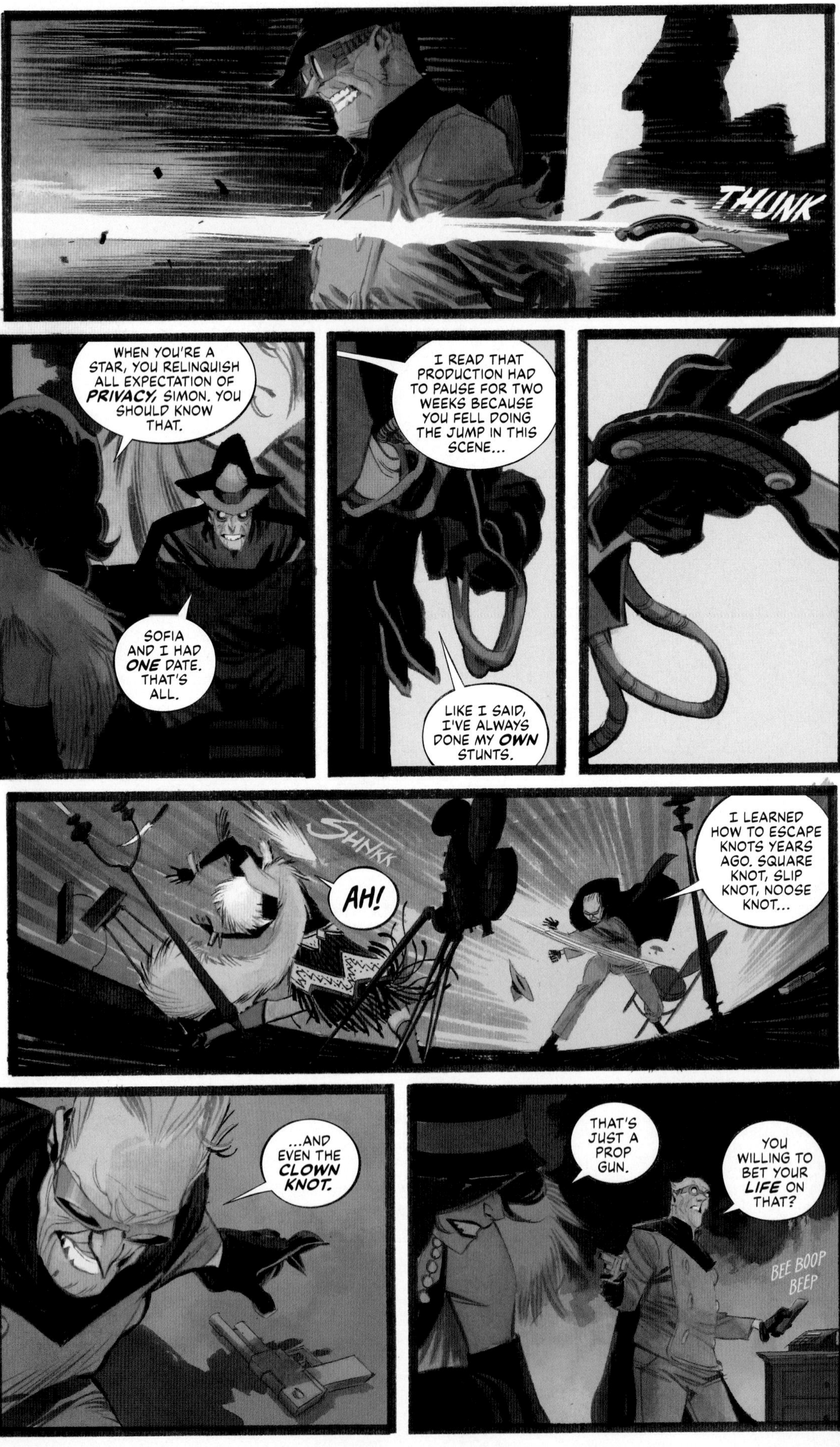

THUNK
WHEN YOU'RE A STAR, YOU RELINQUISH ALL EXPECTATION OF PRIVACY, SIMON. YOU SHOULD KNOW THAT.
SOFIA AND I HAD ONE DATE. THAT'S ALL.
I READ THAT PRODUCTION HAD TO PAUSE FOR TWO WEEKS BECAUSE YOU FELL DOING THE JUMP IN THIS SCENE...
LIKE I SAID, I'VE ALWAYS DONE MY OWN STUNTS.
SHNKK
AH!
I LEARNED HOW TO ESCAPE KNOTS YEARS AGO. SQUARE KNOT, SLIP KNOT, NOOSE KNOT...
...AND EVEN THE CLOWN KNOT.
THAT'S JUST A PROP GUN.
YOU WILLING TO BET YOUR LIFE ON THAT?
BEE BOOP BEEP

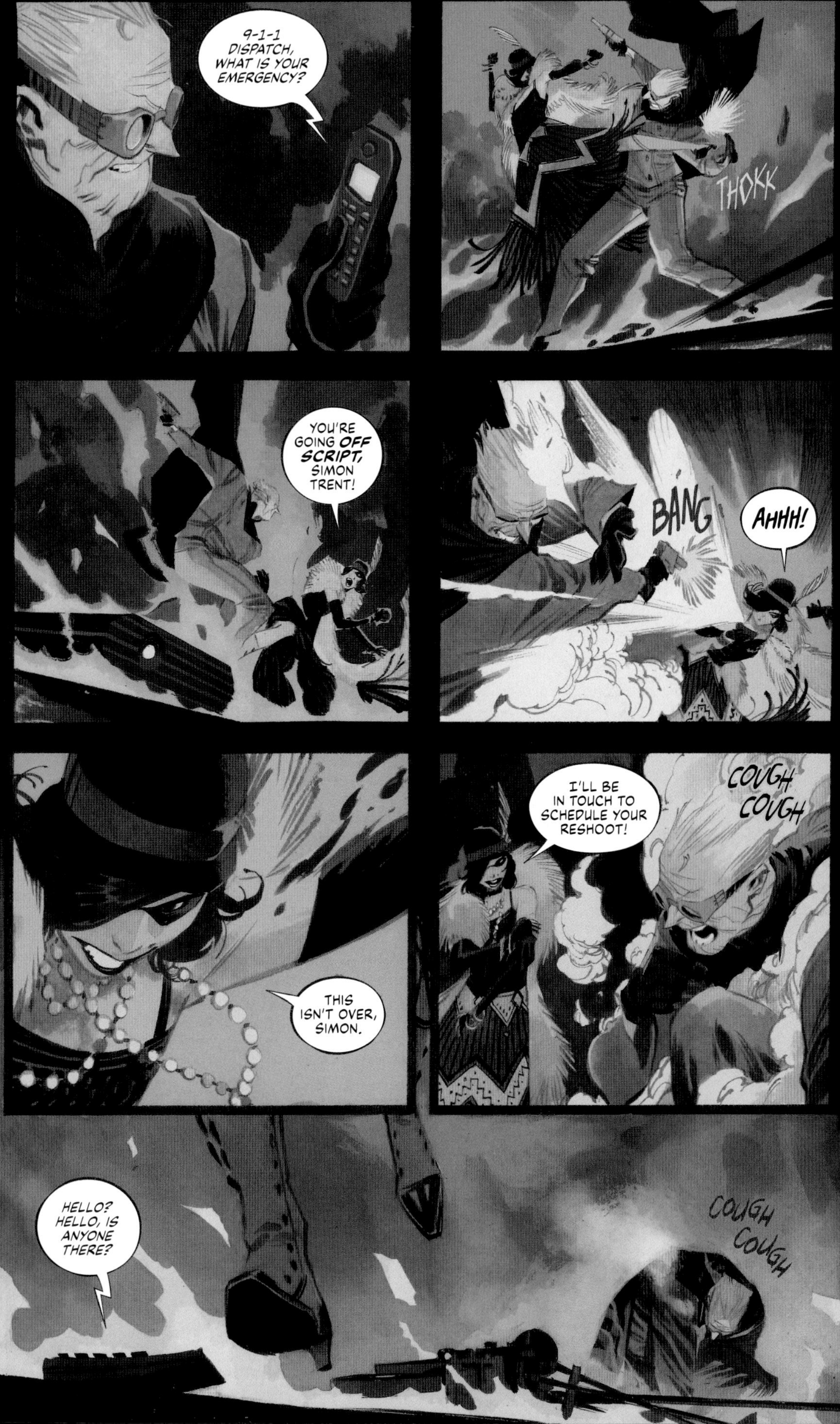
9-1-1 DISPATCH, WHAT IS YOUR EMERGENCY?
THOKK
YOU'RE GOING OFF SCRIPT, SIMON TRENT!
BANG
AHHH!
THIS ISN'T OVER, SIMON.
I'LL BE IN TOUCH TO SCHEDULE YOUR RESHOOT!
COUGH COUGH
HELLO? HELLO, IS ANYONE THERE?
COUGH COUGH

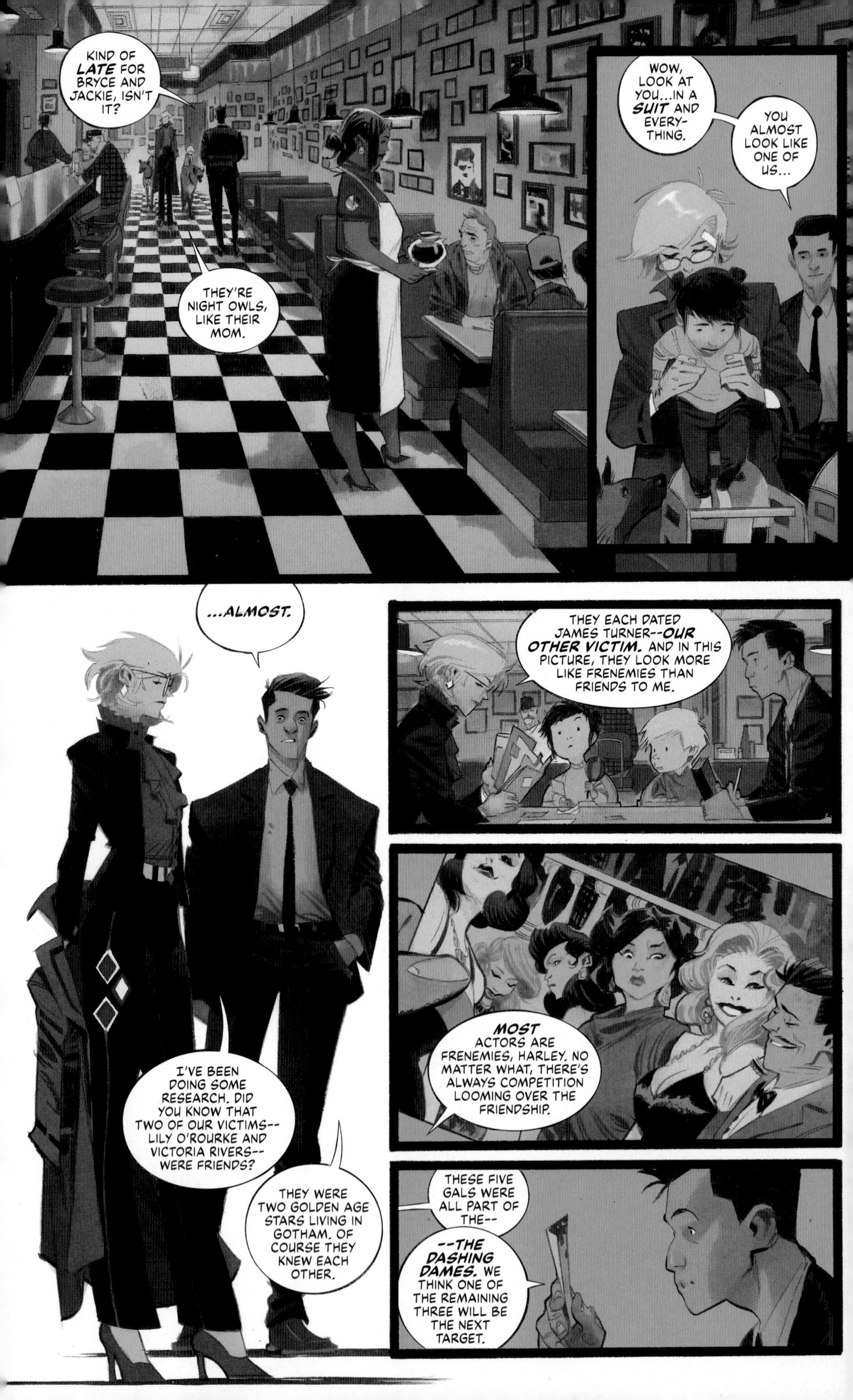
KIND OF LATE FOR BRYCE AND JACKIE, ISN'T IT?
THEY'RE NIGHT OWLS, LIKE THEIR MOM.
WOW, LOOK AT YOU...IN A SUIT AND EVERY-THING.
YOU ALMOST LOOK LIKE ONE OF US...
...ALMOST.
THEY EACH DATED JAMES TURNER--OUR OTHER VICTIM. AND IN THIS PICTURE, THEY LOOK MORE LIKE FRENEMIES THAN FRIENDS TO ME.
I'VE BEEN DOING SOME RESEARCH. DID YOU KNOW THAT TWO OF OUR VICTIMS--LILY O'ROURKE AND VICTORIA RIVERS--WERE FRIENDS?
THEY WERE TWO GOLDEN AGE STARS LIVING IN GOTHAM. OF COURSE THEY KNEW EACH OTHER.
MOST ACTORS ARE FRENEMIES, HARLEY. NO MATTER WHAT, THERE'S ALWAYS COMPETITION LOOMING OVER THE FRIENDSHIP.
THESE FIVE GALS WERE ALL PART OF THE--
--THE DASHING DAMES. WE THINK ONE OF THE REMAINING THREE WILL BE THE NEXT TARGET.

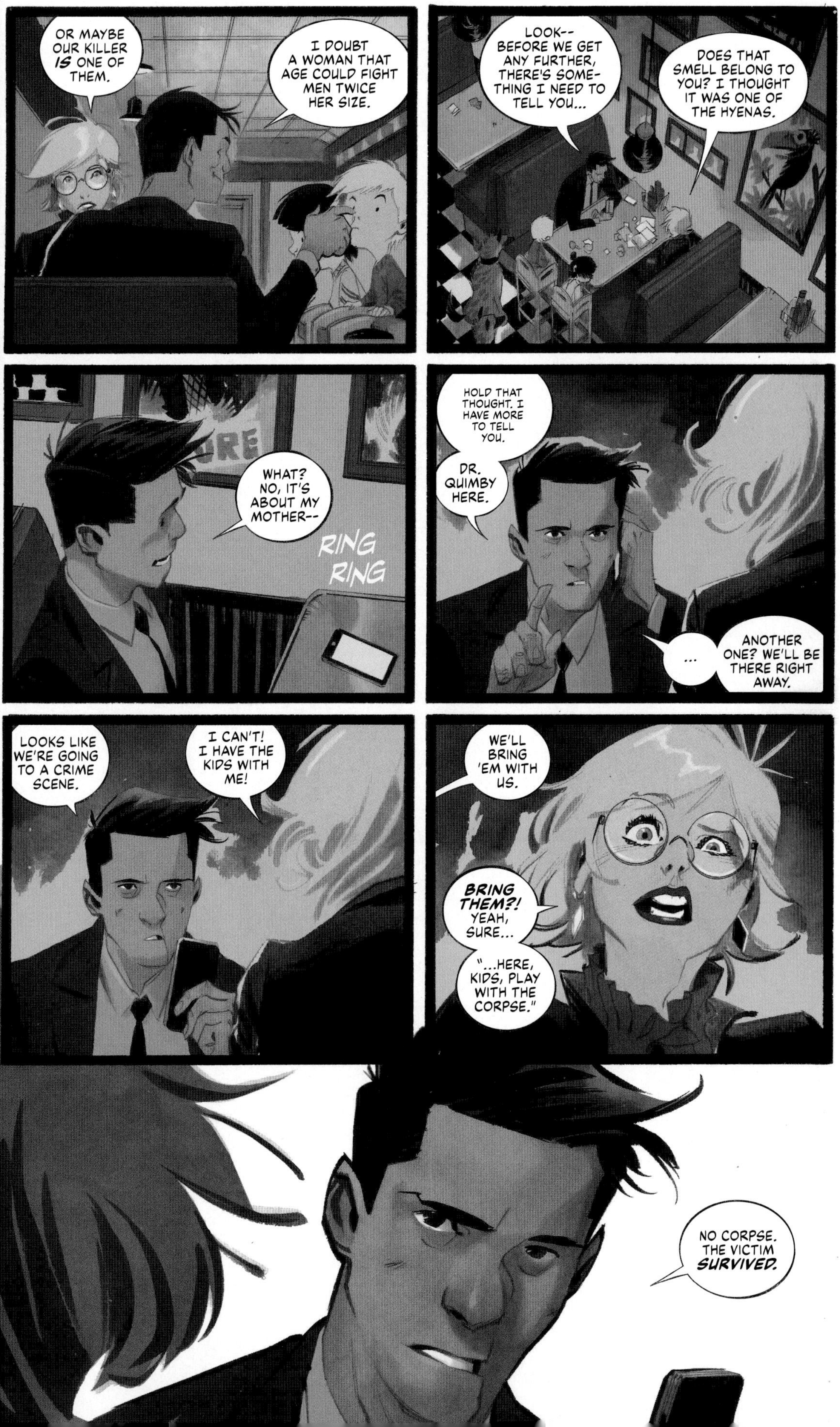
OR MAYBE OUR KILLER *IS* ONE OF THEM.
I DOUBT A WOMAN THAT AGE COULD FIGHT MEN TWICE HER SIZE.
LOOK-- BEFORE WE GET ANY FURTHER, THERE'S SOME-THING I NEED TO TELL YOU...
DOES THAT SMELL BELONG TO YOU? I THOUGHT IT WAS ONE OF THE HYENAS.
WHAT? NO, IT'S ABOUT MY MOTHER--
RING RING
HOLD THAT THOUGHT. I HAVE MORE TO TELL YOU.
DR. QUIMBY HERE.
...
ANOTHER ONE? WE'LL BE THERE RIGHT AWAY.
LOOKS LIKE WE'RE GOING TO A CRIME SCENE.
I CAN'T! I HAVE THE KIDS WITH ME!
WE'LL BRING 'EM WITH US.
BRING THEM?! YEAH, SURE...
"...HERE, KIDS, PLAY WITH THE CORPSE."
NO CORPSE. THE VICTIM *SURVIVED.*

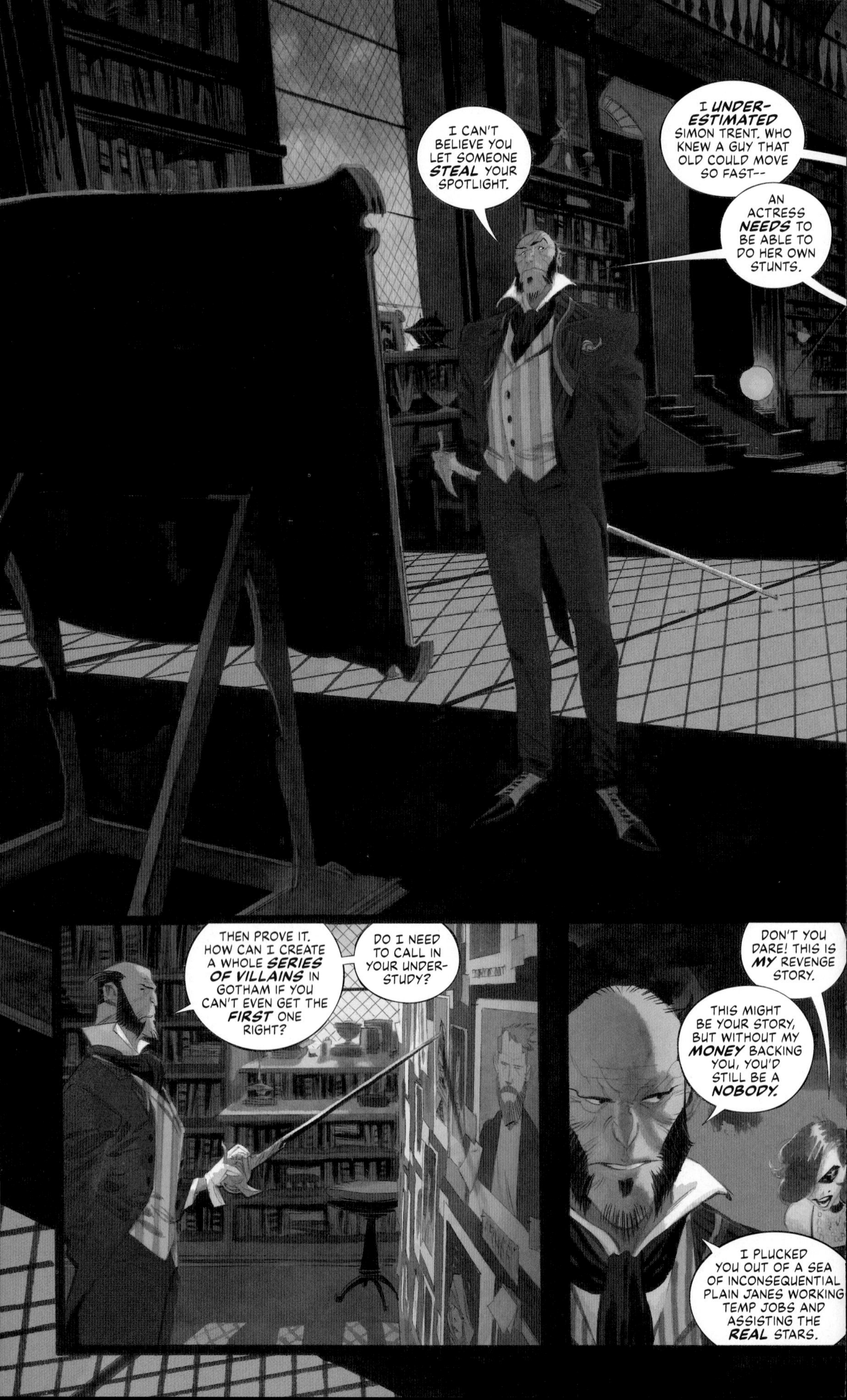
I CAN'T BELIEVE YOU LET SOMEONE STEAL YOUR SPOTLIGHT.
I UNDER-ESTIMATED SIMON TRENT. WHO KNEW A GUY THAT OLD COULD MOVE SO FAST--
AN ACTRESS NEEDS TO BE ABLE TO DO HER OWN STUNTS.
THEN PROVE IT. HOW CAN I CREATE A WHOLE SERIES OF VILLAINS IN GOTHAM IF YOU CAN'T EVEN GET THE FIRST ONE RIGHT?
DO I NEED TO CALL IN YOUR UNDER-STUDY?
DON'T YOU DARE! THIS IS MY REVENGE STORY.
THIS MIGHT BE YOUR STORY, BUT WITHOUT MY MONEY BACKING YOU, YOU'D STILL BE A NOBODY.
I PLUCKED YOU OUT OF A SEA OF INCONSEQUENTIAL PLAIN JANES WORKING TEMP JOBS AND ASSISTING THE REAL STARS.

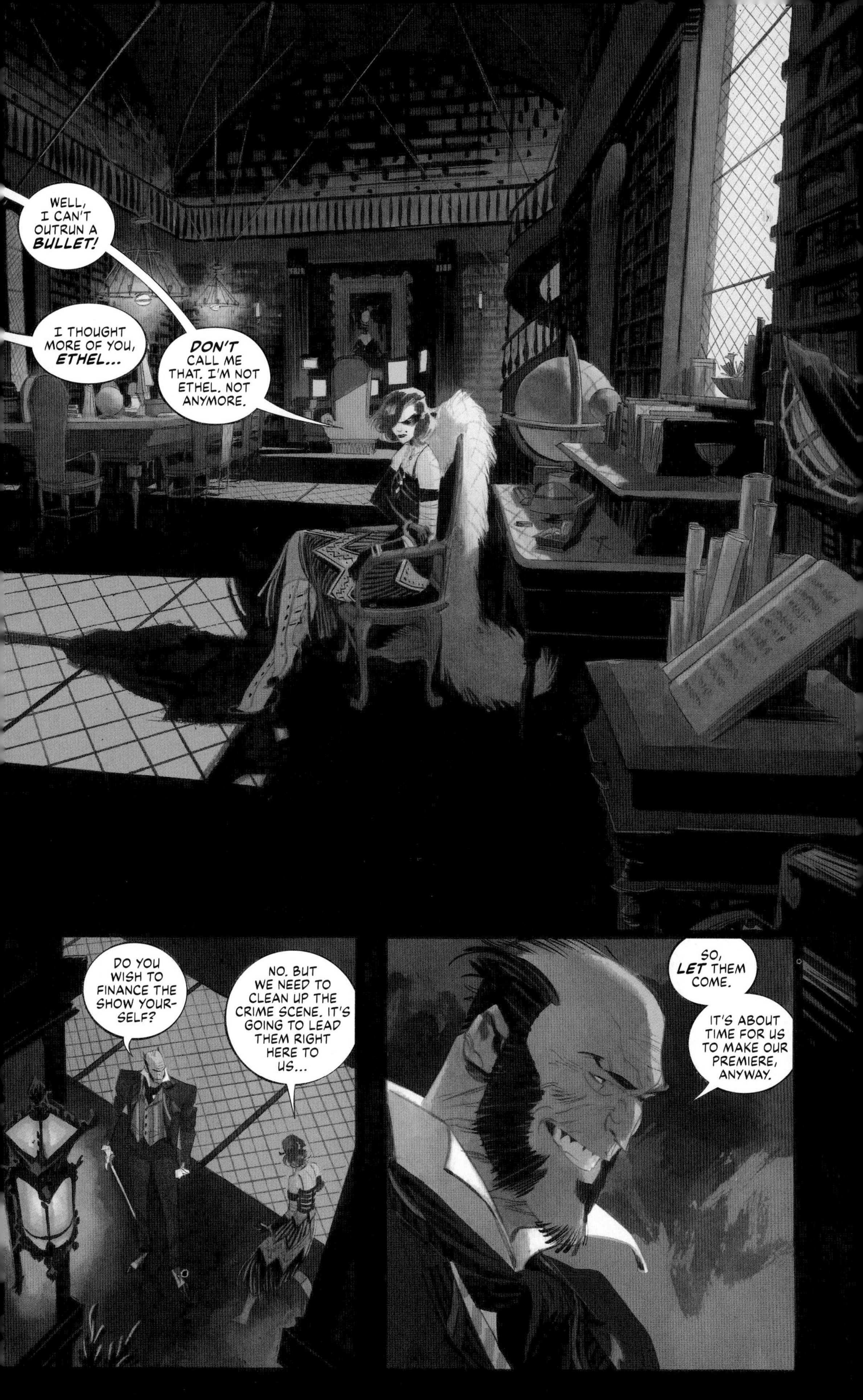
WELL, I CAN'T OUTRUN A BULLET!
I THOUGHT MORE OF YOU, ETHEL...
DON'T CALL ME THAT. I'M NOT ETHEL. NOT ANYMORE.
DO YOU WISH TO FINANCE THE SHOW YOUR-SELF?
NO. BUT WE NEED TO CLEAN UP THE CRIME SCENE. IT'S GOING TO LEAD THEM RIGHT HERE TO US...
SO, LET THEM COME.
IT'S ABOUT TIME FOR US TO MAKE OUR PREMIERE, ANYWAY.

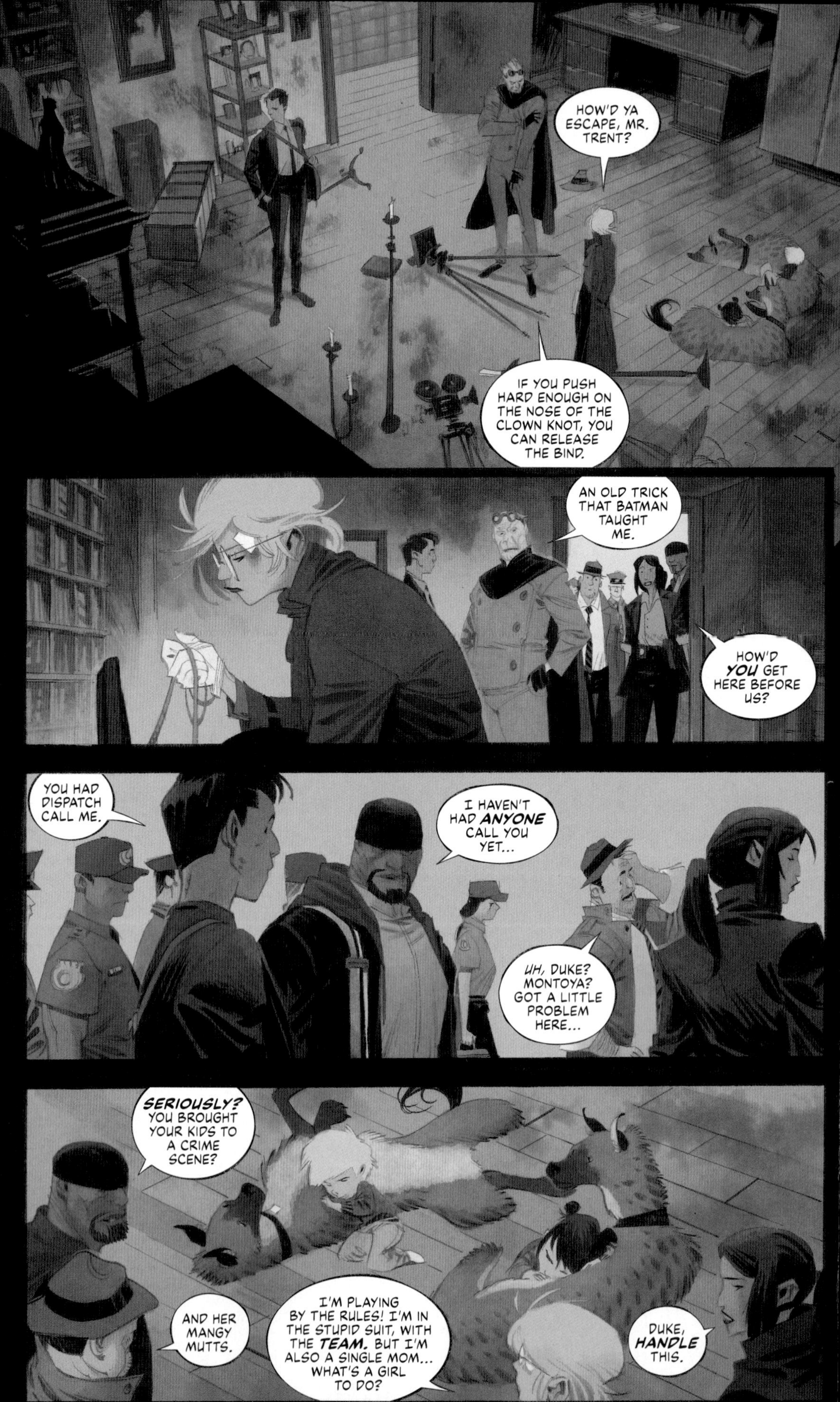

HOW'D YA ESCAPE, MR. TRENT?
IF YOU PUSH HARD ENOUGH ON THE NOSE OF THE CLOWN KNOT, YOU CAN RELEASE THE BIND.
AN OLD TRICK THAT BATMAN TAUGHT ME.
HOW'D *YOU* GET HERE BEFORE US?
YOU HAD DISPATCH CALL ME.
I HAVEN'T HAD ***ANYONE*** CALL YOU YET...
UH, DUKE? MONTOYA? GOT A LITTLE PROBLEM HERE...
SERIOUSLY? YOU BROUGHT YOUR KIDS TO A CRIME SCENE?
AND HER MANGY MUTTS.
I'M PLAYING BY THE RULES! I'M IN THE STUPID SUIT, WITH THE ***TEAM.*** BUT I'M ALSO A SINGLE MOM... WHAT'S A GIRL TO DO?
DUKE, ***HANDLE*** THIS.

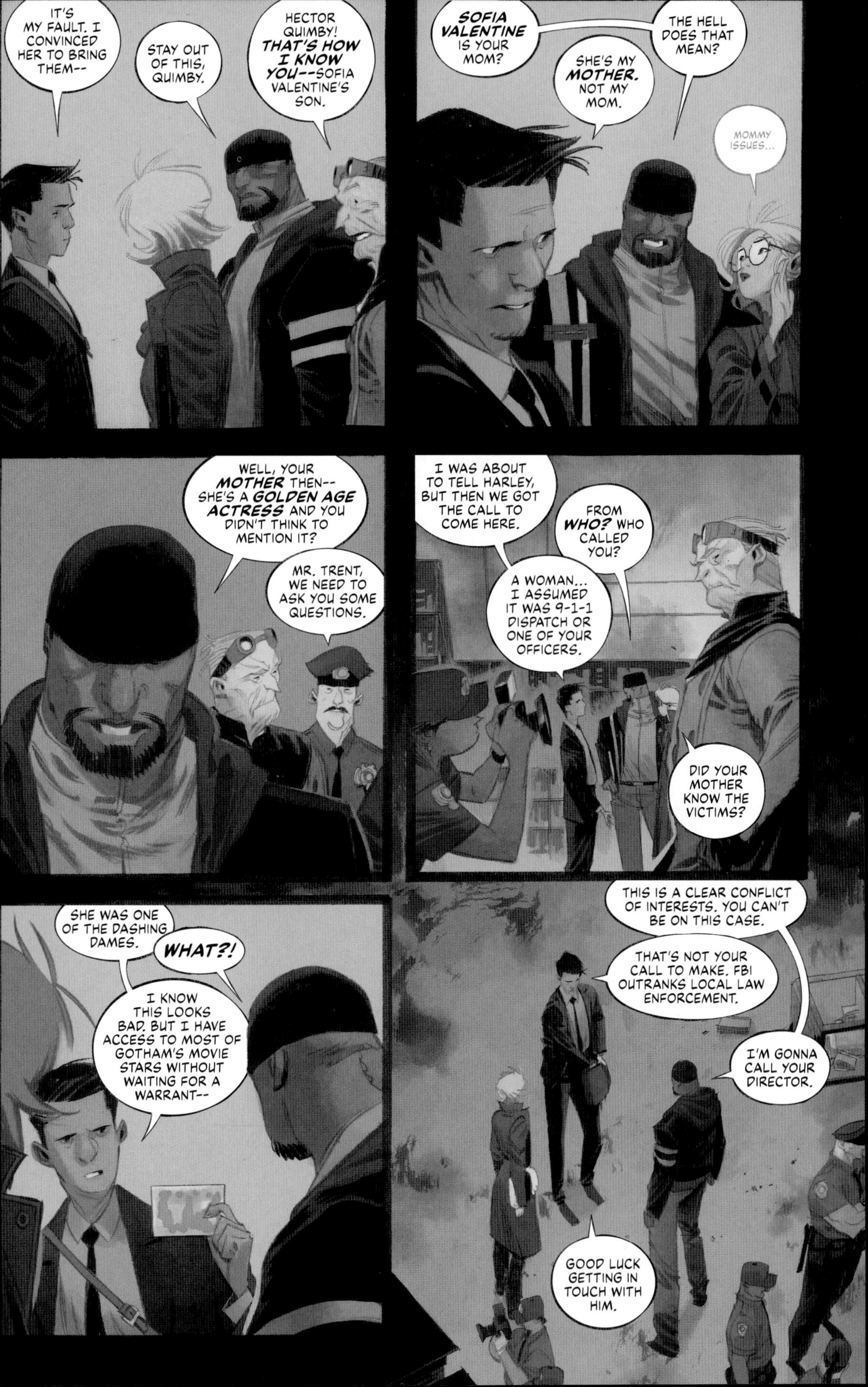
IT'S MY FAULT. I CONVINCED HER TO BRING THEM--
STAY OUT OF THIS, QUIMBY.
HECTOR QUIMBY! THAT'S HOW I KNOW YOU--SOFIA VALENTINE'S SON.
SOFIA VALENTINE IS YOUR MOM?
THE HELL DOES THAT MEAN?
SHE'S MY MOTHER. NOT MY MOM.
MOMMY ISSUES...
WELL, YOUR MOTHER THEN-- SHE'S A GOLDEN AGE ACTRESS AND YOU DIDN'T THINK TO MENTION IT?
MR. TRENT, WE NEED TO ASK YOU SOME QUESTIONS.
I WAS ABOUT TO TELL HARLEY, BUT THEN WE GOT THE CALL TO COME HERE.
FROM WHO? WHO CALLED YOU?
A WOMAN... I ASSUMED IT WAS 9-1-1 DISPATCH OR ONE OF YOUR OFFICERS.
DID YOUR MOTHER KNOW THE VICTIMS?
SHE WAS ONE OF THE DASHING DAMES.
WHAT?!
I KNOW THIS LOOKS BAD. BUT I HAVE ACCESS TO MOST OF GOTHAM'S MOVIE STARS WITHOUT WAITING FOR A WARRANT--
THIS IS A CLEAR CONFLICT OF INTERESTS. YOU CAN'T BE ON THIS CASE.
THAT'S NOT YOUR CALL TO MAKE. FBI OUTRANKS LOCAL LAW ENFORCEMENT.
I'M GONNA CALL YOUR DIRECTOR.
GOOD LUCK GETTING IN TOUCH WITH HIM.

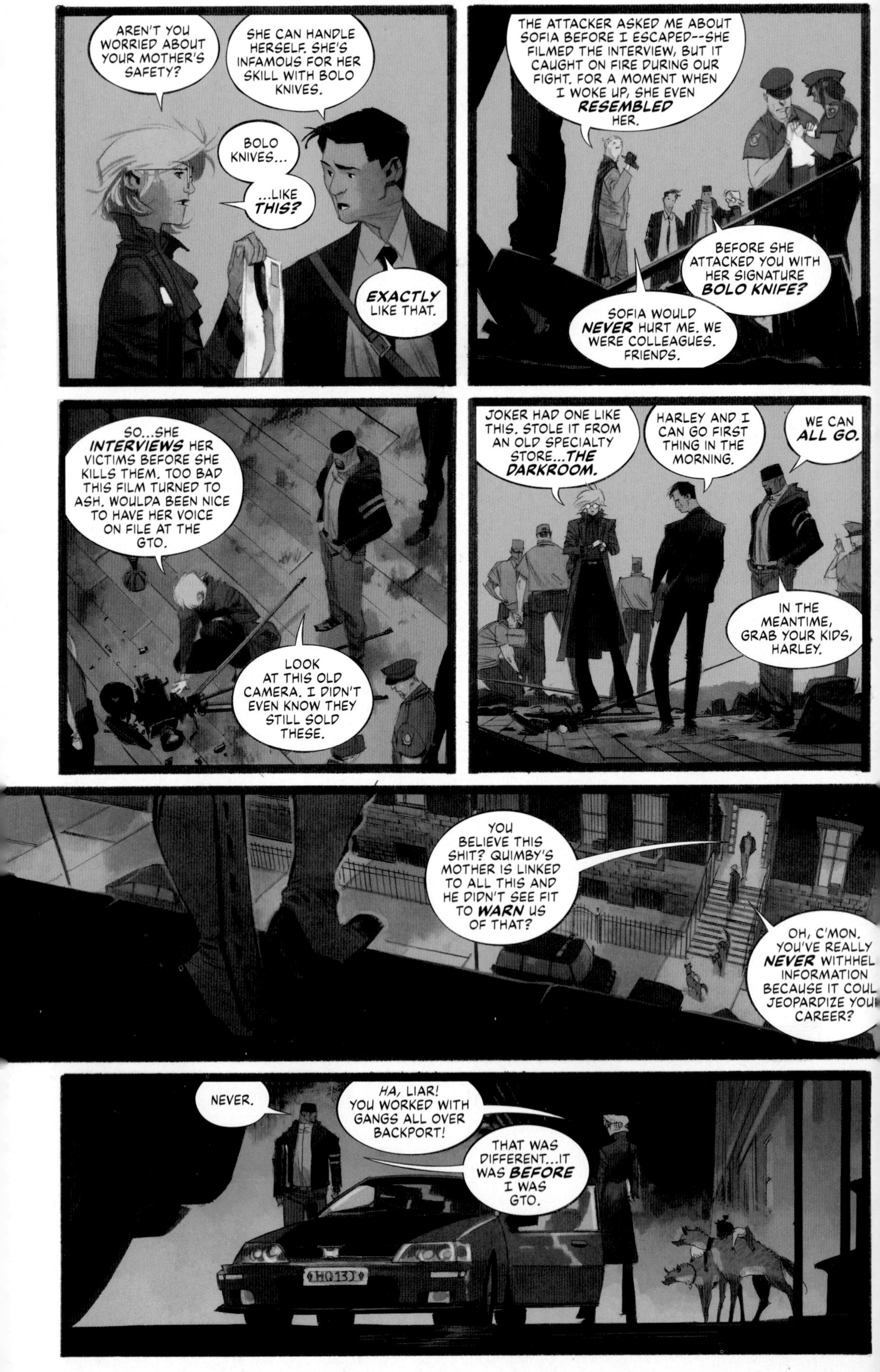
AREN'T YOU WORRIED ABOUT YOUR MOTHER'S SAFETY?
SHE CAN HANDLE HERSELF. SHE'S INFAMOUS FOR HER SKILL WITH BOLO KNIVES.
BOLO KNIVES...
...LIKE THIS?
EXACTLY LIKE THAT.
THE ATTACKER ASKED ME ABOUT SOFIA BEFORE I ESCAPED--SHE FILMED THE INTERVIEW, BUT IT CAUGHT ON FIRE DURING OUR FIGHT. FOR A MOMENT WHEN I WOKE UP, SHE EVEN RESEMBLED HER.
BEFORE SHE ATTACKED YOU WITH HER SIGNATURE BOLO KNIFE?
SOFIA WOULD NEVER HURT ME. WE WERE COLLEAGUES. FRIENDS.
SO...SHE INTERVIEWS HER VICTIMS BEFORE SHE KILLS THEM. TOO BAD THIS FILM TURNED TO ASH. WOULDA BEEN NICE TO HAVE HER VOICE ON FILE AT THE GTO.
LOOK AT THIS OLD CAMERA. I DIDN'T EVEN KNOW THEY STILL SOLD THESE.
JOKER HAD ONE LIKE THIS. STOLE IT FROM AN OLD SPECIALTY STORE...THE DARKROOM.
HARLEY AND I CAN GO FIRST THING IN THE MORNING.
WE CAN ALL GO.
IN THE MEANTIME, GRAB YOUR KIDS, HARLEY.
YOU BELIEVE THIS SHIT? QUIMBY'S MOTHER IS LINKED TO ALL THIS AND HE DIDN'T SEE FIT TO WARN US OF THAT?
OH, C'MON. YOU'VE REALLY NEVER WITHHEL INFORMATION BECAUSE IT COUL JEOPARDIZE YOU CAREER?
NEVER.
HA, LIAR! YOU WORKED WITH GANGS ALL OVER BACKPORT!
THAT WAS DIFFERENT...IT WAS BEFORE I WAS GTO.
HQ13

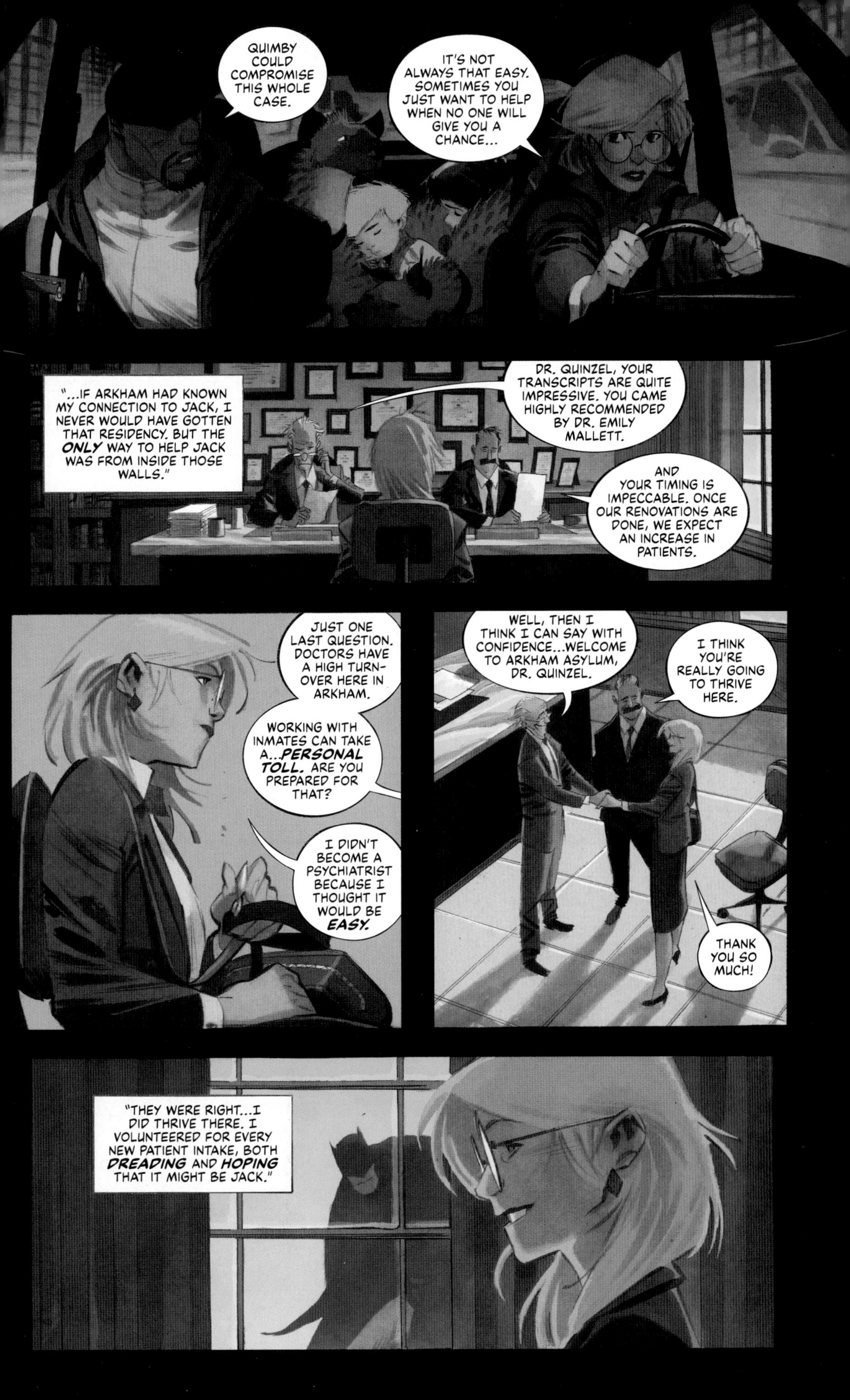
QUIMBY COULD COMPROMISE THIS WHOLE CASE.
IT'S NOT ALWAYS THAT EASY. SOMETIMES YOU JUST WANT TO HELP WHEN NO ONE WILL GIVE YOU A CHANCE...
"...IF ARKHAM HAD KNOWN MY CONNECTION TO JACK, I NEVER WOULD HAVE GOTTEN THAT RESIDENCY. BUT THE ONLY WAY TO HELP JACK WAS FROM INSIDE THOSE WALLS."
DR. QUINZEL, YOUR TRANSCRIPTS ARE QUITE IMPRESSIVE. YOU CAME HIGHLY RECOMMENDED BY DR. EMILY MALLETT.
AND YOUR TIMING IS IMPECCABLE. ONCE OUR RENOVATIONS ARE DONE, WE EXPECT AN INCREASE IN PATIENTS.
JUST ONE LAST QUESTION. DOCTORS HAVE A HIGH TURNOVER HERE IN ARKHAM.
WORKING WITH INMATES CAN TAKE A...PERSONAL TOLL. ARE YOU PREPARED FOR THAT?
I DIDN'T BECOME A PSYCHIATRIST BECAUSE I THOUGHT IT WOULD BE EASY.
WELL, THEN I THINK I CAN SAY WITH CONFIDENCE...WELCOME TO ARKHAM ASYLUM, DR. QUINZEL.
I THINK YOU'RE REALLY GOING TO THRIVE HERE.
THANK YOU SO MUCH!
"THEY WERE RIGHT...I DID THRIVE THERE. I VOLUNTEERED FOR EVERY NEW PATIENT INTAKE, BOTH DREADING AND HOPING THAT IT MIGHT BE JACK."

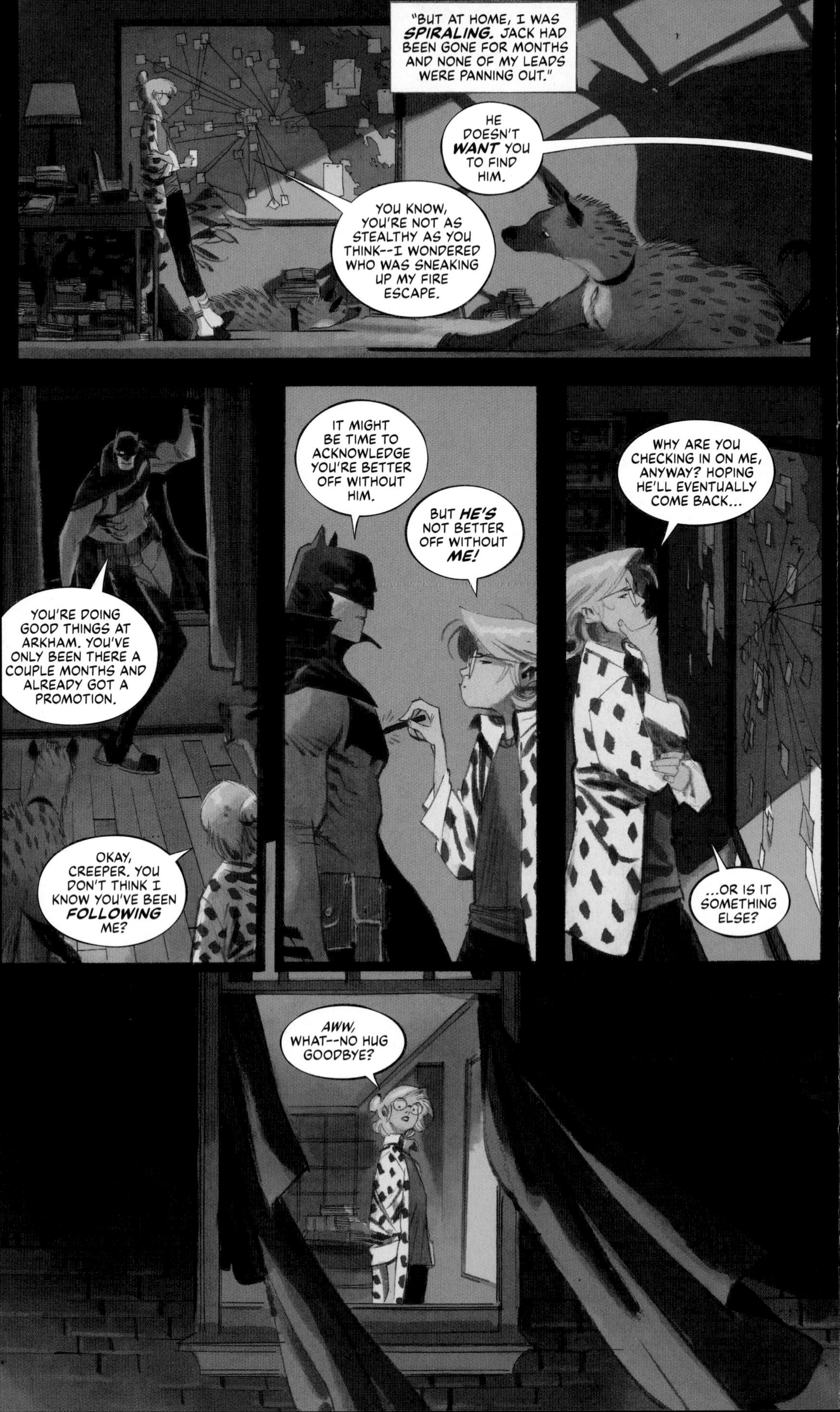
"BUT AT HOME, I WAS SPIRALING. JACK HAD BEEN GONE FOR MONTHS AND NONE OF MY LEADS WERE PANNING OUT."
HE DOESN'T WANT YOU TO FIND HIM.
YOU KNOW, YOU'RE NOT AS STEALTHY AS YOU THINK--I WONDERED WHO WAS SNEAKING UP MY FIRE ESCAPE.
YOU'RE DOING GOOD THINGS AT ARKHAM. YOU'VE ONLY BEEN THERE A COUPLE MONTHS AND ALREADY GOT A PROMOTION.
OKAY, CREEPER. YOU DON'T THINK I KNOW YOU'VE BEEN FOLLOWING ME?
IT MIGHT BE TIME TO ACKNOWLEDGE YOU'RE BETTER OFF WITHOUT HIM.
BUT HE'S NOT BETTER OFF WITHOUT ME!
WHY ARE YOU CHECKING IN ON ME, ANYWAY? HOPING HE'LL EVENTUALLY COME BACK...
...OR IS IT SOMETHING ELSE?
AWW, WHAT--NO HUG GOODBYE?

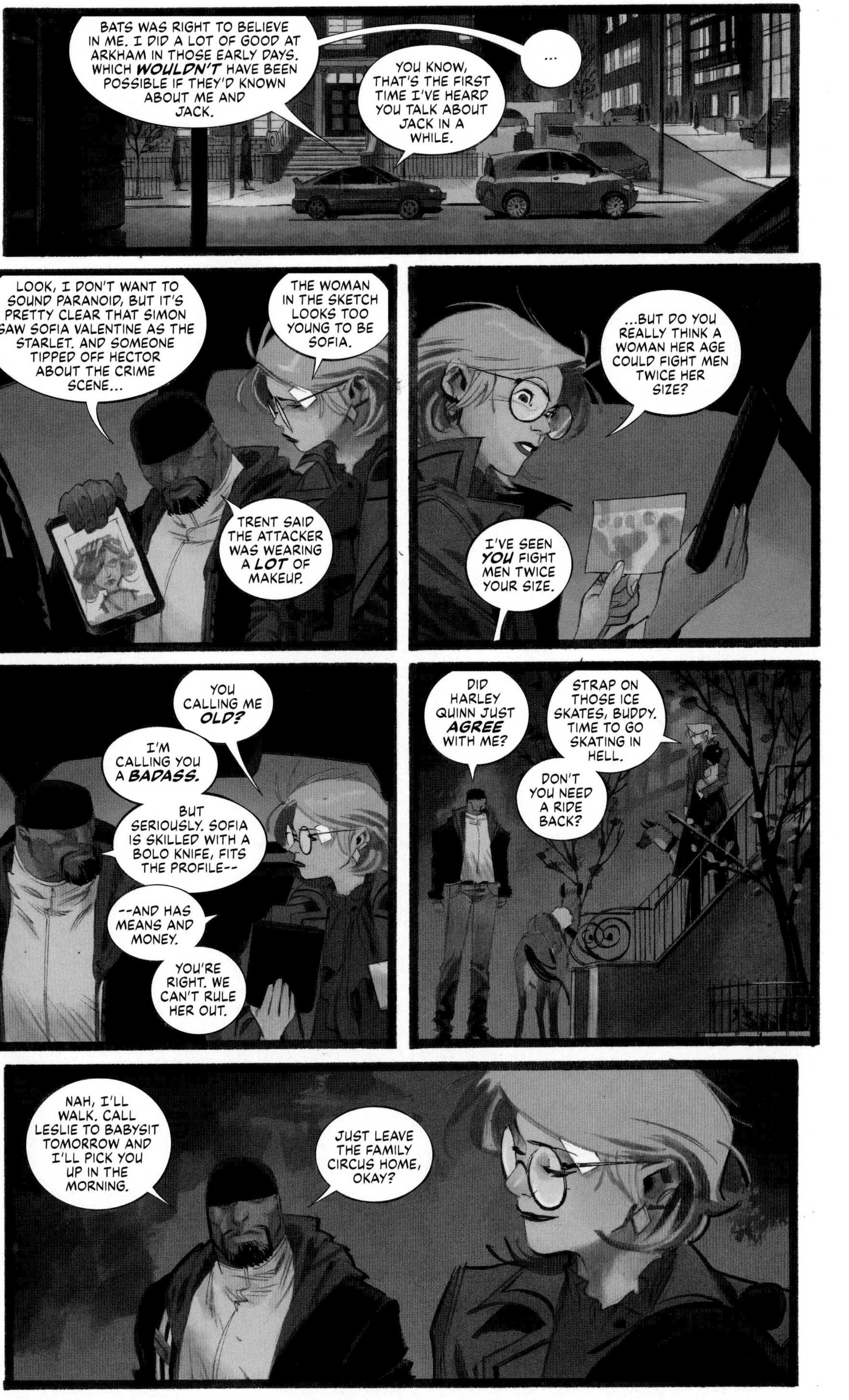
BATS WAS RIGHT TO BELIEVE IN ME. I DID A LOT OF GOOD AT ARKHAM IN THOSE EARLY DAYS. WHICH **WOULDN'T** HAVE BEEN POSSIBLE IF THEY'D KNOWN ABOUT ME AND JACK.
YOU KNOW, THAT'S THE FIRST TIME I'VE HEARD YOU TALK ABOUT JACK IN A WHILE.
...
LOOK, I DON'T WANT TO SOUND PARANOID, BUT IT'S PRETTY CLEAR THAT SIMON SAW SOFIA VALENTINE AS THE STARLET. AND SOMEONE TIPPED OFF HECTOR ABOUT THE CRIME SCENE...
THE WOMAN IN THE SKETCH LOOKS TOO YOUNG TO BE SOFIA.
TRENT SAID THE ATTACKER WAS WEARING A **LOT** OF MAKEUP.
...BUT DO YOU REALLY THINK A WOMAN HER AGE COULD FIGHT MEN TWICE HER SIZE?
I'VE SEEN **YOU** FIGHT MEN TWICE YOUR SIZE.
YOU CALLING ME **OLD?**
I'M CALLING YOU A **BADASS.**
BUT SERIOUSLY. SOFIA IS SKILLED WITH A BOLO KNIFE, FITS THE PROFILE--
--AND HAS MEANS AND MONEY.
YOU'RE RIGHT. WE CAN'T RULE HER OUT.
DID HARLEY QUINN JUST **AGREE** WITH ME?
STRAP ON THOSE ICE SKATES, BUDDY. TIME TO GO SKATING IN HELL.
DON'T YOU NEED A RIDE BACK?
NAH, I'LL WALK. CALL LESLIE TO BABYSIT TOMORROW AND I'LL PICK YOU UP IN THE MORNING.
JUST LEAVE THE FAMILY CIRCUS HOME, OKAY?

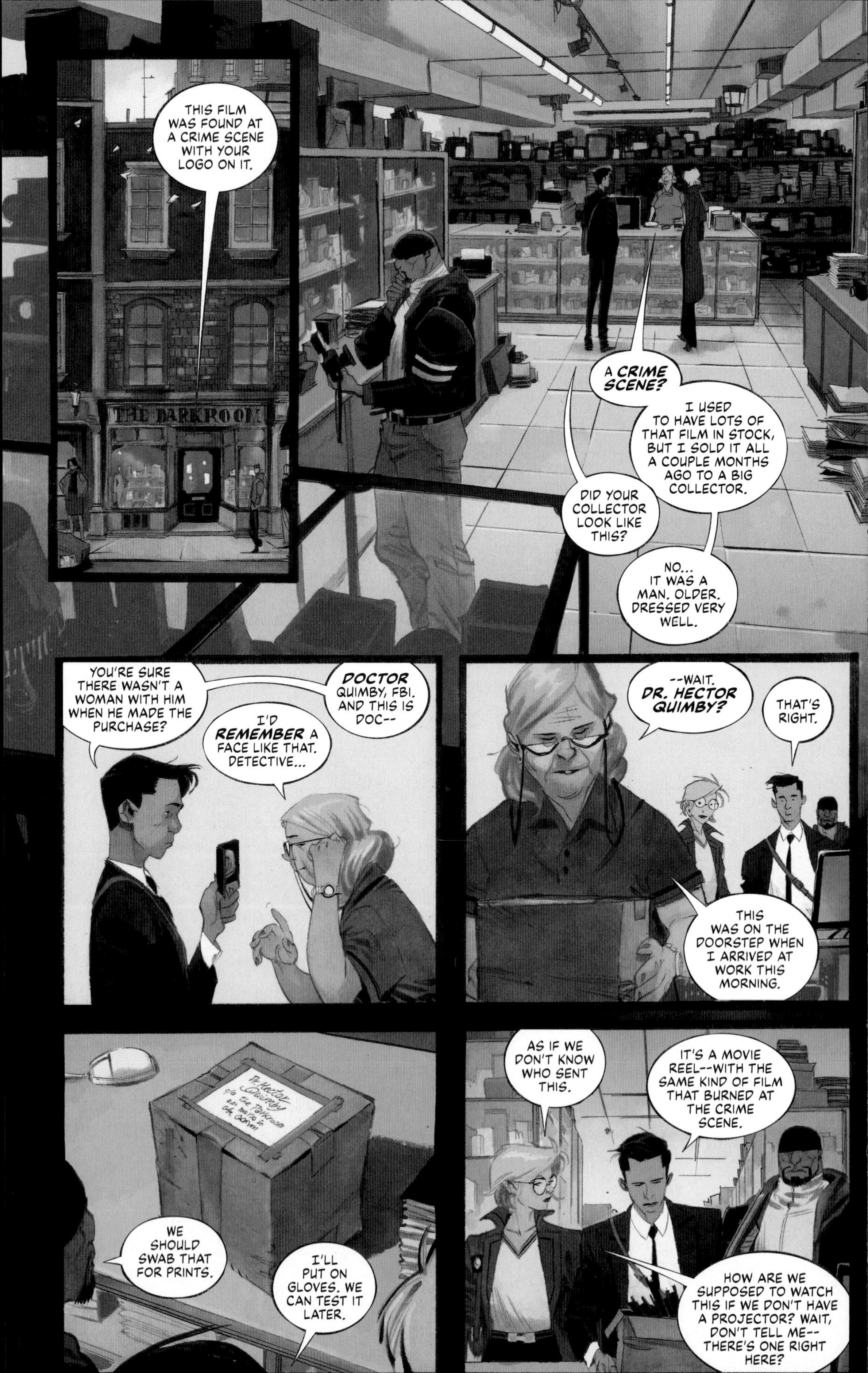
THIS FILM WAS FOUND AT A CRIME SCENE WITH YOUR LOGO ON IT.
THE DARKROOM
A *CRIME SCENE?*
I USED TO HAVE LOTS OF THAT FILM IN STOCK, BUT I SOLD IT ALL A COUPLE MONTHS AGO TO A BIG COLLECTOR.
DID YOUR COLLECTOR LOOK LIKE THIS?
NO... IT WAS A MAN. OLDER. DRESSED VERY WELL.
YOU'RE SURE THERE WASN'T A WOMAN WITH HIM WHEN HE MADE THE PURCHASE?
I'D *REMEMBER* A FACE LIKE THAT. DETECTIVE...
DOCTOR QUIMBY, FBI. AND THIS IS DOC--
--WAIT. *DR. HECTOR QUIMBY?*
THAT'S RIGHT.
THIS WAS ON THE DOORSTEP WHEN I ARRIVED AT WORK THIS MORNING.
WE SHOULD SWAB THAT FOR PRINTS.
I'LL PUT ON GLOVES. WE CAN TEST IT LATER.
AS IF WE DON'T KNOW WHO SENT THIS.
IT'S A MOVIE REEL--WITH THE SAME KIND OF FILM THAT BURNED AT THE CRIME SCENE.
HOW ARE WE SUPPOSED TO WATCH THIS IF WE DON'T HAVE A PROJECTOR? WAIT, DON'T TELL ME-- THERE'S ONE RIGHT HERE?

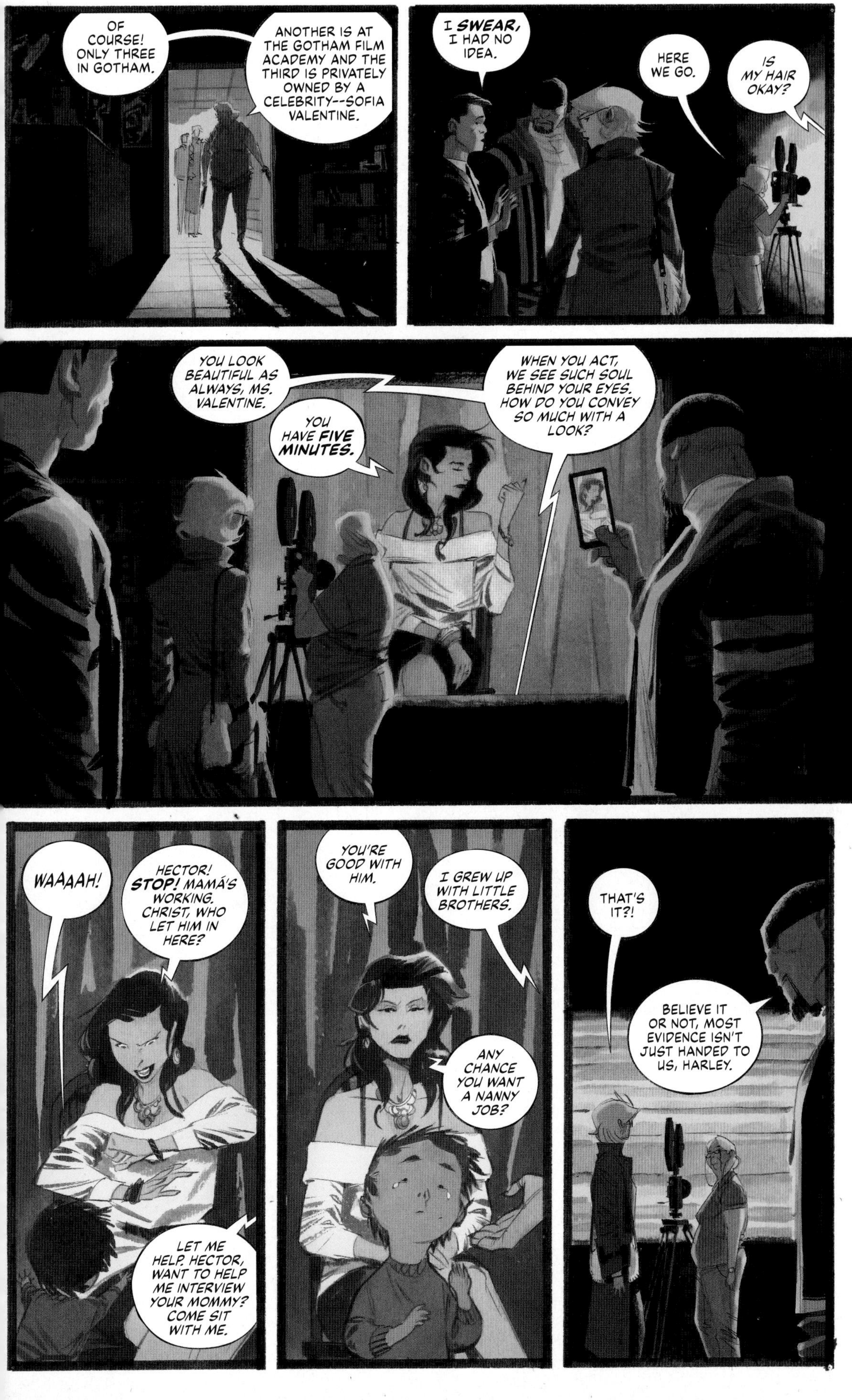
OF COURSE! ONLY THREE IN GOTHAM.
ANOTHER IS AT THE GOTHAM FILM ACADEMY AND THE THIRD IS PRIVATELY OWNED BY A CELEBRITY--SOFIA VALENTINE.
I SWEAR, I HAD NO IDEA.
HERE WE GO.
IS MY HAIR OKAY?
YOU LOOK BEAUTIFUL AS ALWAYS, MS. VALENTINE.
YOU HAVE FIVE MINUTES.
WHEN YOU ACT, WE SEE SUCH SOUL BEHIND YOUR EYES. HOW DO YOU CONVEY SO MUCH WITH A LOOK?
WAAAAH!
HECTOR! STOP! MAMÁ'S WORKING. CHRIST, WHO LET HIM IN HERE?
LET ME HELP. HECTOR, WANT TO HELP ME INTERVIEW YOUR MOMMY? COME SIT WITH ME.
YOU'RE GOOD WITH HIM.
I GREW UP WITH LITTLE BROTHERS.
ANY CHANCE YOU WANT A NANNY JOB?
THAT'S IT?!
BELIEVE IT OR NOT, MOST EVIDENCE ISN'T JUST HANDED TO US, HARLEY.

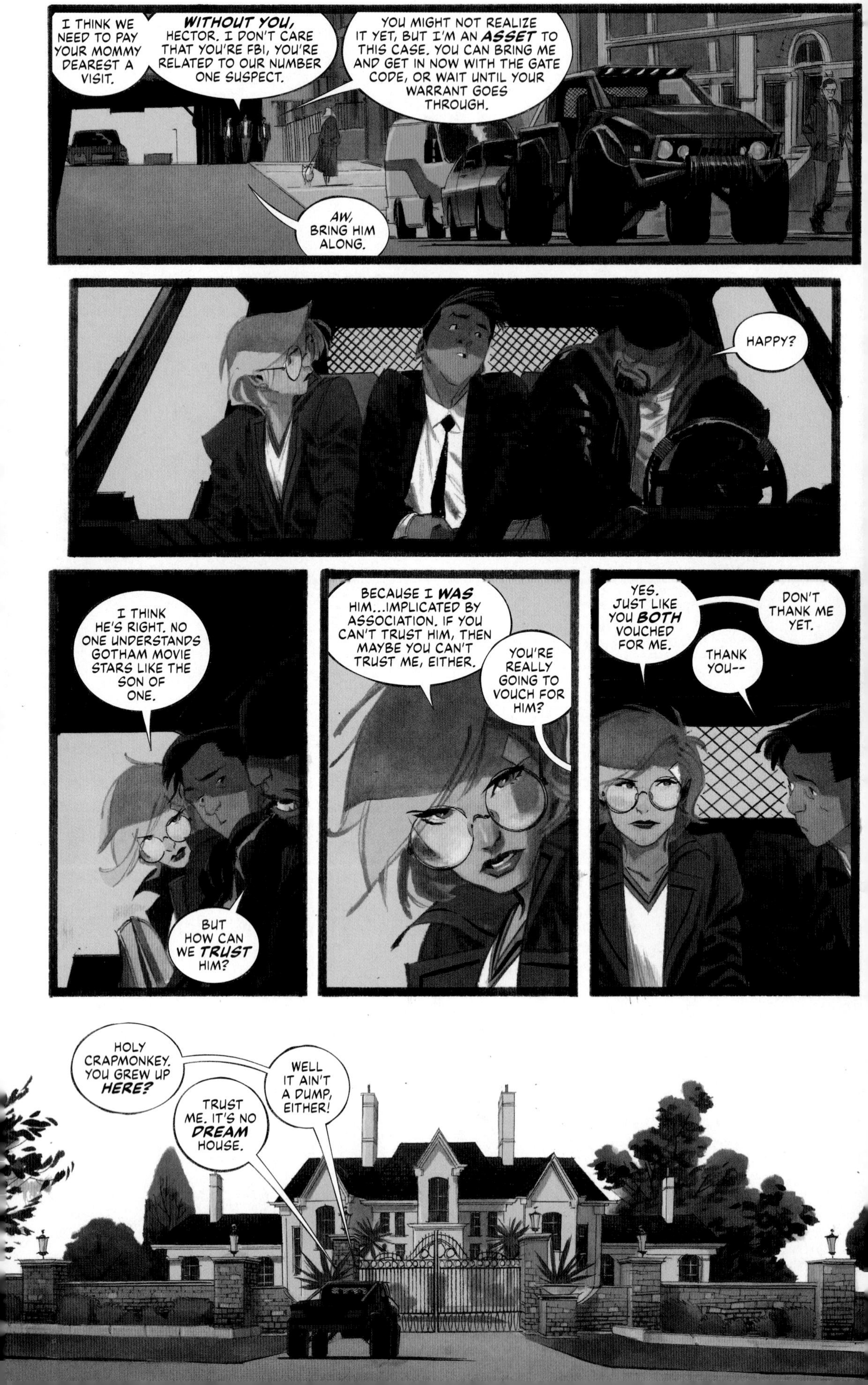
I THINK WE NEED TO PAY YOUR MOMMY DEAREST A VISIT.
WITHOUT YOU, HECTOR. I DON'T CARE THAT YOU'RE FBI, YOU'RE RELATED TO OUR NUMBER ONE SUSPECT.
YOU MIGHT NOT REALIZE IT YET, BUT I'M AN ASSET TO THIS CASE. YOU CAN BRING ME AND GET IN NOW WITH THE GATE CODE, OR WAIT UNTIL YOUR WARRANT GOES THROUGH.
AW, BRING HIM ALONG.
HAPPY?
I THINK HE'S RIGHT. NO ONE UNDERSTANDS GOTHAM MOVIE STARS LIKE THE SON OF ONE.
BUT HOW CAN WE TRUST HIM?
BECAUSE I WAS HIM...IMPLICATED BY ASSOCIATION. IF YOU CAN'T TRUST HIM, THEN MAYBE YOU CAN'T TRUST ME, EITHER.
YOU'RE REALLY GOING TO VOUCH FOR HIM?
YES. JUST LIKE YOU BOTH VOUCHED FOR ME.
THANK YOU--
DON'T THANK ME YET.
HOLY CRAPMONKEY. YOU GREW UP HERE?
TRUST ME. IT'S NO DREAM HOUSE.
WELL IT AIN'T A DUMP, EITHER!

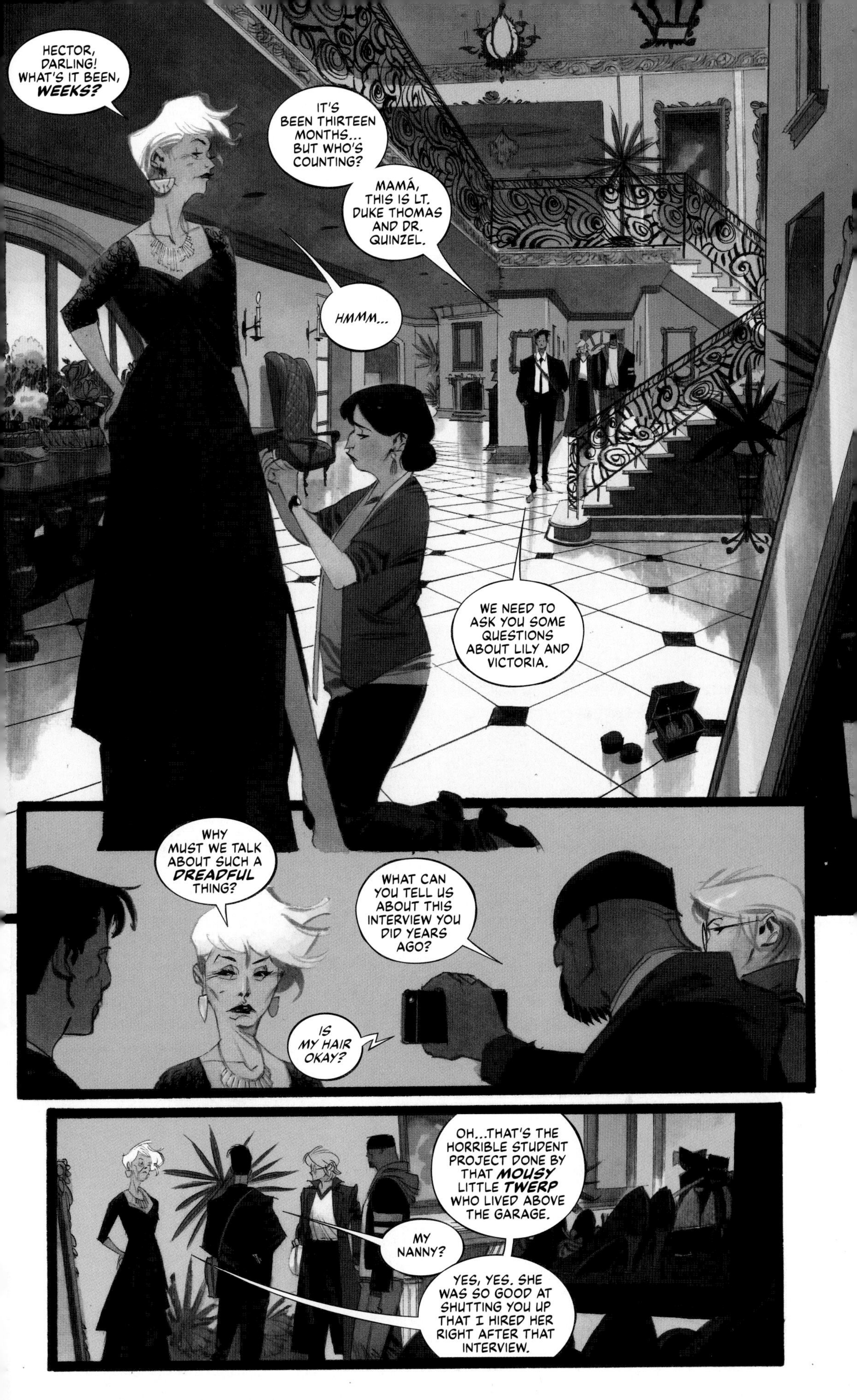
HECTOR, DARLING! WHAT'S IT BEEN, ***WEEKS?***
IT'S BEEN THIRTEEN MONTHS... BUT WHO'S COUNTING?
MAMÁ, THIS IS LT. DUKE THOMAS AND DR. QUINZEL.
HMMM...
WE NEED TO ASK YOU SOME QUESTIONS ABOUT LILY AND VICTORIA.
WHY MUST WE TALK ABOUT SUCH A ***DREADFUL*** THING?
WHAT CAN YOU TELL US ABOUT THIS INTERVIEW YOU DID YEARS AGO?
IS MY HAIR OKAY?
OH...THAT'S THE HORRIBLE STUDENT PROJECT DONE BY THAT ***MOUSY*** LITTLE ***TWERP*** WHO LIVED ABOVE THE GARAGE.
MY NANNY?
YES, YES. SHE WAS SO GOOD AT SHUTTING YOU UP THAT I HIRED HER RIGHT AFTER THAT INTERVIEW.

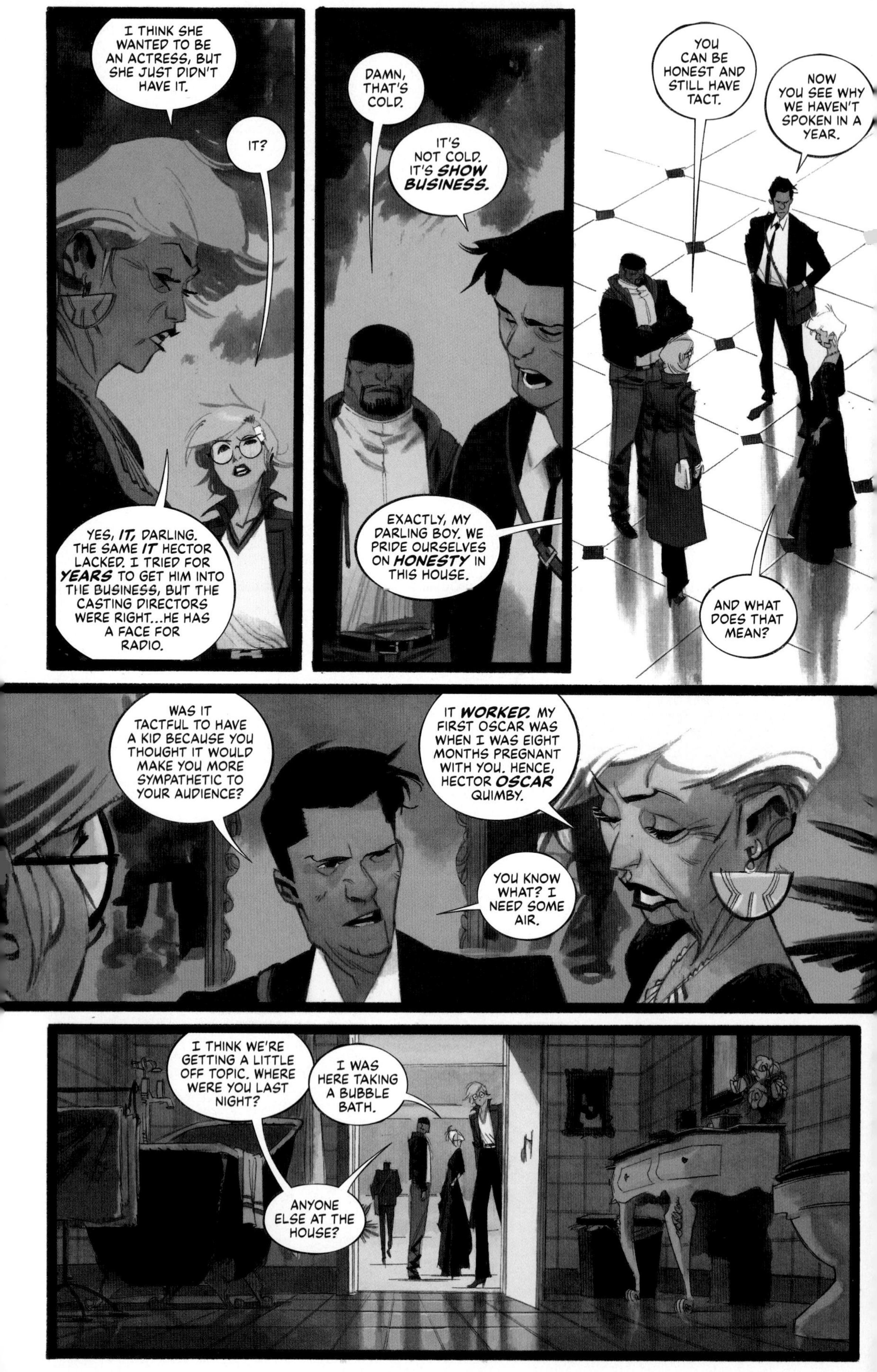

I THINK SHE WANTED TO BE AN ACTRESS, BUT SHE JUST DIDN'T HAVE IT.
IT?
YES, IT, DARLING. THE SAME IT HECTOR LACKED. I TRIED FOR YEARS TO GET HIM INTO THE BUSINESS, BUT THE CASTING DIRECTORS WERE RIGHT...HE HAS A FACE FOR RADIO.
DAMN, THAT'S COLD.
IT'S NOT COLD. IT'S SHOW BUSINESS.
EXACTLY, MY DARLING BOY. WE PRIDE OURSELVES ON HONESTY IN THIS HOUSE.
YOU CAN BE HONEST AND STILL HAVE TACT.
NOW YOU SEE WHY WE HAVEN'T SPOKEN IN A YEAR.
AND WHAT DOES THAT MEAN?
WAS IT TACTFUL TO HAVE A KID BECAUSE YOU THOUGHT IT WOULD MAKE YOU MORE SYMPATHETIC TO YOUR AUDIENCE?
IT WORKED. MY FIRST OSCAR WAS WHEN I WAS EIGHT MONTHS PREGNANT WITH YOU. HENCE, HECTOR OSCAR QUIMBY.
YOU KNOW WHAT? I NEED SOME AIR.
I THINK WE'RE GETTING A LITTLE OFF TOPIC. WHERE WERE YOU LAST NIGHT?
I WAS HERE TAKING A BUBBLE BATH.
ANYONE ELSE AT THE HOUSE?

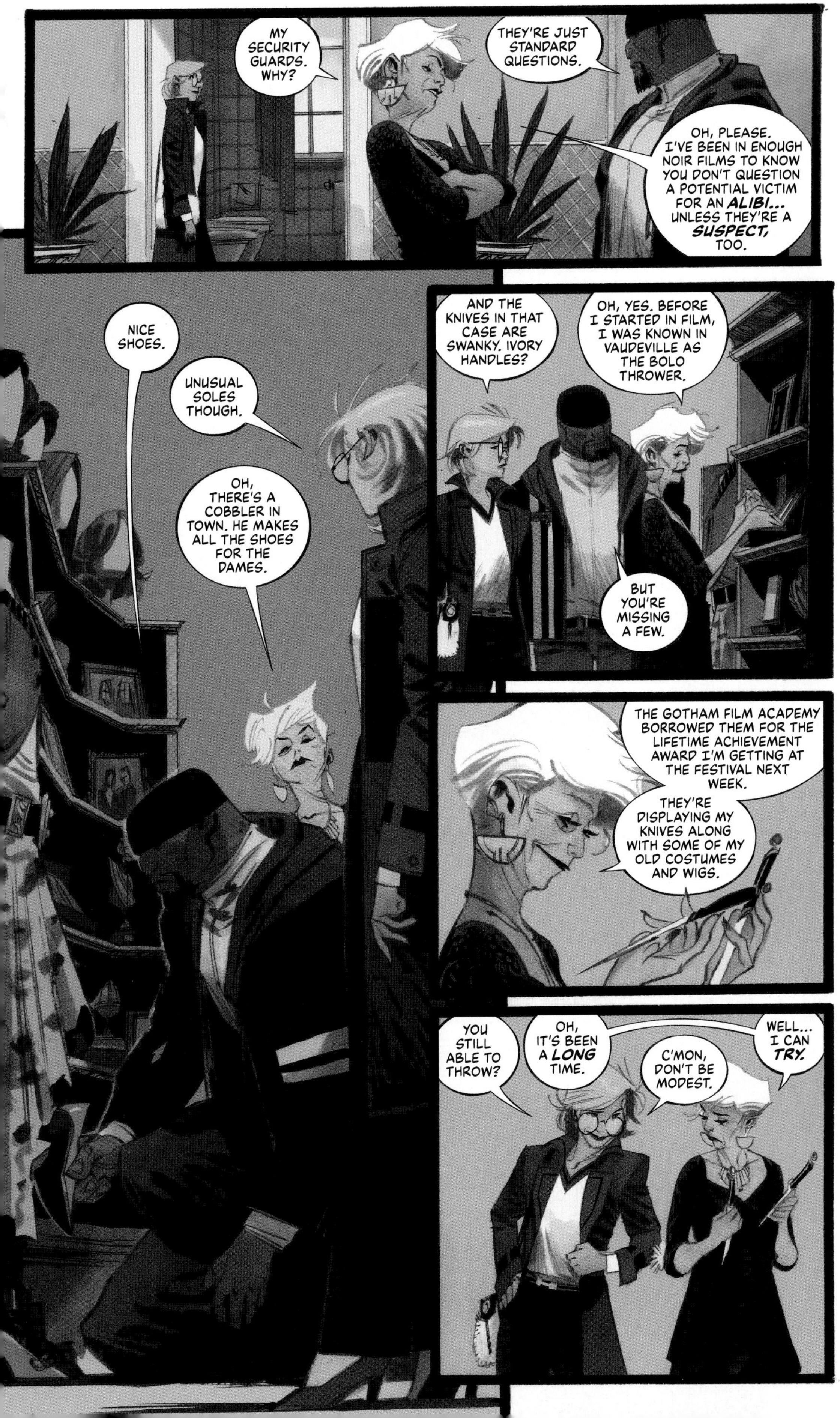

MY SECURITY GUARDS. WHY?
THEY'RE JUST STANDARD QUESTIONS.
OH, PLEASE. I'VE BEEN IN ENOUGH NOIR FILMS TO KNOW YOU DON'T QUESTION A POTENTIAL VICTIM FOR AN ***ALIBI...*** UNLESS THEY'RE A ***SUSPECT,*** TOO.
NICE SHOES.
UNUSUAL SOLES THOUGH.
OH, THERE'S A COBBLER IN TOWN. HE MAKES ALL THE SHOES FOR THE DAMES.
AND THE KNIVES IN THAT CASE ARE SWANKY. IVORY HANDLES?
OH, YES. BEFORE I STARTED IN FILM, I WAS KNOWN IN VAUDEVILLE AS THE BOLO THROWER.
BUT YOU'RE MISSING A FEW.
THE GOTHAM FILM ACADEMY BORROWED THEM FOR THE LIFETIME ACHIEVEMENT AWARD I'M GETTING AT THE FESTIVAL NEXT WEEK.
THEY'RE DISPLAYING MY KNIVES ALONG WITH SOME OF MY OLD COSTUMES AND WIGS.
YOU STILL ABLE TO THROW?
OH, IT'S BEEN A ***LONG*** TIME.
C'MON, DON'T BE MODEST.
WELL... I CAN ***TRY.***

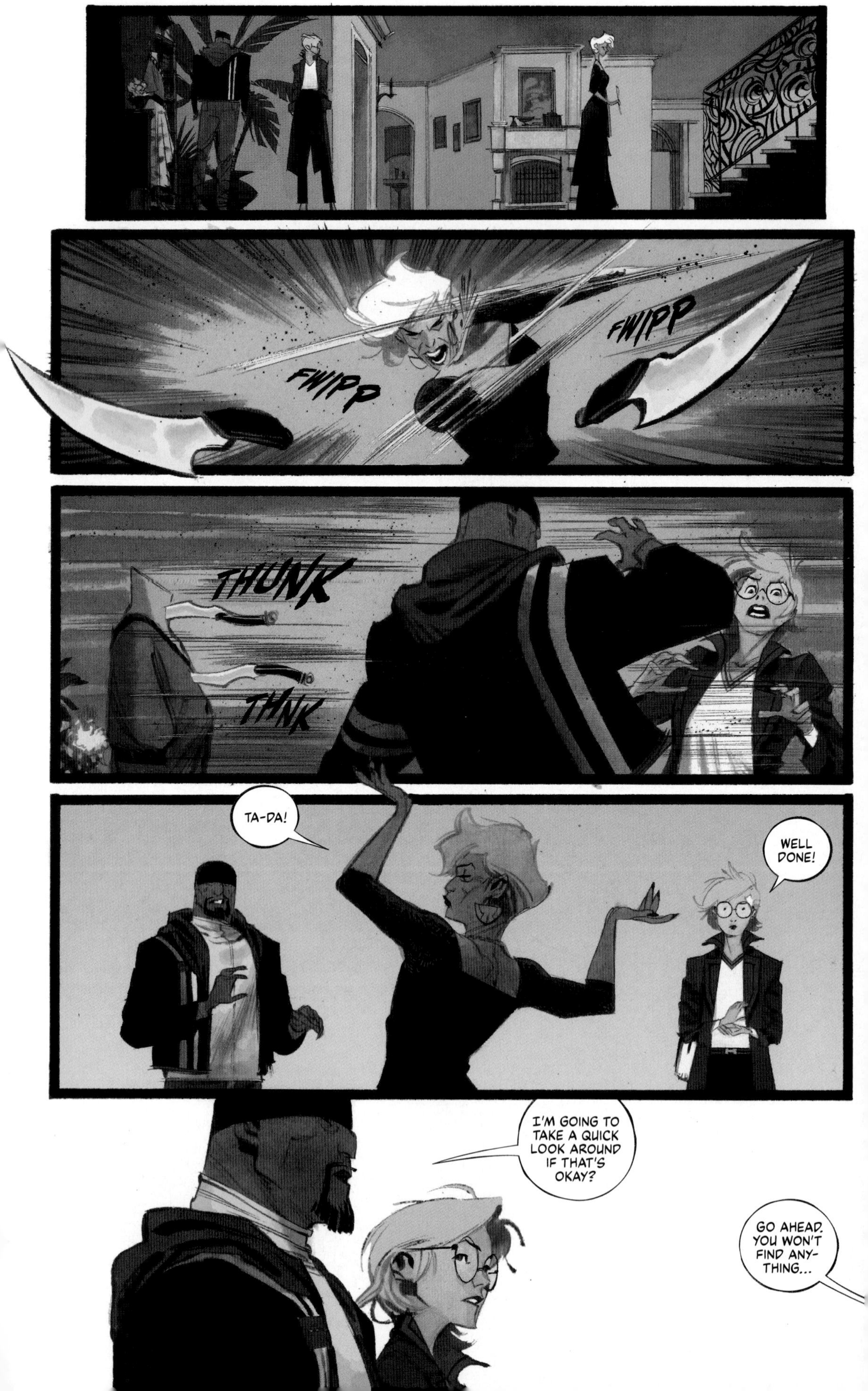
FWIPP
FWIPP
THUNK
THNK
TA-DA!
WELL DONE!
I'M GOING TO TAKE A QUICK LOOK AROUND IF THAT'S OKAY?
GO AHEAD. YOU WON'T FIND ANY-THING...

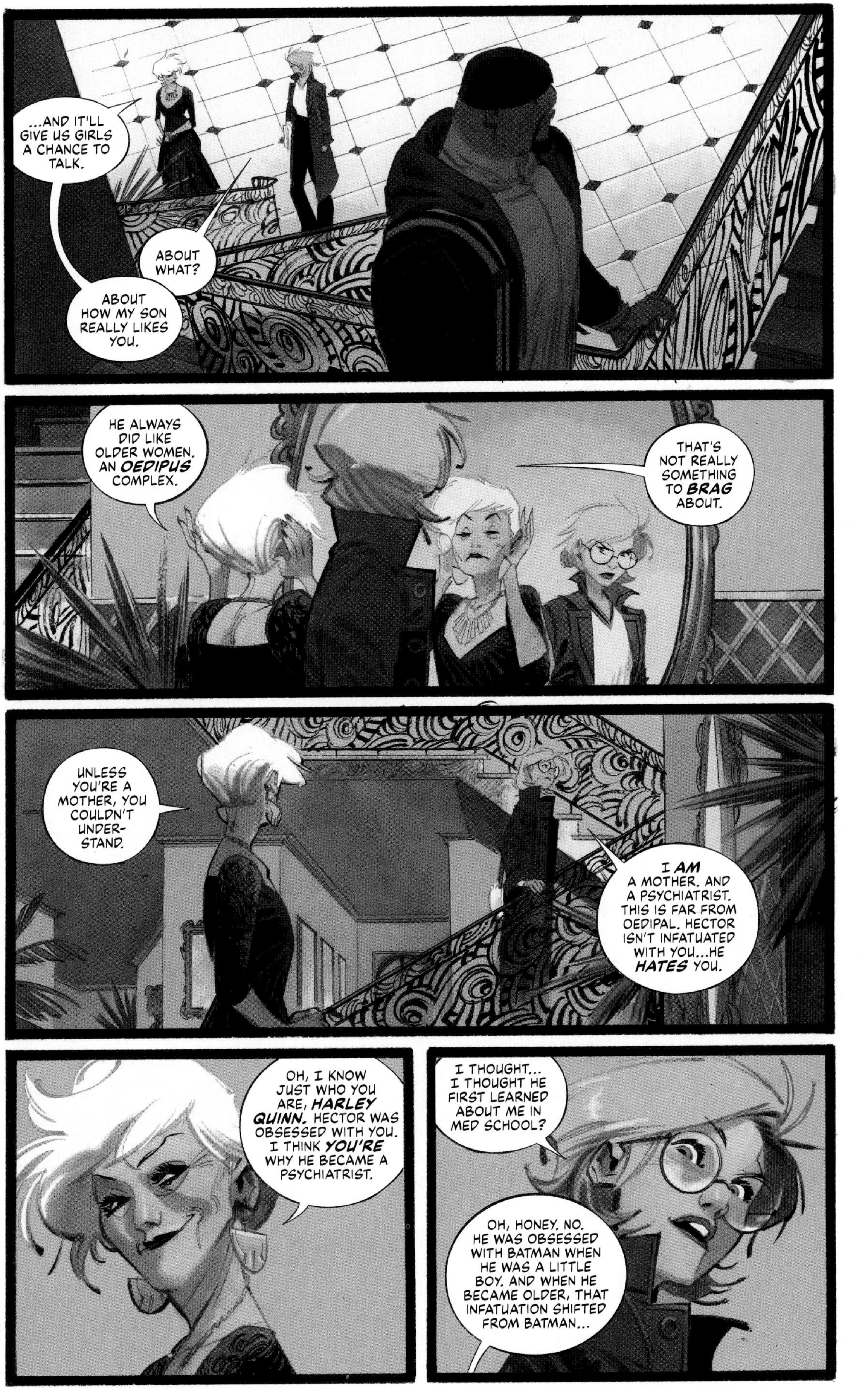

...AND IT'LL GIVE US GIRLS A CHANCE TO TALK.
ABOUT WHAT?
ABOUT HOW MY SON REALLY LIKES YOU.
HE ALWAYS DID LIKE OLDER WOMEN. AN OEDIPUS COMPLEX.
THAT'S NOT REALLY SOMETHING TO BRAG ABOUT.
UNLESS YOU'RE A MOTHER, YOU COULDN'T UNDER-STAND.
I AM A MOTHER. AND A PSYCHIATRIST. THIS IS FAR FROM OEDIPAL. HECTOR ISN'T INFATUATED WITH YOU...HE HATES YOU.
OH, I KNOW JUST WHO YOU ARE, HARLEY QUINN. HECTOR WAS OBSESSED WITH YOU. I THINK YOU'RE WHY HE BECAME A PSYCHIATRIST.
I THOUGHT... I THOUGHT HE FIRST LEARNED ABOUT ME IN MED SCHOOL?
OH, HONEY. NO. HE WAS OBSESSED WITH BATMAN WHEN HE WAS A LITTLE BOY. AND WHEN HE BECAME OLDER, THAT INFATUATION SHIFTED FROM BATMAN...

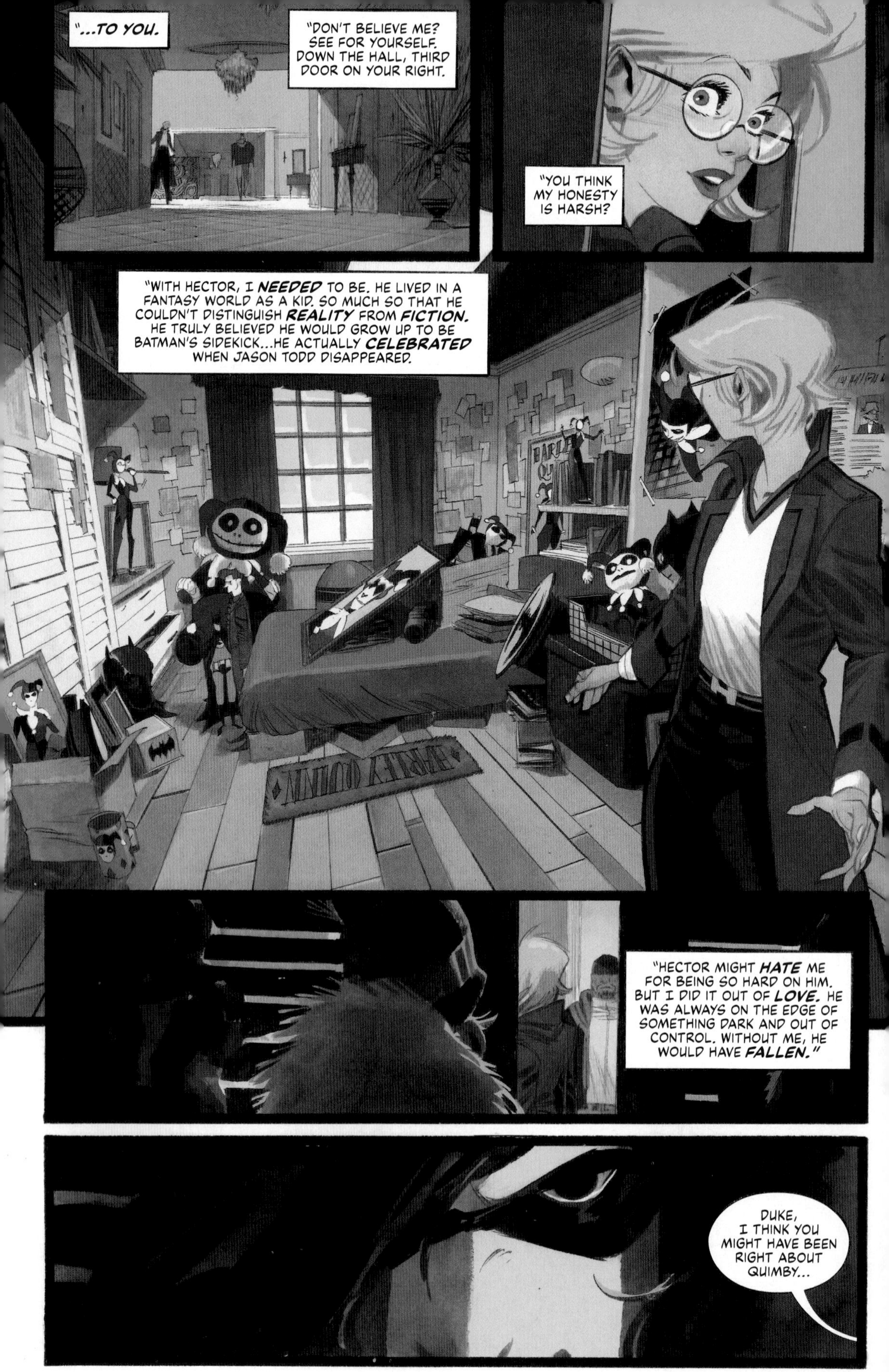
"...TO YOU.
"DON'T BELIEVE ME? SEE FOR YOURSELF. DOWN THE HALL, THIRD DOOR ON YOUR RIGHT.
"YOU THINK MY HONESTY IS HARSH?
"WITH HECTOR, I NEEDED TO BE. HE LIVED IN A FANTASY WORLD AS A KID. SO MUCH SO THAT HE COULDN'T DISTINGUISH REALITY FROM FICTION. HE TRULY BELIEVED HE WOULD GROW UP TO BE BATMAN'S SIDEKICK...HE ACTUALLY CELEBRATED WHEN JASON TODD DISAPPEARED.
"HECTOR MIGHT HATE ME FOR BEING SO HARD ON HIM. BUT I DID IT OUT OF LOVE. HE WAS ALWAYS ON THE EDGE OF SOMETHING DARK AND OUT OF CONTROL. WITHOUT ME, HE WOULD HAVE FALLEN."
DUKE, I THINK YOU MIGHT HAVE BEEN RIGHT ABOUT QUIMBY...

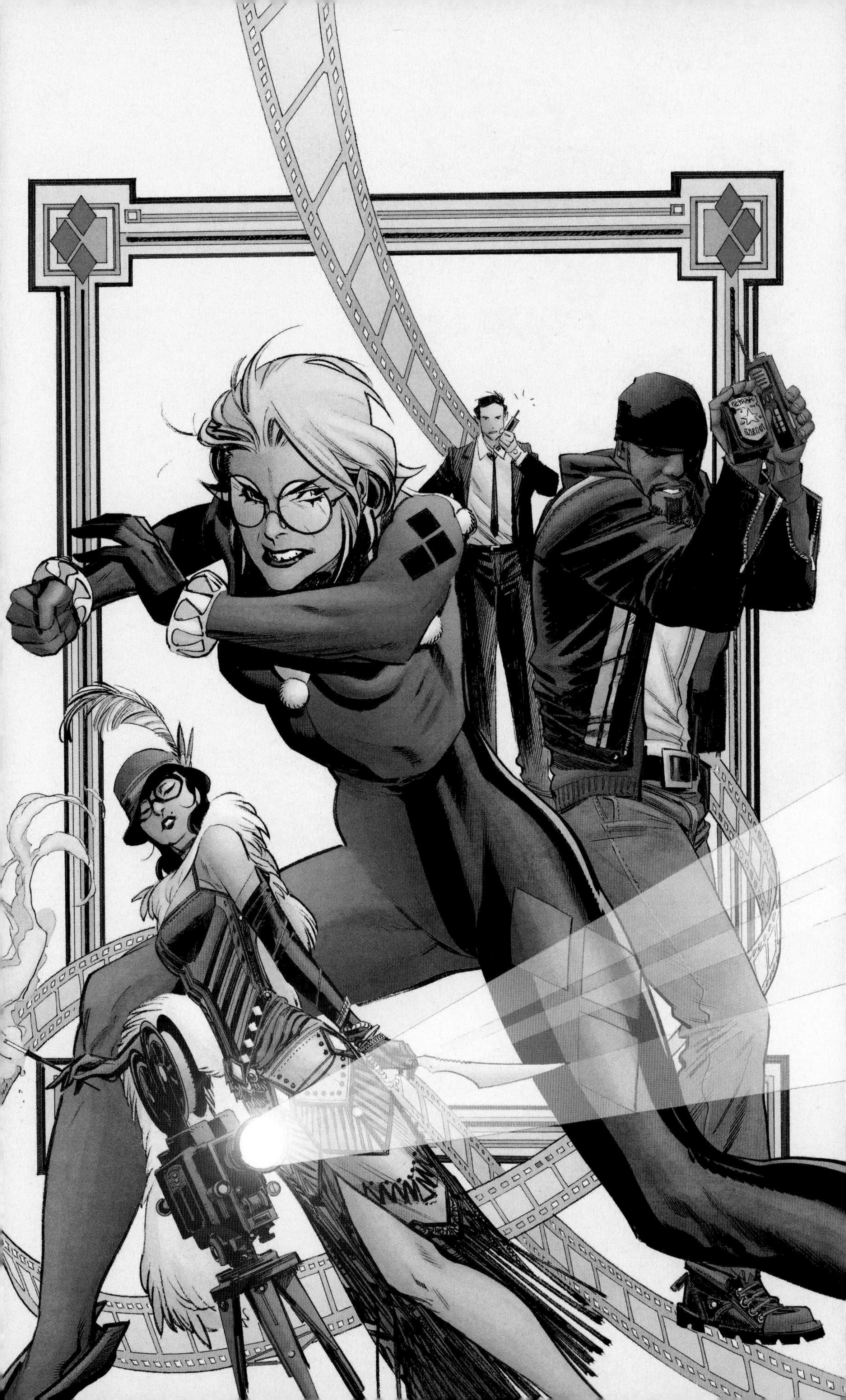

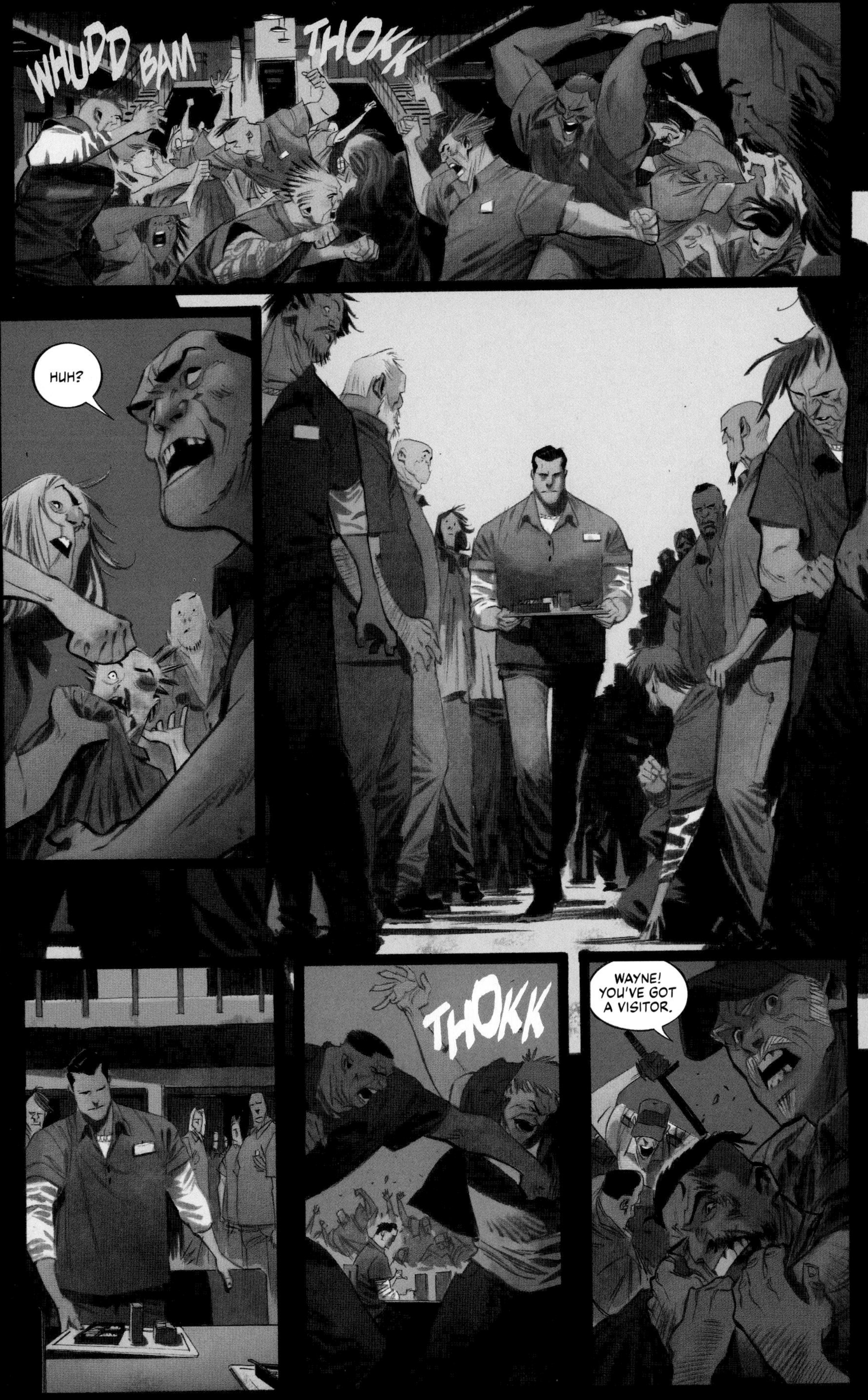

WHUDD
BAM
THOKK
HUH?
THOKK
WAYNE! YOU'VE GOT A VISITOR.

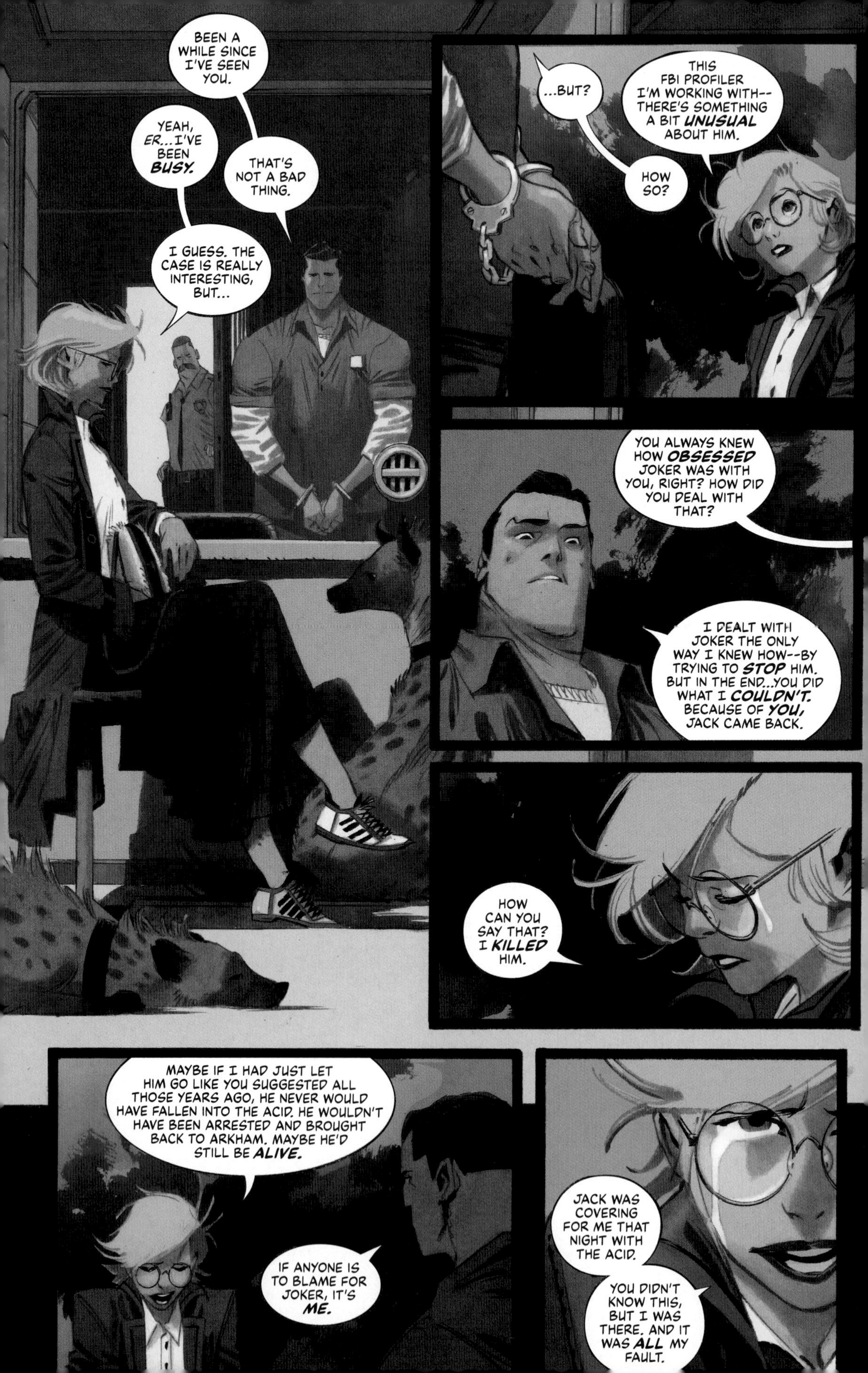
BEEN A WHILE SINCE I'VE SEEN YOU.
YEAH, ER...I'VE BEEN BUSY.
THAT'S NOT A BAD THING.
I GUESS. THE CASE IS REALLY INTERESTING, BUT...
...BUT?
THIS FBI PROFILER I'M WORKING WITH--THERE'S SOMETHING A BIT UNUSUAL ABOUT HIM.
HOW SO?
YOU ALWAYS KNEW HOW OBSESSED JOKER WAS WITH YOU, RIGHT? HOW DID YOU DEAL WITH THAT?
I DEALT WITH JOKER THE ONLY WAY I KNEW HOW--BY TRYING TO STOP HIM. BUT IN THE END...YOU DID WHAT I COULDN'T. BECAUSE OF YOU, JACK CAME BACK.
HOW CAN YOU SAY THAT? I KILLED HIM.
MAYBE IF I HAD JUST LET HIM GO LIKE YOU SUGGESTED ALL THOSE YEARS AGO, HE NEVER WOULD HAVE FALLEN INTO THE ACID. HE WOULDN'T HAVE BEEN ARRESTED AND BROUGHT BACK TO ARKHAM. MAYBE HE'D STILL BE ALIVE.
IF ANYONE IS TO BLAME FOR JOKER, IT'S ME.
JACK WAS COVERING FOR ME THAT NIGHT WITH THE ACID.
YOU DIDN'T KNOW THIS, BUT I WAS THERE, AND IT WAS ALL MY FAULT.

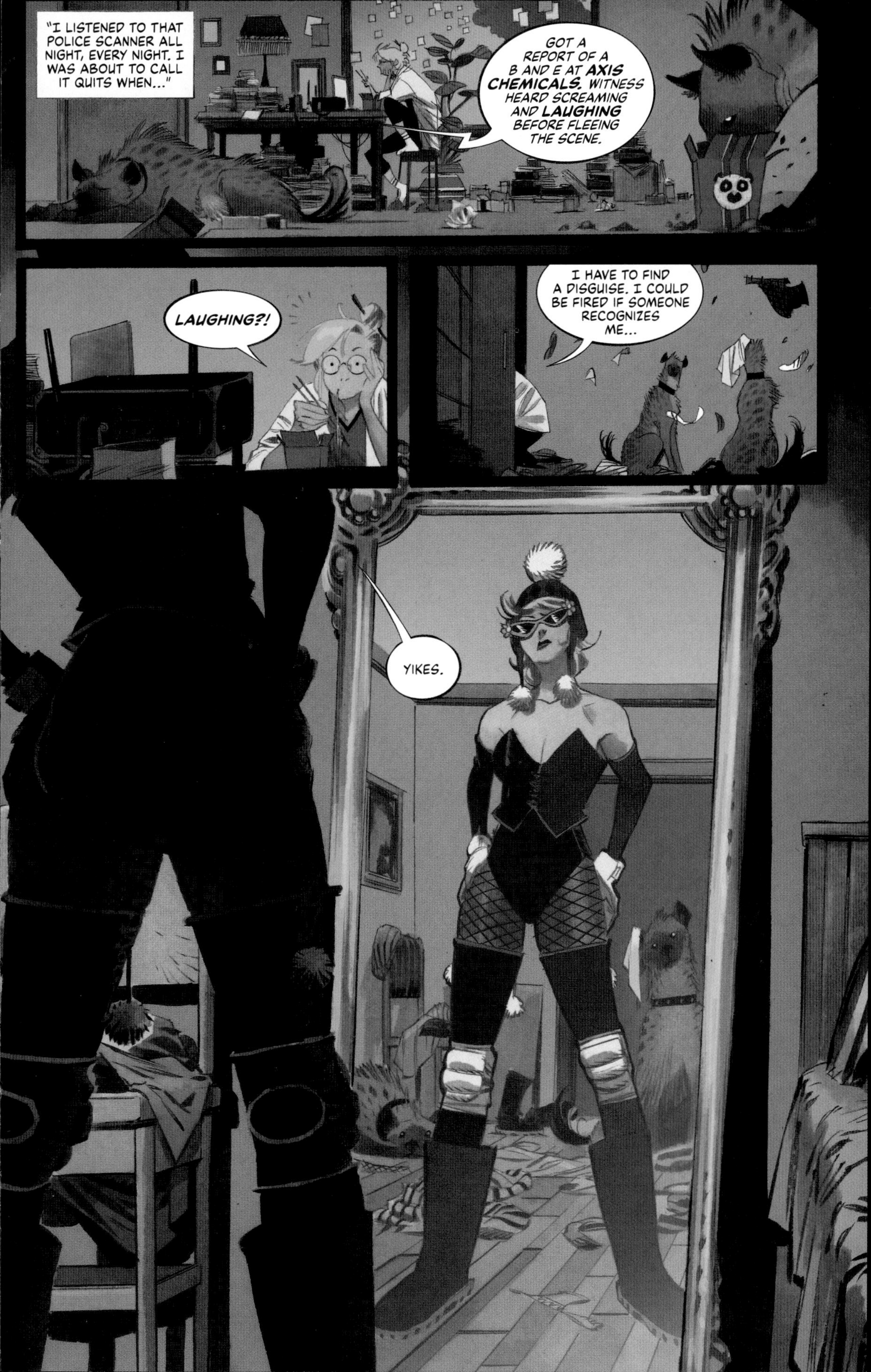
"I LISTENED TO THAT POLICE SCANNER ALL NIGHT, EVERY NIGHT. I WAS ABOUT TO CALL IT QUITS WHEN..."
GOT A REPORT OF A B AND E AT AXIS CHEMICALS. WITNESS HEARD SCREAMING AND LAUGHING BEFORE FLEEING THE SCENE.
LAUGHING?!
I HAVE TO FIND A DISGUISE. I COULD BE FIRED IF SOMEONE RECOGNIZES ME...
YIKES.

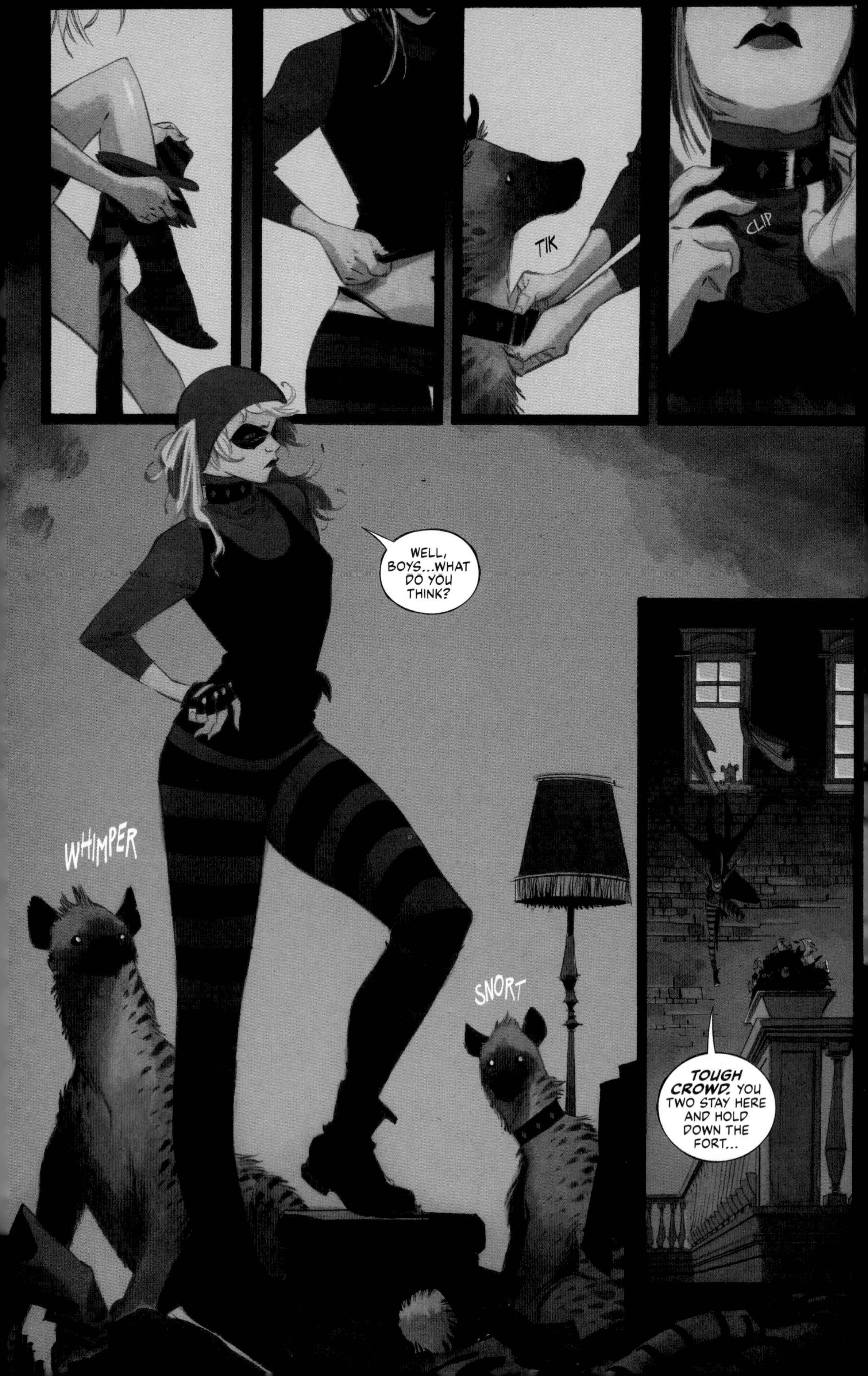
TIK
CLIP
WELL, BOYS...WHAT DO YOU THINK?
WHIMPER
SNORT
TOUGH CROWD. YOU TWO STAY HERE AND HOLD DOWN THE FORT...

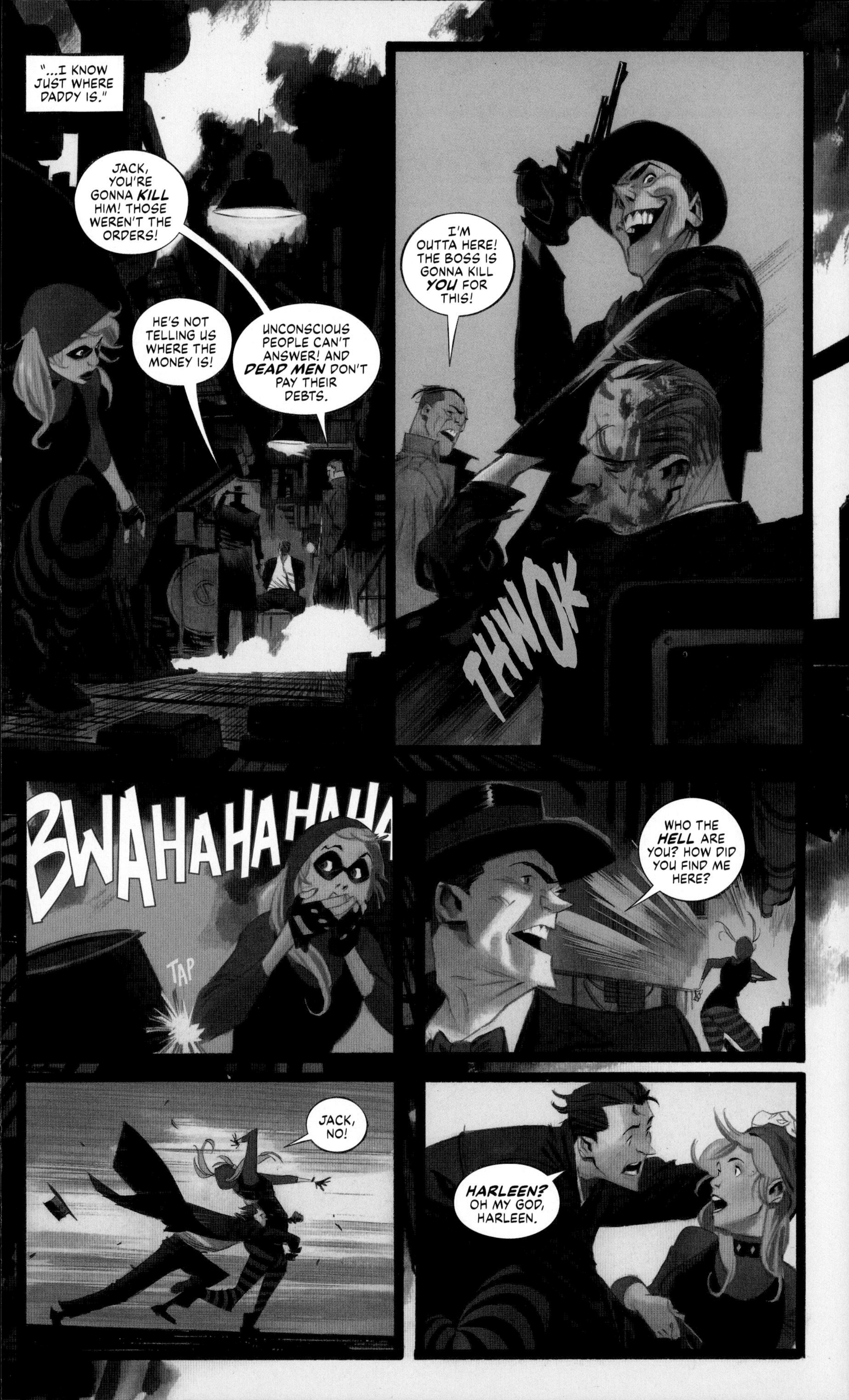
"...I KNOW JUST WHERE DADDY IS."
JACK, YOU'RE GONNA KILL HIM! THOSE WEREN'T THE ORDERS!
HE'S NOT TELLING US WHERE THE MONEY IS!
UNCONSCIOUS PEOPLE CAN'T ANSWER! AND DEAD MEN DON'T PAY THEIR DEBTS.
I'M OUTTA HERE! THE BOSS IS GONNA KILL YOU FOR THIS!
THWOK
BWAHAHAHAHAHA
TAP
WHO THE HELL ARE YOU? HOW DID YOU FIND ME HERE?
JACK, NO!
HARLEEN? OH MY GOD, HARLEEN.

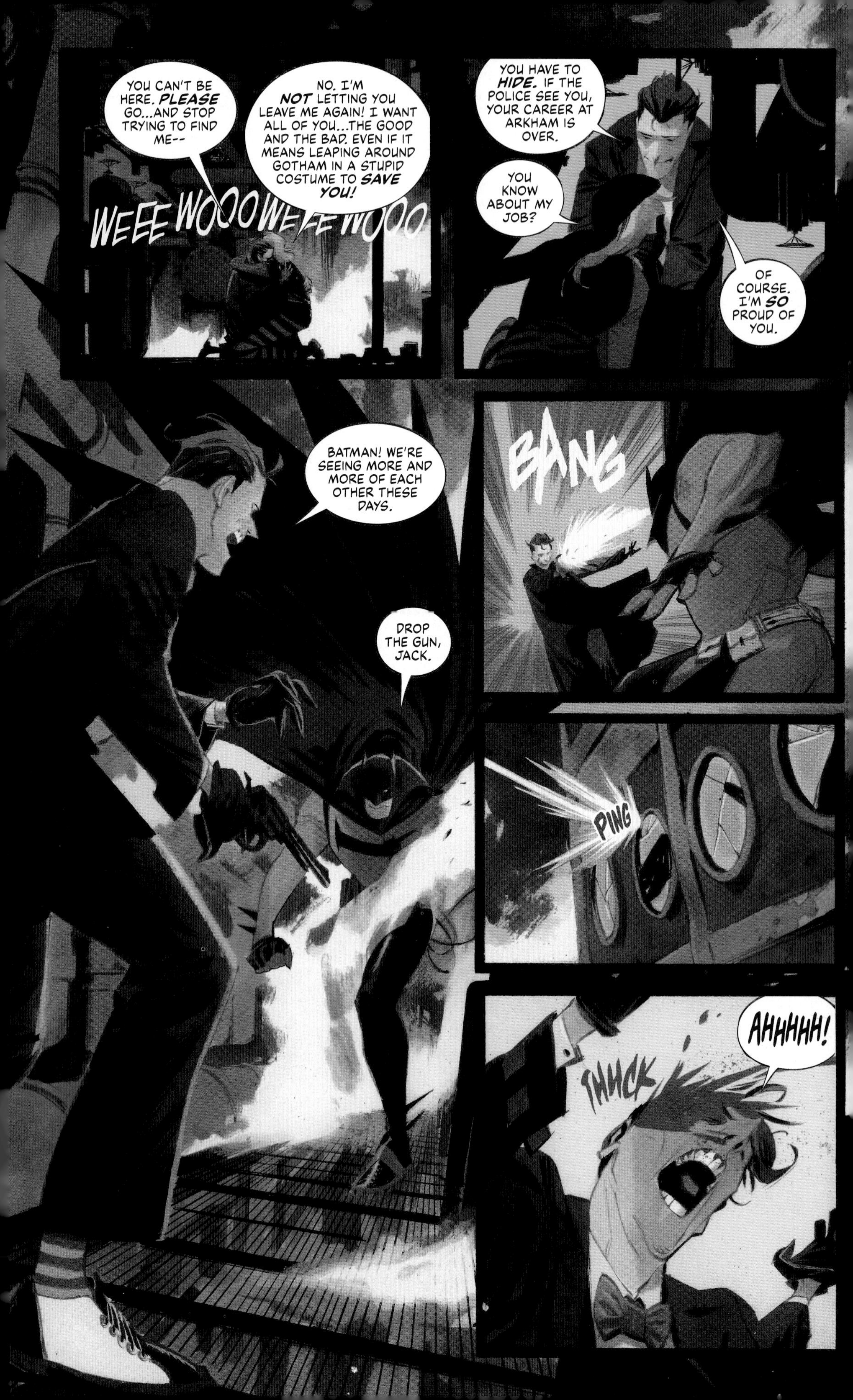
YOU CAN'T BE HERE. PLEASE GO...AND STOP TRYING TO FIND ME--
NO. I'M NOT LETTING YOU LEAVE ME AGAIN! I WANT ALL OF YOU...THE GOOD AND THE BAD. EVEN IF IT MEANS LEAPING AROUND GOTHAM IN A STUPID COSTUME TO SAVE YOU!
WEEE WOOO WEEE WOOO
YOU HAVE TO HIDE. IF THE POLICE SEE YOU, YOUR CAREER AT ARKHAM IS OVER.
YOU KNOW ABOUT MY JOB?
OF COURSE. I'M SO PROUD OF YOU.
BATMAN! WE'RE SEEING MORE AND MORE OF EACH OTHER THESE DAYS.
DROP THE GUN, JACK.
BANG
PING
THUCK
AHHHHH!

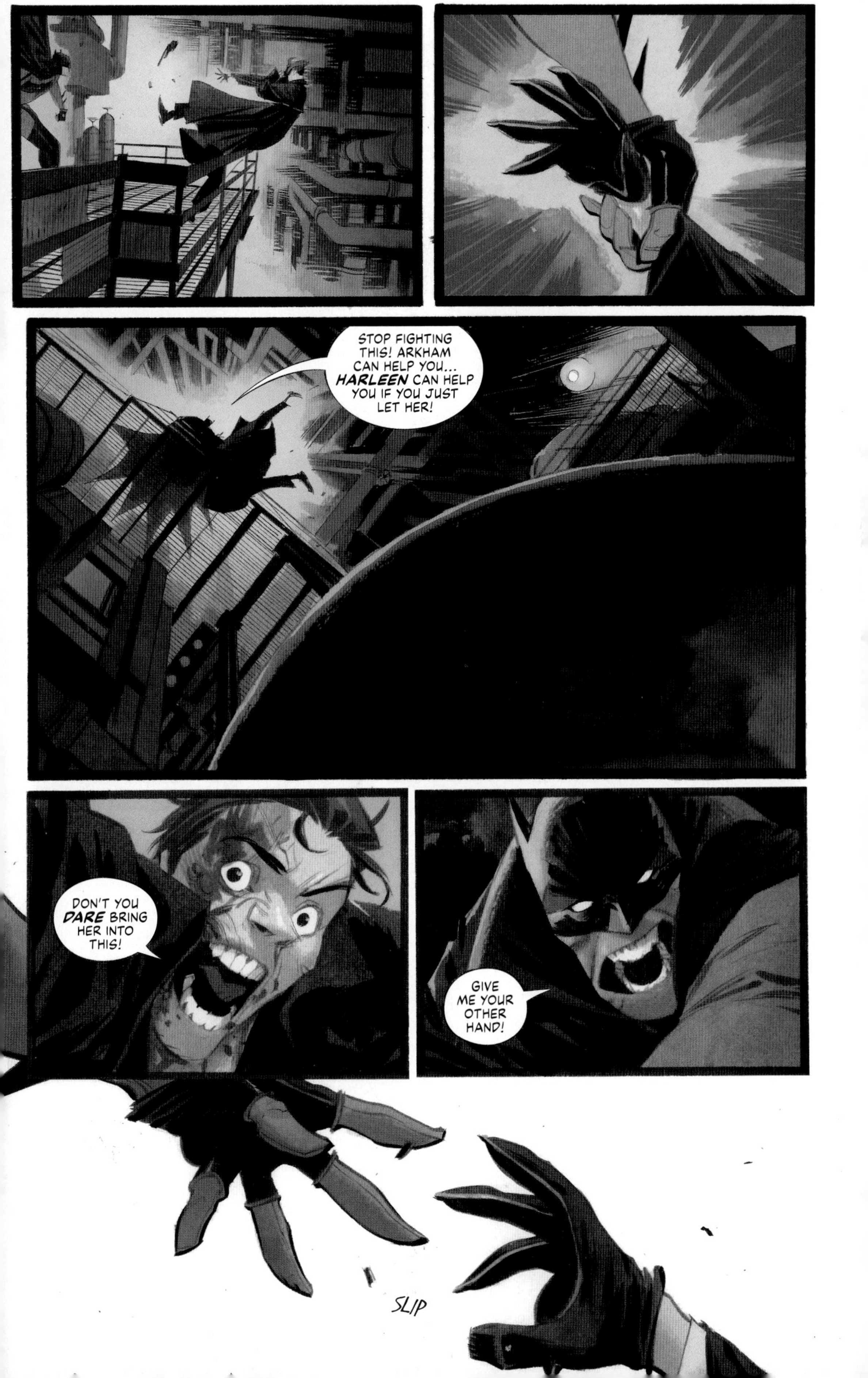
STOP FIGHTING THIS! ARKHAM CAN HELP YOU... HARLEEN CAN HELP YOU IF YOU JUST LET HER!
DON'T YOU DARE BRING HER INTO THIS!
GIVE ME YOUR OTHER HAND!
SLIP

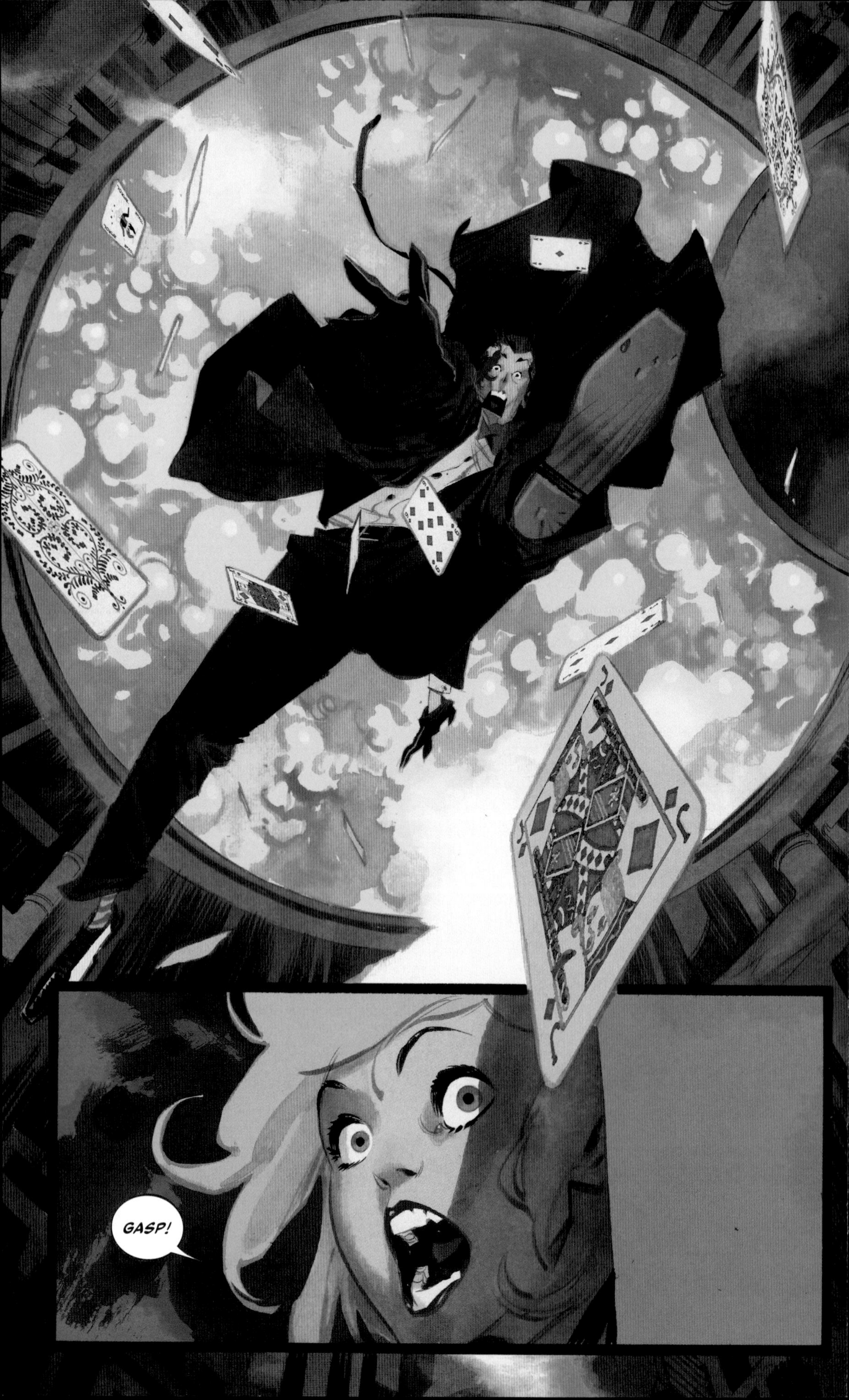
GASP!

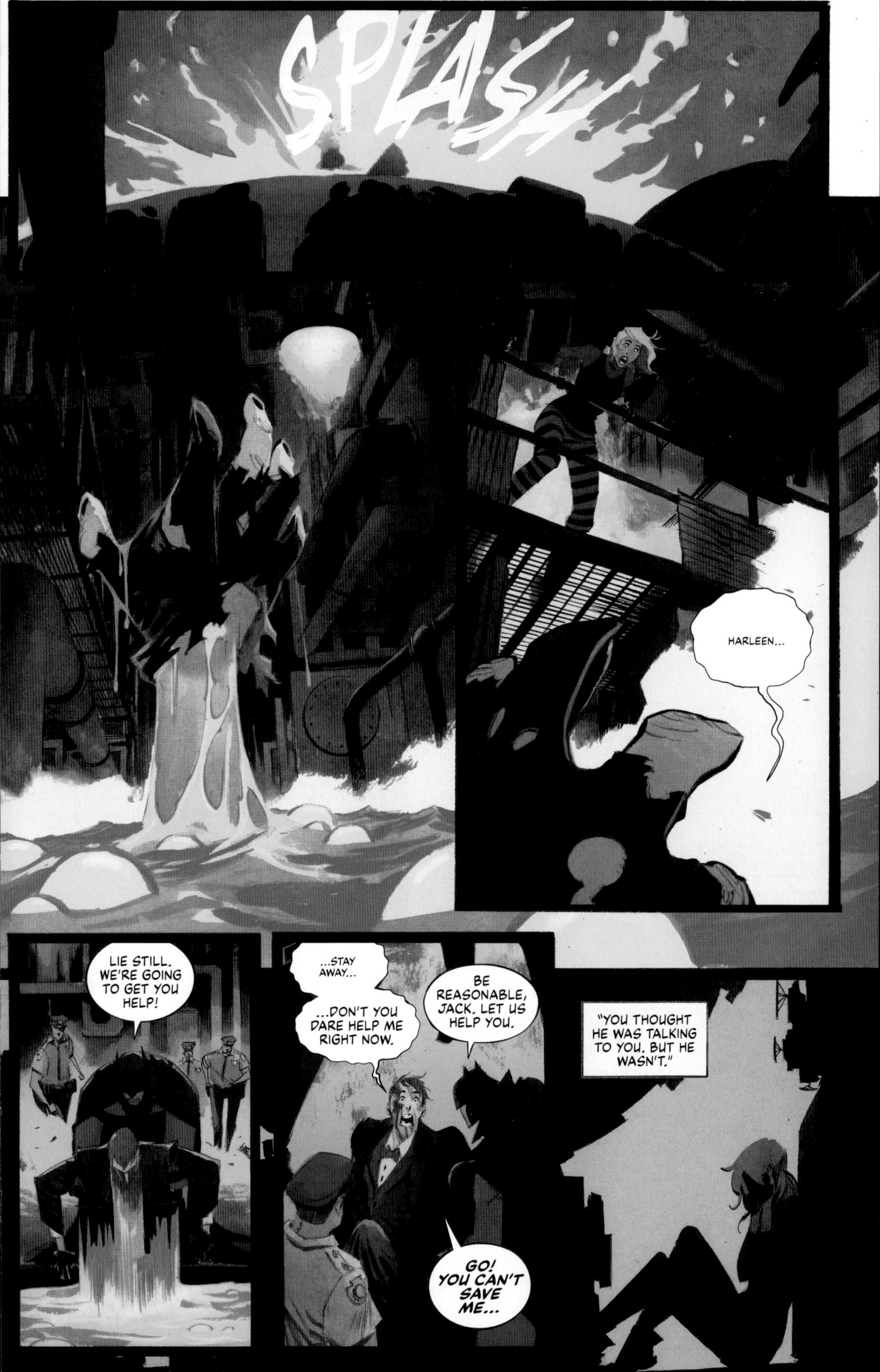
SPLASH
HARLEEN...
LIE STILL. WE'RE GOING TO GET YOU HELP!
...STAY AWAY...
...DON'T YOU DARE HELP ME RIGHT NOW.
BE REASONABLE, JACK. LET US HELP YOU.
GO! YOU CAN'T SAVE ME...
"YOU THOUGHT HE WAS TALKING TO YOU. BUT HE WASN'T."

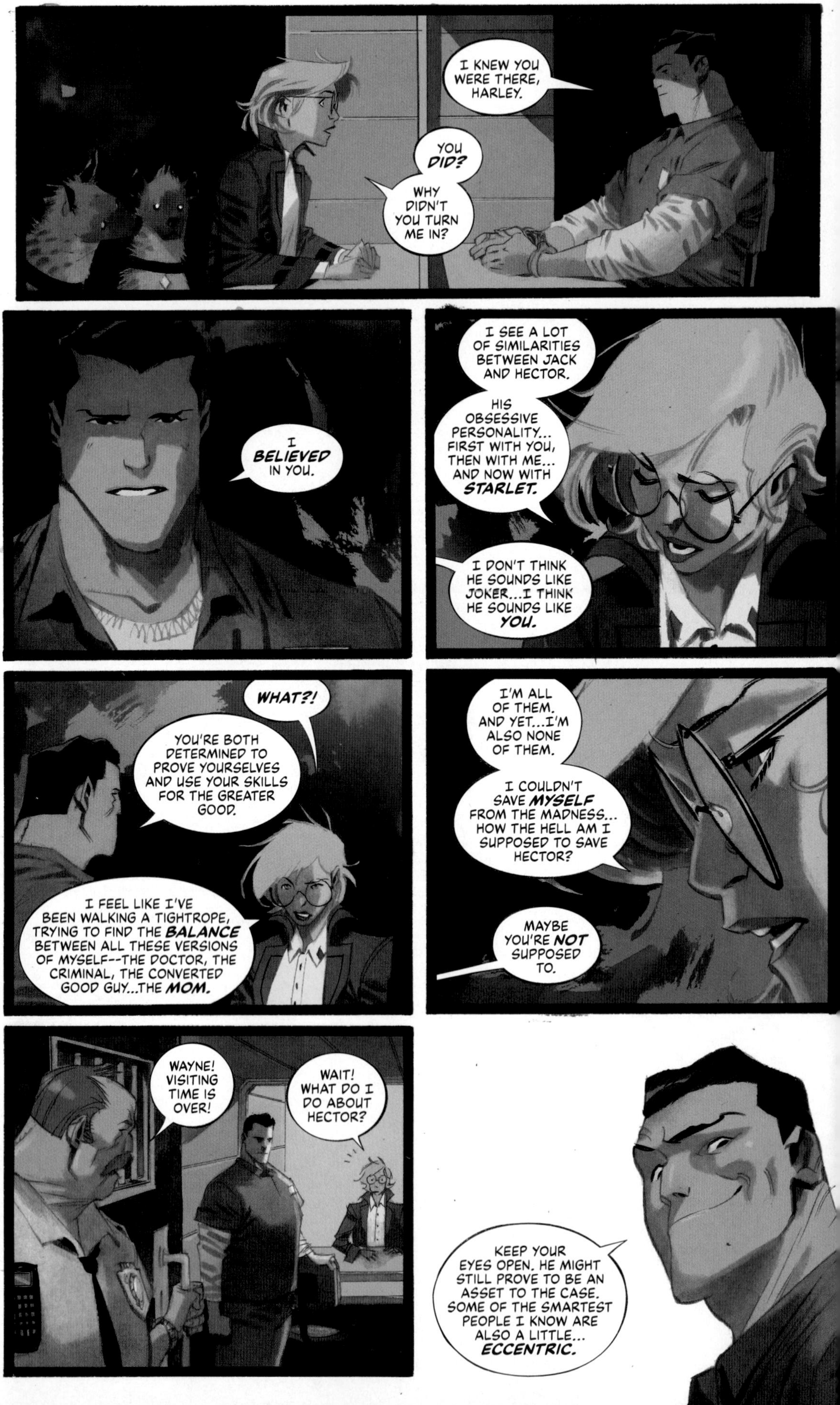
I KNEW YOU WERE THERE, HARLEY.
YOU DID?
WHY DIDN'T YOU TURN ME IN?
I BELIEVED IN YOU.
I SEE A LOT OF SIMILARITIES BETWEEN JACK AND HECTOR.
HIS OBSESSIVE PERSONALITY... FIRST WITH YOU, THEN WITH ME... AND NOW WITH STARLET.
I DON'T THINK HE SOUNDS LIKE JOKER...I THINK HE SOUNDS LIKE YOU.
WHAT?!
YOU'RE BOTH DETERMINED TO PROVE YOURSELVES AND USE YOUR SKILLS FOR THE GREATER GOOD.
I FEEL LIKE I'VE BEEN WALKING A TIGHTROPE, TRYING TO FIND THE BALANCE BETWEEN ALL THESE VERSIONS OF MYSELF--THE DOCTOR, THE CRIMINAL, THE CONVERTED GOOD GUY...THE MOM.
I'M ALL OF THEM. AND YET...I'M ALSO NONE OF THEM.
I COULDN'T SAVE MYSELF FROM THE MADNESS... HOW THE HELL AM I SUPPOSED TO SAVE HECTOR?
MAYBE YOU'RE NOT SUPPOSED TO.
WAYNE! VISITING TIME IS OVER!
WAIT! WHAT DO I DO ABOUT HECTOR?
KEEP YOUR EYES OPEN. HE MIGHT STILL PROVE TO BE AN ASSET TO THE CASE. SOME OF THE SMARTEST PEOPLE I KNOW ARE ALSO A LITTLE... ECCENTRIC.

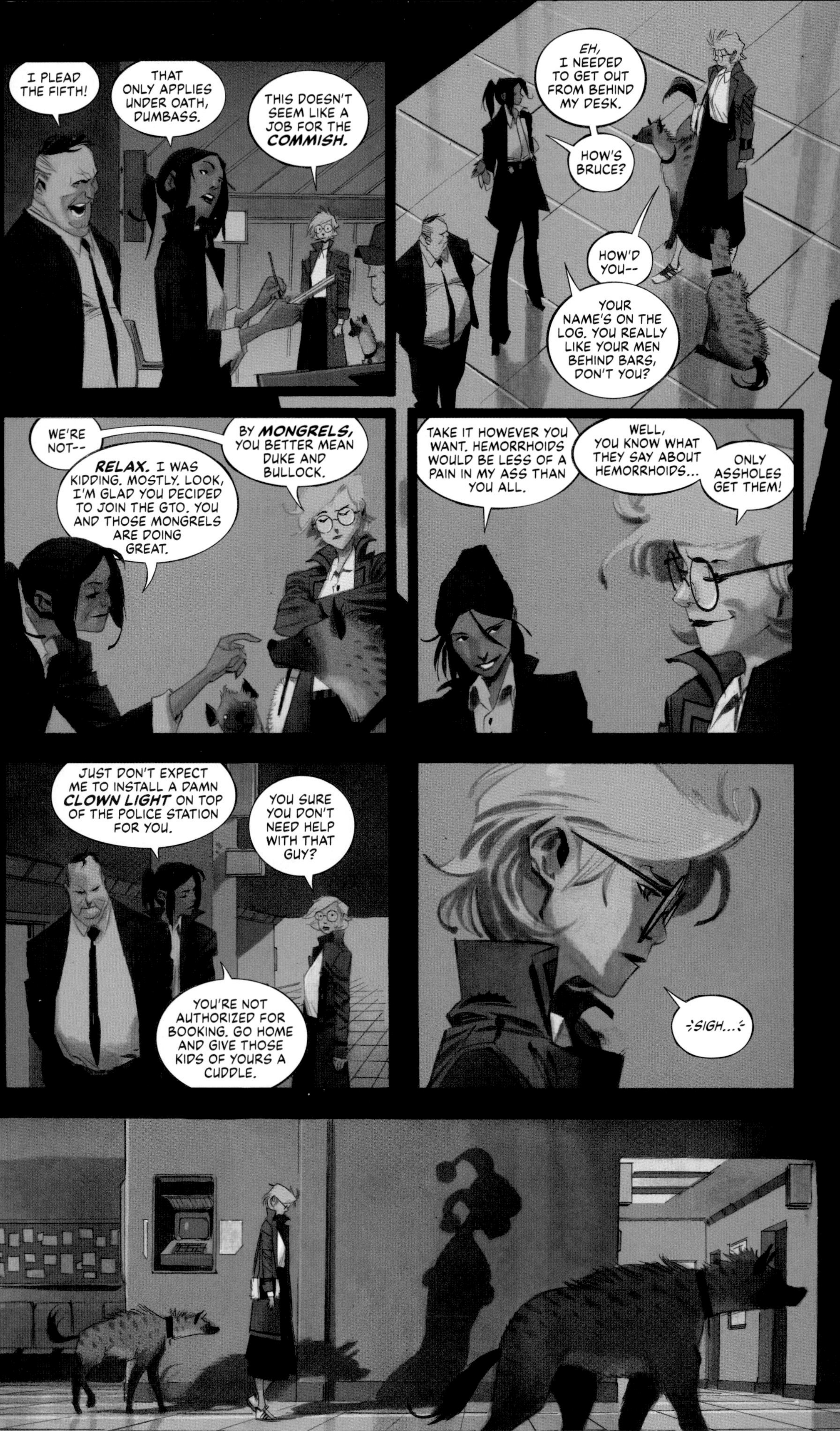
I PLEAD THE FIFTH!
THAT ONLY APPLIES UNDER OATH, DUMBASS.
THIS DOESN'T SEEM LIKE A JOB FOR THE COMMISH.
EH, I NEEDED TO GET OUT FROM BEHIND MY DESK.
HOW'S BRUCE?
HOW'D YOU--
YOUR NAME'S ON THE LOG. YOU REALLY LIKE YOUR MEN BEHIND BARS, DON'T YOU?
WE'RE NOT--
RELAX. I WAS KIDDING. MOSTLY. LOOK, I'M GLAD YOU DECIDED TO JOIN THE GTO. YOU AND THOSE MONGRELS ARE DOING GREAT.
BY MONGRELS, YOU BETTER MEAN DUKE AND BULLOCK.
TAKE IT HOWEVER YOU WANT. HEMORRHOIDS WOULD BE LESS OF A PAIN IN MY ASS THAN YOU ALL.
WELL, YOU KNOW WHAT THEY SAY ABOUT HEMORRHOIDS...
ONLY ASSHOLES GET THEM!
JUST DON'T EXPECT ME TO INSTALL A DAMN CLOWN LIGHT ON TOP OF THE POLICE STATION FOR YOU.
YOU SURE YOU DON'T NEED HELP WITH THAT GUY?
YOU'RE NOT AUTHORIZED FOR BOOKING. GO HOME AND GIVE THOSE KIDS OF YOURS A CUDDLE.
SIGH...

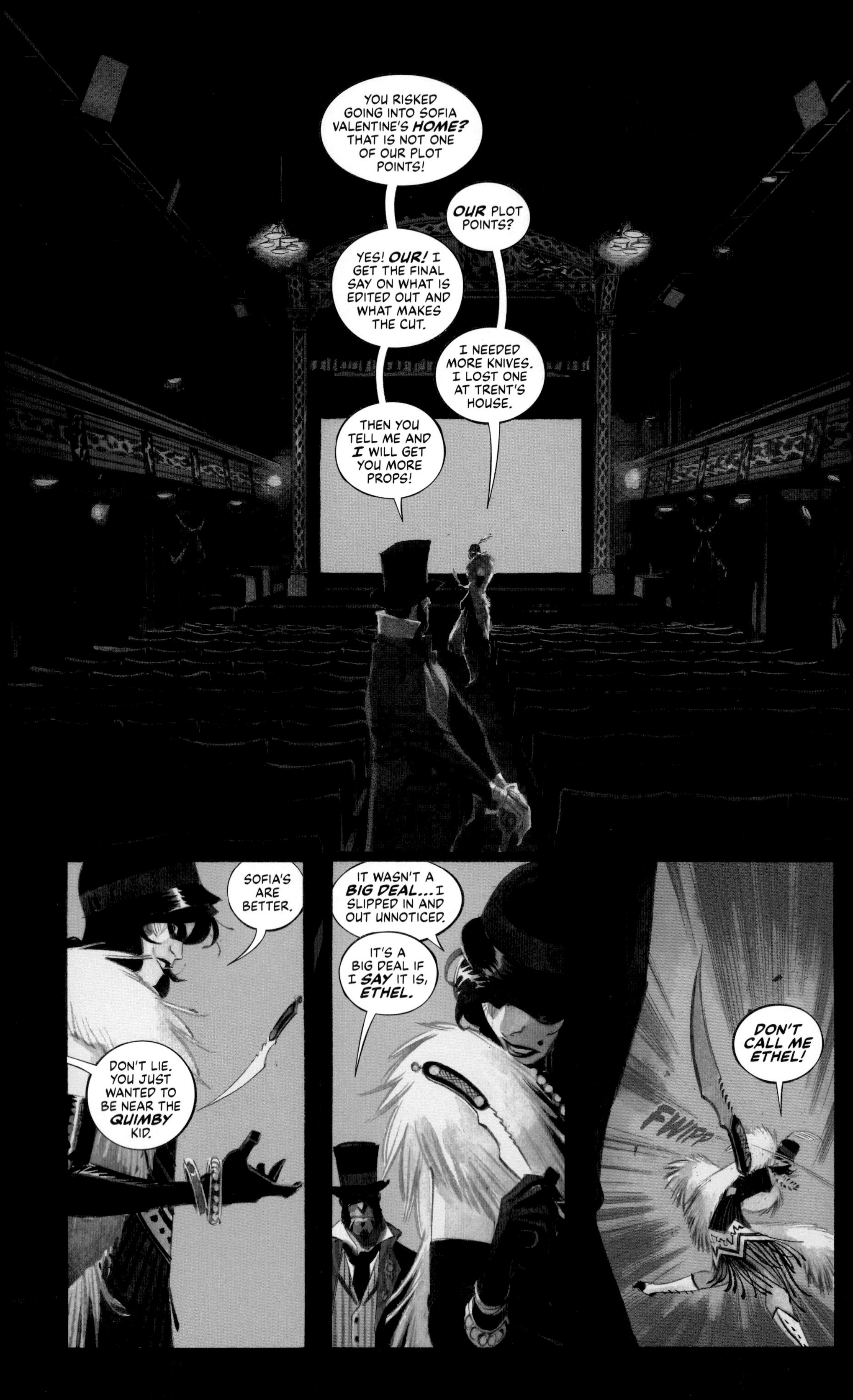
YOU RISKED GOING INTO SOFIA VALENTINE'S HOME? THAT IS NOT ONE OF OUR PLOT POINTS!
OUR PLOT POINTS?
YES! OUR! I GET THE FINAL SAY ON WHAT IS EDITED OUT AND WHAT MAKES THE CUT.
I NEEDED MORE KNIVES. I LOST ONE AT TRENT'S HOUSE.
THEN YOU TELL ME AND I WILL GET YOU MORE PROPS!
SOFIA'S ARE BETTER.
DON'T LIE. YOU JUST WANTED TO BE NEAR THE QUIMBY KID.
IT WASN'T A BIG DEAL... I SLIPPED IN AND OUT UNNOTICED.
IT'S A BIG DEAL IF I SAY IT IS, ETHEL.
FWIPP
DON'T CALL ME ETHEL!

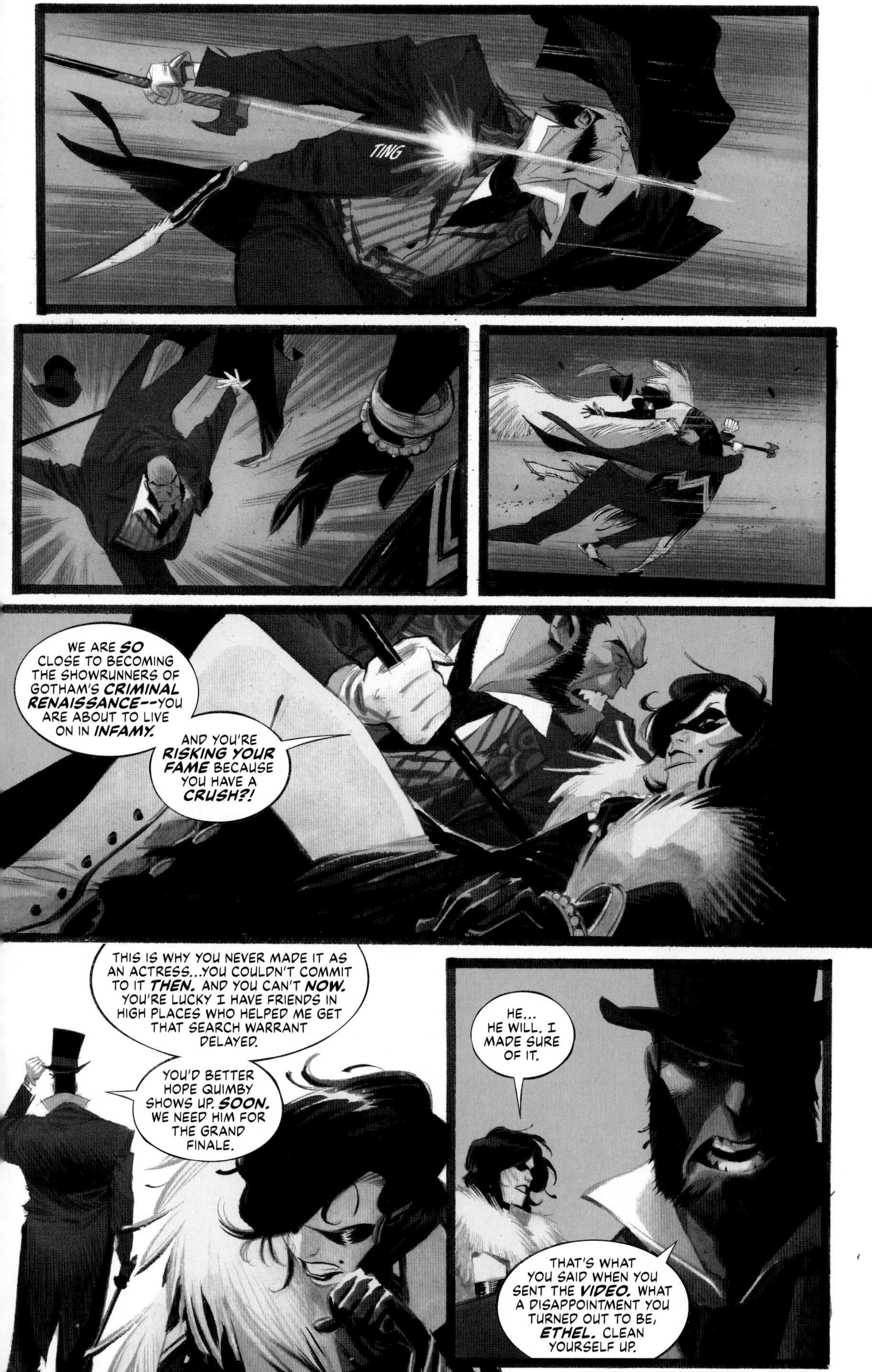
TING
WE ARE SO CLOSE TO BECOMING THE SHOWRUNNERS OF GOTHAM'S CRIMINAL RENAISSANCE--YOU ARE ABOUT TO LIVE ON IN INFAMY.
AND YOU'RE RISKING YOUR FAME BECAUSE YOU HAVE A CRUSH?!
THIS IS WHY YOU NEVER MADE IT AS AN ACTRESS...YOU COULDN'T COMMIT TO IT THEN. AND YOU CAN'T NOW. YOU'RE LUCKY I HAVE FRIENDS IN HIGH PLACES WHO HELPED ME GET THAT SEARCH WARRANT DELAYED.
YOU'D BETTER HOPE QUIMBY SHOWS UP. SOON. WE NEED HIM FOR THE GRAND FINALE.
HE... HE WILL. I MADE SURE OF IT.
THAT'S WHAT YOU SAID WHEN YOU SENT THE VIDEO. WHAT A DISAPPOINTMENT YOU TURNED OUT TO BE, ETHEL. CLEAN YOURSELF UP.

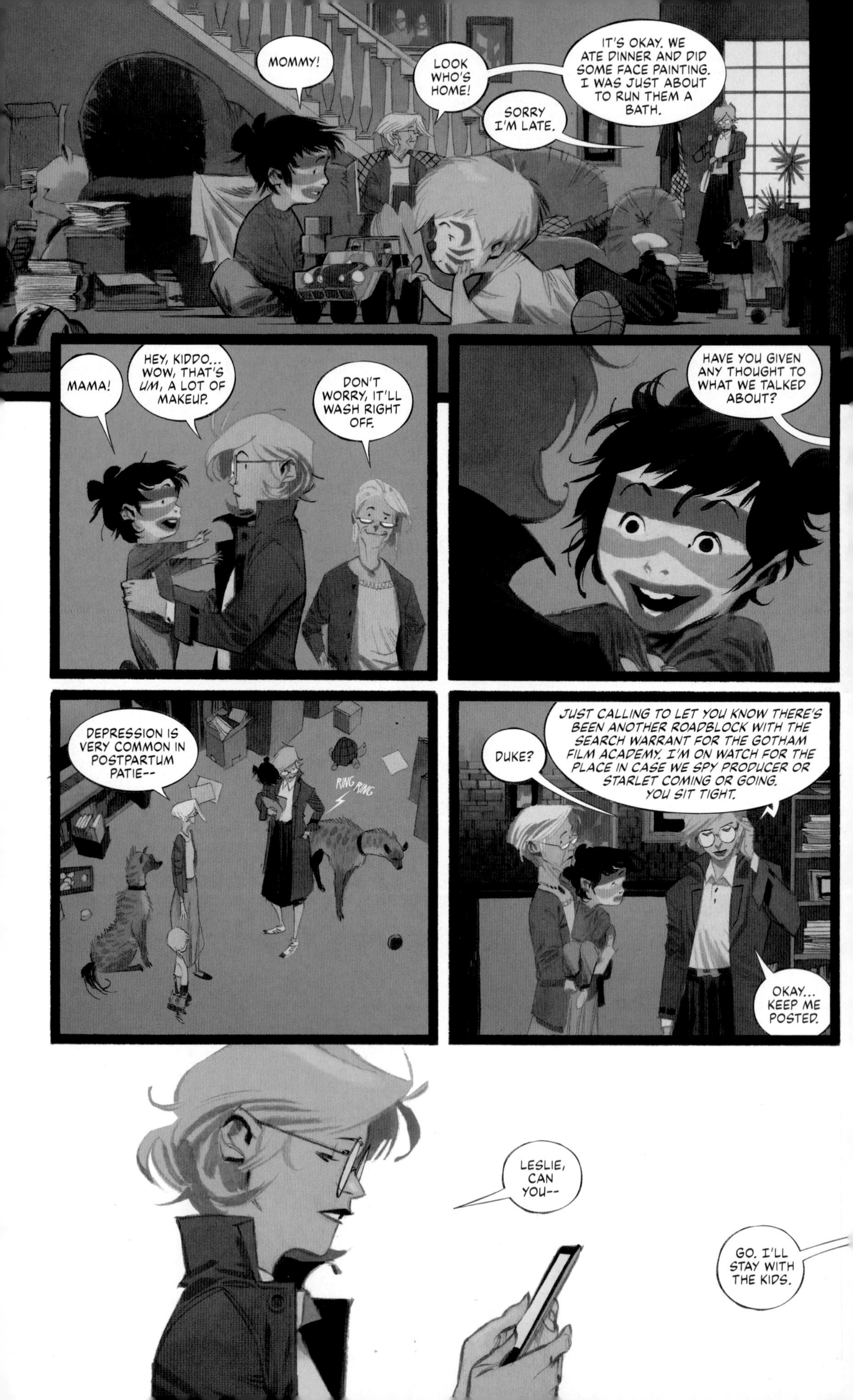
MOMMY!
LOOK WHO'S HOME!
SORRY I'M LATE.
IT'S OKAY. WE ATE DINNER AND DID SOME FACE PAINTING. I WAS JUST ABOUT TO RUN THEM A BATH.
MAMA!
HEY, KIDDO... WOW, THAT'S UM, A LOT OF MAKEUP.
DON'T WORRY, IT'LL WASH RIGHT OFF.
HAVE YOU GIVEN ANY THOUGHT TO WHAT WE TALKED ABOUT?
DEPRESSION IS VERY COMMON IN POSTPARTUM PATIE--
RING RING
DUKE?
JUST CALLING TO LET YOU KNOW THERE'S BEEN ANOTHER ROADBLOCK WITH THE SEARCH WARRANT FOR THE GOTHAM FILM ACADEMY. I'M ON WATCH FOR THE PLACE IN CASE WE SPY PRODUCER OR STARLET COMING OR GOING. YOU SIT TIGHT.
OKAY... KEEP ME POSTED.
LESLIE, CAN YOU--
GO. I'LL STAY WITH THE KIDS.

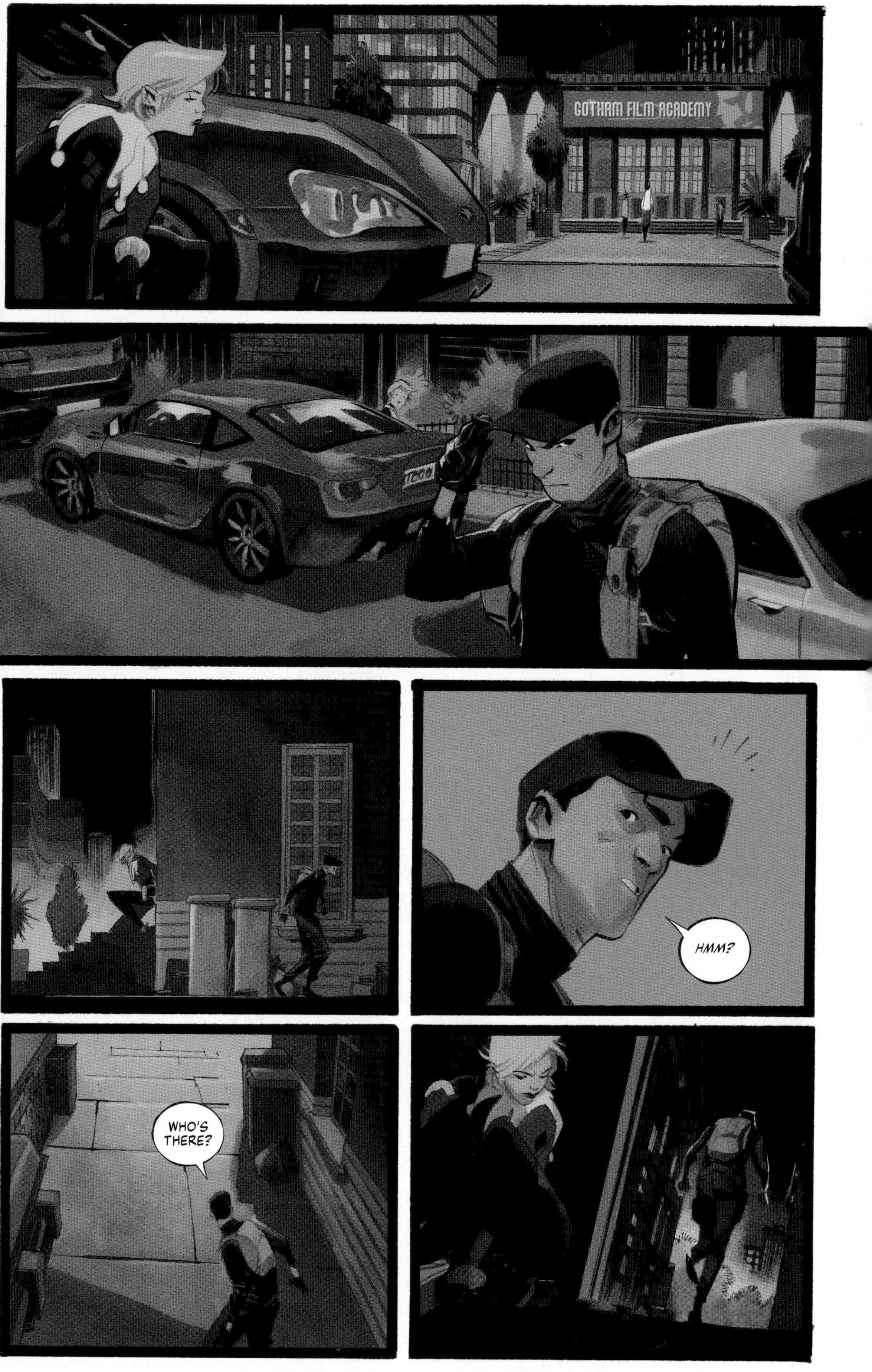
GOTHAM FILM ACADEMY
HMM?
WHO'S THERE?

YOU'RE USING THE WRONG SIDE...

✳

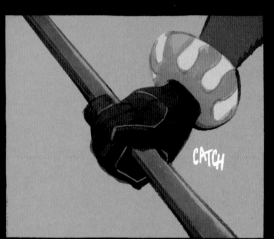
CATCH

WHAT ARE YOU DOING HERE?

WHAT AM I DOING HERE?

IN CASE YOU DIDN'T NOTICE, BENDING THE RULES IS KIND OF MY THING. WHAT THE HELL ARE YOU DOING HERE?

THIS WAS ON MY CAR TODAY. I TOOK IT TO THE JUDGE HOPING TO SPEED UP THE WARRANT, AND HE COMPLETELY DISMISSED IT! SAID IT STILL WASN'T ENOUGH TO GET IN HERE! I THOUGHT IF I COULD SNEAK IN, MAYBE HAVE A LOOK AROUND--

YEAH, WELL, YOU KIND OF SUCK AT SNEAKING AROUND.

SAYS THE GIRL DRESSED IN BRIGHT RED.

NEWS FLASH... YOU BOTH SUCK AT SNEAKING AROUND.

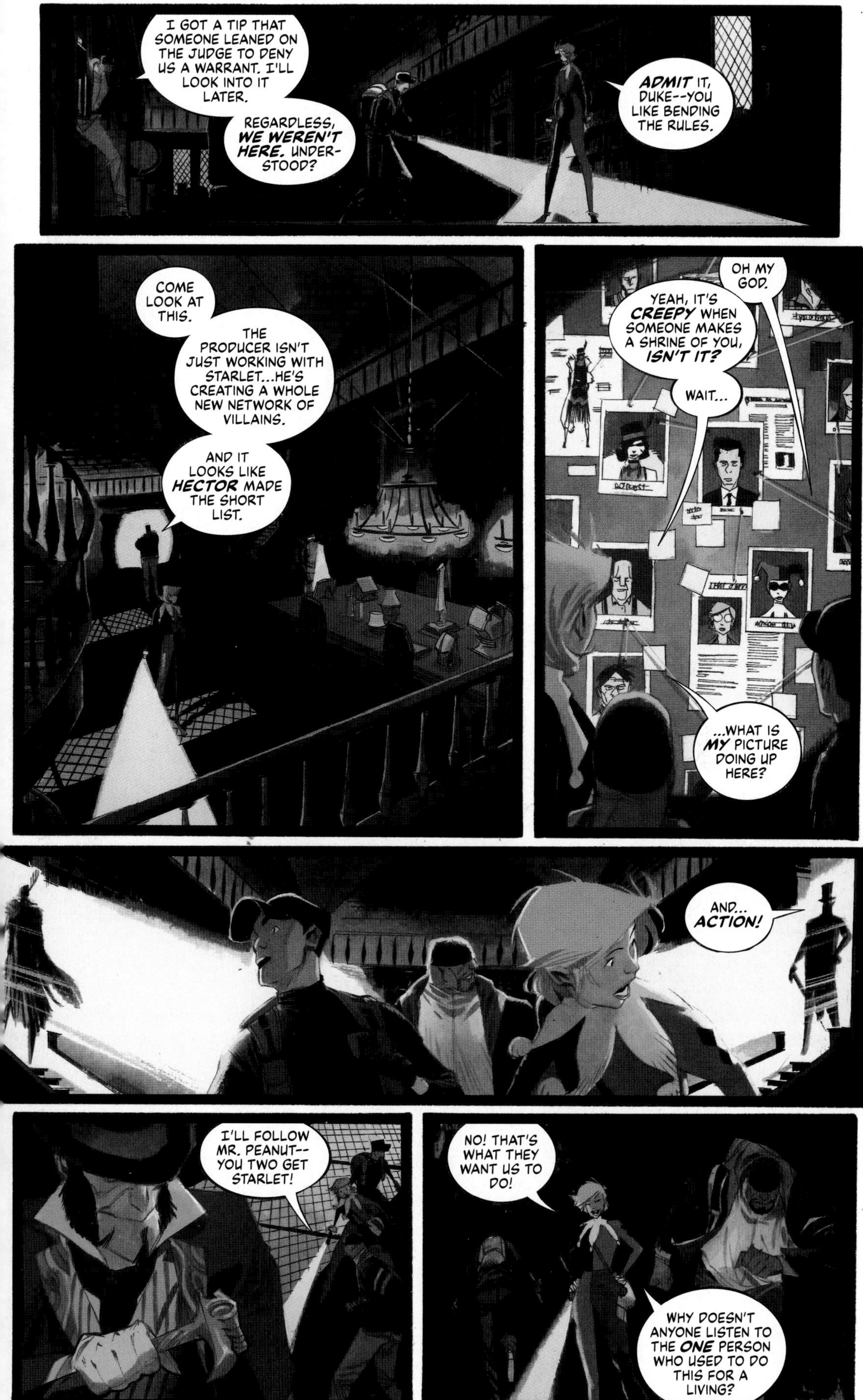
I GOT A TIP THAT SOMEONE LEANED ON THE JUDGE TO DENY US A WARRANT. I'LL LOOK INTO IT LATER.
REGARDLESS, ***WE WEREN'T HERE.*** UNDER-STOOD?
ADMIT IT, DUKE--YOU LIKE BENDING THE RULES.
COME LOOK AT THIS.
THE PRODUCER ISN'T JUST WORKING WITH STARLET...HE'S CREATING A WHOLE NEW NETWORK OF VILLAINS.
AND IT LOOKS LIKE ***HECTOR*** MADE THE SHORT LIST.
OH MY GOD.
YEAH, IT'S ***CREEPY*** WHEN SOMEONE MAKES A SHRINE OF YOU, ***ISN'T IT?***
WAIT...
...WHAT IS ***MY*** PICTURE DOING UP HERE?
AND... ***ACTION!***
I'LL FOLLOW MR. PEANUT--YOU TWO GET STARLET!
NO! THAT'S WHAT THEY WANT US TO DO!
WHY DOESN'T ANYONE LISTEN TO THE ***ONE*** PERSON WHO USED TO DO THIS FOR A LIVING?

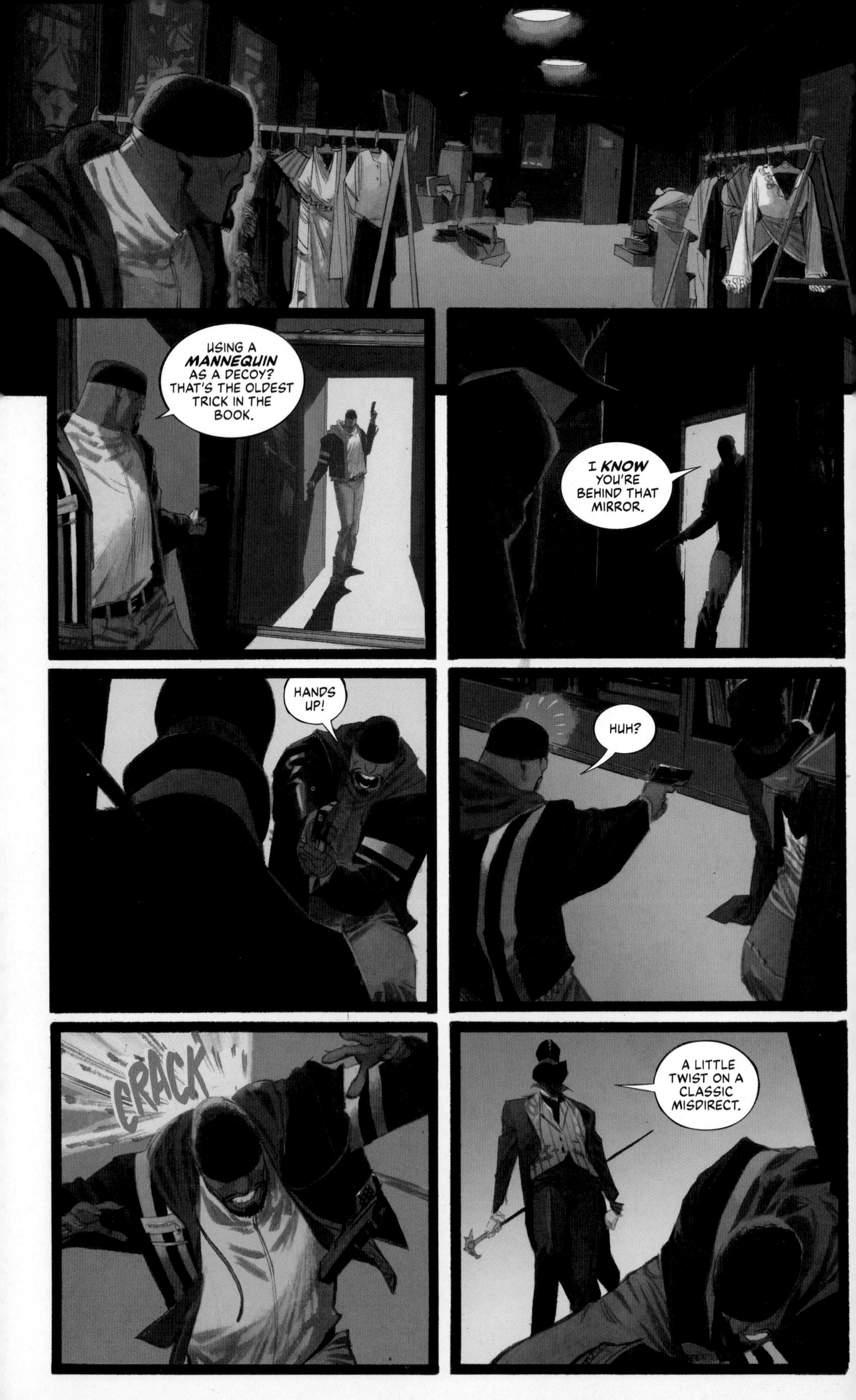
USING A MANNEQUIN AS A DECOY? THAT'S THE OLDEST TRICK IN THE BOOK.
I KNOW YOU'RE BEHIND THAT MIRROR.
HANDS UP!
HUH?
CRACK
A LITTLE TWIST ON A CLASSIC MISDIRECT.

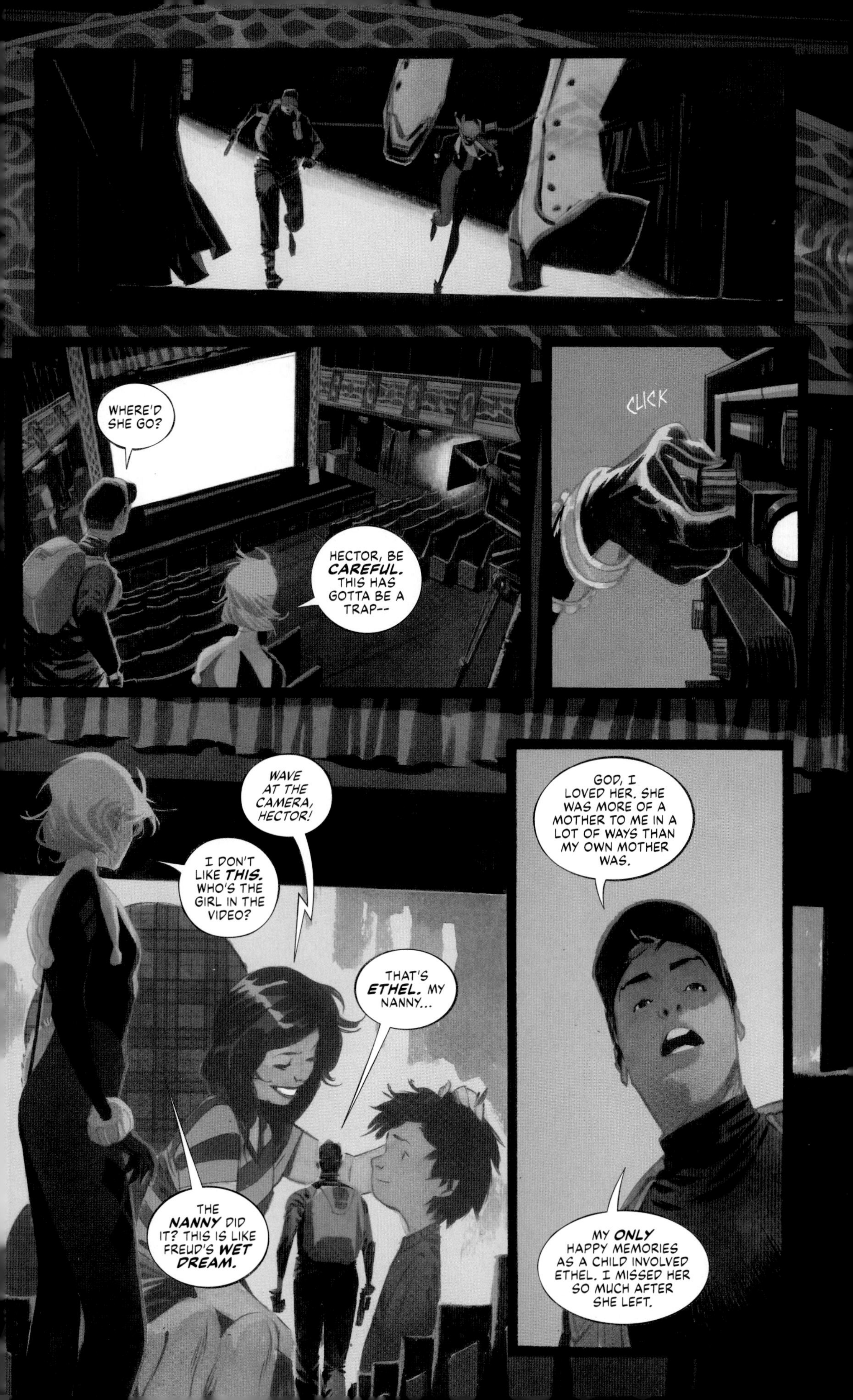
WHERE'D SHE GO?
HECTOR, BE CAREFUL. THIS HAS GOTTA BE A TRAP--
CLICK
WAVE AT THE CAMERA, HECTOR!
I DON'T LIKE THIS. WHO'S THE GIRL IN THE VIDEO?
THAT'S ETHEL. MY NANNY...
THE NANNY DID IT? THIS IS LIKE FREUD'S WET DREAM.
GOD, I LOVED HER. SHE WAS MORE OF A MOTHER TO ME IN A LOT OF WAYS THAN MY OWN MOTHER WAS.
MY ONLY HAPPY MEMORIES AS A CHILD INVOLVED ETHEL. I MISSED HER SO MUCH AFTER SHE LEFT.

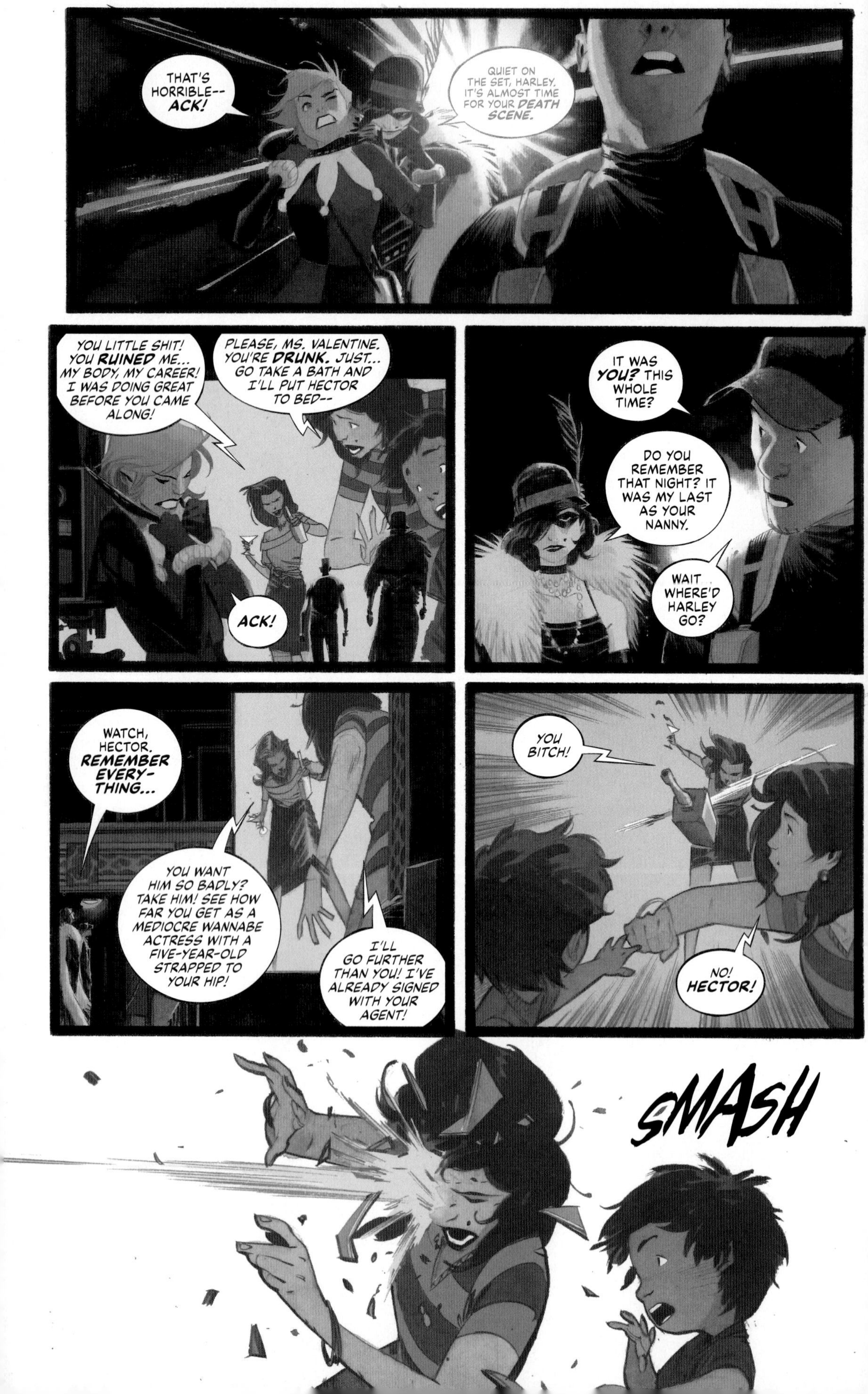

THAT'S HORRIBLE-- ACK!
QUIET ON THE SET, HARLEY. IT'S ALMOST TIME FOR YOUR DEATH SCENE.
YOU LITTLE SHIT! YOU RUINED ME... MY BODY, MY CAREER! I WAS DOING GREAT BEFORE YOU CAME ALONG!
PLEASE, MS. VALENTINE. YOU'RE DRUNK. JUST... GO TAKE A BATH AND I'LL PUT HECTOR TO BED--
ACK!
IT WAS YOU? THIS WHOLE TIME?
DO YOU REMEMBER THAT NIGHT? IT WAS MY LAST AS YOUR NANNY.
WAIT. WHERE'D HARLEY GO?
WATCH, HECTOR. REMEMBER EVERY-THING...
YOU WANT HIM SO BADLY? TAKE HIM! SEE HOW FAR YOU GET AS A MEDIOCRE WANNABE ACTRESS WITH A FIVE-YEAR-OLD STRAPPED TO YOUR HIP!
I'LL GO FURTHER THAN YOU! I'VE ALREADY SIGNED WITH YOUR AGENT!
YOU BITCH!
NO! HECTOR!
SMASH

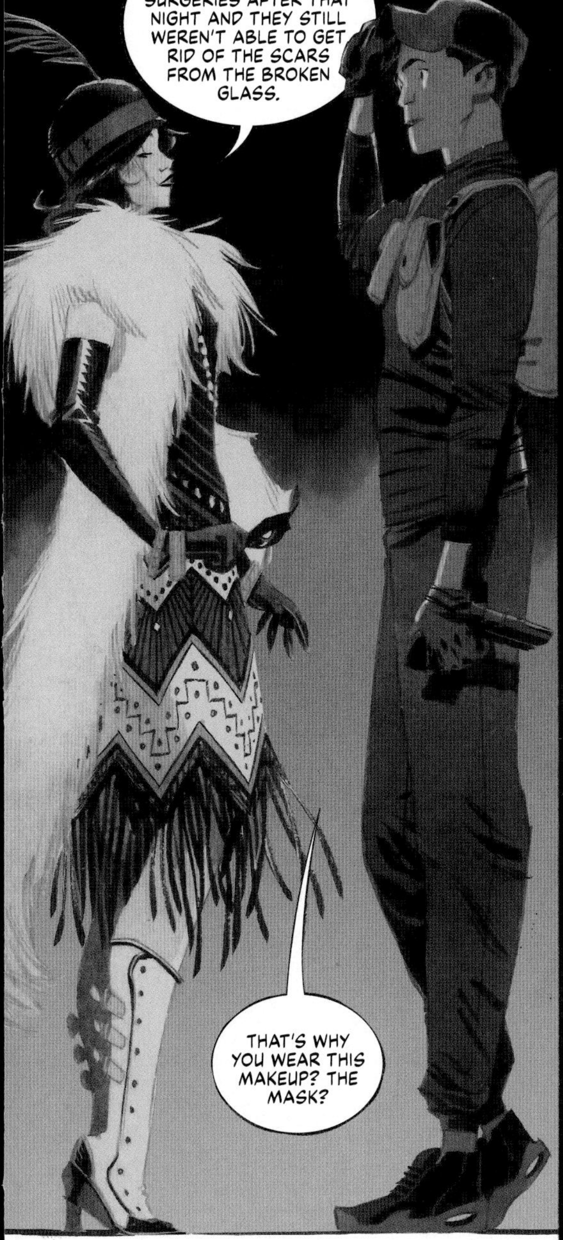
I NEEDED THREE RECONSTRUCTIVE SURGERIES AFTER THAT NIGHT AND THEY STILL WEREN'T ABLE TO GET RID OF THE SCARS FROM THE BROKEN GLASS.
THAT'S WHY YOU WEAR THIS MAKEUP? THE MASK?

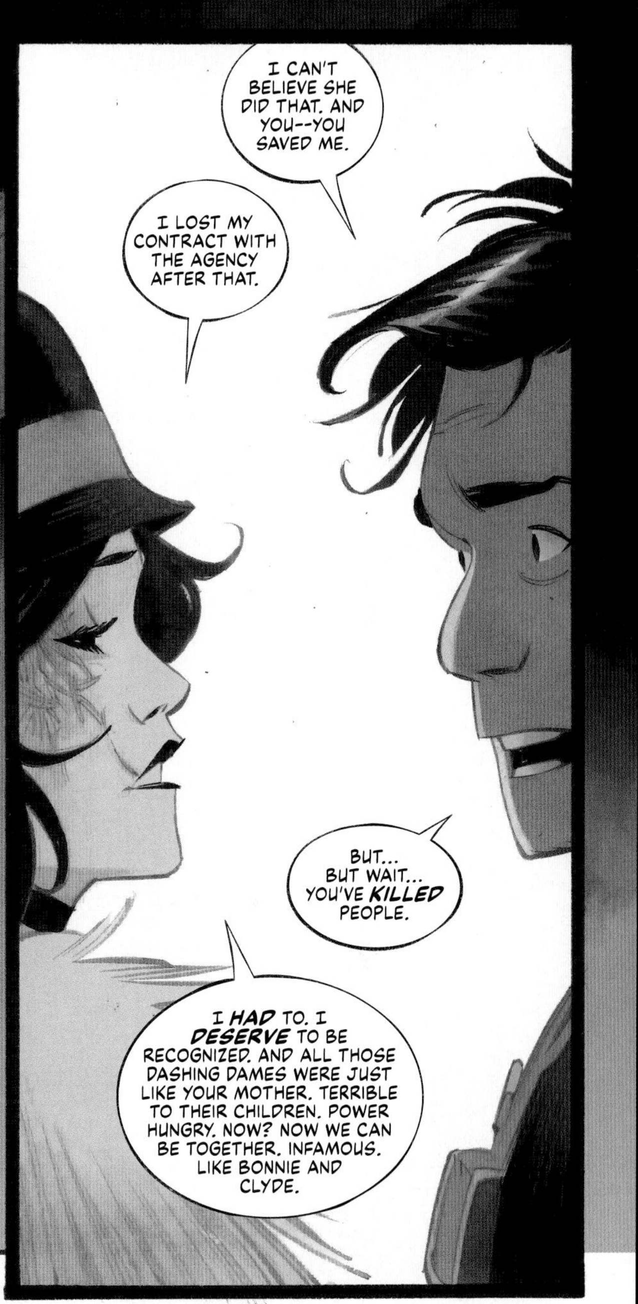
I CAN'T BELIEVE SHE DID THAT. AND YOU--YOU SAVED ME.
I LOST MY CONTRACT WITH THE AGENCY AFTER THAT.
BUT... BUT WAIT... YOU'VE *KILLED* PEOPLE.
I *HAD* TO. I *DESERVE* TO BE RECOGNIZED. AND ALL THOSE DASHING DAMES WERE JUST LIKE YOUR MOTHER. TERRIBLE TO THEIR CHILDREN. POWER HUNGRY. NOW? NOW WE CAN BE TOGETHER. INFAMOUS. LIKE BONNIE AND CLYDE.

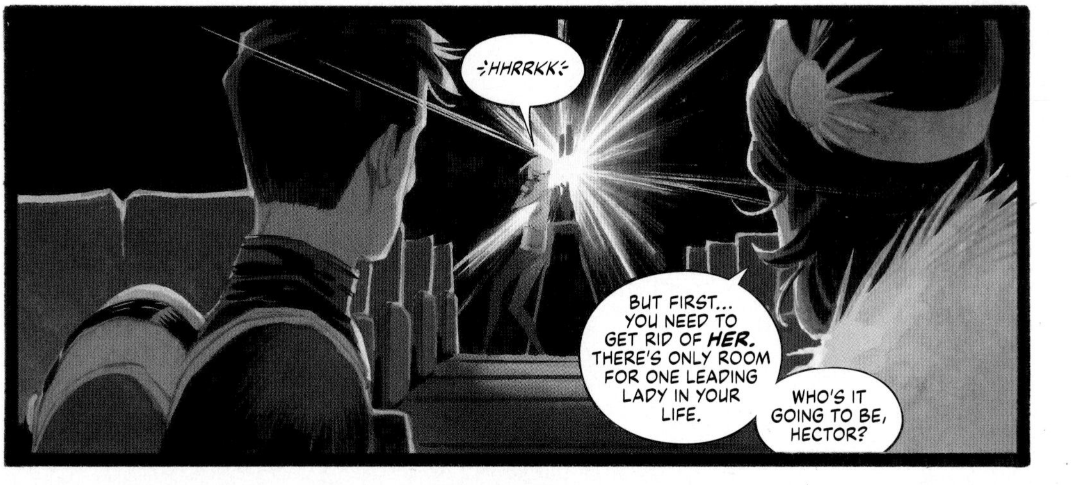
HHRRKK
BUT FIRST... YOU NEED TO GET RID OF *HER.* THERE'S ONLY ROOM FOR ONE LEADING LADY IN YOUR LIFE.
WHO'S IT GOING TO BE, HECTOR?

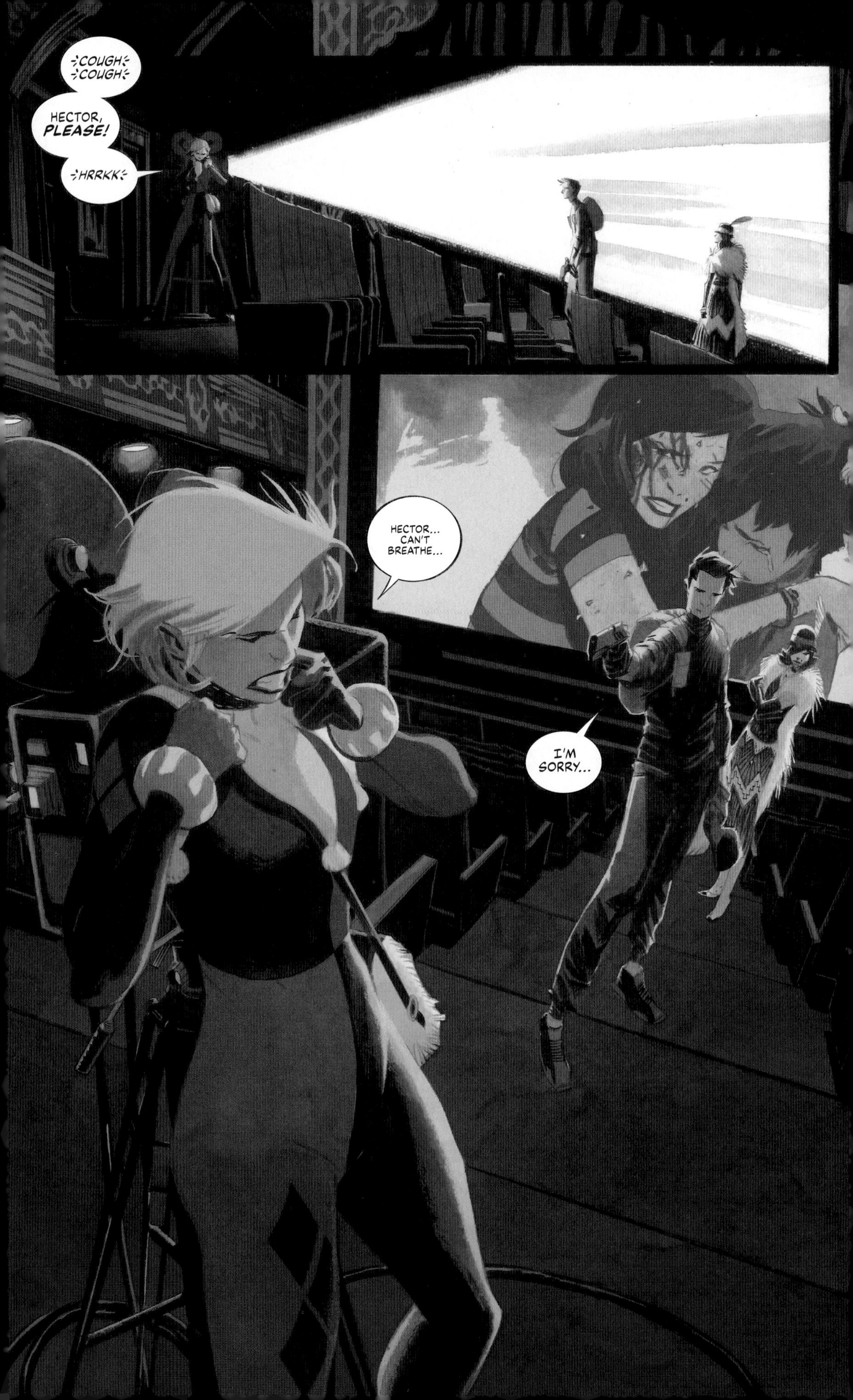

COUGH *COUGH*
HECTOR, **PLEASE!**
HRRKK
HECTOR... CAN'T BREATHE...
I'M SORRY...

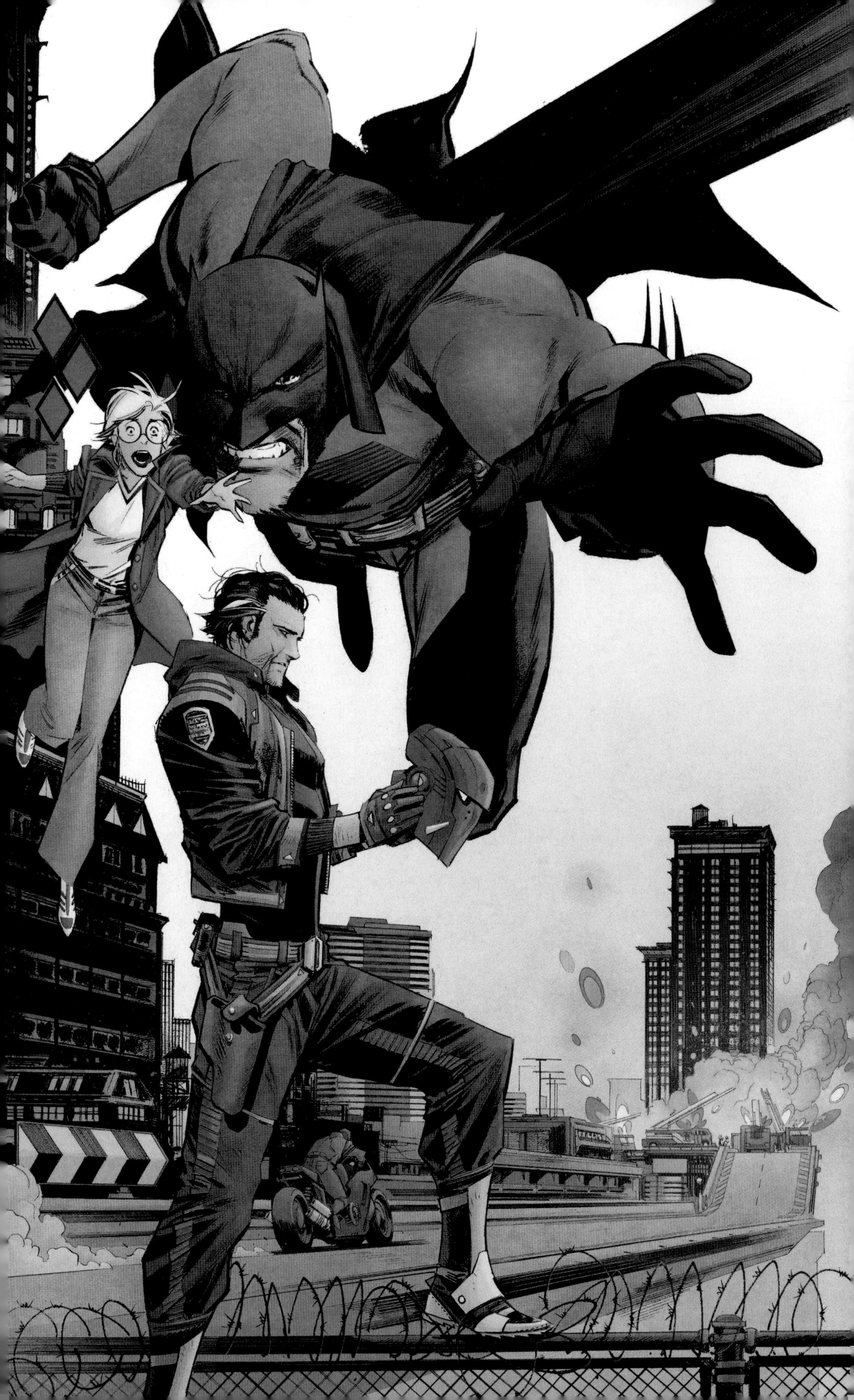

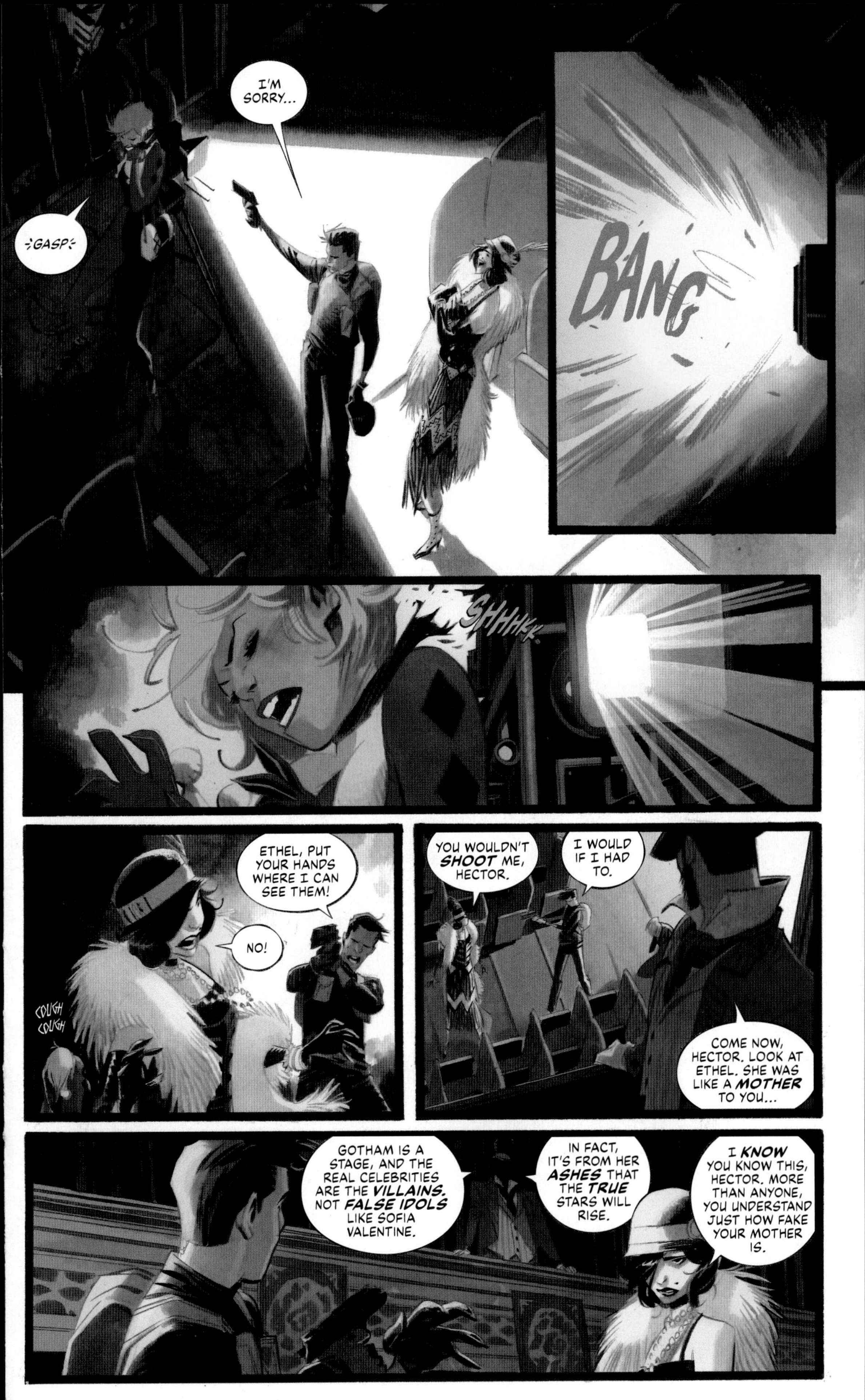
-GASP-
I'M SORRY...
BANG
SHHHKK
ETHEL, PUT YOUR HANDS WHERE I CAN SEE THEM!
NO!
COUGH COUGH
YOU WOULDN'T SHOOT ME, HECTOR.
I WOULD IF I HAD TO.
COME NOW, HECTOR. LOOK AT ETHEL. SHE WAS LIKE A MOTHER TO YOU...
GOTHAM IS A STAGE, AND THE REAL CELEBRITIES ARE THE VILLAINS. NOT FALSE IDOLS LIKE SOFIA VALENTINE.
IN FACT, IT'S FROM HER ASHES THAT THE TRUE STARS WILL RISE.
I KNOW YOU KNOW THIS, HECTOR. MORE THAN ANYONE, YOU UNDERSTAND JUST HOW FAKE YOUR MOTHER IS.

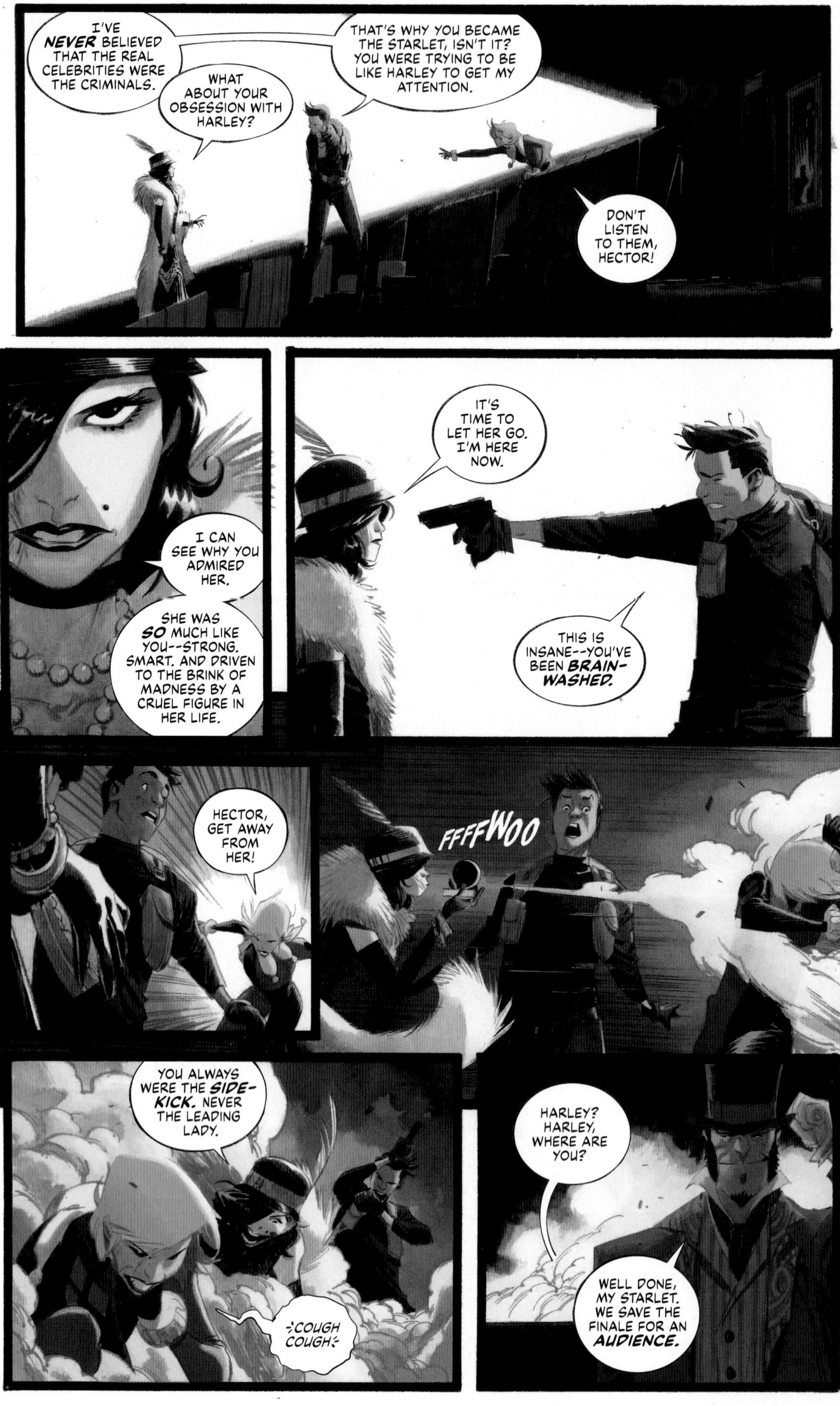
I'VE NEVER BELIEVED THAT THE REAL CELEBRITIES WERE THE CRIMINALS.
WHAT ABOUT YOUR OBSESSION WITH HARLEY?
THAT'S WHY YOU BECAME THE STARLET, ISN'T IT? YOU WERE TRYING TO BE LIKE HARLEY TO GET MY ATTENTION.
DON'T LISTEN TO THEM, HECTOR!
I CAN SEE WHY YOU ADMIRED HER.
SHE WAS SO MUCH LIKE YOU--STRONG. SMART. AND DRIVEN TO THE BRINK OF MADNESS BY A CRUEL FIGURE IN HER LIFE.
IT'S TIME TO LET HER GO. I'M HERE NOW.
THIS IS INSANE--YOU'VE BEEN BRAIN-WASHED.
HECTOR, GET AWAY FROM HER!
FFFFWOO
YOU ALWAYS WERE THE SIDE-KICK. NEVER THE LEADING LADY.
COUGH COUGH
HARLEY? HARLEY, WHERE ARE YOU?
WELL DONE, MY STARLET. WE SAVE THE FINALE FOR AN AUDIENCE.

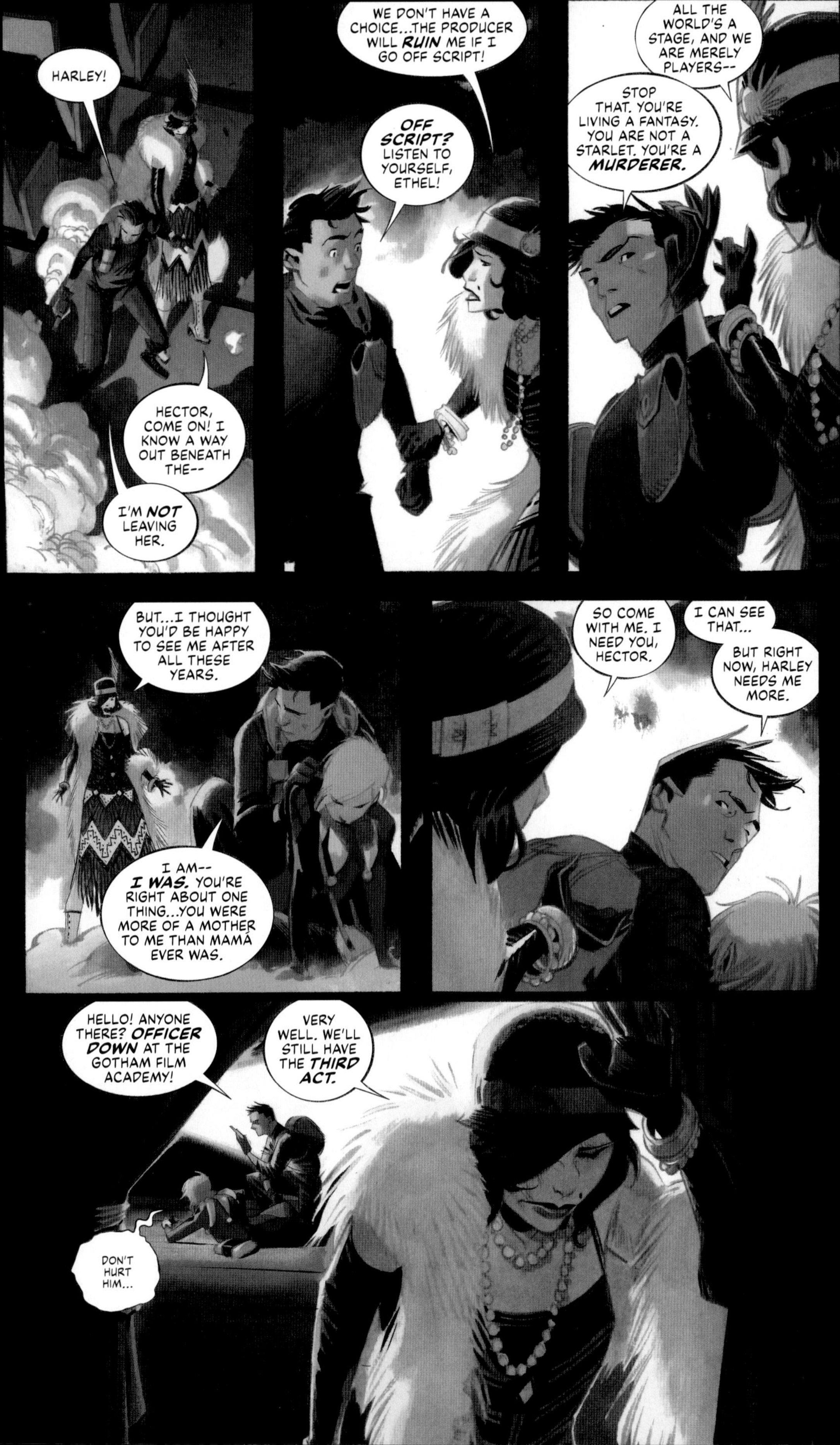
HARLEY!
HECTOR, COME ON! I KNOW A WAY OUT BENEATH THE--
I'M **NOT** LEAVING HER.
WE DON'T HAVE A CHOICE...THE PRODUCER WILL **RUIN** ME IF I GO OFF SCRIPT!
OFF SCRIPT? LISTEN TO YOURSELF, ETHEL!
ALL THE WORLD'S A STAGE, AND WE ARE MERELY PLAYERS--
STOP THAT. YOU'RE LIVING A FANTASY. YOU ARE NOT A STARLET. YOU'RE A **MURDERER.**
BUT...I THOUGHT YOU'D BE HAPPY TO SEE ME AFTER ALL THESE YEARS.
I AM-- **I WAS.** YOU'RE RIGHT ABOUT ONE THING...YOU WERE MORE OF A MOTHER TO ME THAN MAMÁ EVER WAS.
SO COME WITH ME. I NEED YOU, HECTOR.
I CAN SEE THAT...
BUT RIGHT NOW, HARLEY NEEDS ME MORE.
HELLO! ANYONE THERE? **OFFICER DOWN** AT THE GOTHAM FILM ACADEMY!
VERY WELL. WE'LL STILL HAVE THE **THIRD ACT.**
DON'T HURT HIM...

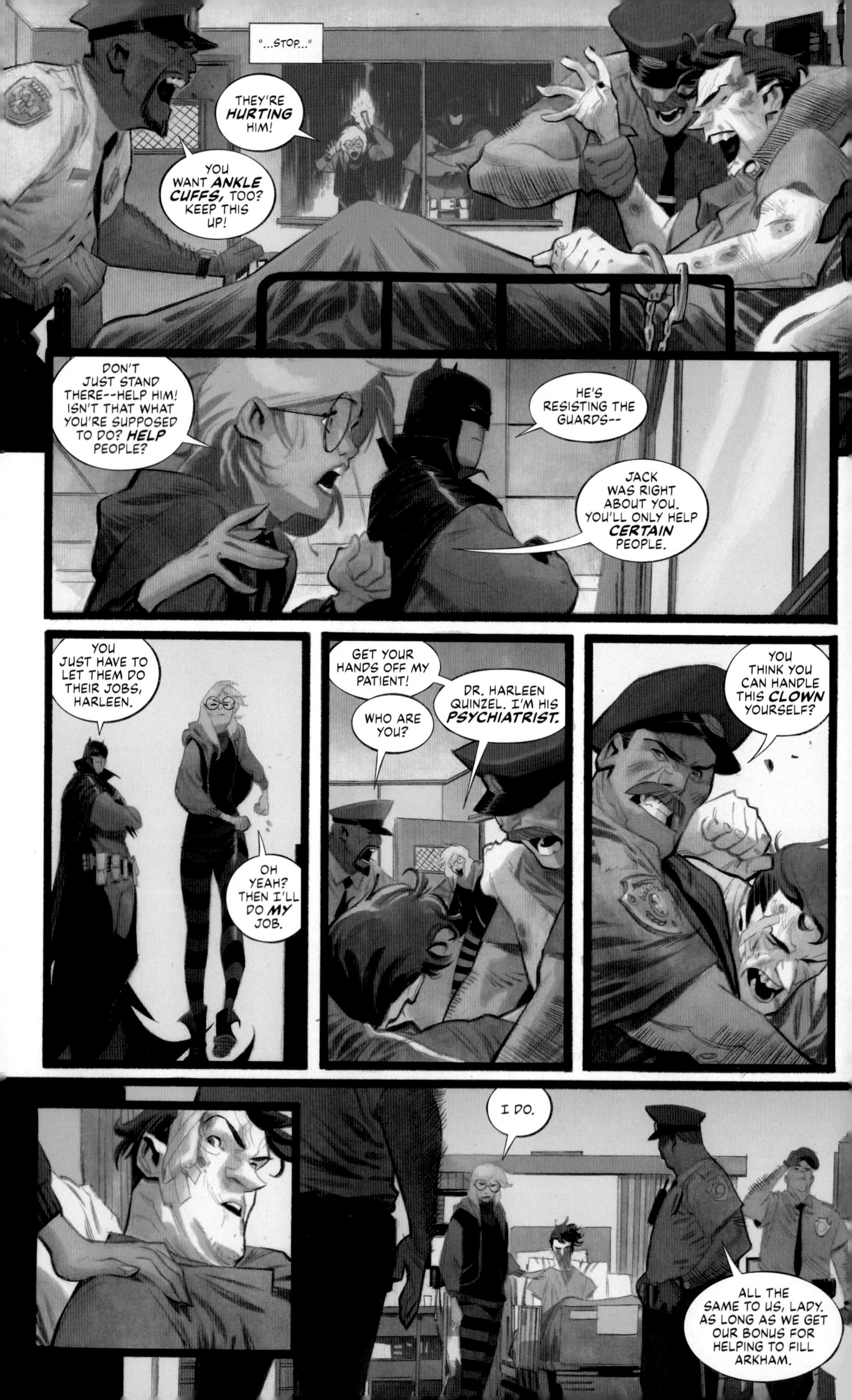
"...STOP..."
THEY'RE HURTING HIM!
YOU WANT ANKLE CUFFS, TOO? KEEP THIS UP!
DON'T JUST STAND THERE--HELP HIM! ISN'T THAT WHAT YOU'RE SUPPOSED TO DO? HELP PEOPLE?
HE'S RESISTING THE GUARDS--
JACK WAS RIGHT ABOUT YOU. YOU'LL ONLY HELP CERTAIN PEOPLE.
YOU JUST HAVE TO LET THEM DO THEIR JOBS, HARLEEN.
OH YEAH? THEN I'LL DO MY JOB.
GET YOUR HANDS OFF MY PATIENT!
WHO ARE YOU?
DR. HARLEEN QUINZEL. I'M HIS PSYCHIATRIST.
YOU THINK YOU CAN HANDLE THIS CLOWN YOURSELF?
I DO.
ALL THE SAME TO US, LADY. AS LONG AS WE GET OUR BONUS FOR HELPING TO FILL ARKHAM.

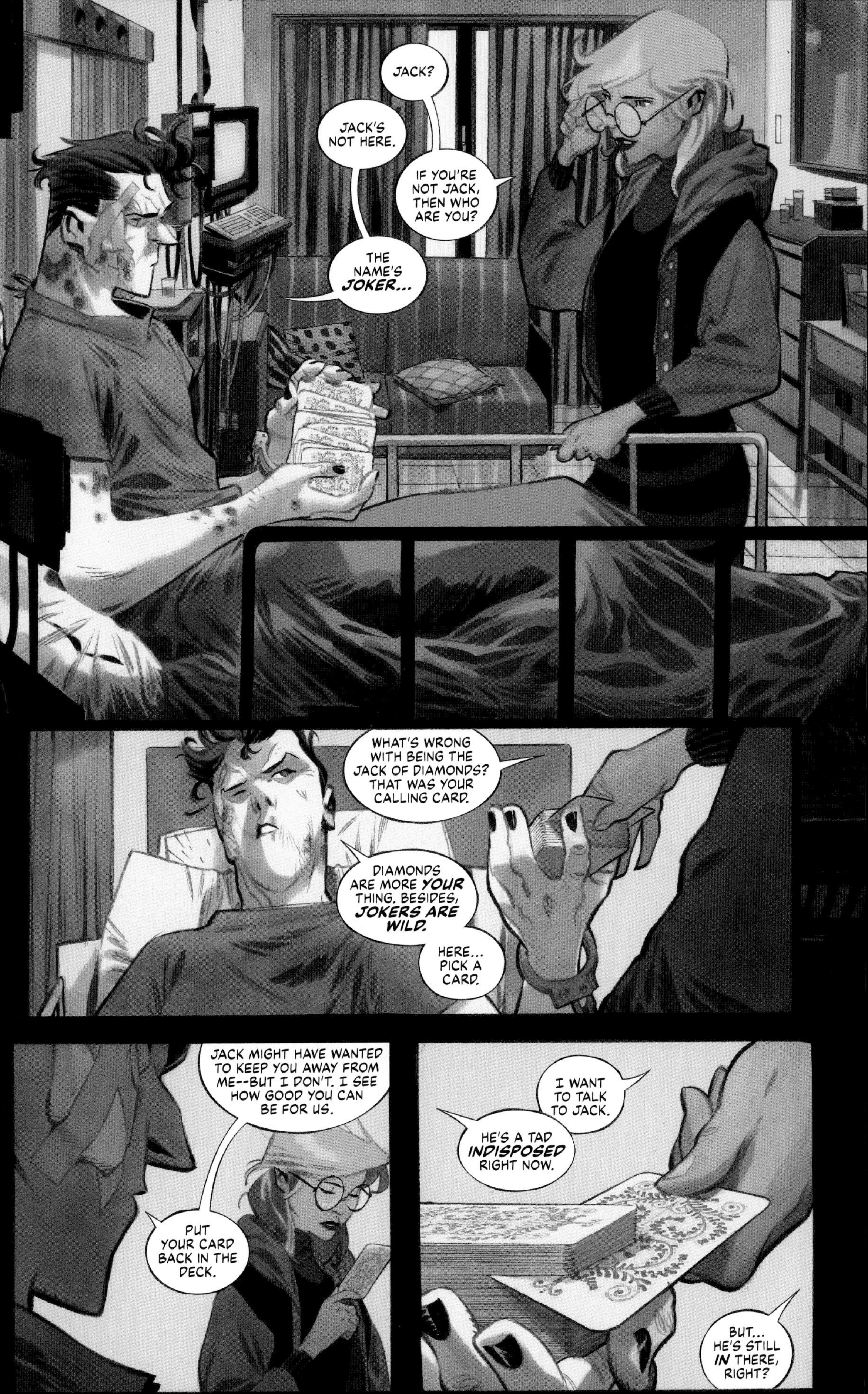
JACK?
JACK'S NOT HERE.
IF YOU'RE NOT JACK, THEN WHO ARE YOU?
THE NAME'S JOKER...
WHAT'S WRONG WITH BEING THE JACK OF DIAMONDS? THAT WAS YOUR CALLING CARD.
DIAMONDS ARE MORE YOUR THING. BESIDES, JOKERS ARE WILD.
HERE... PICK A CARD.
JACK MIGHT HAVE WANTED TO KEEP YOU AWAY FROM ME--BUT I DON'T. I SEE HOW GOOD YOU CAN BE FOR US.
PUT YOUR CARD BACK IN THE DECK.
I WANT TO TALK TO JACK.
HE'S A TAD INDISPOSED RIGHT NOW.
BUT... HE'S STILL IN THERE, RIGHT?

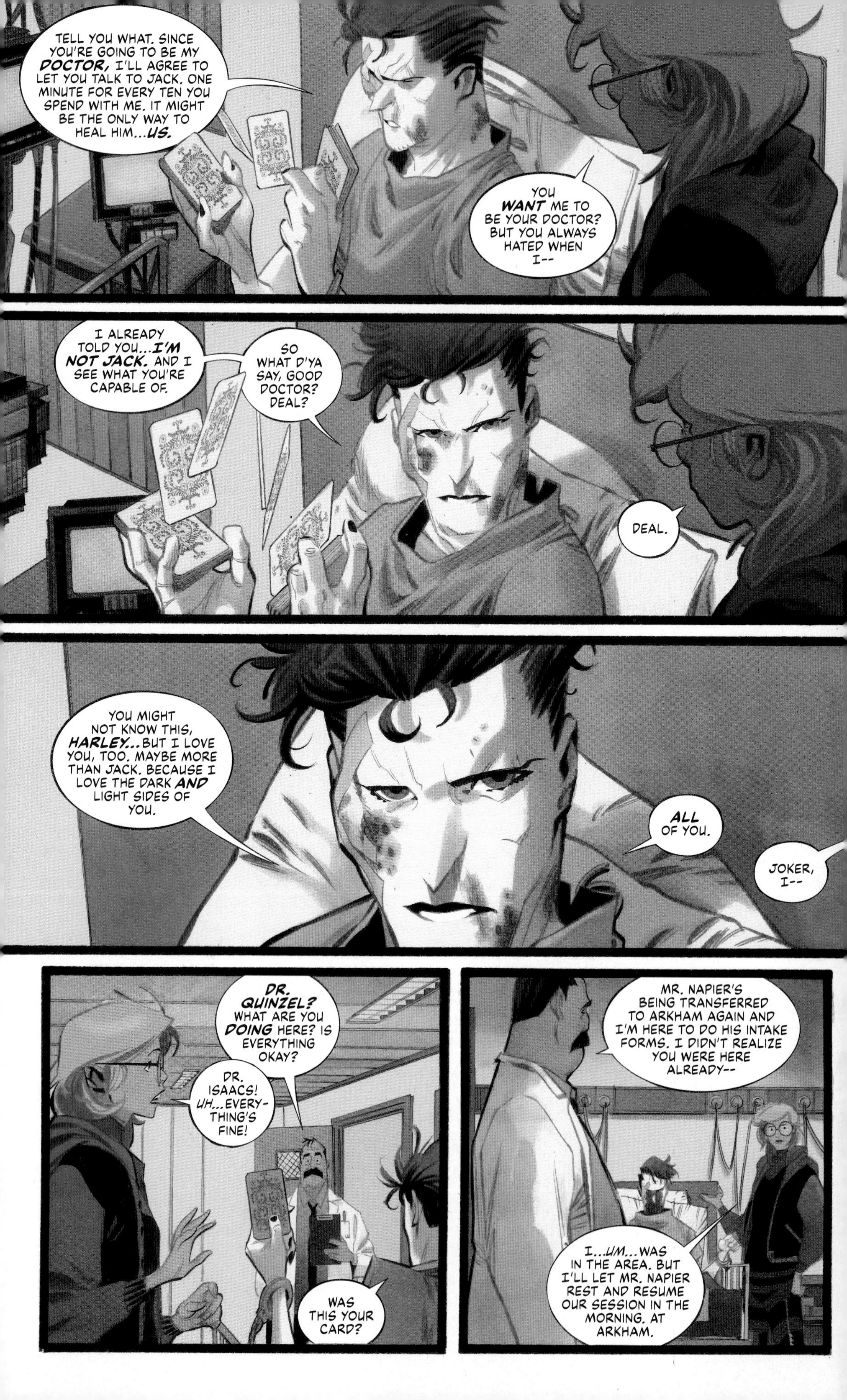
TELL YOU WHAT. SINCE YOU'RE GOING TO BE MY DOCTOR, I'LL AGREE TO LET YOU TALK TO JACK. ONE MINUTE FOR EVERY TEN YOU SPEND WITH ME. IT MIGHT BE THE ONLY WAY TO HEAL HIM...US.
YOU WANT ME TO BE YOUR DOCTOR? BUT YOU ALWAYS HATED WHEN I--
I ALREADY TOLD YOU...I'M NOT JACK. AND I SEE WHAT YOU'RE CAPABLE OF.
SO WHAT D'YA SAY, GOOD DOCTOR? DEAL?
DEAL.
YOU MIGHT NOT KNOW THIS, HARLEY...BUT I LOVE YOU, TOO. MAYBE MORE THAN JACK. BECAUSE I LOVE THE DARK AND LIGHT SIDES OF YOU.
ALL OF YOU.
JOKER, I--
DR. QUINZEL? WHAT ARE YOU DOING HERE? IS EVERYTHING OKAY?
DR. ISAACS! UH...EVERY-THING'S FINE!
WAS THIS YOUR CARD?
MR. NAPIER'S BEING TRANSFERRED TO ARKHAM AGAIN AND I'M HERE TO DO HIS INTAKE FORMS. I DIDN'T REALIZE YOU WERE HERE ALREADY--
I...UM...WAS IN THE AREA. BUT I'LL LET MR. NAPIER REST AND RESUME OUR SESSION IN THE MORNING. AT ARKHAM.

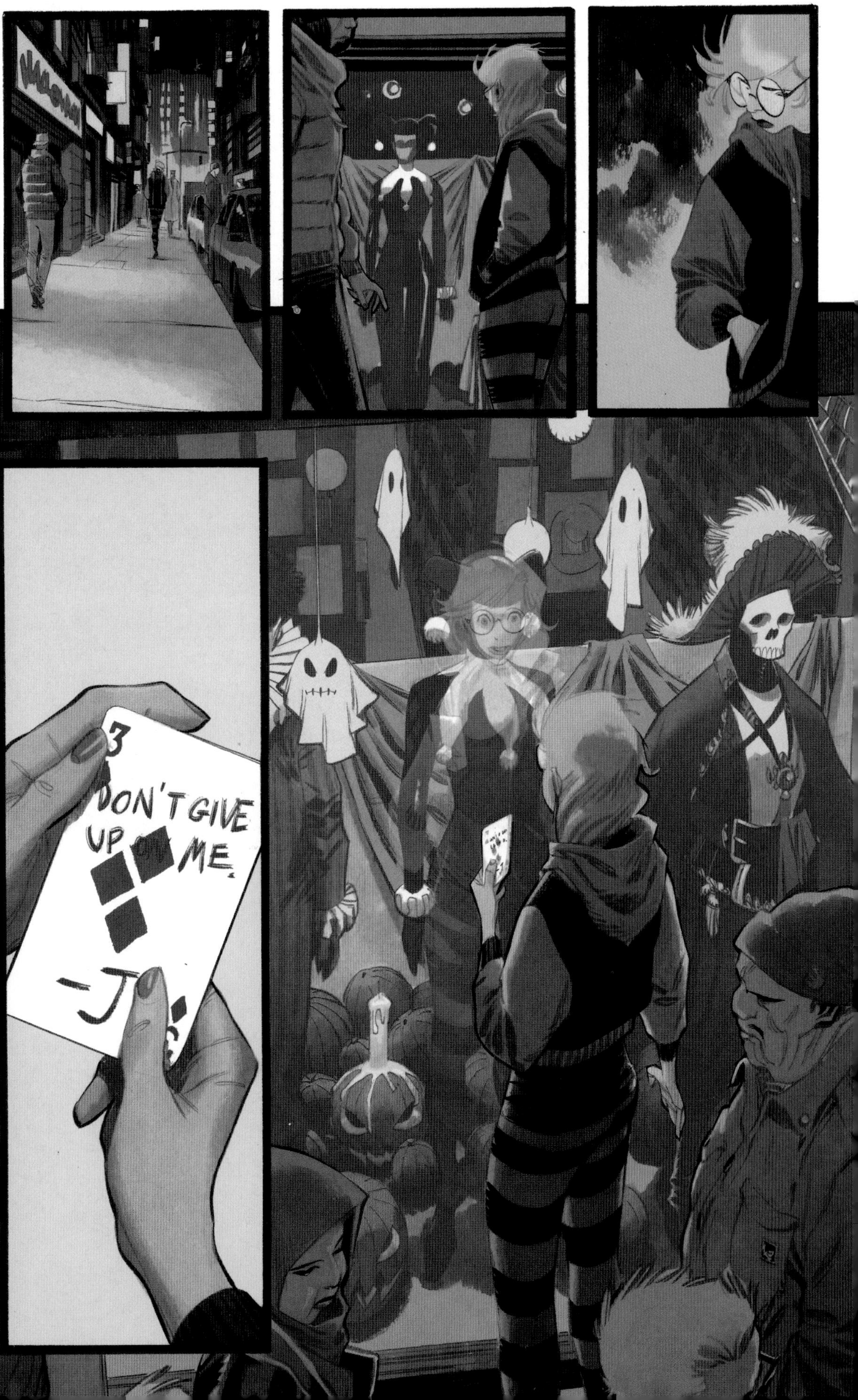

3
DON'T GIVE
UP ME.
-J

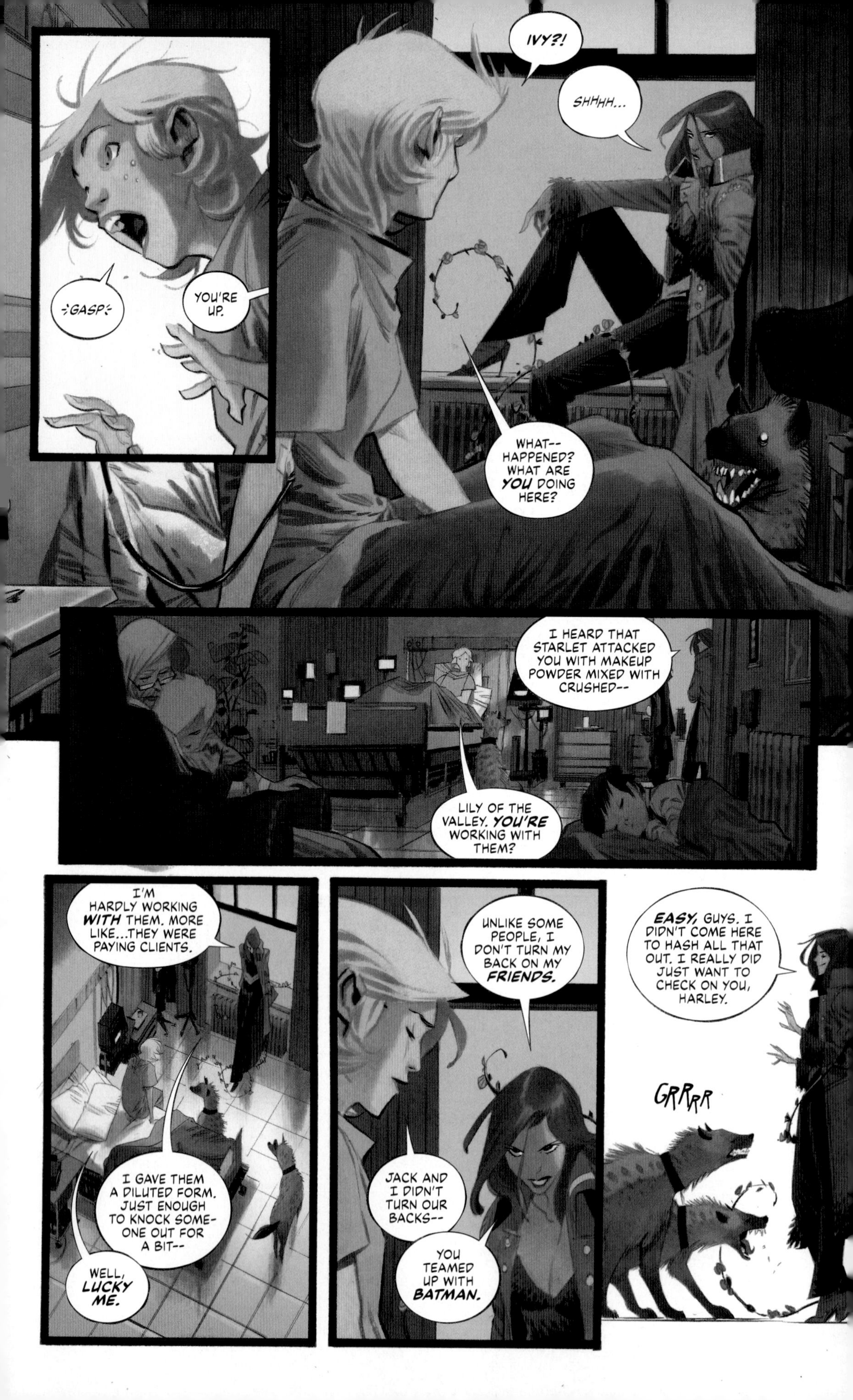
IVY?!
SHHHH...
-GASP-
YOU'RE UP.
WHAT-- HAPPENED? WHAT ARE YOU DOING HERE?
I HEARD THAT STARLET ATTACKED YOU WITH MAKEUP POWDER MIXED WITH CRUSHED--
LILY OF THE VALLEY. YOU'RE WORKING WITH THEM?
I'M HARDLY WORKING WITH THEM. MORE LIKE...THEY WERE PAYING CLIENTS.
I GAVE THEM A DILUTED FORM. JUST ENOUGH TO KNOCK SOME-ONE OUT FOR A BIT--
WELL, LUCKY ME.
UNLIKE SOME PEOPLE, I DON'T TURN MY BACK ON MY FRIENDS.
JACK AND I DIDN'T TURN OUR BACKS--
YOU TEAMED UP WITH BATMAN.
EASY, GUYS. I DIDN'T COME HERE TO HASH ALL THAT OUT. I REALLY DID JUST WANT TO CHECK ON YOU, HARLEY.
GRRRR

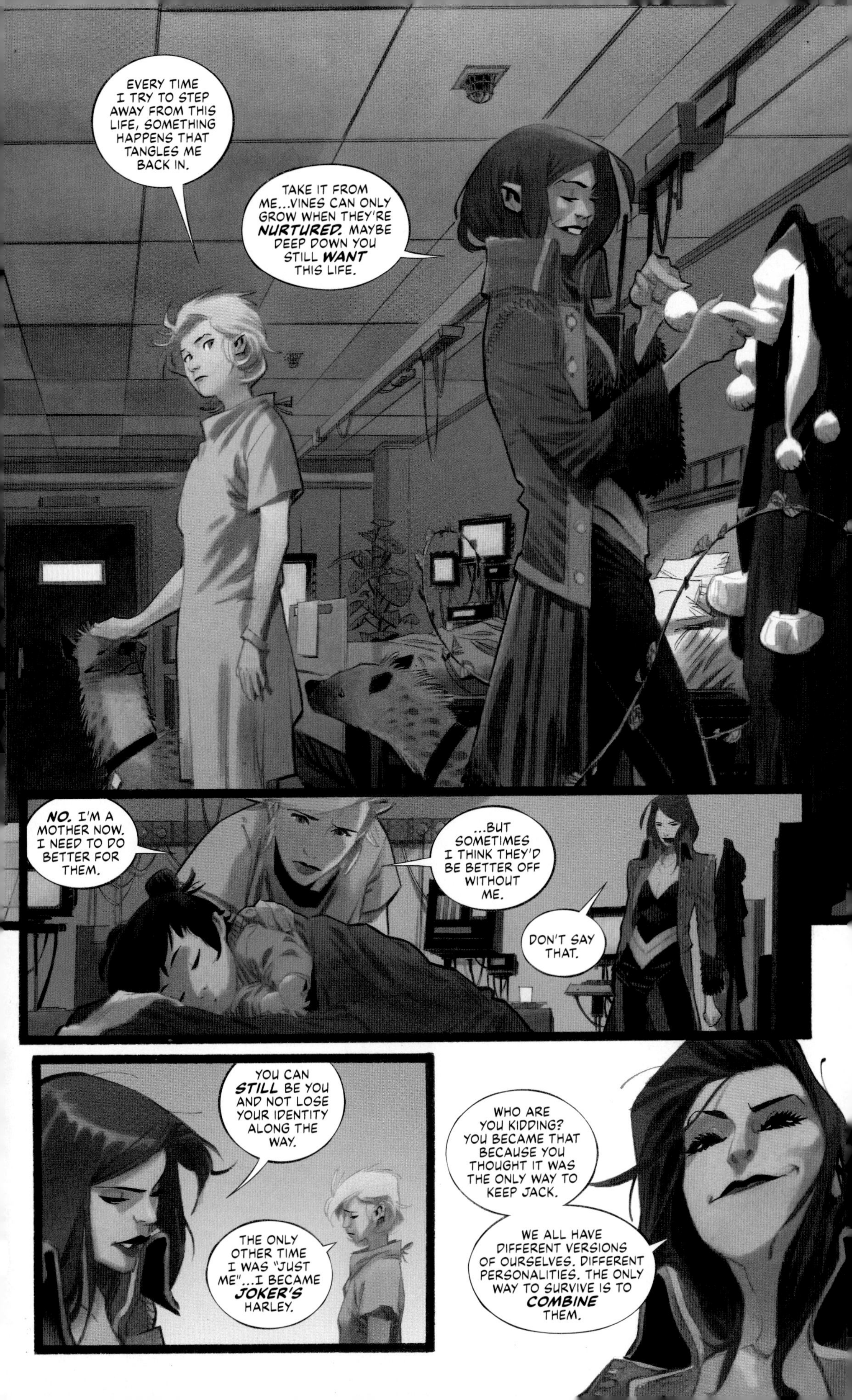
EVERY TIME I TRY TO STEP AWAY FROM THIS LIFE, SOMETHING HAPPENS THAT TANGLES ME BACK IN.
TAKE IT FROM ME...VINES CAN ONLY GROW WHEN THEY'RE NURTURED. MAYBE DEEP DOWN YOU STILL WANT THIS LIFE.
NO. I'M A MOTHER NOW. I NEED TO DO BETTER FOR THEM.
...BUT SOMETIMES I THINK THEY'D BE BETTER OFF WITHOUT ME.
DON'T SAY THAT.
YOU CAN STILL BE YOU AND NOT LOSE YOUR IDENTITY ALONG THE WAY.
THE ONLY OTHER TIME I WAS "JUST ME"...I BECAME JOKER'S HARLEY.
WHO ARE YOU KIDDING? YOU BECAME THAT BECAUSE YOU THOUGHT IT WAS THE ONLY WAY TO KEEP JACK.
WE ALL HAVE DIFFERENT VERSIONS OF OURSELVES. DIFFERENT PERSONALITIES. THE ONLY WAY TO SURVIVE IS TO COMBINE THEM.

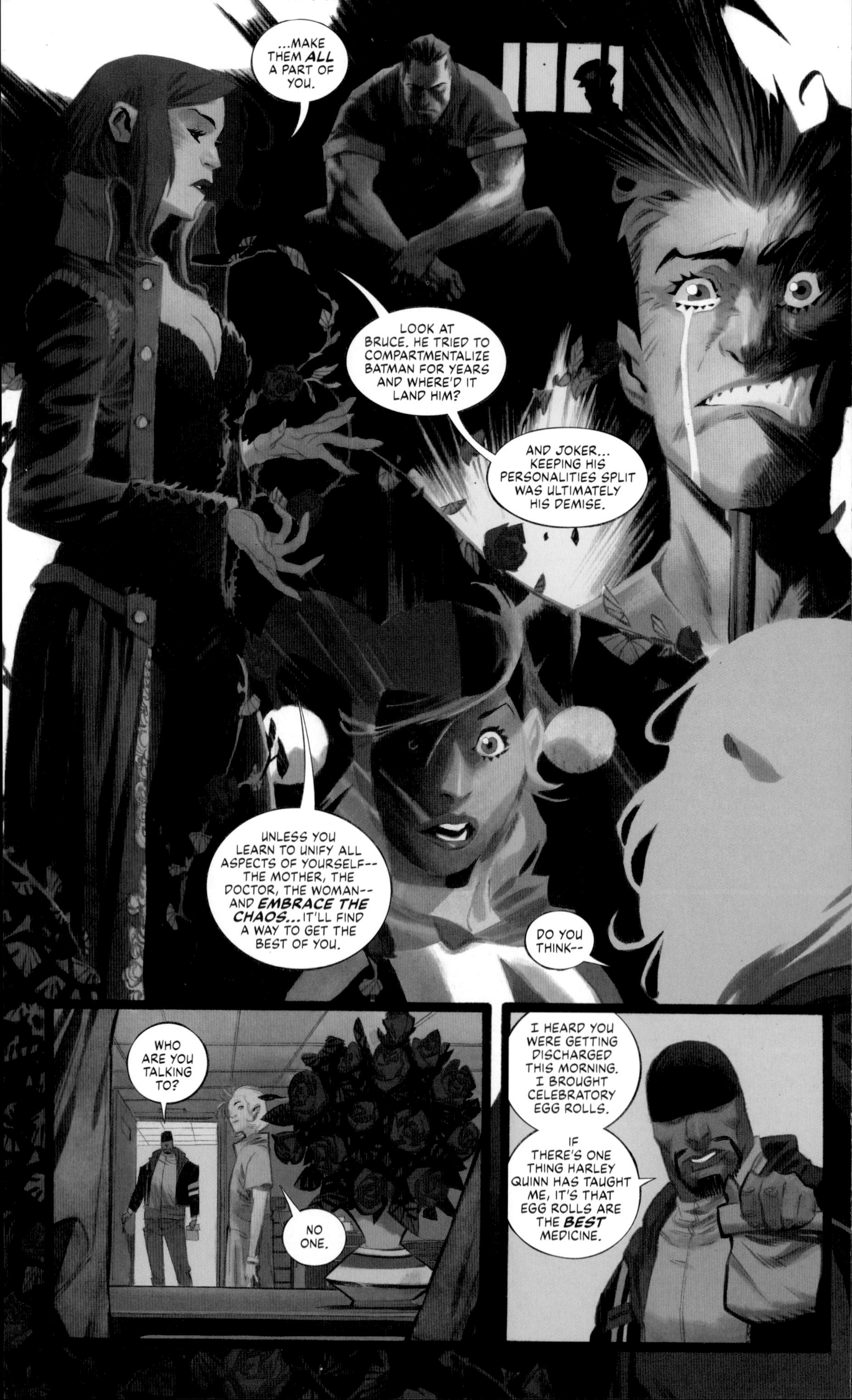
...MAKE THEM ALL A PART OF YOU.
LOOK AT BRUCE. HE TRIED TO COMPARTMENTALIZE BATMAN FOR YEARS AND WHERE'D IT LAND HIM?
AND JOKER... KEEPING HIS PERSONALITIES SPLIT WAS ULTIMATELY HIS DEMISE.
UNLESS YOU LEARN TO UNIFY ALL ASPECTS OF YOURSELF-- THE MOTHER, THE DOCTOR, THE WOMAN-- AND EMBRACE THE CHAOS... IT'LL FIND A WAY TO GET THE BEST OF YOU.
DO YOU THINK--
WHO ARE YOU TALKING TO?
NO ONE.
I HEARD YOU WERE GETTING DISCHARGED THIS MORNING. I BROUGHT CELEBRATORY EGG ROLLS.
IF THERE'S ONE THING HARLEY QUINN HAS TAUGHT ME, IT'S THAT EGG ROLLS ARE THE BEST MEDICINE.

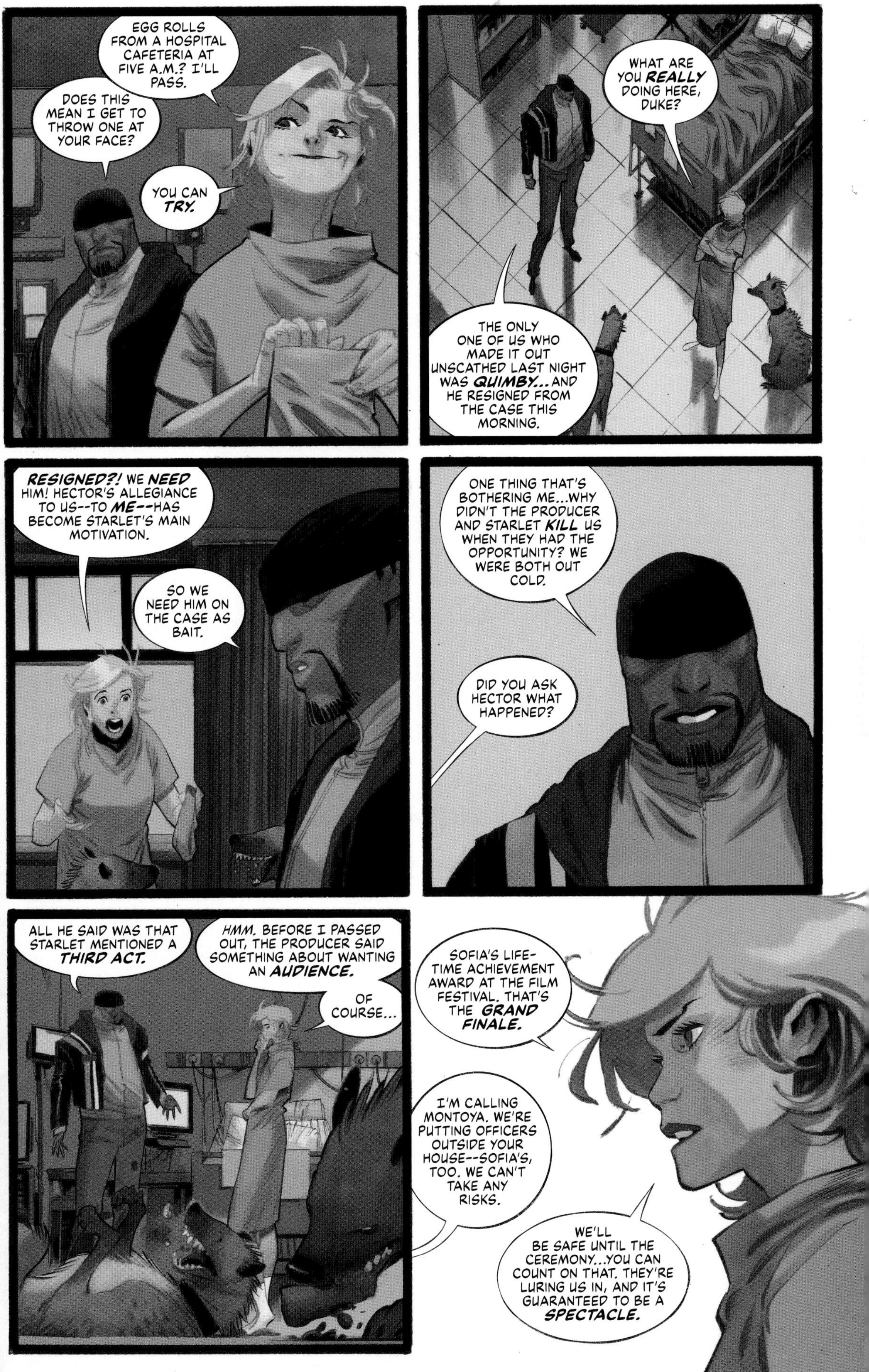
EGG ROLLS FROM A HOSPITAL CAFETERIA AT FIVE A.M.? I'LL PASS.
DOES THIS MEAN I GET TO THROW ONE AT YOUR FACE?
YOU CAN TRY.
WHAT ARE YOU REALLY DOING HERE, DUKE?
THE ONLY ONE OF US WHO MADE IT OUT UNSCATHED LAST NIGHT WAS QUIMBY... AND HE RESIGNED FROM THE CASE THIS MORNING.
RESIGNED?! WE NEED HIM! HECTOR'S ALLEGIANCE TO US--TO ME--HAS BECOME STARLET'S MAIN MOTIVATION.
SO WE NEED HIM ON THE CASE AS BAIT.
ONE THING THAT'S BOTHERING ME...WHY DIDN'T THE PRODUCER AND STARLET KILL US WHEN THEY HAD THE OPPORTUNITY? WE WERE BOTH OUT COLD.
DID YOU ASK HECTOR WHAT HAPPENED?
ALL HE SAID WAS THAT STARLET MENTIONED A THIRD ACT.
HMM. BEFORE I PASSED OUT, THE PRODUCER SAID SOMETHING ABOUT WANTING AN AUDIENCE.
OF COURSE...
SOFIA'S LIFE-TIME ACHIEVEMENT AWARD AT THE FILM FESTIVAL. THAT'S THE GRAND FINALE.
I'M CALLING MONTOYA. WE'RE PUTTING OFFICERS OUTSIDE YOUR HOUSE--SOFIA'S, TOO. WE CAN'T TAKE ANY RISKS.
WE'LL BE SAFE UNTIL THE CEREMONY...YOU CAN COUNT ON THAT. THEY'RE LURING US IN, AND IT'S GUARANTEED TO BE A SPECTACLE.

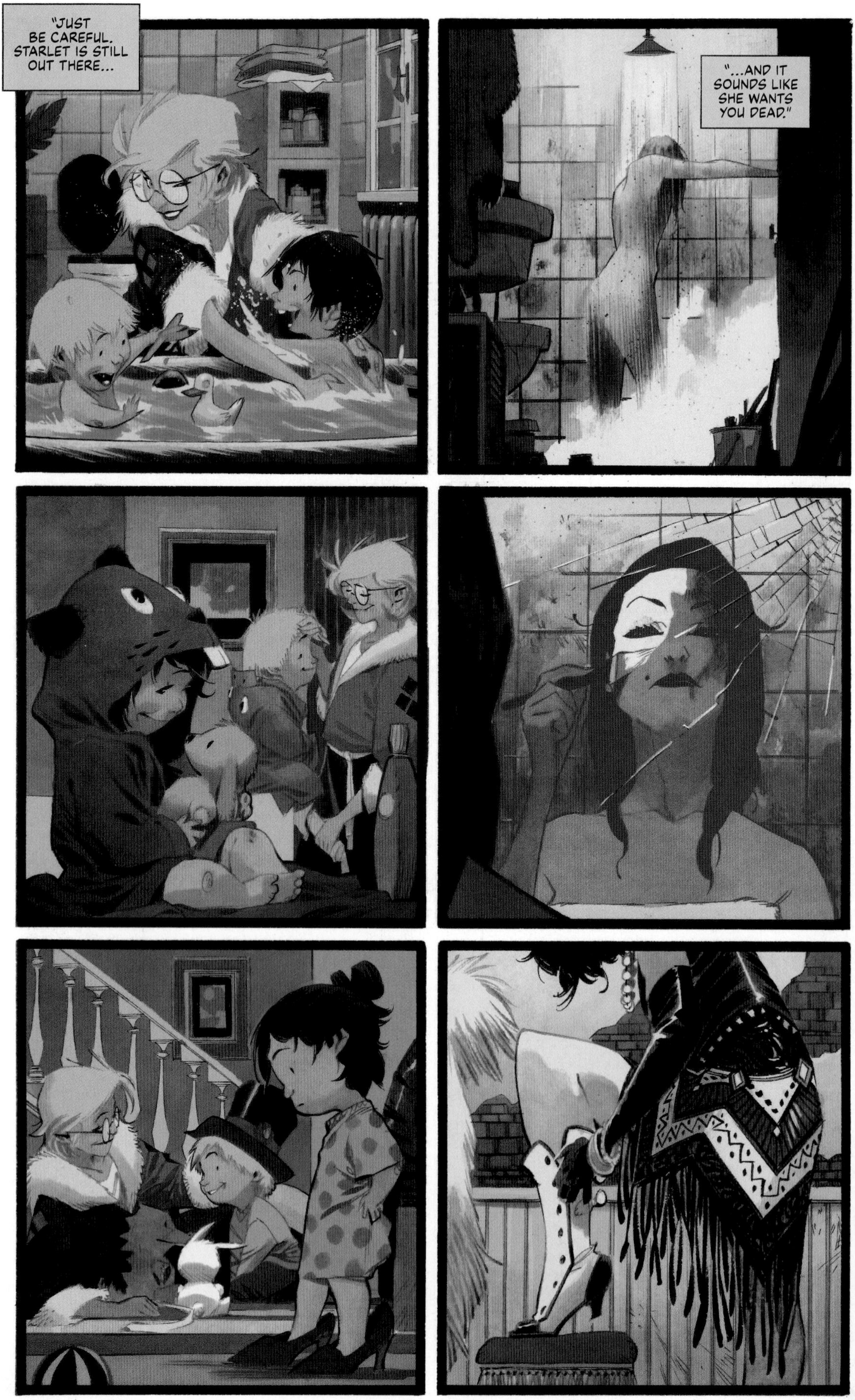
"JUST
BE CAREFUL.
STARLET IS STILL
OUT THERE...
"...AND IT
SOUNDS LIKE
SHE WANTS
YOU DEAD."

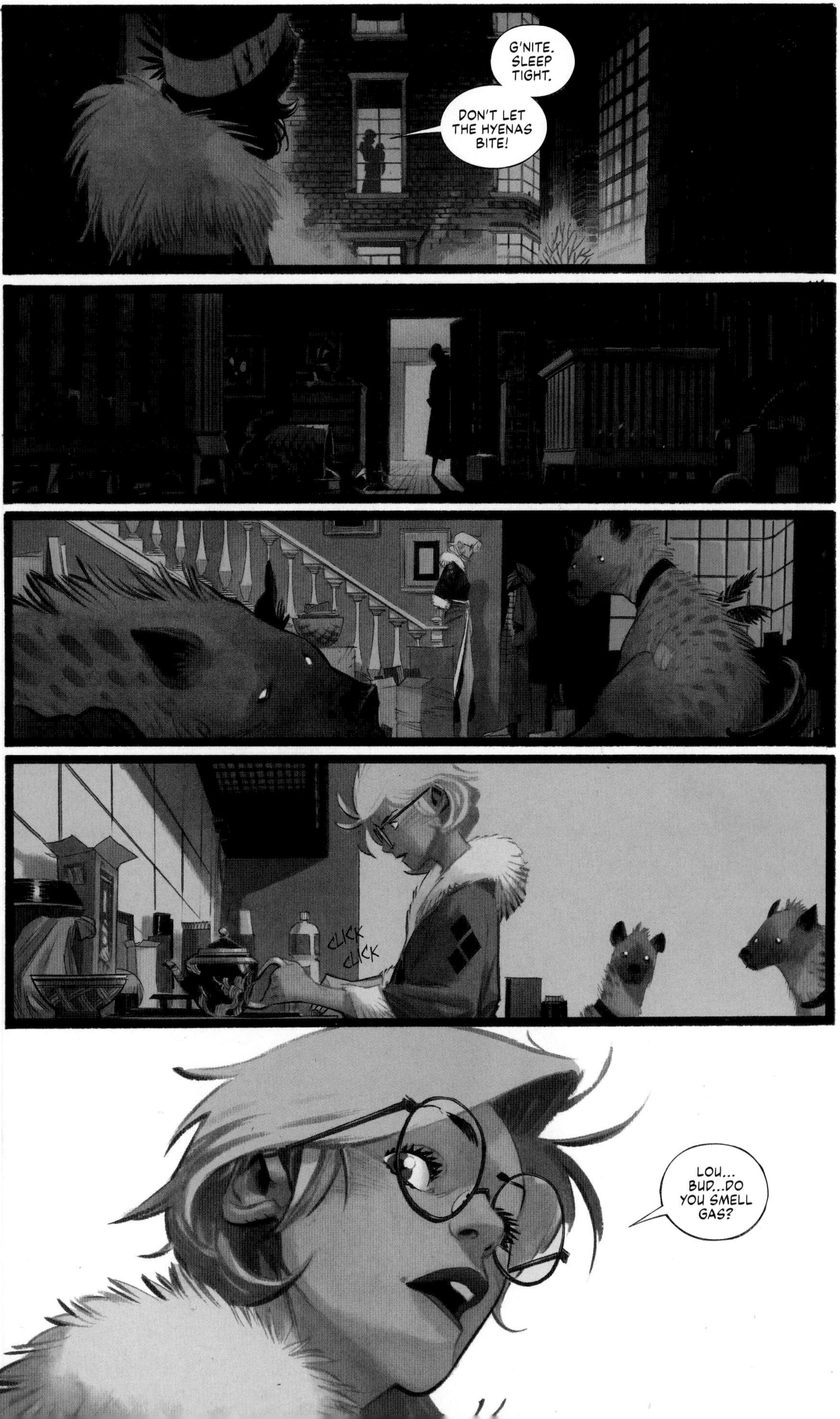
G'NITE. SLEEP TIGHT.
DON'T LET THE HYENAS BITE!
CLICK CLICK
LOU... BUD...DO YOU SMELL GAS?

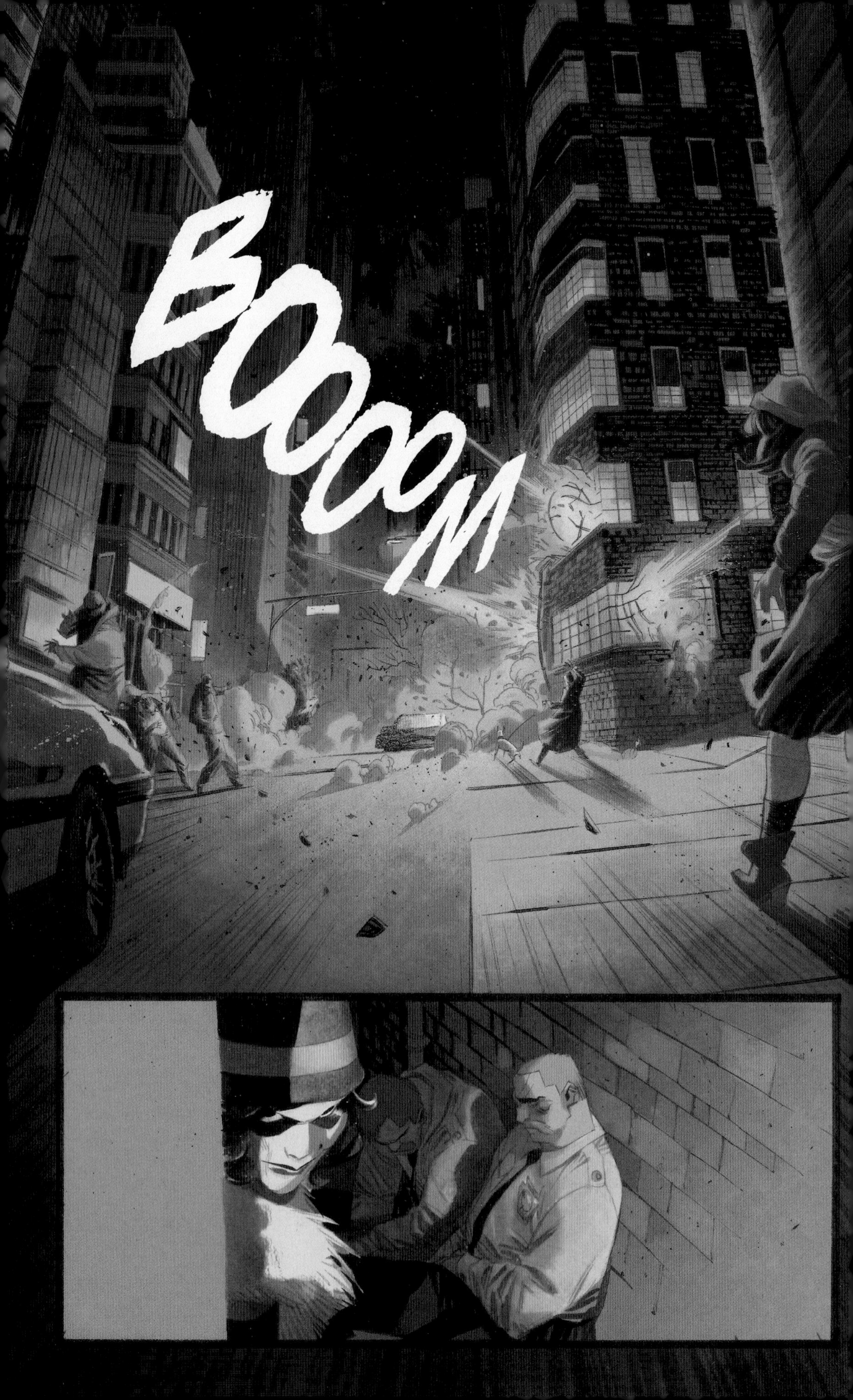
BOOOOM

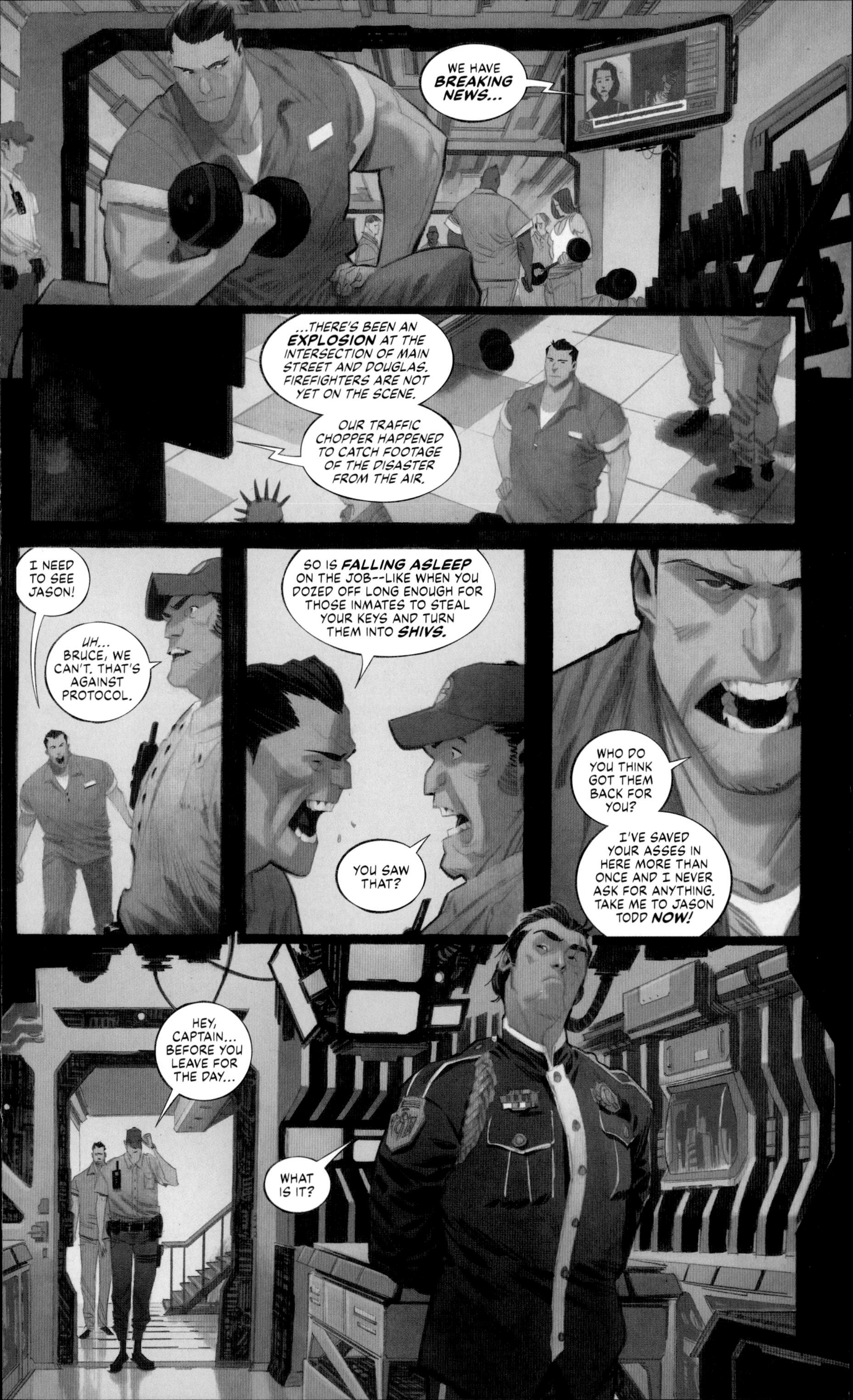

WE HAVE BREAKING NEWS...
...THERE'S BEEN AN EXPLOSION AT THE INTERSECTION OF MAIN STREET AND DOUGLAS. FIREFIGHTERS ARE NOT YET ON THE SCENE.
OUR TRAFFIC CHOPPER HAPPENED TO CATCH FOOTAGE OF THE DISASTER FROM THE AIR.
I NEED TO SEE JASON!
UH... BRUCE, WE CAN'T. THAT'S AGAINST PROTOCOL.
SO IS FALLING ASLEEP ON THE JOB--LIKE WHEN YOU DOZED OFF LONG ENOUGH FOR THOSE INMATES TO STEAL YOUR KEYS AND TURN THEM INTO SHIVS.
YOU SAW THAT?
WHO DO YOU THINK GOT THEM BACK FOR YOU?
I'VE SAVED YOUR ASSES IN HERE MORE THAN ONCE AND I NEVER ASK FOR ANYTHING. TAKE ME TO JASON TODD NOW!
HEY, CAPTAIN... BEFORE YOU LEAVE FOR THE DAY...
WHAT IS IT?

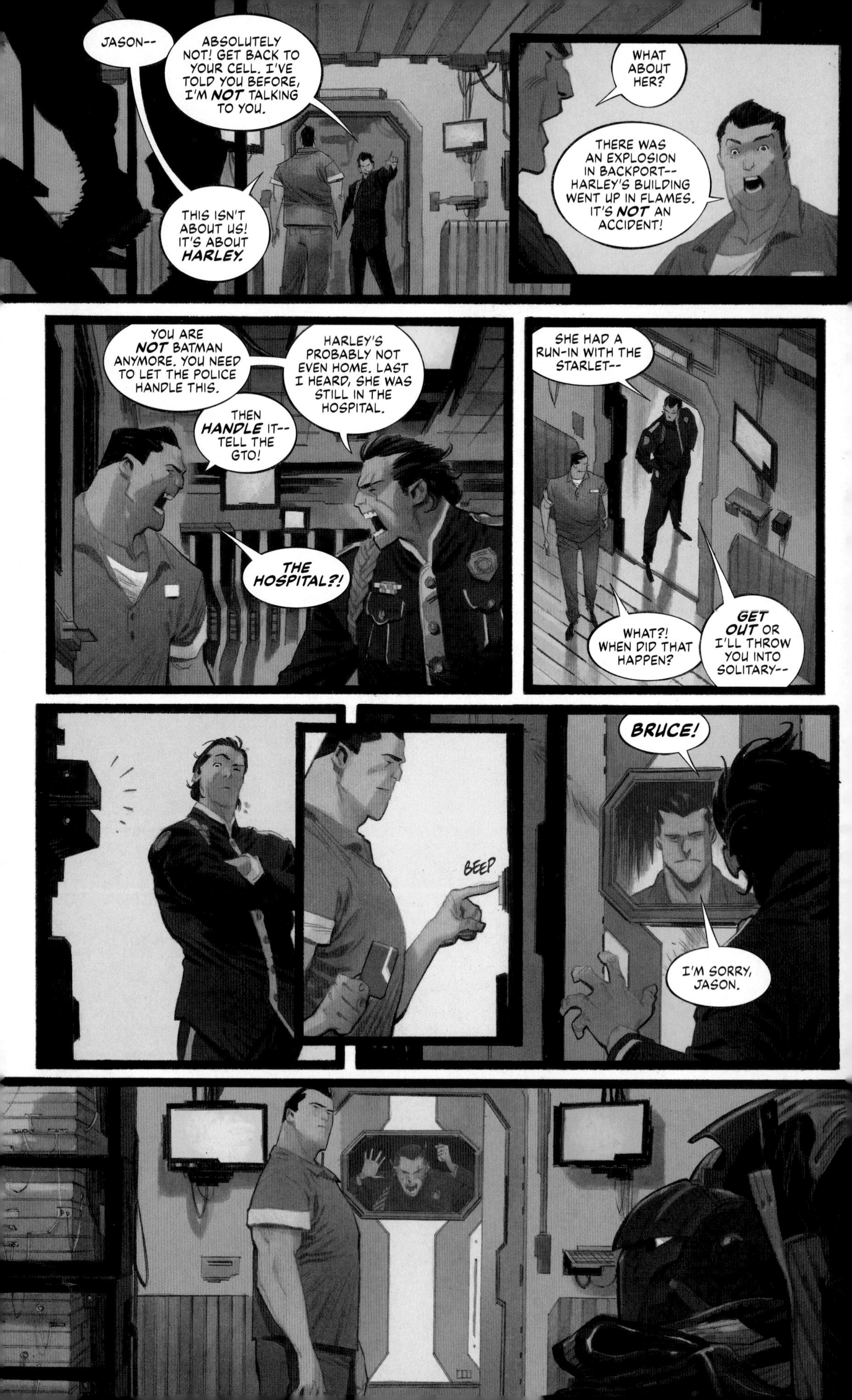

JASON--
ABSOLUTELY NOT! GET BACK TO YOUR CELL. I'VE TOLD YOU BEFORE, I'M NOT TALKING TO YOU.
THIS ISN'T ABOUT US! IT'S ABOUT HARLEY.
WHAT ABOUT HER?
THERE WAS AN EXPLOSION IN BACKPORT-- HARLEY'S BUILDING WENT UP IN FLAMES. IT'S NOT AN ACCIDENT!
YOU ARE NOT BATMAN ANYMORE. YOU NEED TO LET THE POLICE HANDLE THIS.
HARLEY'S PROBABLY NOT EVEN HOME. LAST I HEARD, SHE WAS STILL IN THE HOSPITAL.
THEN HANDLE IT-- TELL THE GTO!
THE HOSPITAL?!
SHE HAD A RUN-IN WITH THE STARLET--
WHAT?! WHEN DID THAT HAPPEN?
GET OUT OR I'LL THROW YOU INTO SOLITARY--
BEEP
BRUCE!
I'M SORRY, JASON.

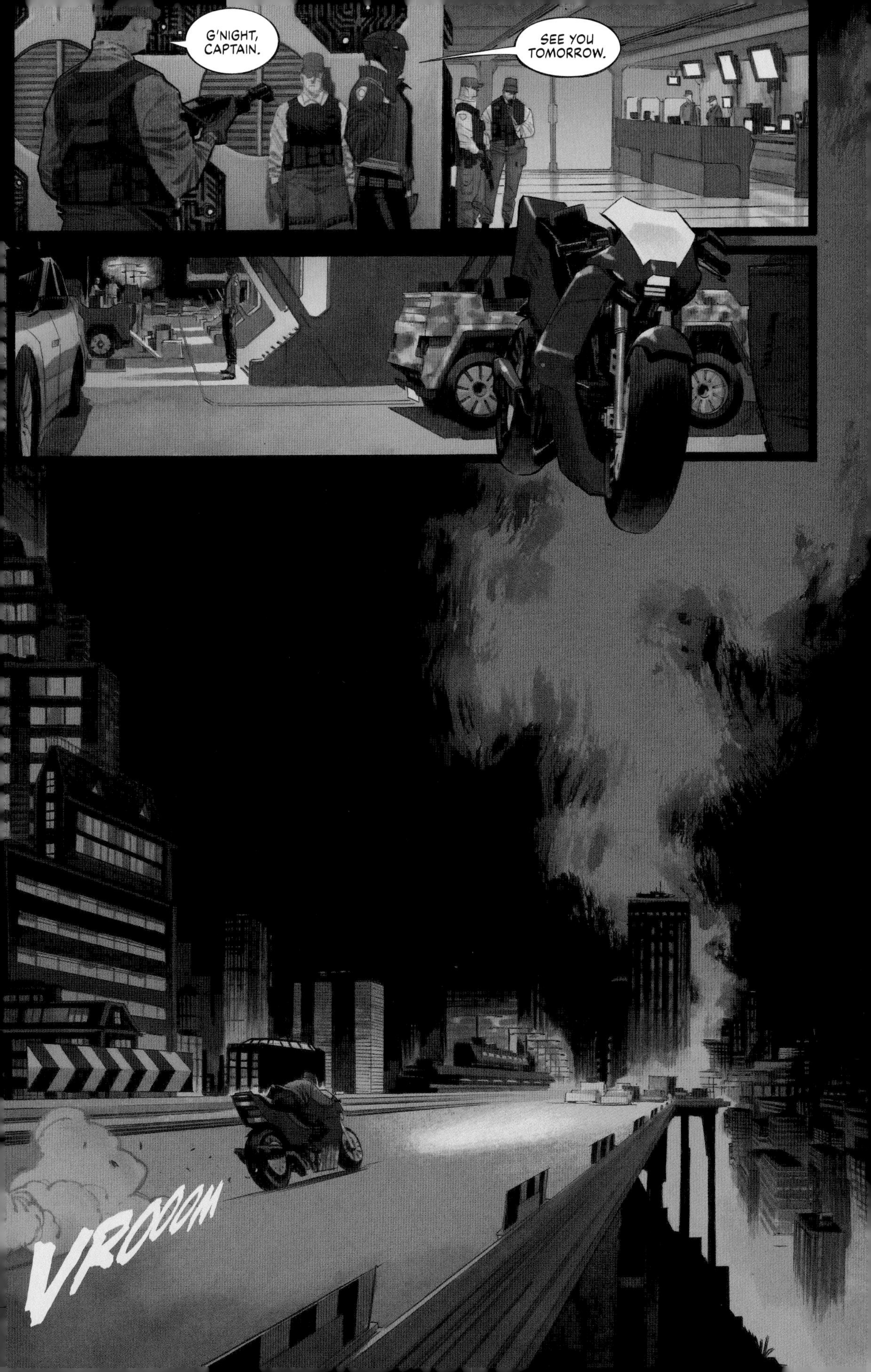
G'NIGHT, CAPTAIN.
SEE YOU TOMORROW.
VROOOM

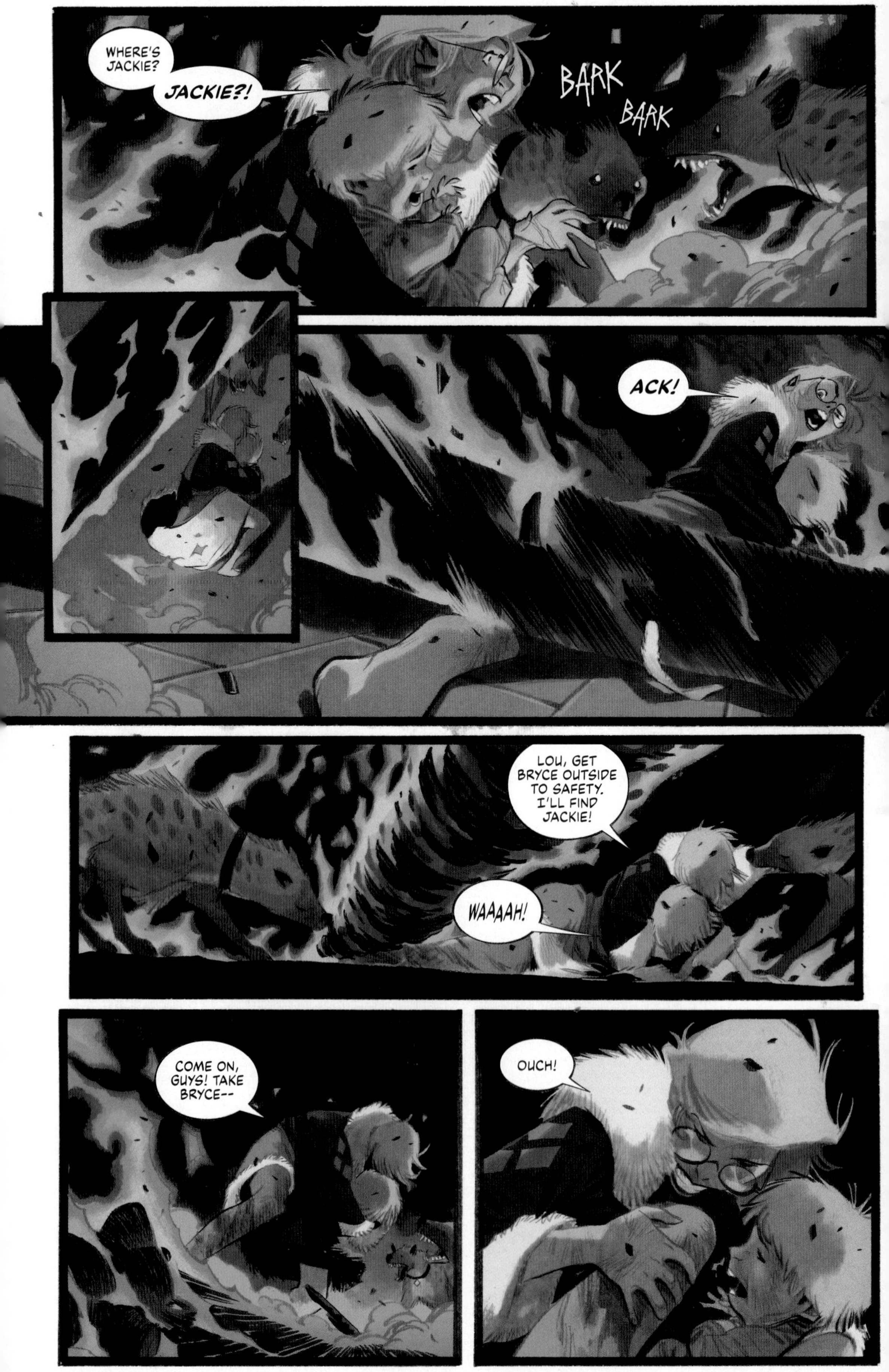
WHERE'S JACKIE?
JACKIE?!
BARK
BARK
ACK!
LOU, GET BRYCE OUTSIDE TO SAFETY. I'LL FIND JACKIE!
WAAAAH!
COME ON, GUYS! TAKE BRYCE--
OUCH!

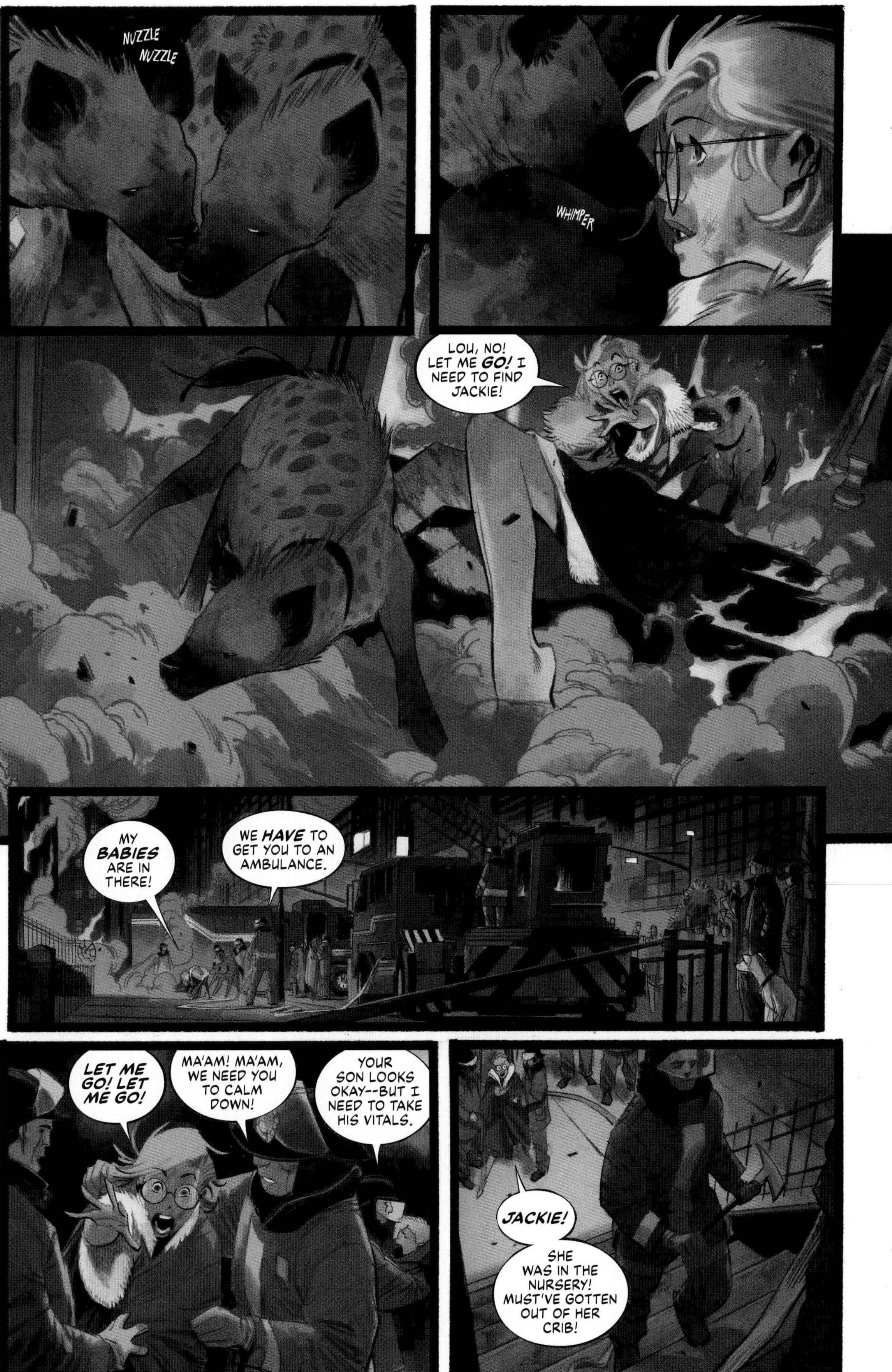
NUZZLE
NUZZLE
WHIMPER
LOU, NO! LET ME GO! I NEED TO FIND JACKIE!
MY BABIES ARE IN THERE!
WE HAVE TO GET YOU TO AN AMBULANCE.
LET ME GO! LET ME GO!
MA'AM! MA'AM, WE NEED YOU TO CALM DOWN!
YOUR SON LOOKS OKAY--BUT I NEED TO TAKE HIS VITALS.
JACKIE!
SHE WAS IN THE NURSERY! MUST'VE GOTTEN OUT OF HER CRIB!

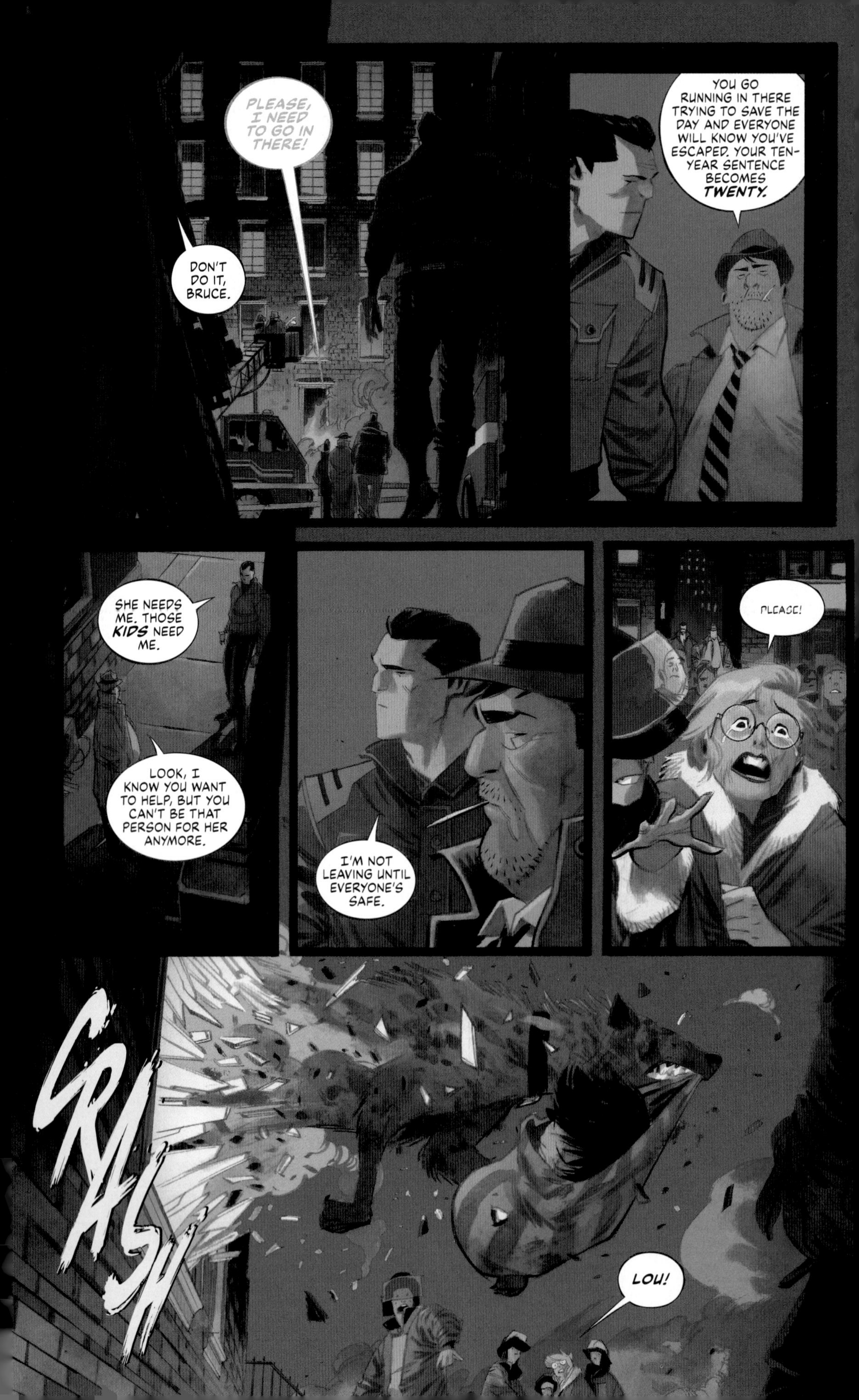
PLEASE, I NEED TO GO IN THERE!
DON'T DO IT, BRUCE.
YOU GO RUNNING IN THERE TRYING TO SAVE THE DAY AND EVERYONE WILL KNOW YOU'VE ESCAPED. YOUR TEN-YEAR SENTENCE BECOMES TWENTY.
SHE NEEDS ME. THOSE KIDS NEED ME.
LOOK, I KNOW YOU WANT TO HELP, BUT YOU CAN'T BE THAT PERSON FOR HER ANYMORE.
I'M NOT LEAVING UNTIL EVERYONE'S SAFE.
PLEASE!
CRASH
LOU!

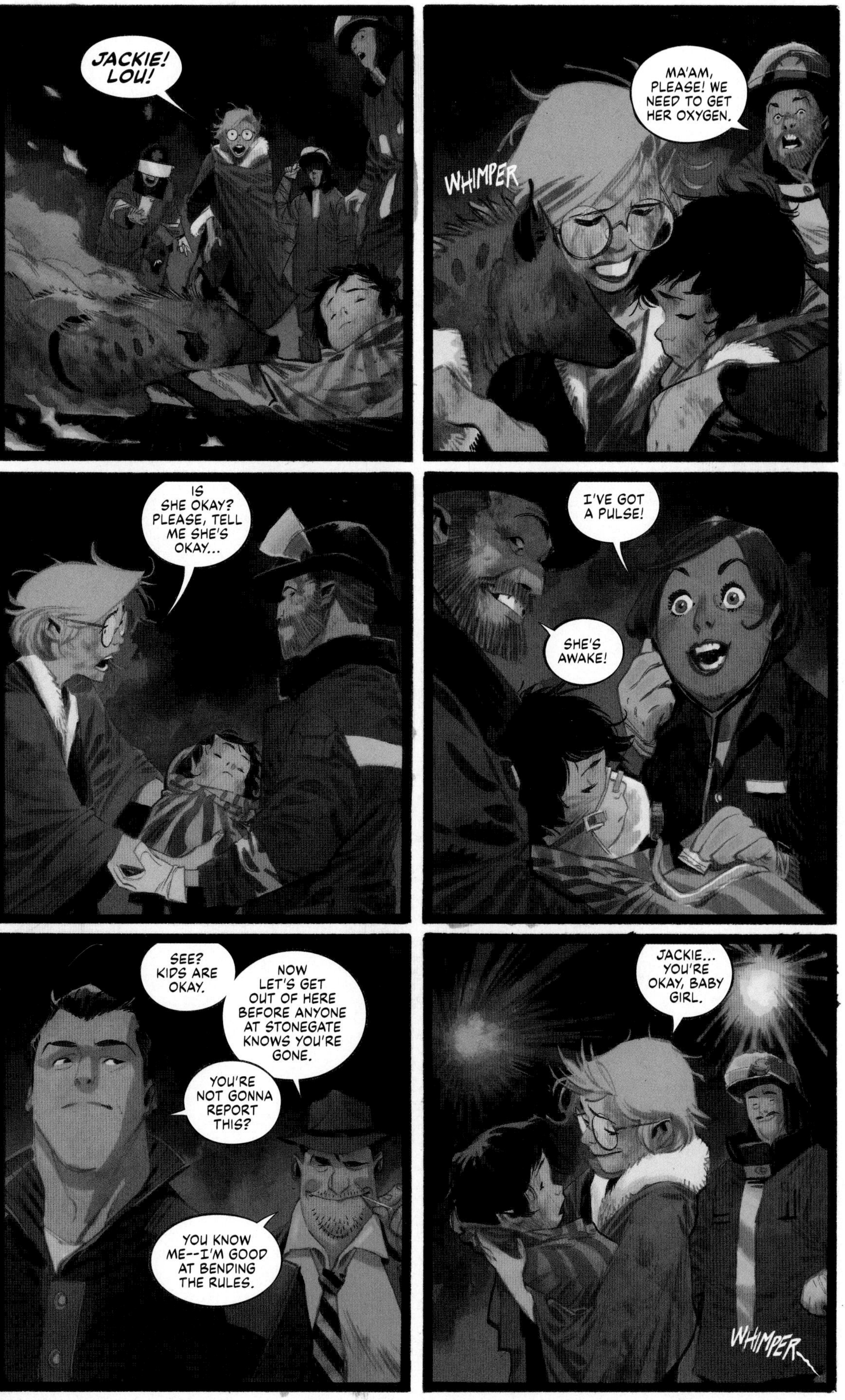
JACKIE! LOU!
MA'AM, PLEASE! WE NEED TO GET HER OXYGEN.
WHIMPER
IS SHE OKAY? PLEASE, TELL ME SHE'S OKAY...
I'VE GOT A PULSE!
SHE'S AWAKE!
SEE? KIDS ARE OKAY.
NOW LET'S GET OUT OF HERE BEFORE ANYONE AT STONEGATE KNOWS YOU'RE GONE.
YOU'RE NOT GONNA REPORT THIS?
YOU KNOW ME--I'M GOOD AT BENDING THE RULES.
JACKIE... YOU'RE OKAY, BABY GIRL.
WHIMPER

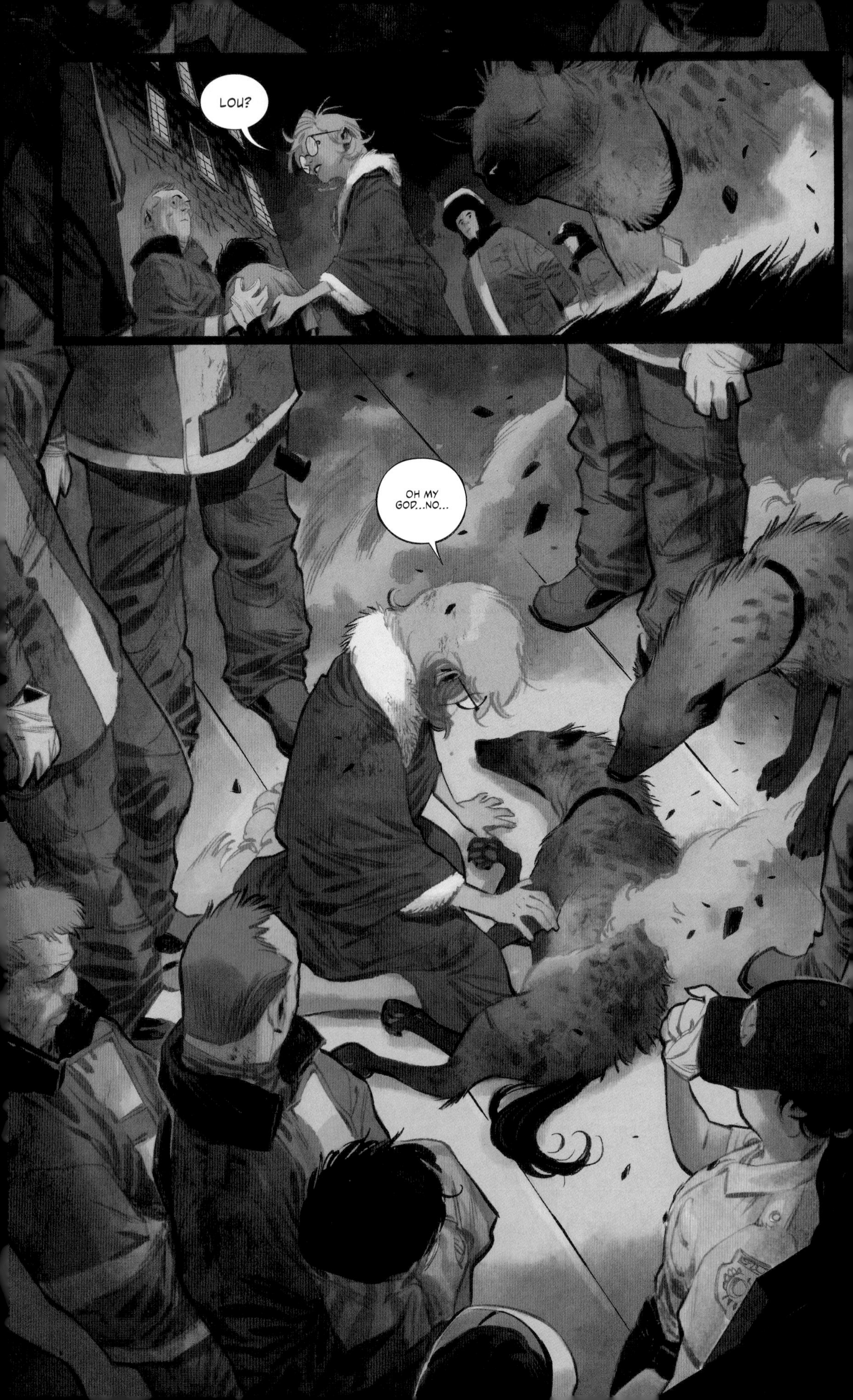
LOU?
OH MY GOD...NO...

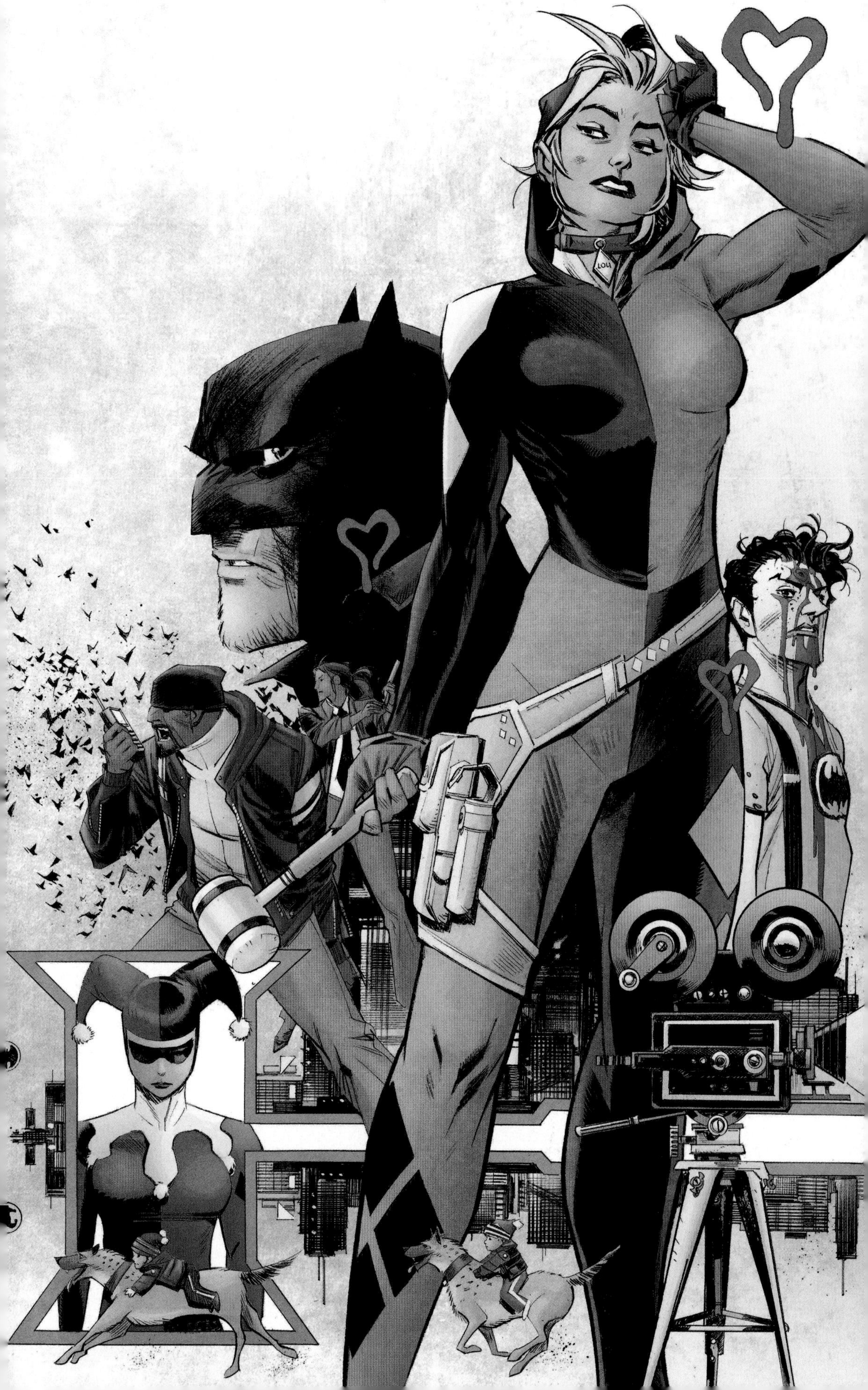

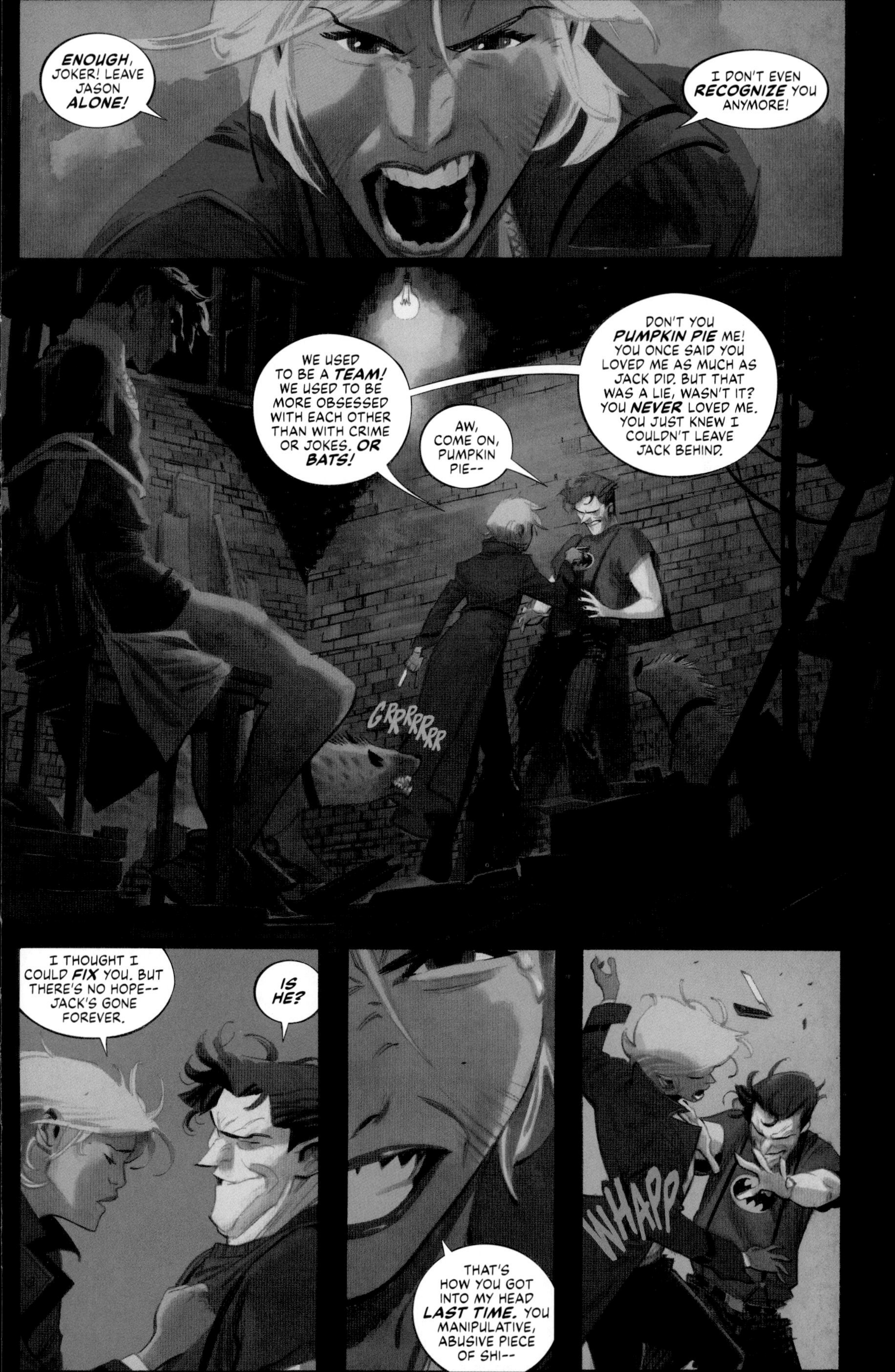
ENOUGH, JOKER! LEAVE JASON ALONE!
I DON'T EVEN RECOGNIZE YOU ANYMORE!
WE USED TO BE A TEAM! WE USED TO BE MORE OBSESSED WITH EACH OTHER THAN WITH CRIME OR JOKES. OR BATS!
AW, COME ON, PUMPKIN PIE--
DON'T YOU PUMPKIN PIE ME! YOU ONCE SAID YOU LOVED ME AS MUCH AS JACK DID. BUT THAT WAS A LIE, WASN'T IT? YOU NEVER LOVED ME. YOU JUST KNEW I COULDN'T LEAVE JACK BEHIND.
GRRRRRR
I THOUGHT I COULD FIX YOU. BUT THERE'S NO HOPE-- JACK'S GONE FOREVER.
IS HE?
THAT'S HOW YOU GOT INTO MY HEAD LAST TIME. YOU MANIPULATIVE, ABUSIVE PIECE OF SHI--
WHAPP

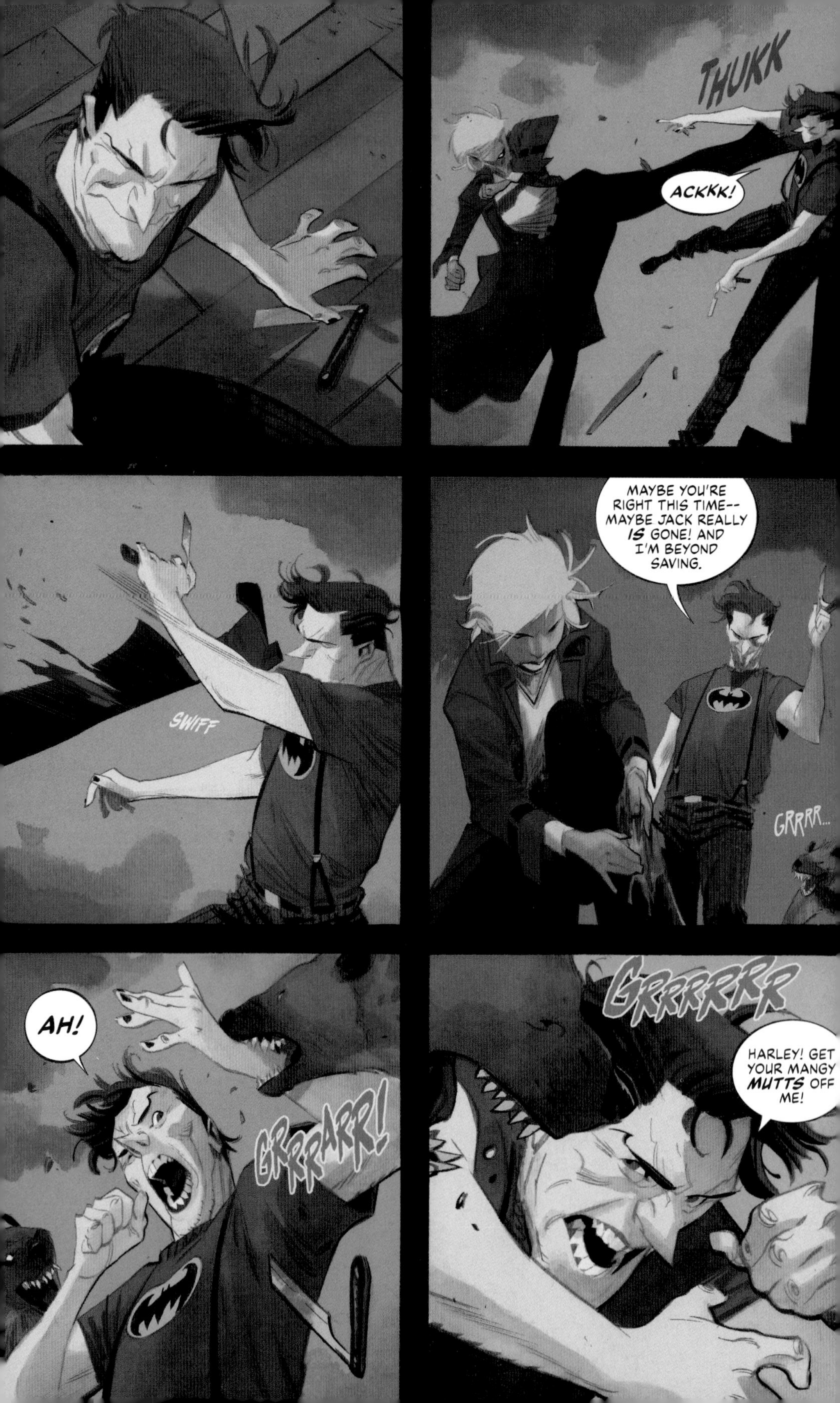
THUKK
ACKKK!
SWIFF
MAYBE YOU'RE RIGHT THIS TIME-- MAYBE JACK REALLY *IS* GONE! AND I'M BEYOND SAVING.
GRRRR...
AH!
GRRRARR!
GRRRRRR
HARLEY! GET YOUR MANGY *MUTTS* OFF ME!

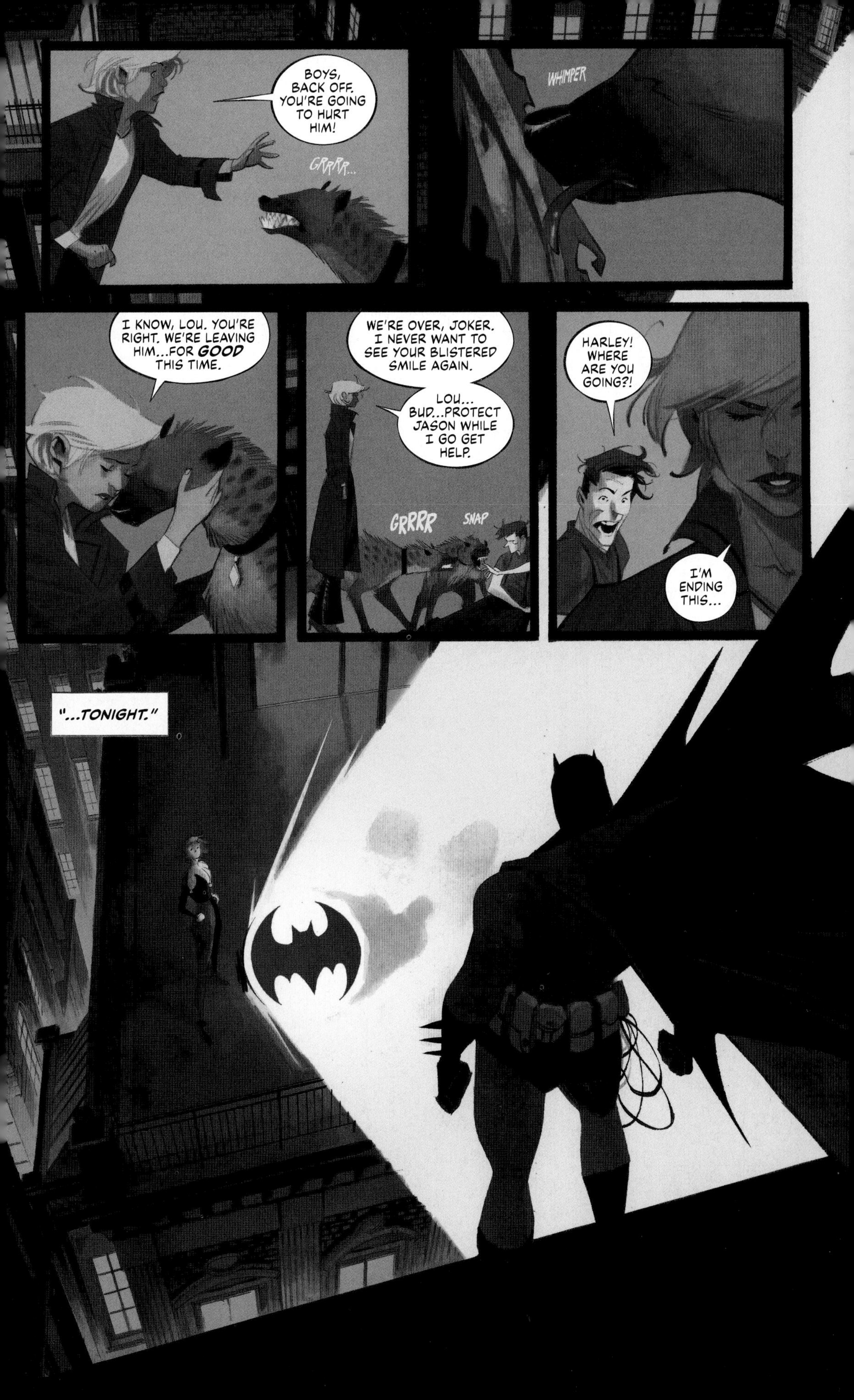
BOYS, BACK OFF. YOU'RE GOING TO HURT HIM!
GRRRR...
WHIMPER
I KNOW, LOU. YOU'RE RIGHT. WE'RE LEAVING HIM...FOR GOOD THIS TIME.
WE'RE OVER, JOKER. I NEVER WANT TO SEE YOUR BLISTERED SMILE AGAIN.
LOU... BUD...PROTECT JASON WHILE I GO GET HELP.
GRRRR
SNAP
HARLEY! WHERE ARE YOU GOING?!
I'M ENDING THIS...
"...TONIGHT."

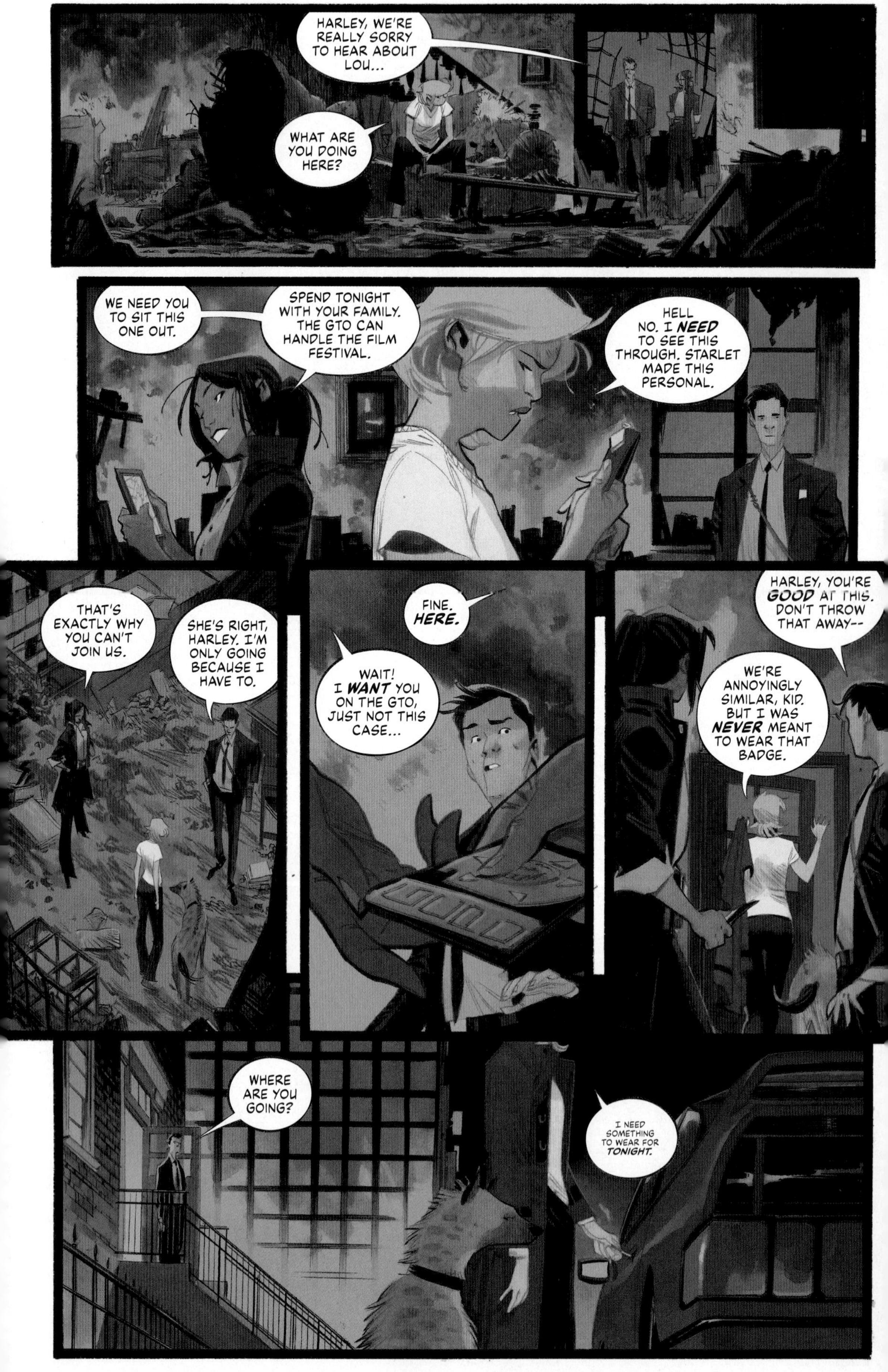
HARLEY, WE'RE REALLY SORRY TO HEAR ABOUT LOU...
WHAT ARE YOU DOING HERE?
WE NEED YOU TO SIT THIS ONE OUT.
SPEND TONIGHT WITH YOUR FAMILY. THE GTO CAN HANDLE THE FILM FESTIVAL.
HELL NO. I NEED TO SEE THIS THROUGH. STARLET MADE THIS PERSONAL.
THAT'S EXACTLY WHY YOU CAN'T JOIN US.
SHE'S RIGHT, HARLEY. I'M ONLY GOING BECAUSE I HAVE TO.
FINE. HERE.
WAIT! I WANT YOU ON THE GTO, JUST NOT THIS CASE...
HARLEY, YOU'RE GOOD AT THIS. DON'T THROW THAT AWAY--
WE'RE ANNOYINGLY SIMILAR, KID. BUT I WAS NEVER MEANT TO WEAR THAT BADGE.
WHERE ARE YOU GOING?
I NEED SOMETHING TO WEAR FOR TONIGHT.

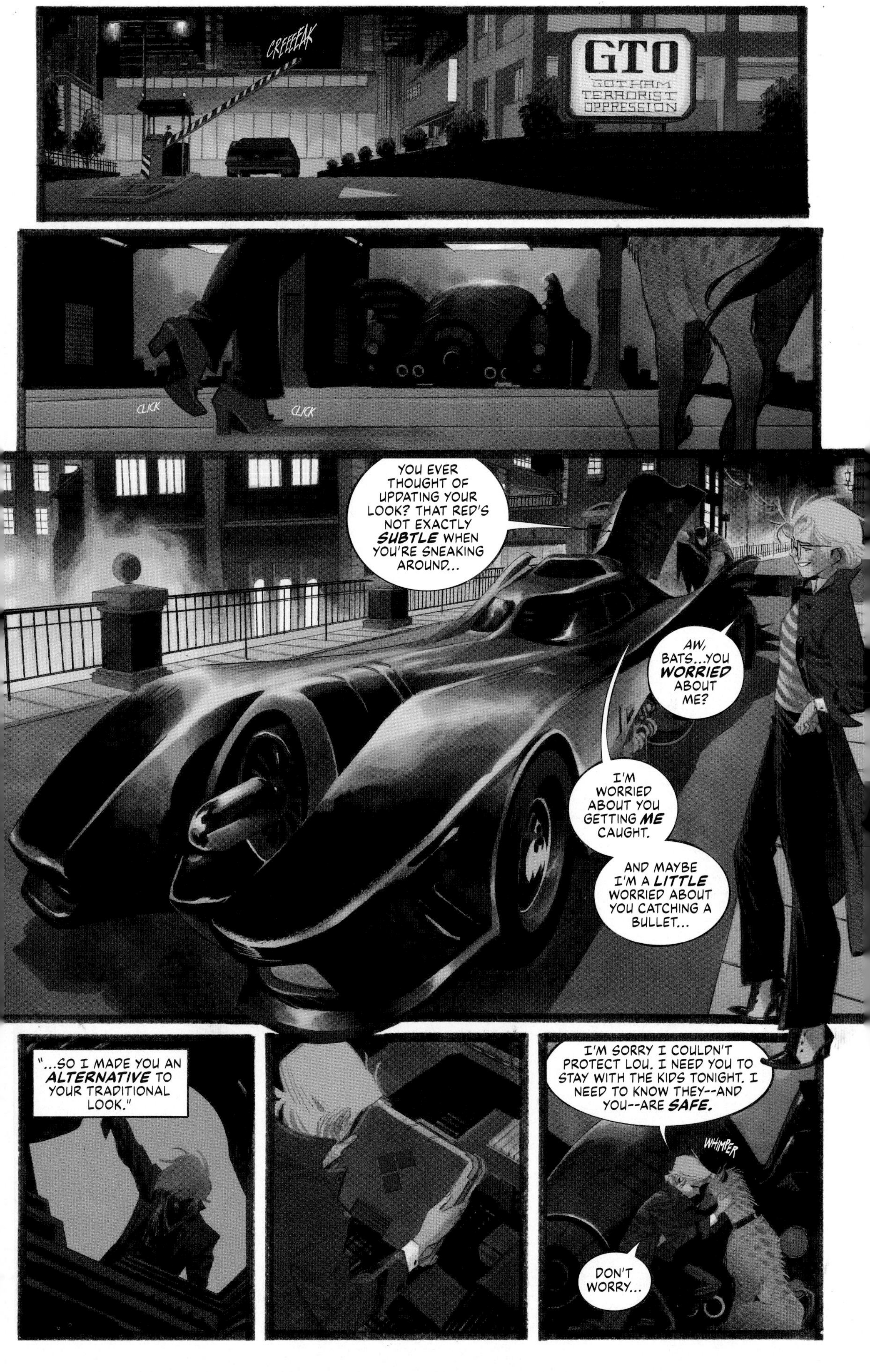
CREEEEAK
GTO
GOTHAM
TERRORIST
OPPRESSION
CLICK
CLICK
YOU EVER THOUGHT OF UPDATING YOUR LOOK? THAT RED'S NOT EXACTLY SUBTLE WHEN YOU'RE SNEAKING AROUND...
AW, BATS...YOU WORRIED ABOUT ME?
I'M WORRIED ABOUT YOU GETTING ME CAUGHT.
AND MAYBE I'M A LITTLE WORRIED ABOUT YOU CATCHING A BULLET...
"...SO I MADE YOU AN ALTERNATIVE TO YOUR TRADITIONAL LOOK."
I'M SORRY I COULDN'T PROTECT LOU. I NEED YOU TO STAY WITH THE KIDS TONIGHT. I NEED TO KNOW THEY--AND YOU--ARE SAFE.
WHIMPER
DON'T WORRY...

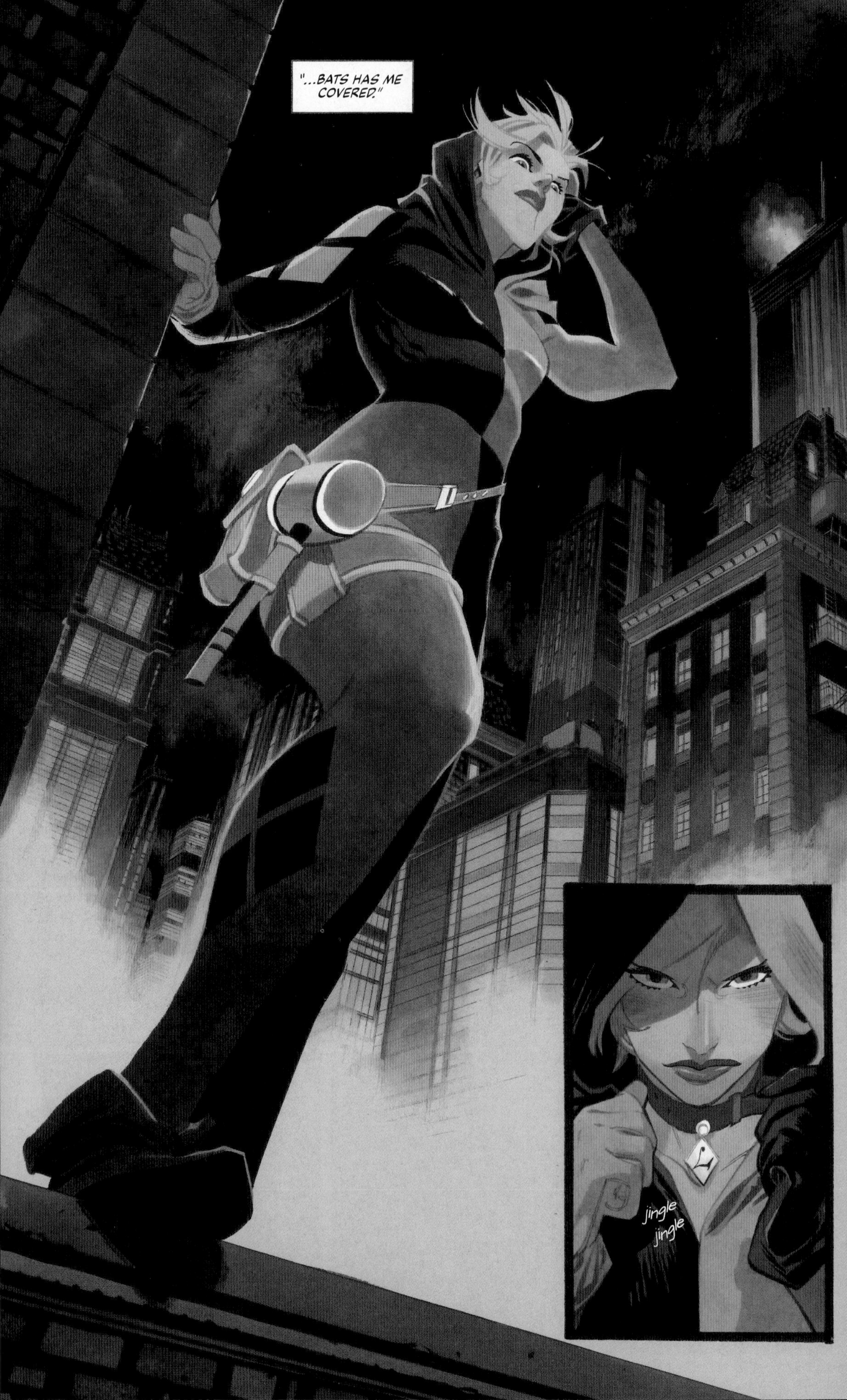
"...BATS HAS ME COVERED."
jingle
jingle

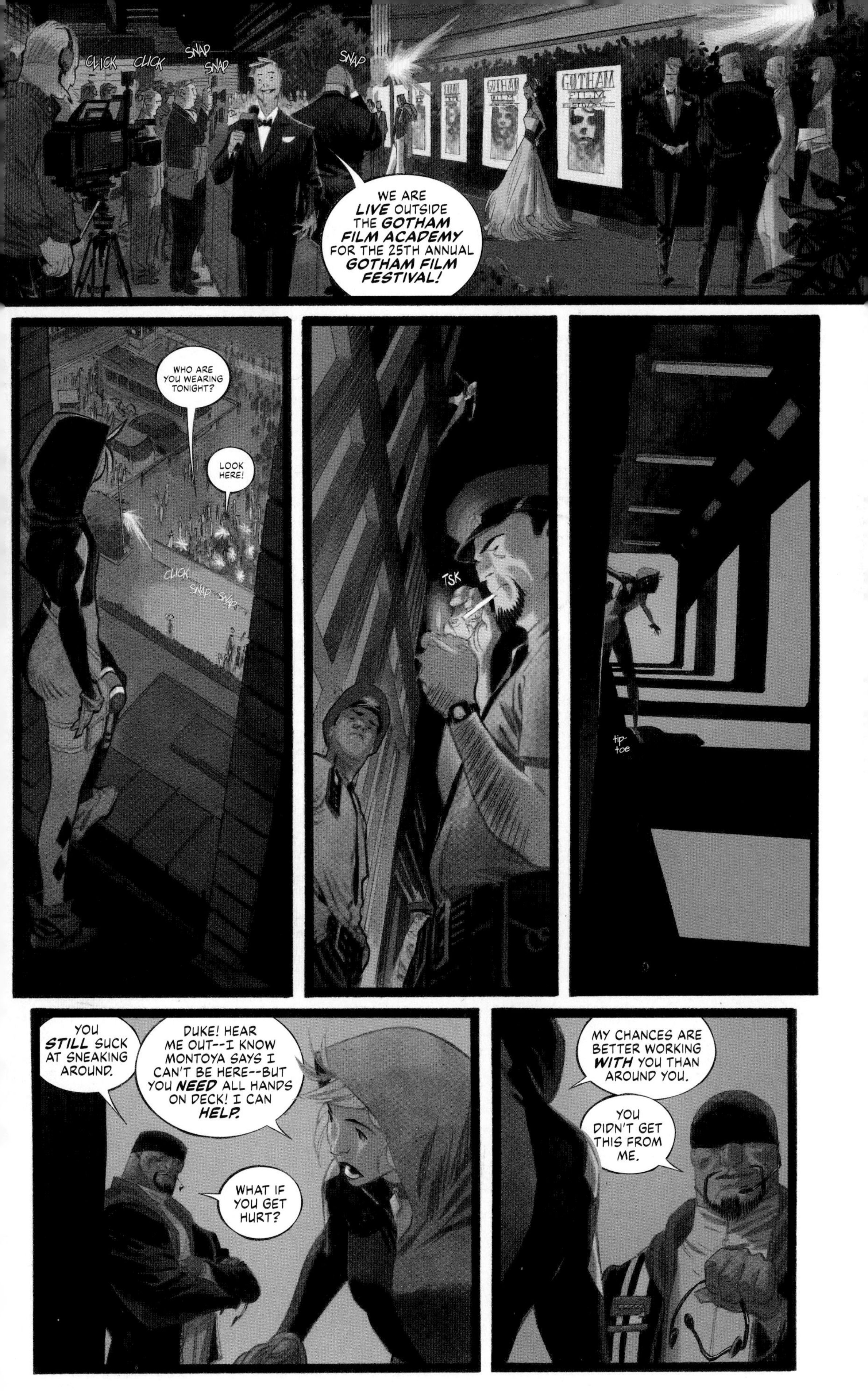
CLICK CLICK
SNAP SNAP
SNAP
WE ARE LIVE OUTSIDE THE GOTHAM FILM ACADEMY FOR THE 25TH ANNUAL GOTHAM FILM FESTIVAL!
WHO ARE YOU WEARING TONIGHT?
LOOK HERE!
CLICK SNAP SNAP
TSK
tip-toe
YOU STILL SUCK AT SNEAKING AROUND.
DUKE! HEAR ME OUT--I KNOW MONTOYA SAYS I CAN'T BE HERE--BUT YOU NEED ALL HANDS ON DECK! I CAN HELP.
WHAT IF YOU GET HURT?
MY CHANCES ARE BETTER WORKING WITH YOU THAN AROUND YOU.
YOU DIDN'T GET THIS FROM ME.

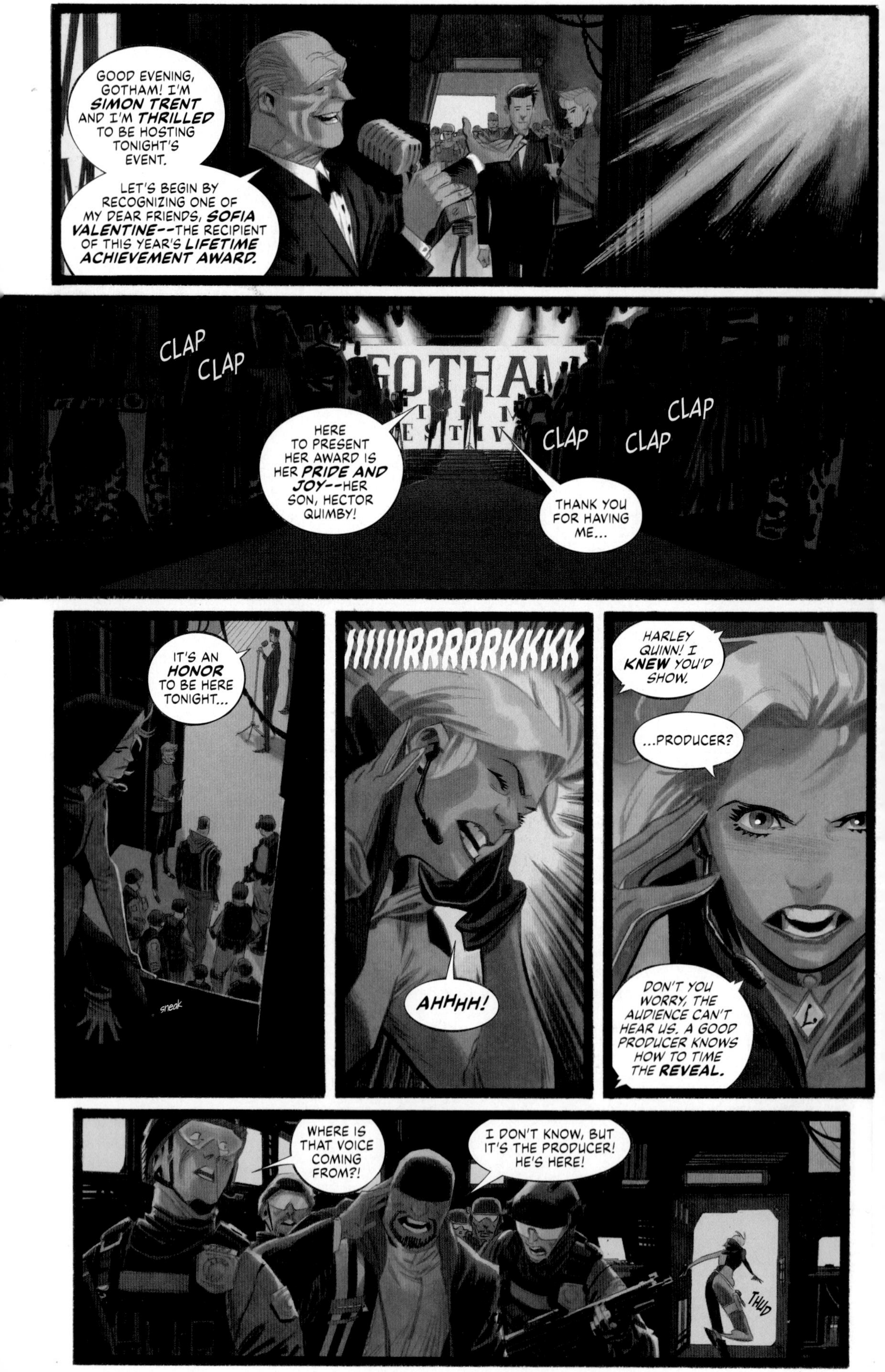
GOOD EVENING, GOTHAM! I'M SIMON TRENT AND I'M THRILLED TO BE HOSTING TONIGHT'S EVENT.
LET'S BEGIN BY RECOGNIZING ONE OF MY DEAR FRIENDS, SOFIA VALENTINE--THE RECIPIENT OF THIS YEAR'S LIFETIME ACHIEVEMENT AWARD.
CLAP CLAP
GOTHAM
HERE TO PRESENT HER AWARD IS HER PRIDE AND JOY--HER SON, HECTOR QUIMBY!
CLAP CLAP CLAP
THANK YOU FOR HAVING ME...
IT'S AN HONOR TO BE HERE TONIGHT...
sneak
IIIIIIRRRRRRKKKK
AHHHH!
HARLEY QUINN! I KNEW YOU'D SHOW.
...PRODUCER?
DON'T YOU WORRY, THE AUDIENCE CAN'T HEAR US. A GOOD PRODUCER KNOWS HOW TO TIME THE REVEAL.
WHERE IS THAT VOICE COMING FROM?!
I DON'T KNOW, BUT IT'S THE PRODUCER! HE'S HERE!
THUD

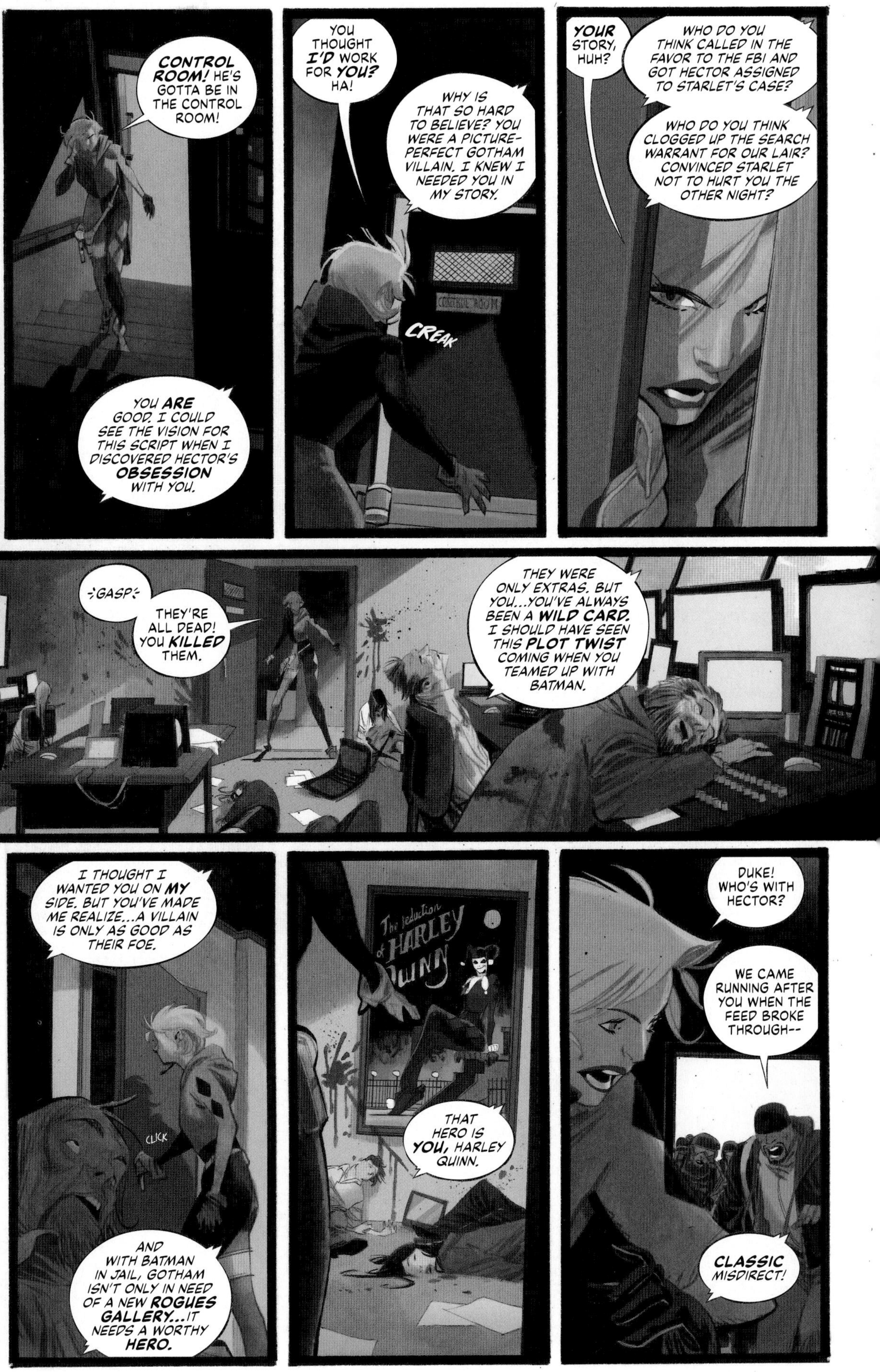
CONTROL ROOM! HE'S GOTTA BE IN THE CONTROL ROOM!
YOU ARE GOOD. I COULD SEE THE VISION FOR THIS SCRIPT WHEN I DISCOVERED HECTOR'S OBSESSION WITH YOU.
YOU THOUGHT I'D WORK FOR YOU? HA!
WHY IS THAT SO HARD TO BELIEVE? YOU WERE A PICTURE-PERFECT GOTHAM VILLAIN. I KNEW I NEEDED YOU IN MY STORY.
CONTROL ROOM
CREAK
YOUR STORY, HUH?
WHO DO YOU THINK CALLED IN THE FAVOR TO THE FBI AND GOT HECTOR ASSIGNED TO STARLET'S CASE?
WHO DO YOU THINK CLOGGED UP THE SEARCH WARRANT FOR OUR LAIR? CONVINCED STARLET NOT TO HURT YOU THE OTHER NIGHT?
-GASP- THEY'RE ALL DEAD! YOU KILLED THEM.
THEY WERE ONLY EXTRAS. BUT YOU...YOU'VE ALWAYS BEEN A WILD CARD. I SHOULD HAVE SEEN THIS PLOT TWIST COMING WHEN YOU TEAMED UP WITH BATMAN.
I THOUGHT I WANTED YOU ON MY SIDE. BUT YOU'VE MADE ME REALIZE...A VILLAIN IS ONLY AS GOOD AS THEIR FOE.
CLICK
AND WITH BATMAN IN JAIL, GOTHAM ISN'T ONLY IN NEED OF A NEW ROGUES GALLERY...IT NEEDS A WORTHY HERO.
HARLEY
THAT HERO IS YOU, HARLEY QUINN.
DUKE! WHO'S WITH HECTOR?
WE CAME RUNNING AFTER YOU WHEN THE FEED BROKE THROUGH--
CLASSIC MISDIRECT!

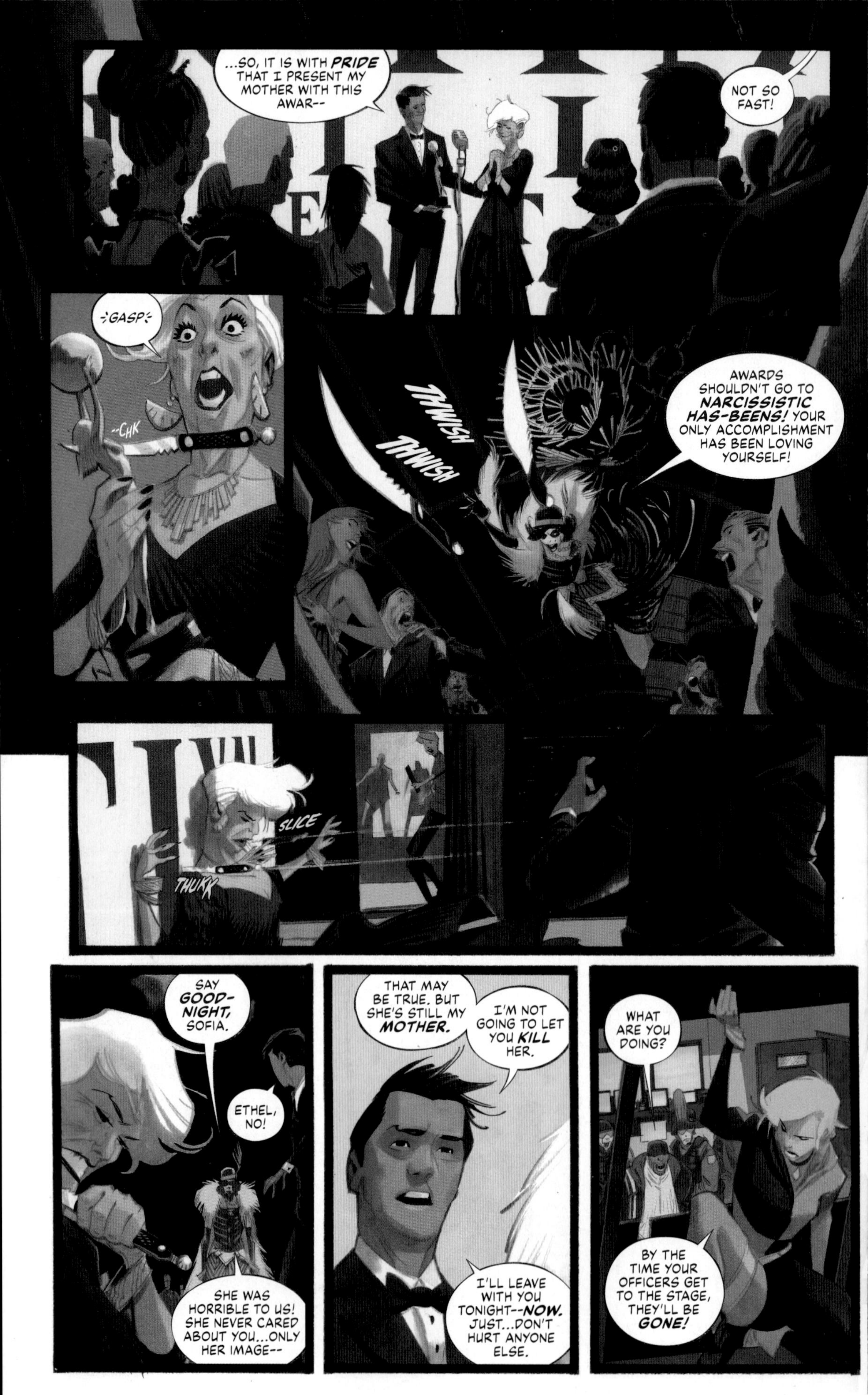
...SO, IT IS WITH PRIDE THAT I PRESENT MY MOTHER WITH THIS AWAR--
NOT SO FAST!
GASP
--CHK
THWISH
THWISH
AWARDS SHOULDN'T GO TO NARCISSISTIC HAS-BEENS! YOUR ONLY ACCOMPLISHMENT HAS BEEN LOVING YOURSELF!
SLICE
THUKK
SAY GOOD-NIGHT, SOFIA.
ETHEL, NO!
SHE WAS HORRIBLE TO US! SHE NEVER CARED ABOUT YOU...ONLY HER IMAGE--
THAT MAY BE TRUE. BUT SHE'S STILL MY MOTHER.
I'M NOT GOING TO LET YOU KILL HER.
I'LL LEAVE WITH YOU TONIGHT--NOW. JUST...DON'T HURT ANYONE ELSE.
WHAT ARE YOU DOING?
BY THE TIME YOUR OFFICERS GET TO THE STAGE, THEY'LL BE GONE!

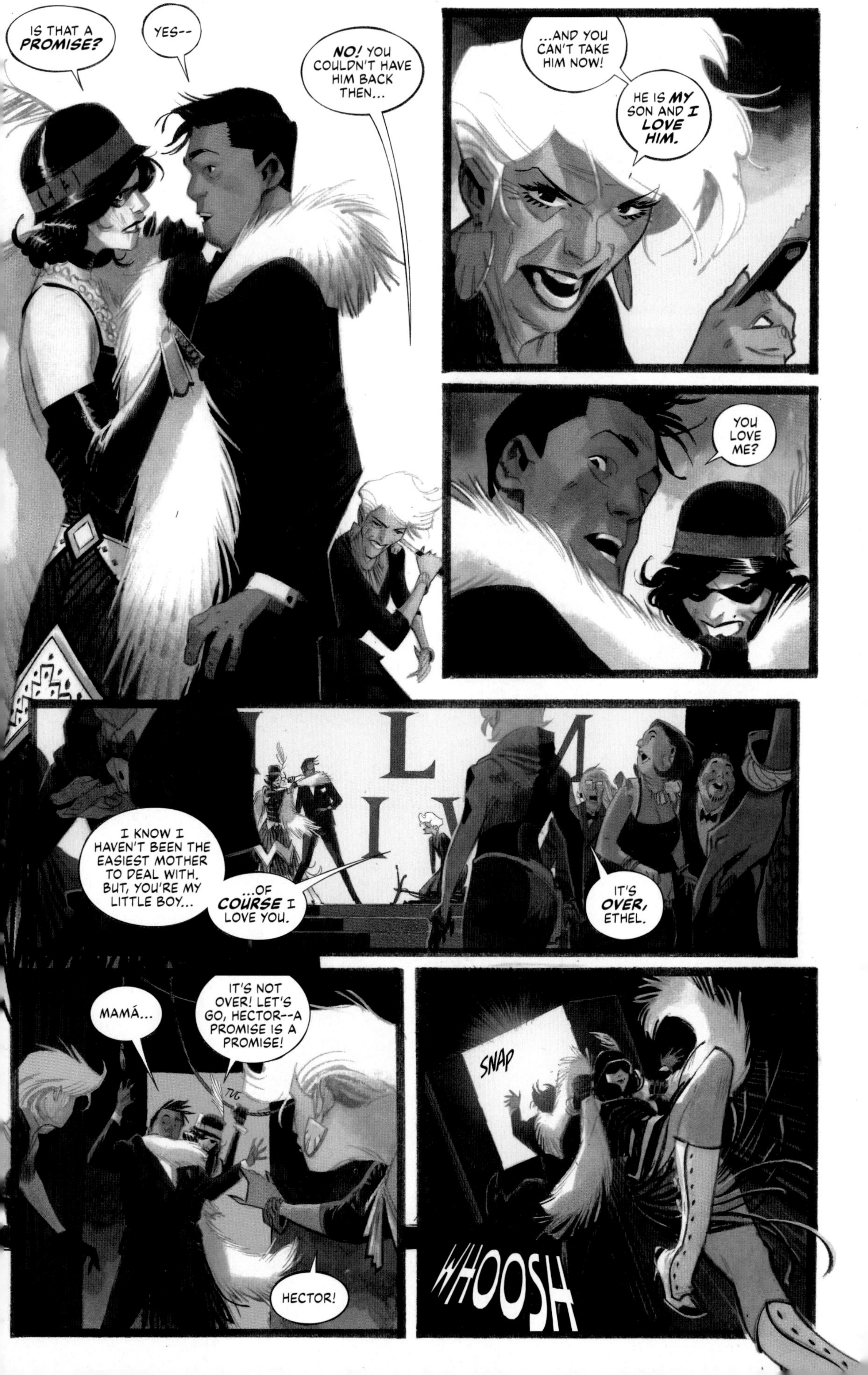

IS THAT A PROMISE?
YES--
NO! YOU COULDN'T HAVE HIM BACK THEN...
...AND YOU CAN'T TAKE HIM NOW!
HE IS MY SON AND I LOVE HIM.
YOU LOVE ME?
I KNOW I HAVEN'T BEEN THE EASIEST MOTHER TO DEAL WITH. BUT, YOU'RE MY LITTLE BOY...
...OF COURSE I LOVE YOU.
IT'S OVER, ETHEL.
MAMÁ...
IT'S NOT OVER! LET'S GO, HECTOR--A PROMISE IS A PROMISE!
HECTOR!
SNAP
WHOOSH

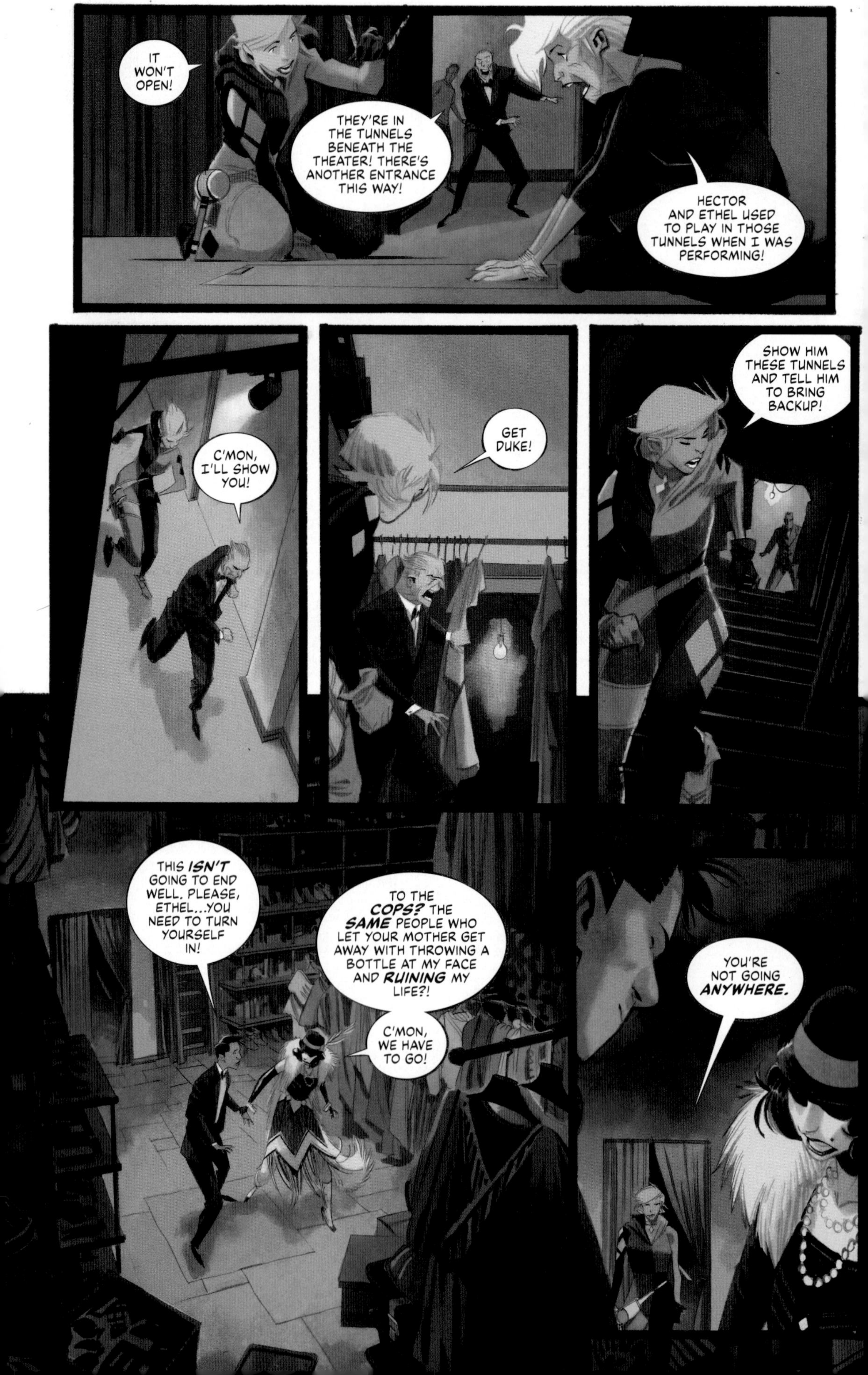
IT WON'T OPEN!
THEY'RE IN THE TUNNELS BENEATH THE THEATER! THERE'S ANOTHER ENTRANCE THIS WAY!
HECTOR AND ETHEL USED TO PLAY IN THOSE TUNNELS WHEN I WAS PERFORMING!
C'MON, I'LL SHOW YOU!
GET DUKE!
SHOW HIM THESE TUNNELS AND TELL HIM TO BRING BACKUP!
THIS ISN'T GOING TO END WELL. PLEASE, ETHEL...YOU NEED TO TURN YOURSELF IN!
TO THE COPS? THE SAME PEOPLE WHO LET YOUR MOTHER GET AWAY WITH THROWING A BOTTLE AT MY FACE AND RUINING MY LIFE?!
C'MON, WE HAVE TO GO!
YOU'RE NOT GOING ANYWHERE.

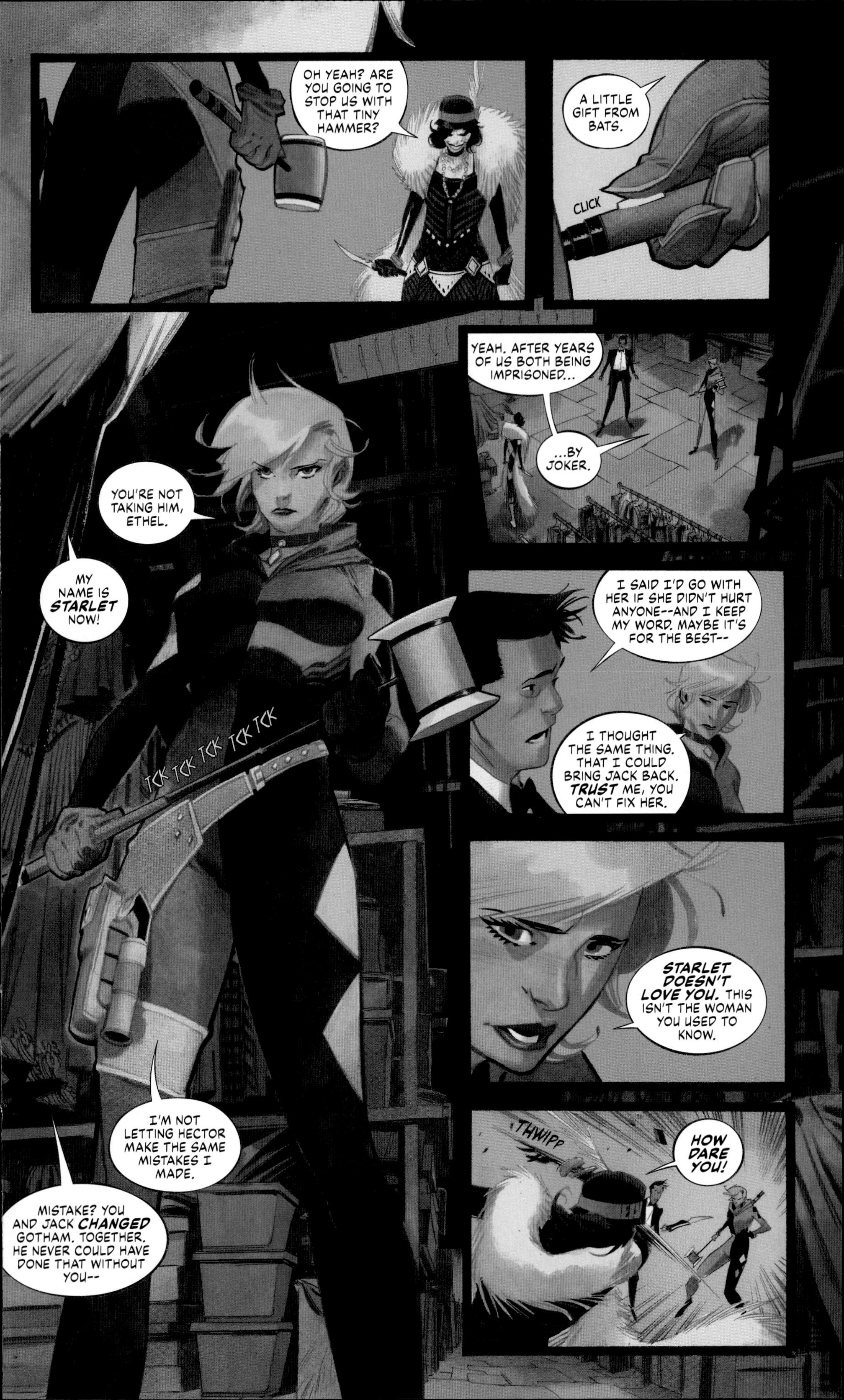

OH YEAH? ARE YOU GOING TO STOP US WITH THAT TINY HAMMER?
A LITTLE GIFT FROM BATS.
CLICK
YEAH. AFTER YEARS OF US BOTH BEING IMPRISONED...
...BY JOKER.
YOU'RE NOT TAKING HIM, ETHEL.
MY NAME IS STARLET NOW!
TCK TCK TCK TCK TCK
I SAID I'D GO WITH HER IF SHE DIDN'T HURT ANYONE--AND I KEEP MY WORD. MAYBE IT'S FOR THE BEST--
I THOUGHT THE SAME THING. THAT I COULD BRING JACK BACK. TRUST ME, YOU CAN'T FIX HER.
STARLET DOESN'T LOVE YOU. THIS ISN'T THE WOMAN YOU USED TO KNOW.
I'M NOT LETTING HECTOR MAKE THE SAME MISTAKES I MADE.
MISTAKE? YOU AND JACK CHANGED GOTHAM. TOGETHER. HE NEVER COULD HAVE DONE THAT WITHOUT YOU--
THWIPP
HOW DARE YOU!

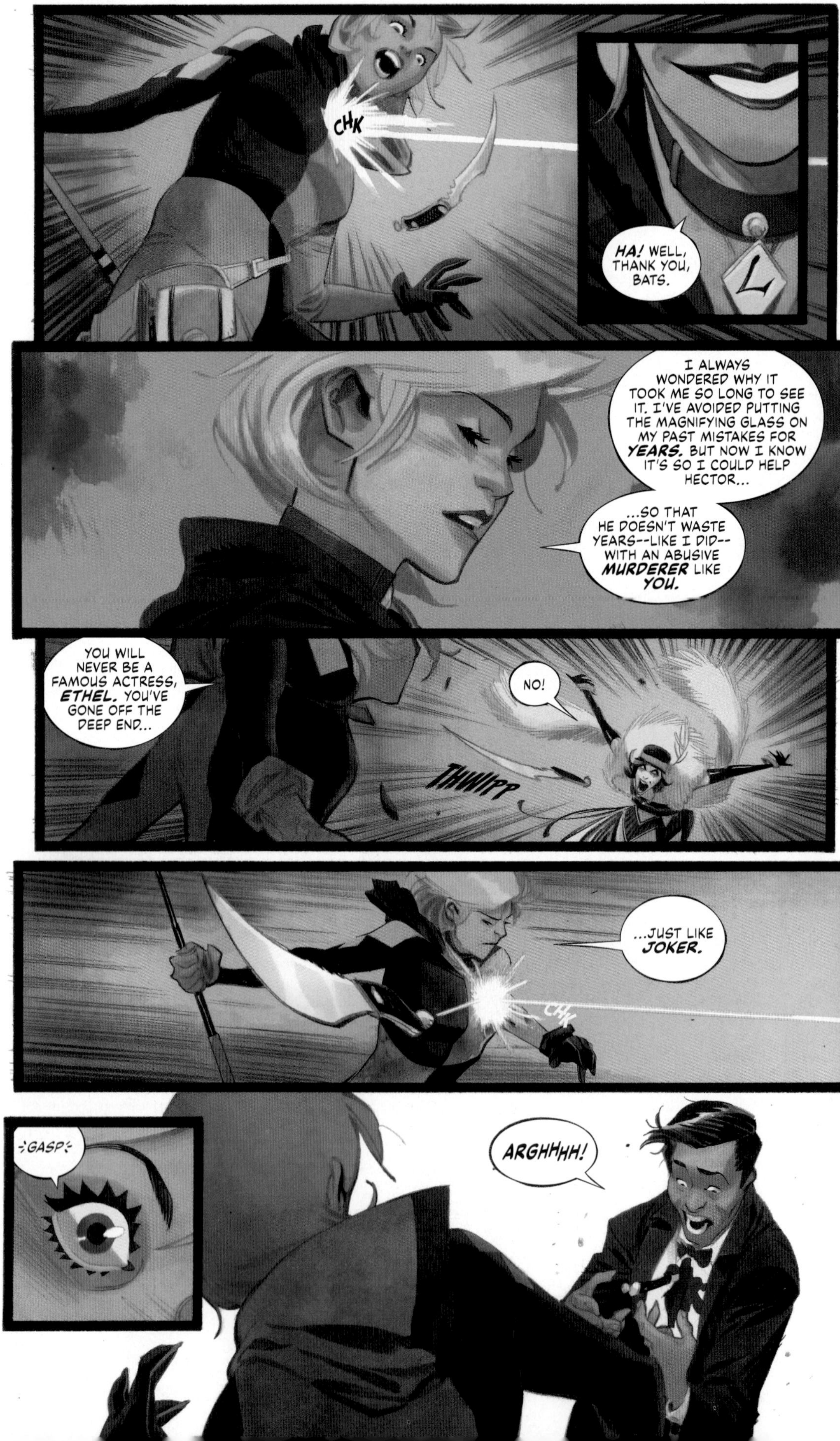
CHK
HA! WELL, THANK YOU, BATS.
I ALWAYS WONDERED WHY IT TOOK ME SO LONG TO SEE IT. I'VE AVOIDED PUTTING THE MAGNIFYING GLASS ON MY PAST MISTAKES FOR YEARS. BUT NOW I KNOW IT'S SO I COULD HELP HECTOR...
...SO THAT HE DOESN'T WASTE YEARS--LIKE I DID--WITH AN ABUSIVE MURDERER LIKE YOU.
YOU WILL NEVER BE A FAMOUS ACTRESS, ETHEL. YOU'VE GONE OFF THE DEEP END...
NO!
THWIPP
...JUST LIKE JOKER.
CHK
GASP
ARGHHHH!

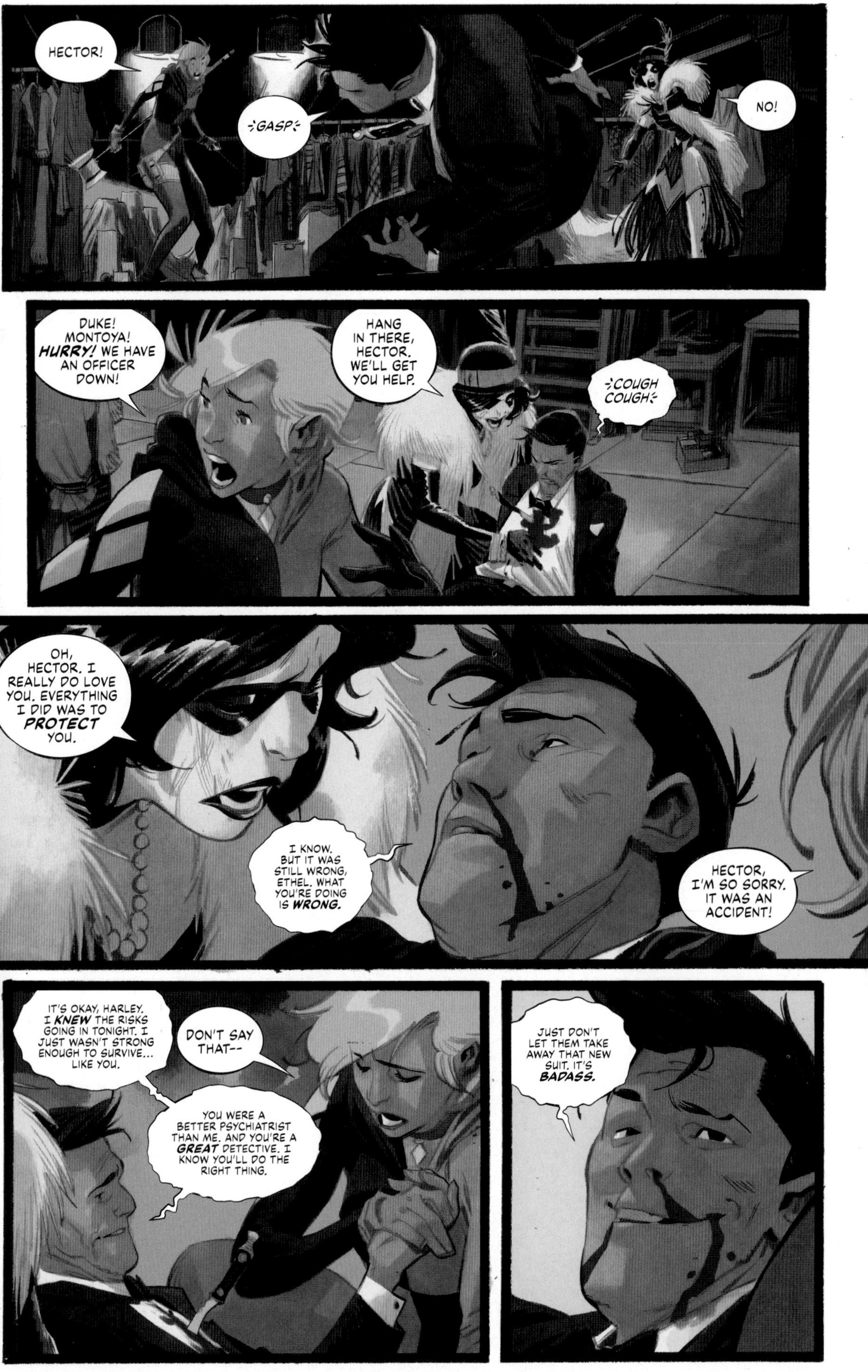
HECTOR!
GASP
NO!
DUKE! MONTOYA! HURRY! WE HAVE AN OFFICER DOWN!
HANG IN THERE, HECTOR. WE'LL GET YOU HELP.
COUGH COUGH
OH, HECTOR. I REALLY DO LOVE YOU. EVERYTHING I DID WAS TO PROTECT YOU.
I KNOW. BUT IT WAS STILL WRONG, ETHEL. WHAT YOU'RE DOING IS WRONG.
HECTOR, I'M SO SORRY. IT WAS AN ACCIDENT!
IT'S OKAY, HARLEY. I KNEW THE RISKS GOING IN TONIGHT. I JUST WASN'T STRONG ENOUGH TO SURVIVE... LIKE YOU.
DON'T SAY THAT--
YOU WERE A BETTER PSYCHIATRIST THAN ME. AND YOU'RE A GREAT DETECTIVE. I KNOW YOU'LL DO THE RIGHT THING.
JUST DON'T LET THEM TAKE AWAY THAT NEW SUIT. IT'S BADASS.

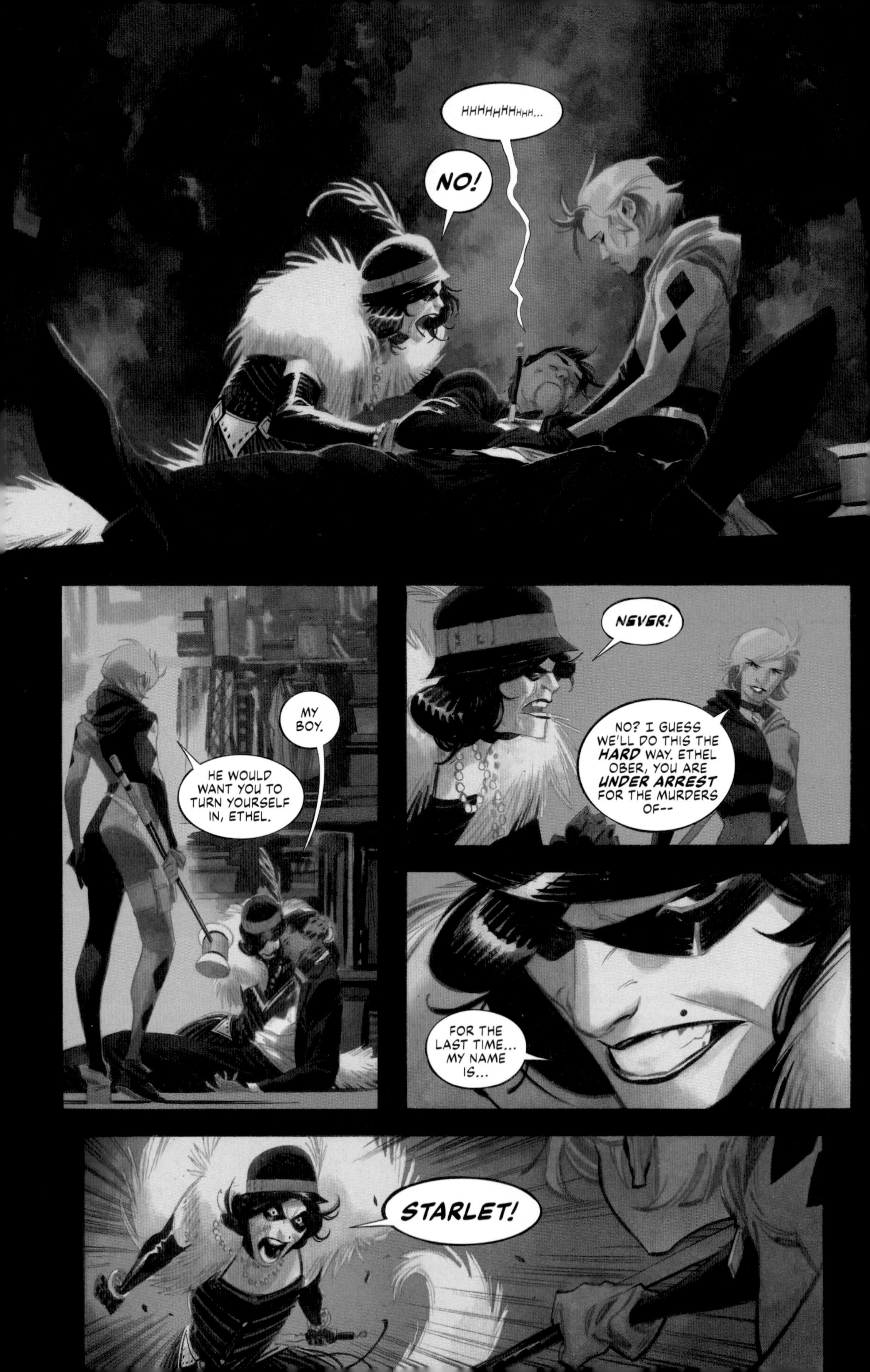
HHHHHHHhhh...
NO!
MY BOY.
HE WOULD WANT YOU TO TURN YOURSELF IN, ETHEL.
NEVER!
NO? I GUESS WE'LL DO THIS THE HARD WAY. ETHEL OBER, YOU ARE UNDER ARREST FOR THE MURDERS OF--
FOR THE LAST TIME... MY NAME IS...
STARLET!

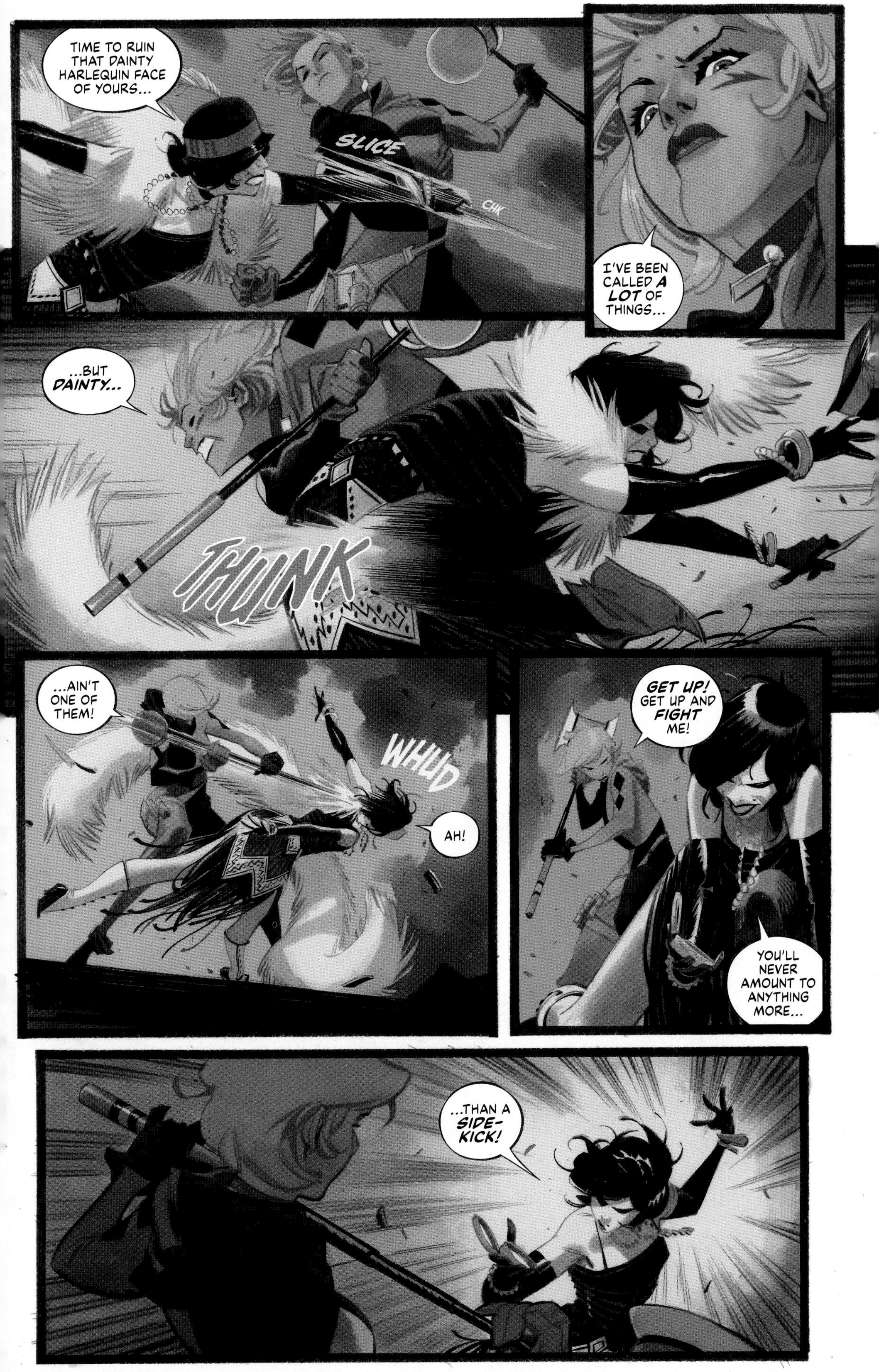

TIME TO RUIN THAT DAINTY HARLEQUIN FACE OF YOURS...
SLICE
CHK
I'VE BEEN CALLED **A LOT** OF THINGS...
...BUT ***DAINTY...***
THUNK
...AIN'T ONE OF THEM!
WHUD
AH!
GET UP! GET UP AND ***FIGHT*** ME!
YOU'LL NEVER AMOUNT TO ANYTHING MORE...
...THAN A ***SIDE-KICK!***

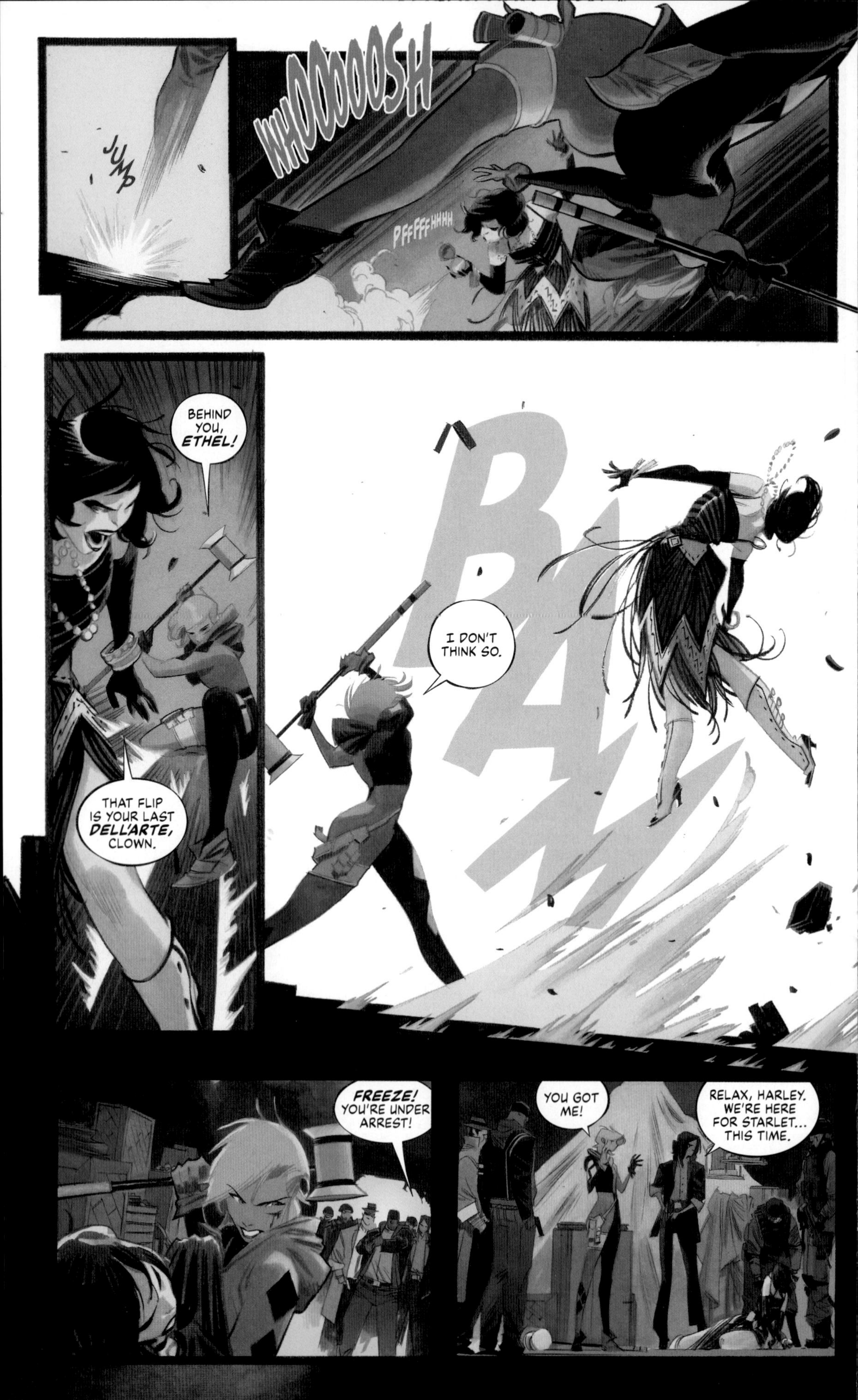
JUMP
WHOOOOOSH
PFFFFFHHHH
BEHIND YOU, *ETHEL!*
THAT FLIP IS YOUR LAST *DELL'ARTE,* CLOWN.
I DON'T THINK SO.
BRAAM
FREEZE! YOU'RE UNDER ARREST!
YOU GOT ME!
RELAX, HARLEY. WE'RE HERE FOR STARLET... THIS TIME.

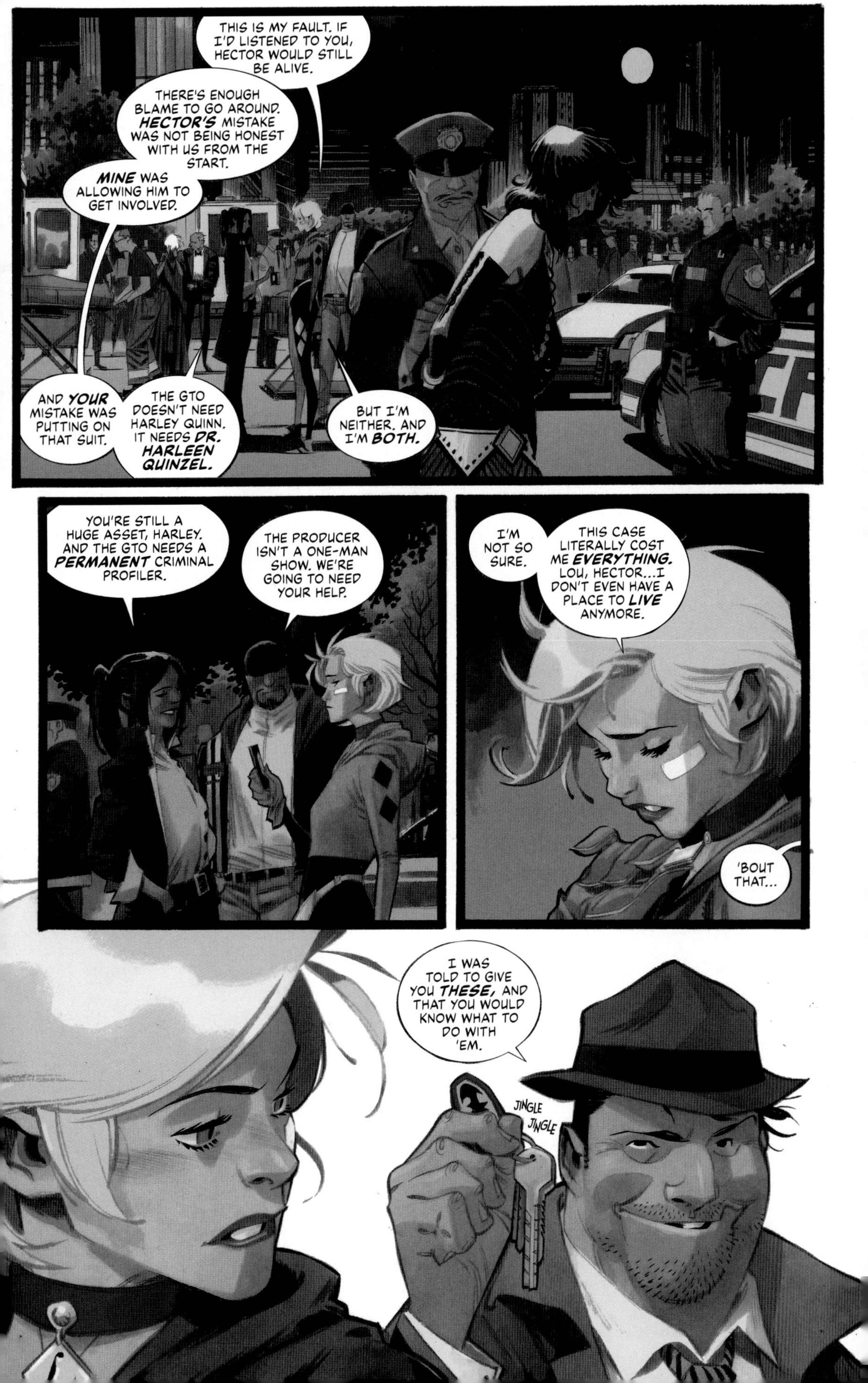
THIS IS MY FAULT. IF I'D LISTENED TO YOU, HECTOR WOULD STILL BE ALIVE.
THERE'S ENOUGH BLAME TO GO AROUND. HECTOR'S MISTAKE WAS NOT BEING HONEST WITH US FROM THE START.
MINE WAS ALLOWING HIM TO GET INVOLVED.
AND YOUR MISTAKE WAS PUTTING ON THAT SUIT.
THE GTO DOESN'T NEED HARLEY QUINN. IT NEEDS DR. HARLEEN QUINZEL.
BUT I'M NEITHER. AND I'M BOTH.
YOU'RE STILL A HUGE ASSET, HARLEY. AND THE GTO NEEDS A PERMANENT CRIMINAL PROFILER.
THE PRODUCER ISN'T A ONE-MAN SHOW. WE'RE GOING TO NEED YOUR HELP.
I'M NOT SO SURE.
THIS CASE LITERALLY COST ME EVERYTHING. LOU, HECTOR...I DON'T EVEN HAVE A PLACE TO LIVE ANYMORE.
'BOUT THAT...
I WAS TOLD TO GIVE YOU THESE, AND THAT YOU WOULD KNOW WHAT TO DO WITH 'EM.
JINGLE
JINGLE

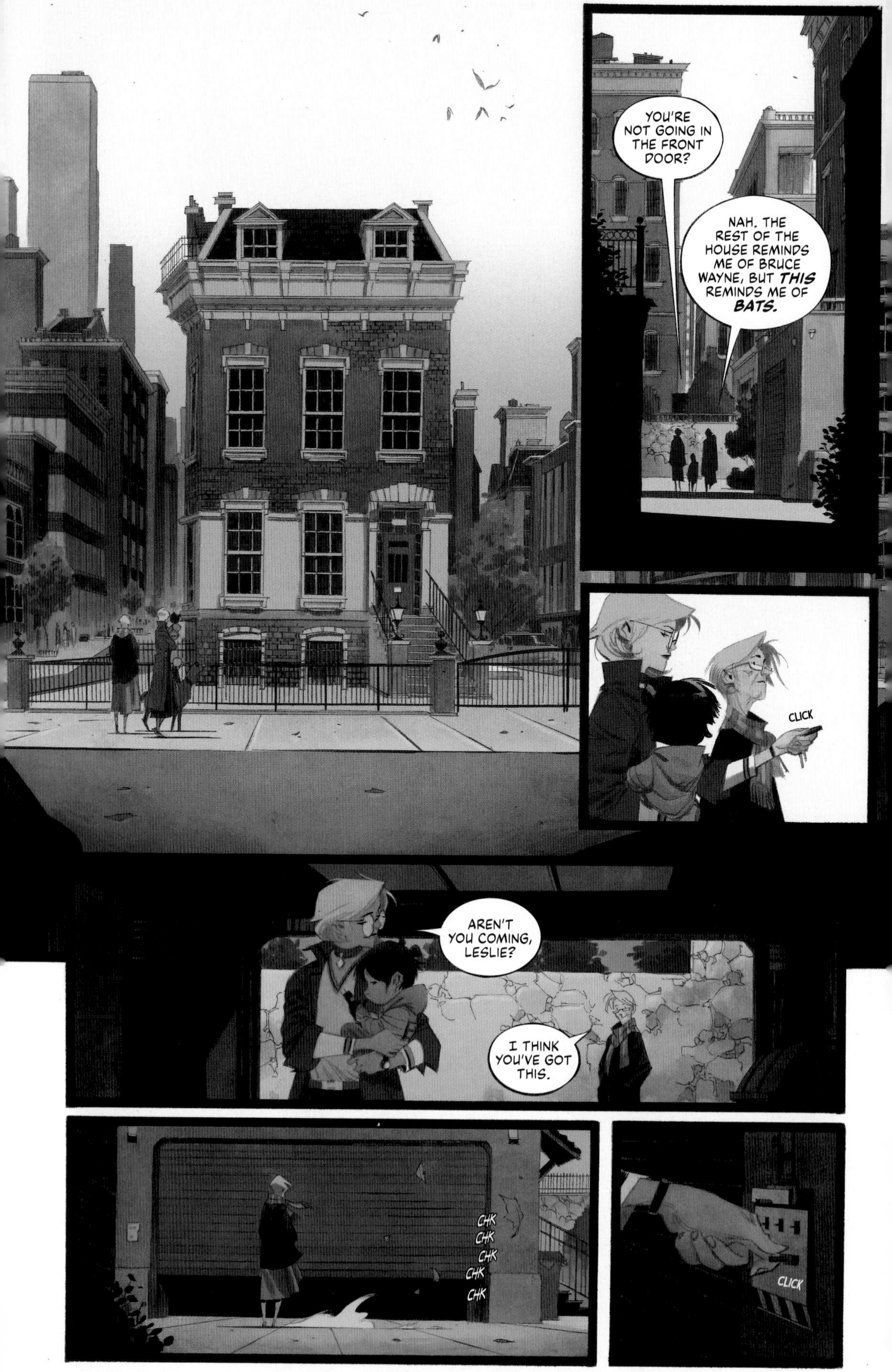
YOU'RE NOT GOING IN THE FRONT DOOR?
NAH. THE REST OF THE HOUSE REMINDS ME OF BRUCE WAYNE, BUT THIS REMINDS ME OF BATS.
CLICK
AREN'T YOU COMING, LESLIE?
I THINK YOU'VE GOT THIS.
CHK
CHK
CHK
CHK
CHK
CLICK

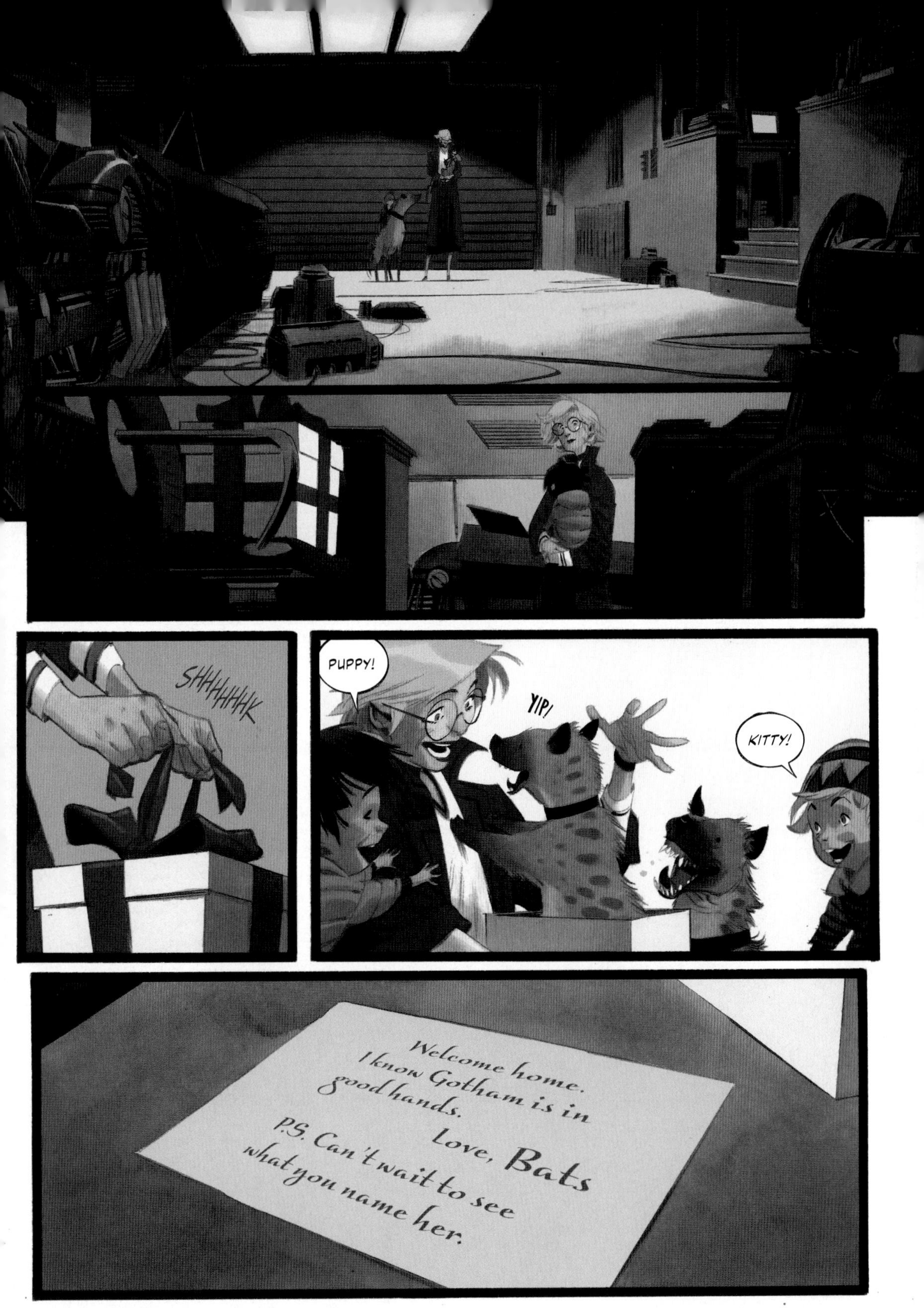
SHHHHHHK
PUPPY!
YIP!
KITTY!
Welcome home.
I know Gotham is in
good hands.
Love, Bats
P.S. Can't wait to see
what you name her.

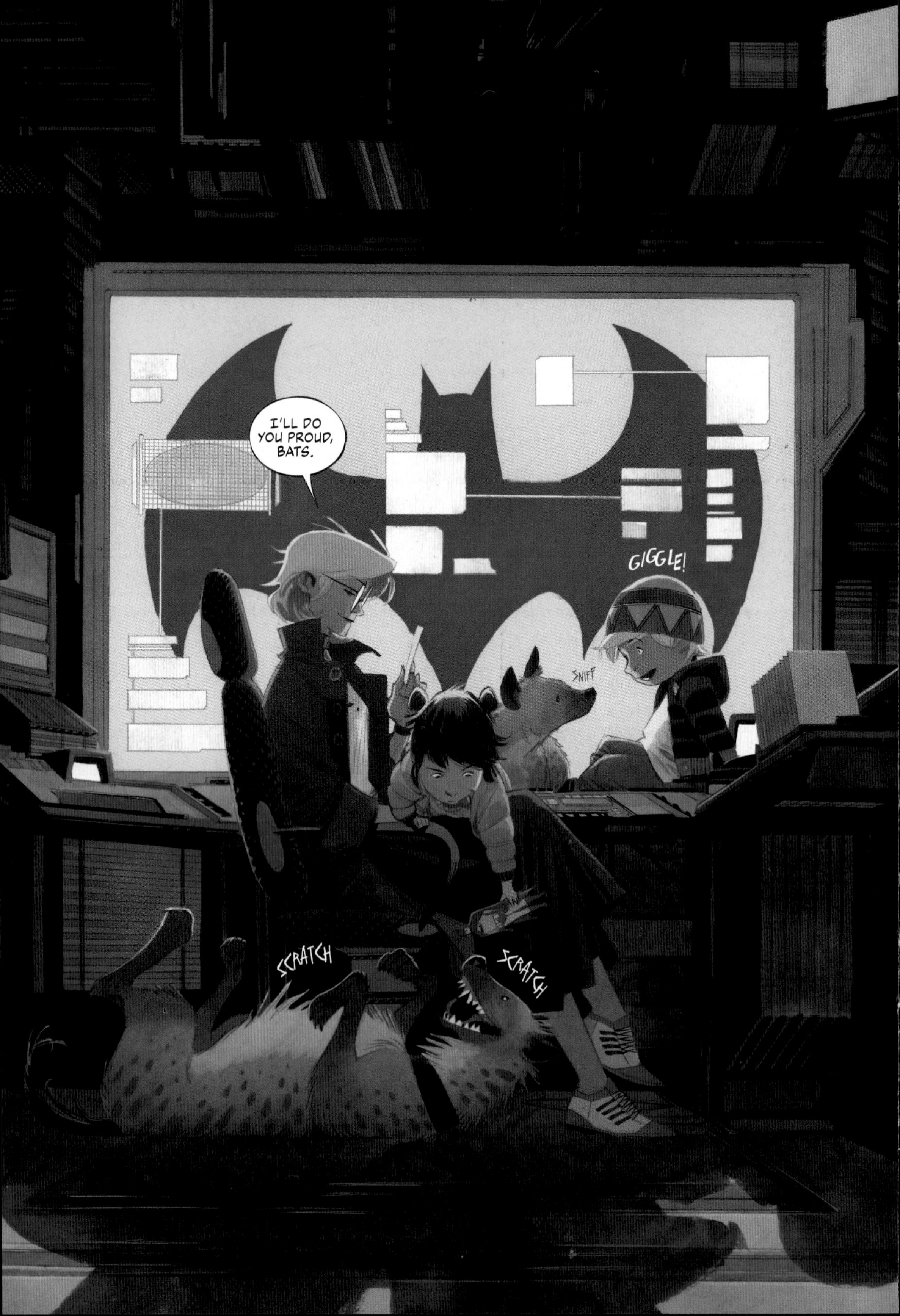
I'LL DO YOU PROUD, BATS.
GIGGLE!
SNIFF
SCRATCH
SCRATCH

Issue #1 variant cover art by
Matteo Scalera and **Matt Hollingsworth**

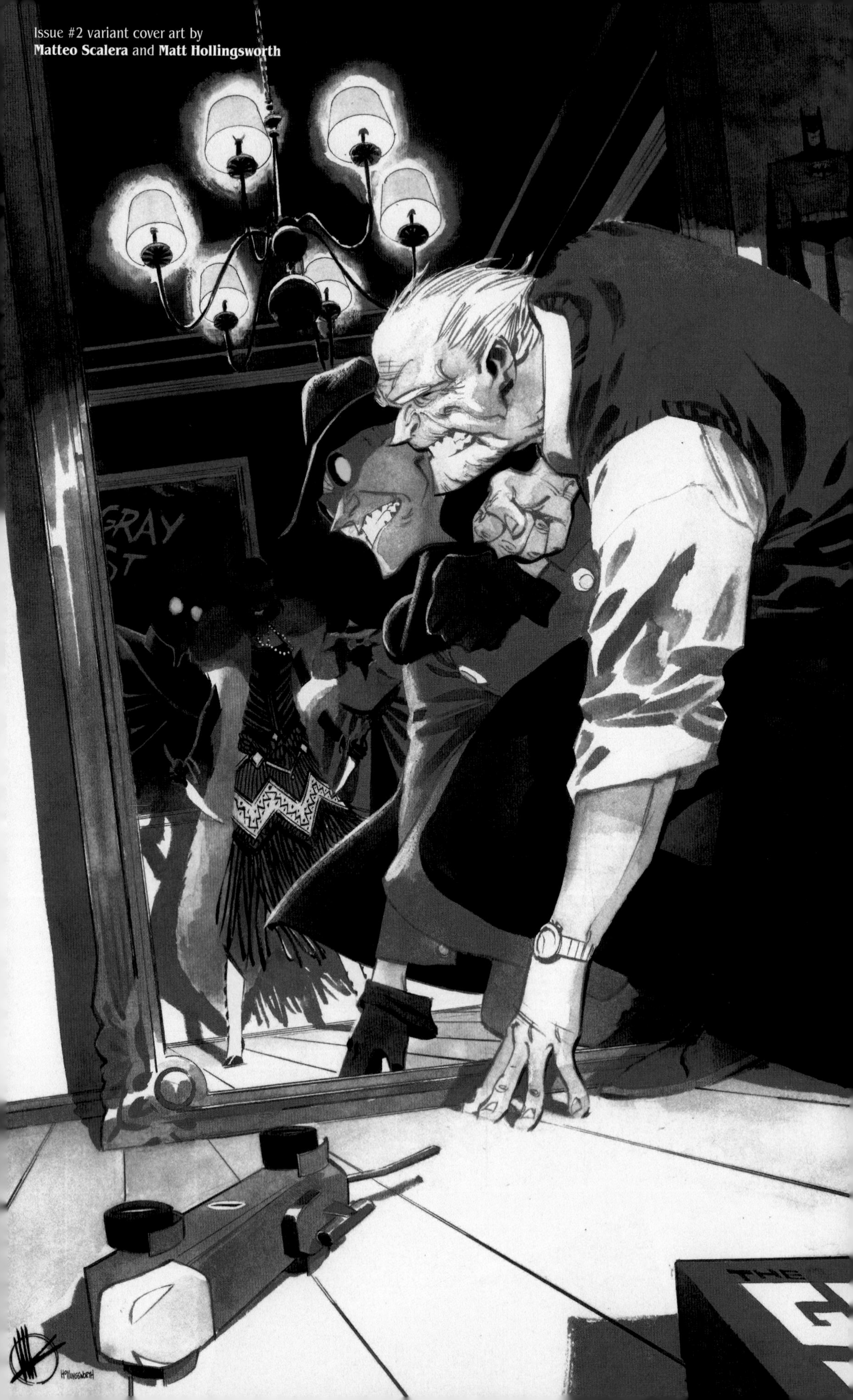
GRAY
THE
HOLLINGSWORTH

Issue #2 variant cover art by
Matteo Scalera and **Matt Hollingsworth**

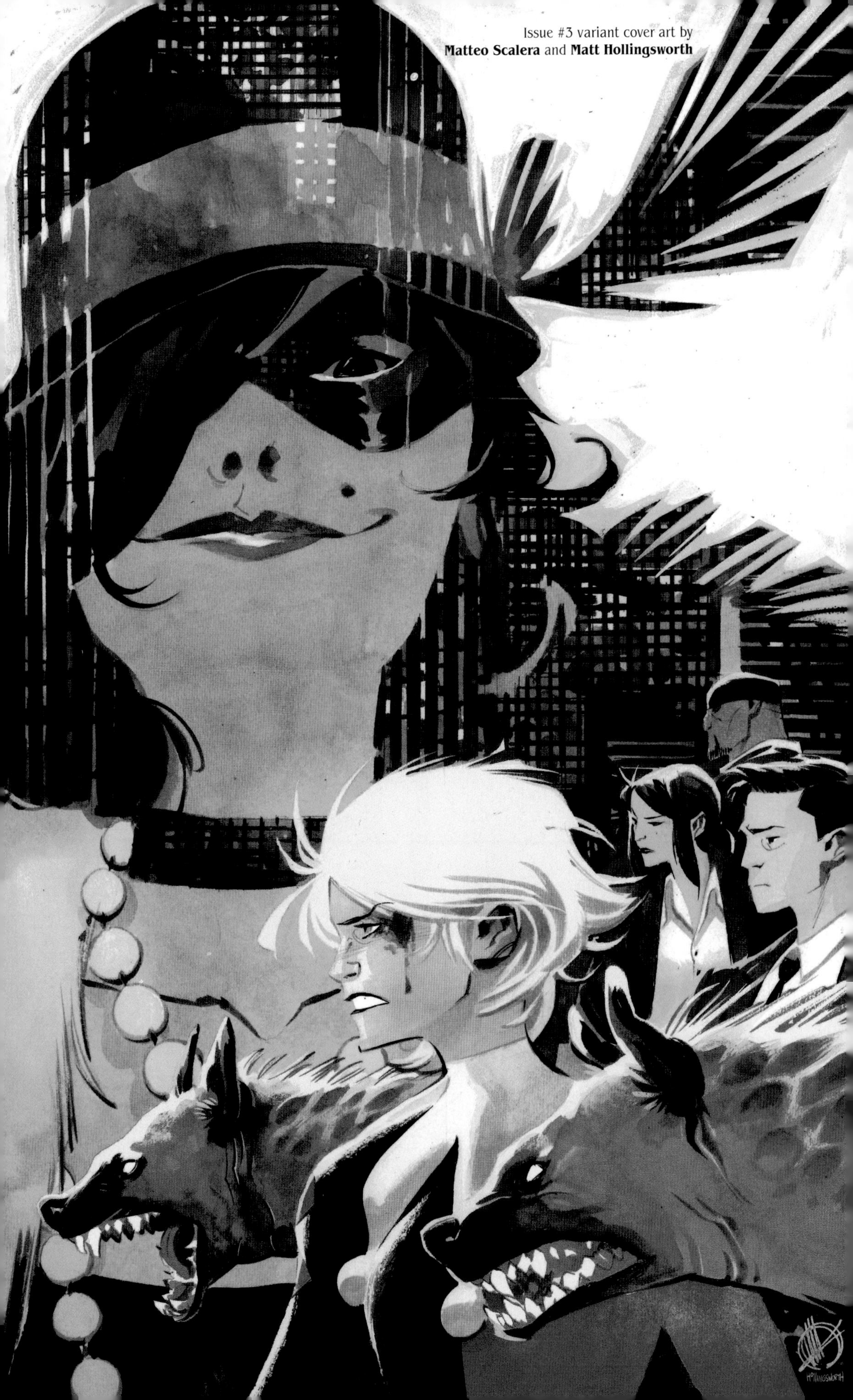
HOLLINGSWORTH

Issue #3 variant cover art by
Matteo Scalera and **Matt Hollingsworth**

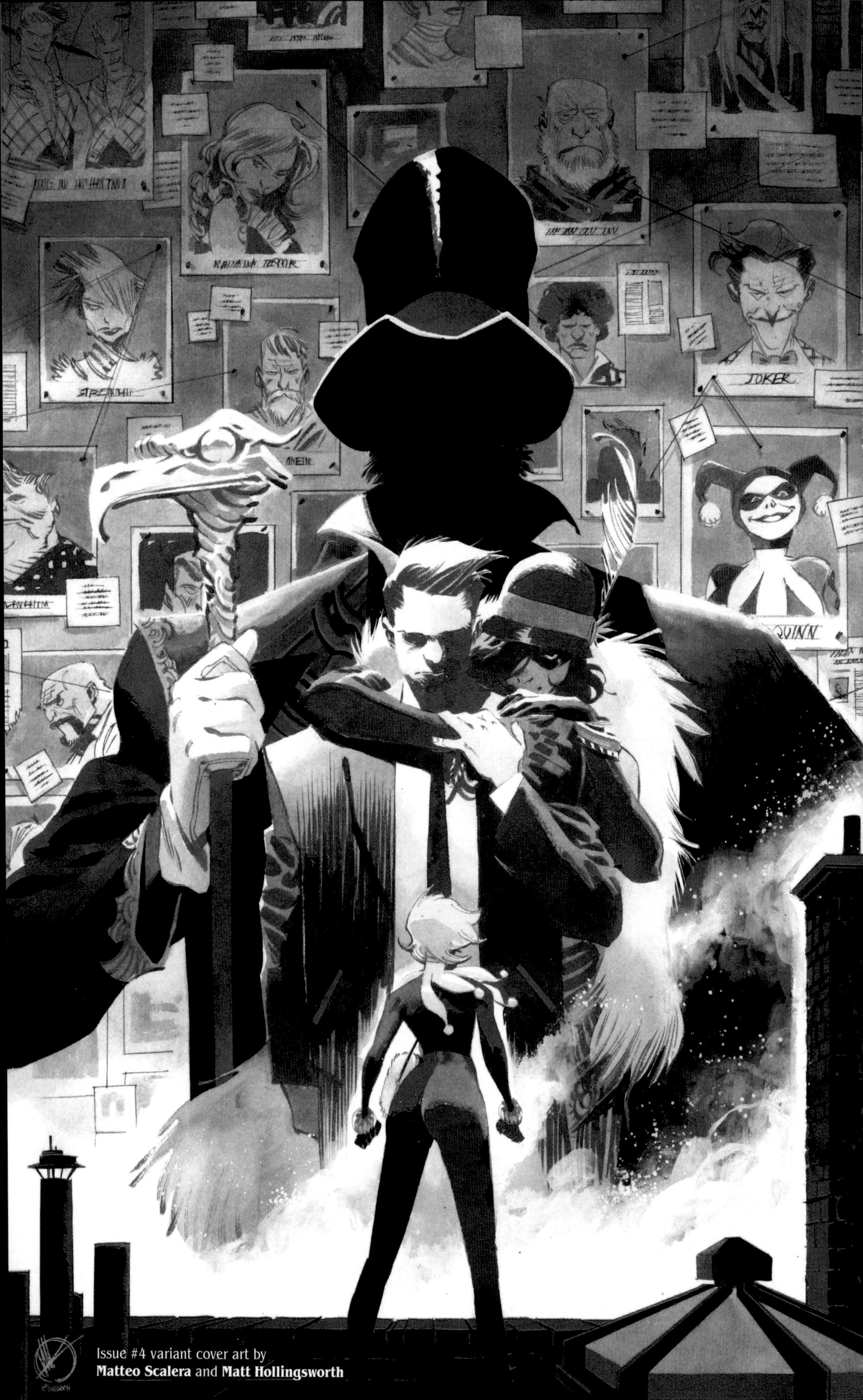
JOKER
QUINN

Issue #4 variant cover art by
Matteo Scalera and **Matt Hollingsworth**

Issue #5 variant cover art by
Matteo Scalera and **Matt Hollingsworth**

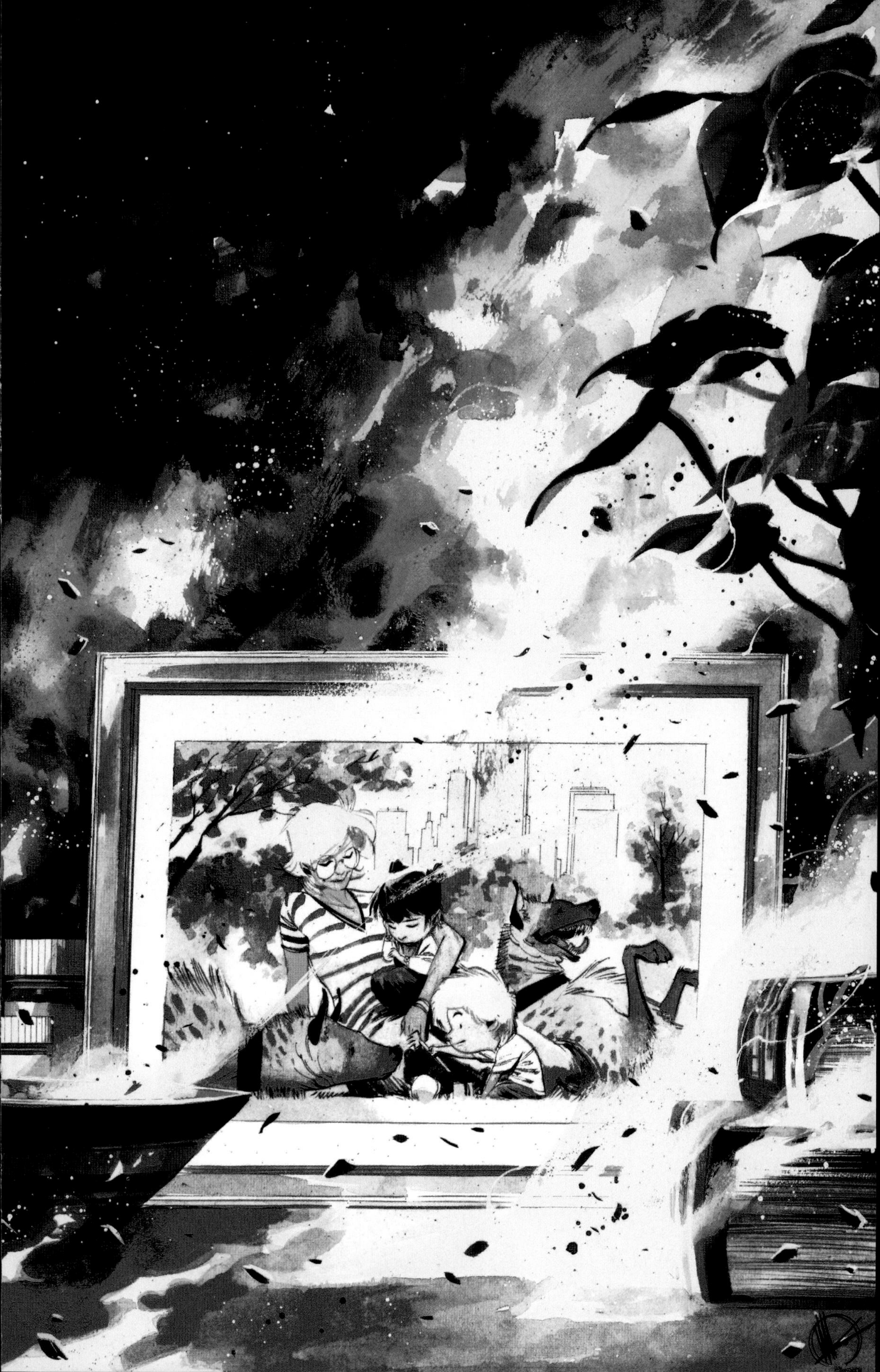

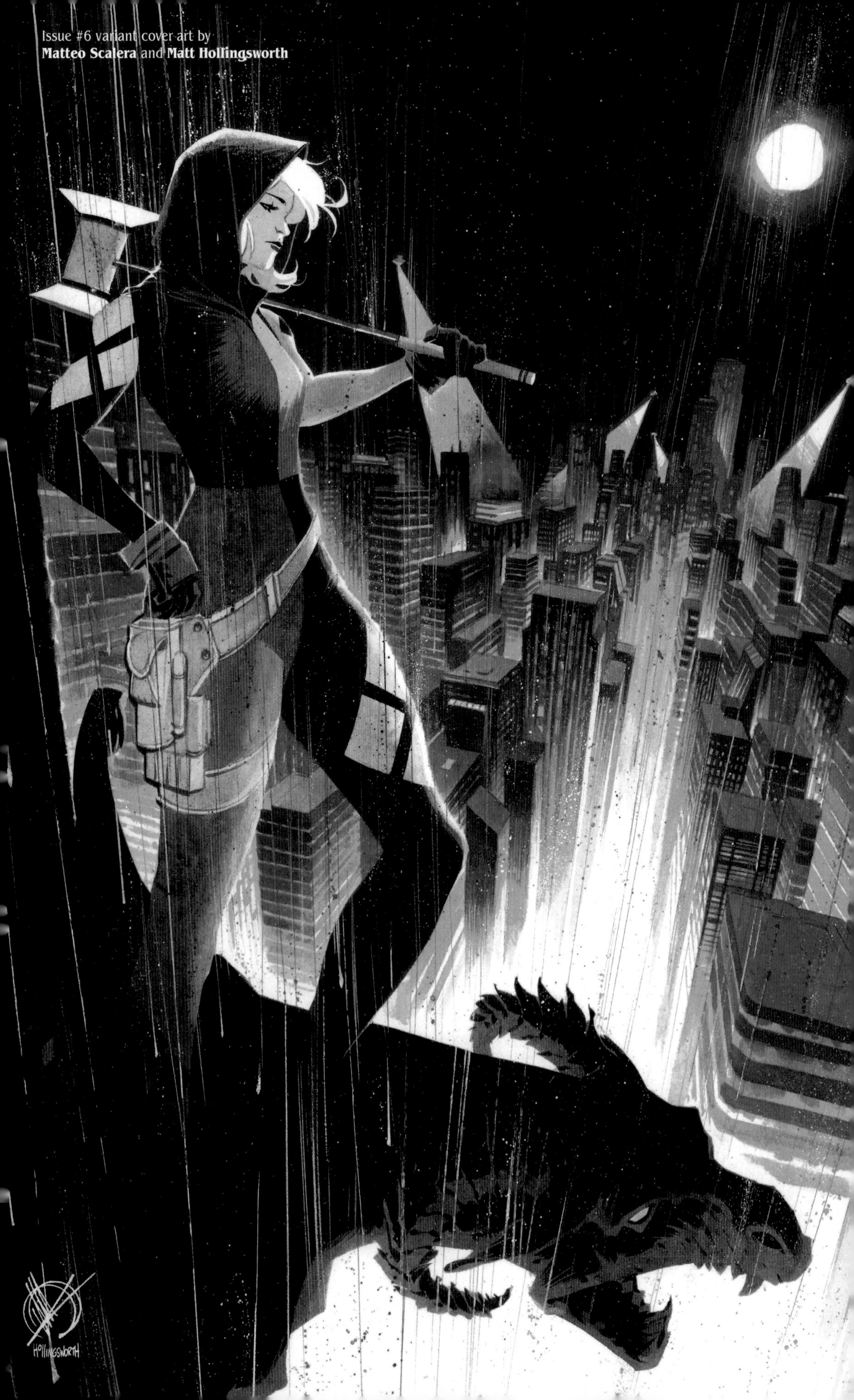
HOLLINGSWORTH

Issue #6 variant cover art by
Matteo Scalera and **Matt Hollingsworth**

Harley Quinn
BLACK and WHITE + RED

DC DIGITAL FIRST

CHAPTER SIX

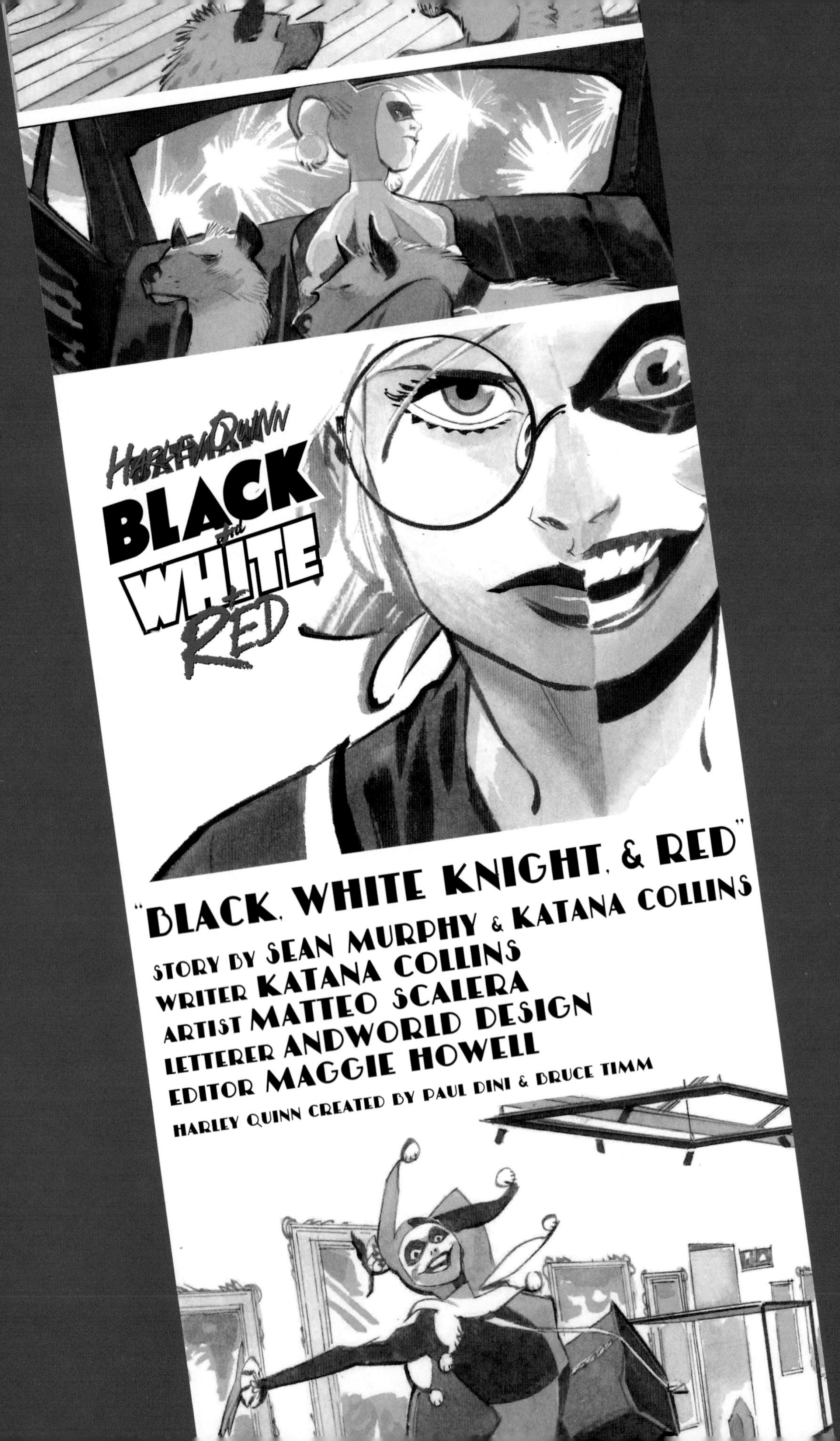
HARLEY QUINN
BLACK and WHITE + RED
"BLACK, WHITE KNIGHT, & RED"
STORY BY SEAN MURPHY & KATANA COLLINS
WRITER KATANA COLLINS
ARTIST MATTEO SCALERA
LETTERER ANDWORLD DESIGN
EDITOR MAGGIE HOWELL
HARLEY QUINN CREATED BY PAUL DINI & BRUCE TIMM

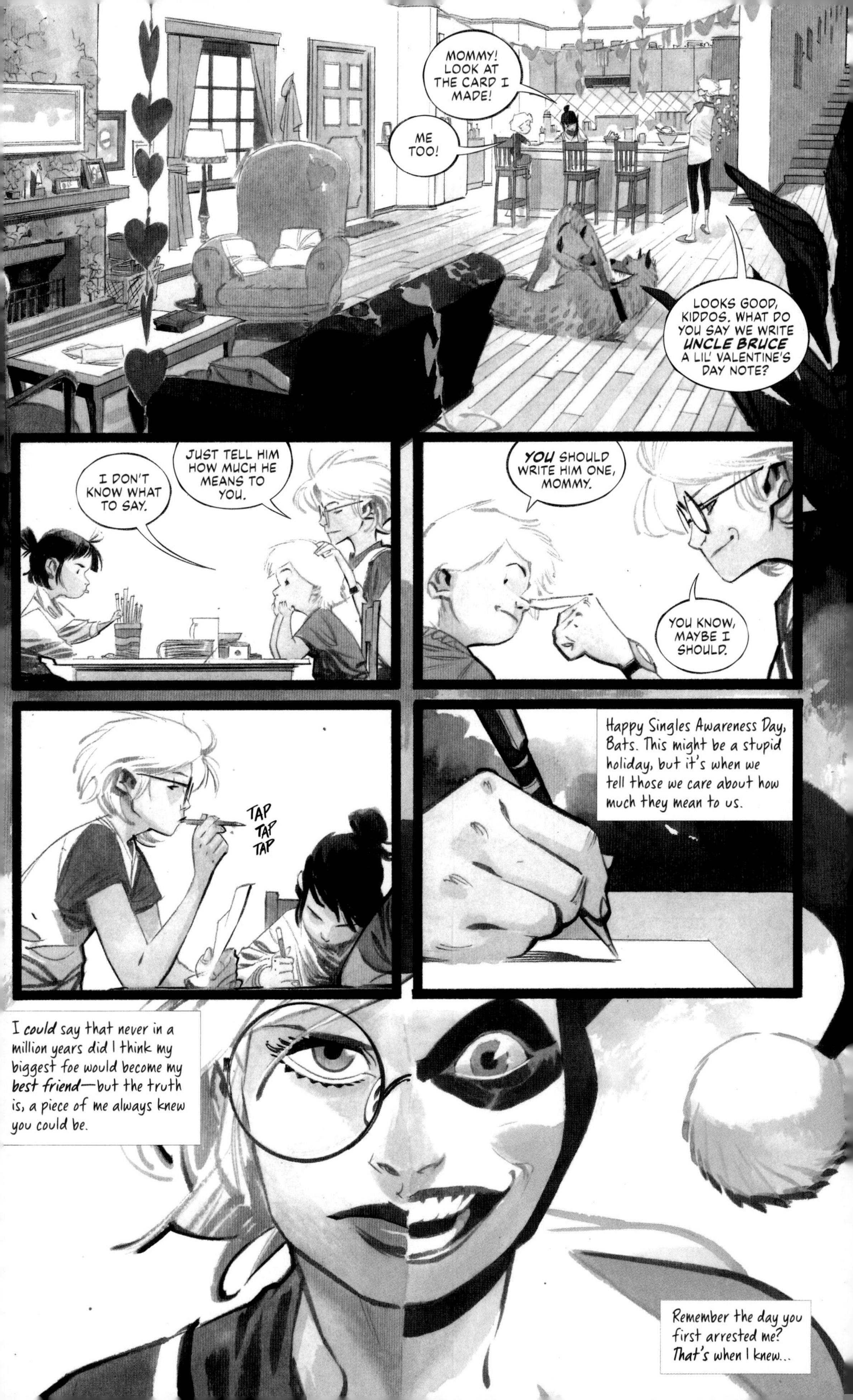

MOMMY! LOOK AT THE CARD I MADE!
ME TOO!
LOOKS GOOD, KIDDOS. WHAT DO YOU SAY WE WRITE UNCLE BRUCE A LIL' VALENTINE'S DAY NOTE?
I DON'T KNOW WHAT TO SAY.
JUST TELL HIM HOW MUCH HE MEANS TO YOU.
YOU SHOULD WRITE HIM ONE, MOMMY.
YOU KNOW, MAYBE I SHOULD.
TAP TAP TAP
Happy Singles Awareness Day, Bats. This might be a stupid holiday, but it's when we tell those we care about how much they mean to us.
I could say that never in a million years did I think my biggest foe would become my best friend—but the truth is, a piece of me always knew you could be.
Remember the day you first arrested me? That's when I knew...

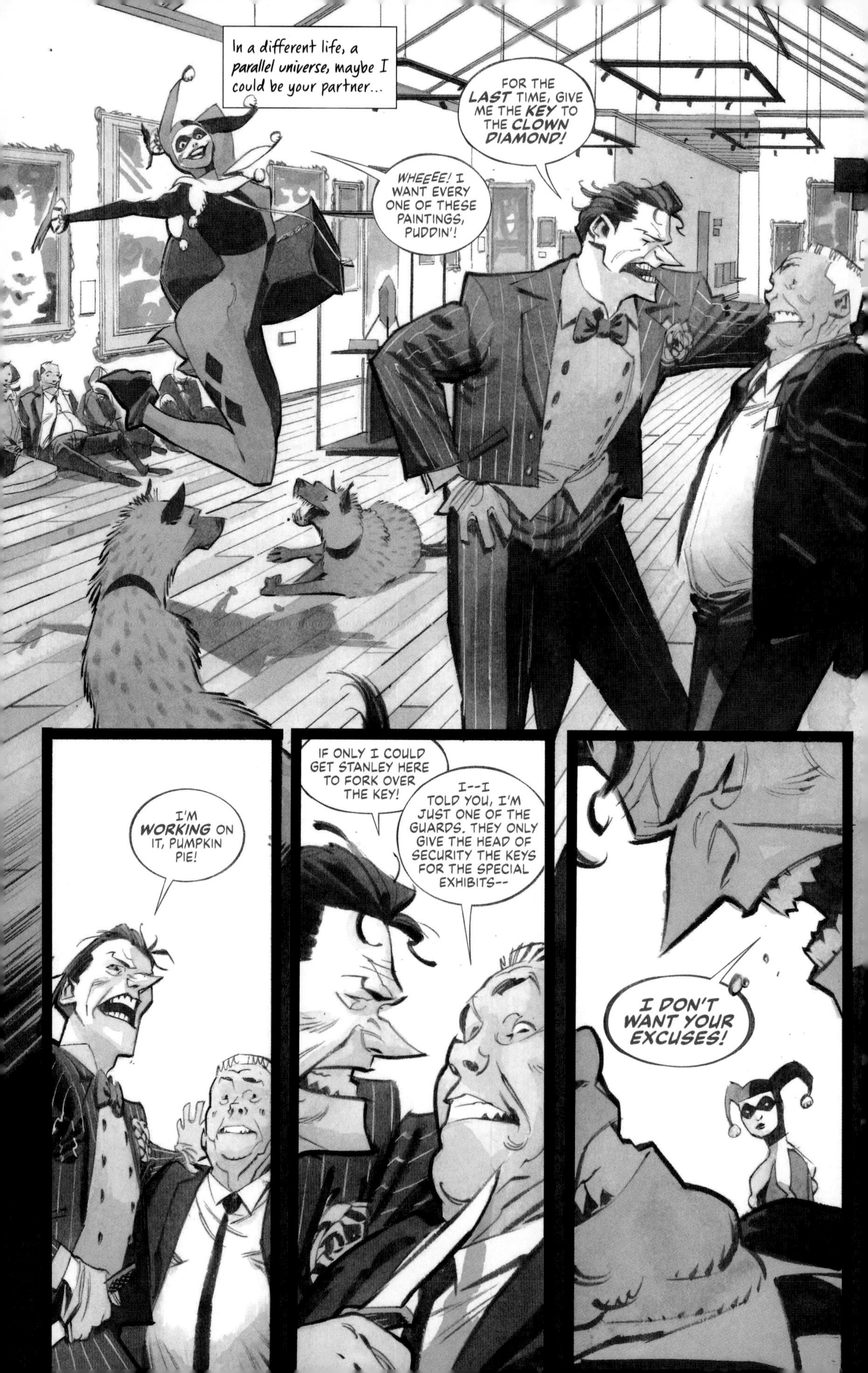
In a different life, a parallel universe, maybe I could be your partner...
FOR THE LAST TIME, GIVE ME THE KEY TO THE CLOWN DIAMOND!
WHEEEE! I WANT EVERY ONE OF THESE PAINTINGS, PUDDIN'!
I'M WORKING ON IT, PUMPKIN PIE!
IF ONLY I COULD GET STANLEY HERE TO FORK OVER THE KEY!
I--I TOLD YOU, I'M JUST ONE OF THE GUARDS. THEY ONLY GIVE THE HEAD OF SECURITY THE KEYS FOR THE SPECIAL EXHIBITS--
I DON'T WANT YOUR EXCUSES!

WHOA, WHOA, MR. J! I THOUGHT WE WERE JUST HERE FOR A LIL' FUN!

YOU DON'T FIND THIS *FUN*, HARLEY?

MAYBE WE SHOULD JUST TAKE SOME OF THE *PAINTINGS.* THEY'RE WORTH A PRETTY PENNY--

WE *CAME* FOR THE INFAMOUS DIAMOND, AND *THAT'S* WHAT WE'RE LEAVING WITH.

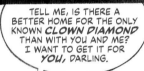

TELL ME, IS THERE A BETTER HOME FOR THE ONLY KNOWN *CLOWN DIAMOND* THAN WITH YOU AND ME? I WANT TO GET IT FOR *YOU*, DARLING.

AWWWW!

WE CAN HAVE IT MADE INTO SOME JEWELRY! A BRACELET, EARRINGS, A RING--

A RING?!

NOT *THAT* KIND OF RING. BUT FIRST...

...WE *NEED THAT KEY!*

AND SOMETIMES, YOU NEED TO SEND A LITTLE *MESSAGE.*

UH, PUDDIN'?

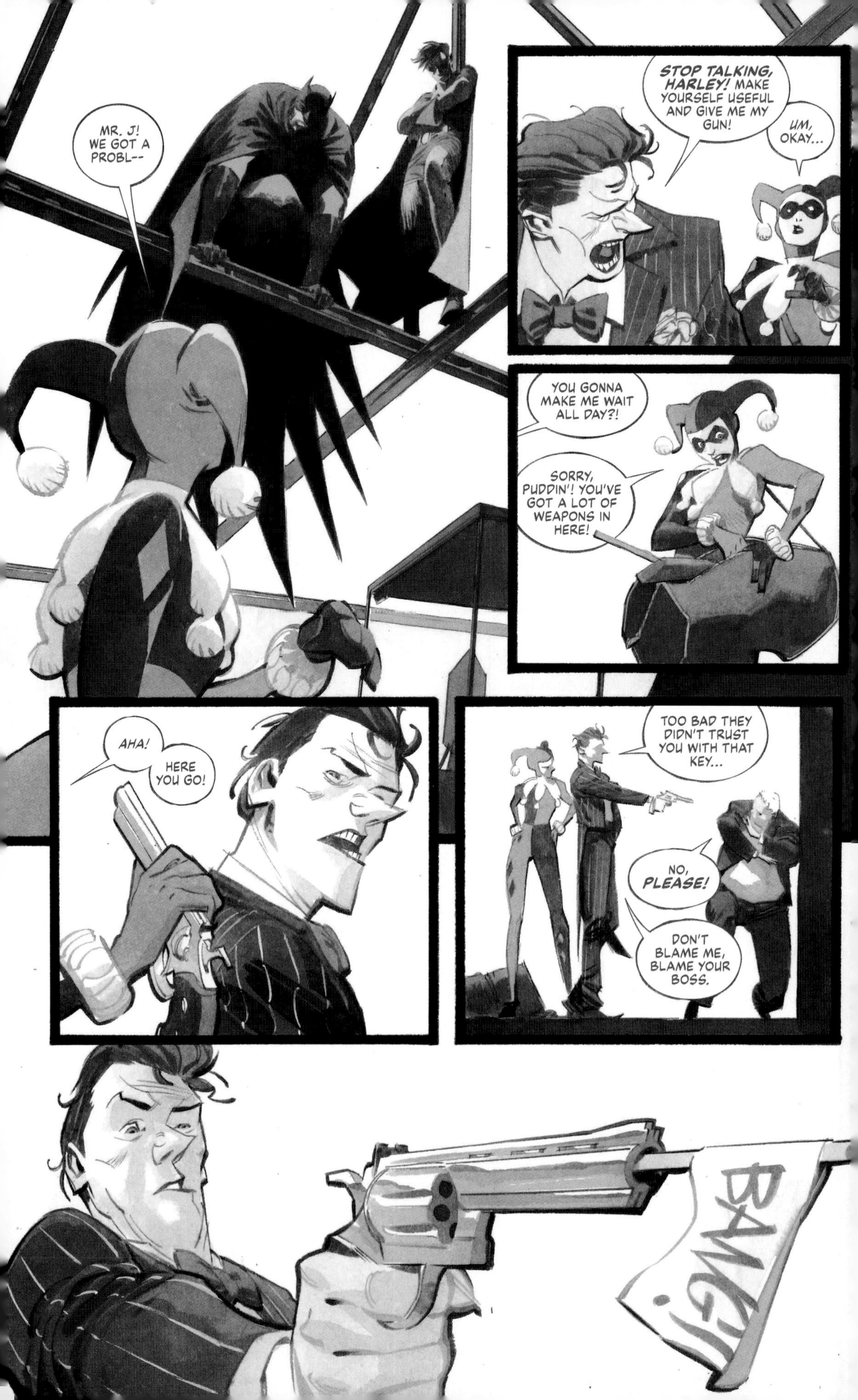
MR. J! WE GOT A PROBL--
STOP TALKING, HARLEY! MAKE YOURSELF USEFUL AND GIVE ME MY GUN!
UM, OKAY...
YOU GONNA MAKE ME WAIT ALL DAY?!
SORRY, PUDDIN'! YOU'VE GOT A LOT OF WEAPONS IN HERE!
AHA!
HERE YOU GO!
TOO BAD THEY DIDN'T TRUST YOU WITH THAT KEY...
NO, PLEASE!
DON'T BLAME ME, BLAME YOUR BOSS.
BANG!

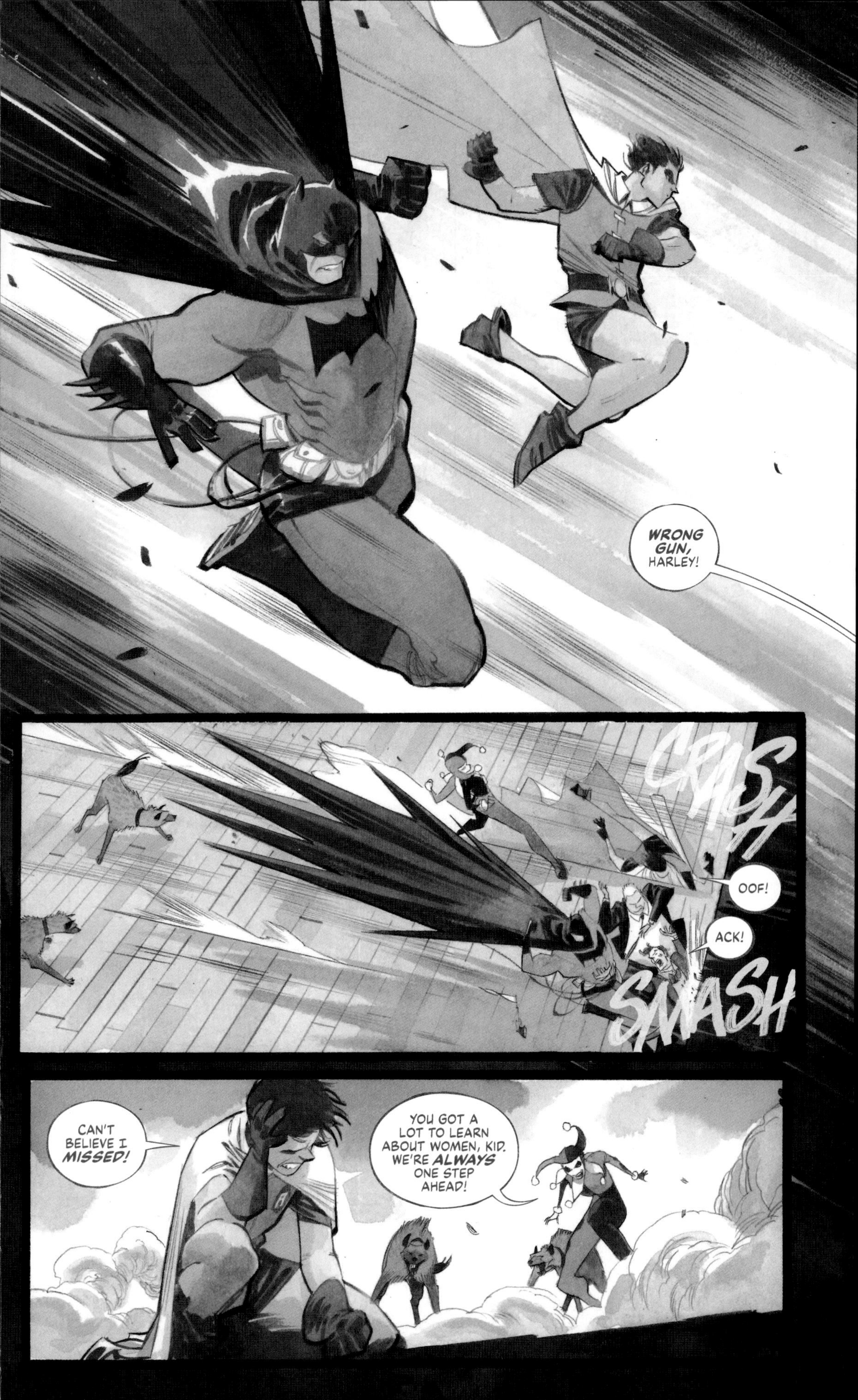

WRONG GUN, HARLEY!
CRASH
OOF!
ACK!
SMASH
CAN'T BELIEVE I MISSED!
YOU GOT A LOT TO LEARN ABOUT WOMEN, KID. WE'RE ALWAYS ONE STEP AHEAD!

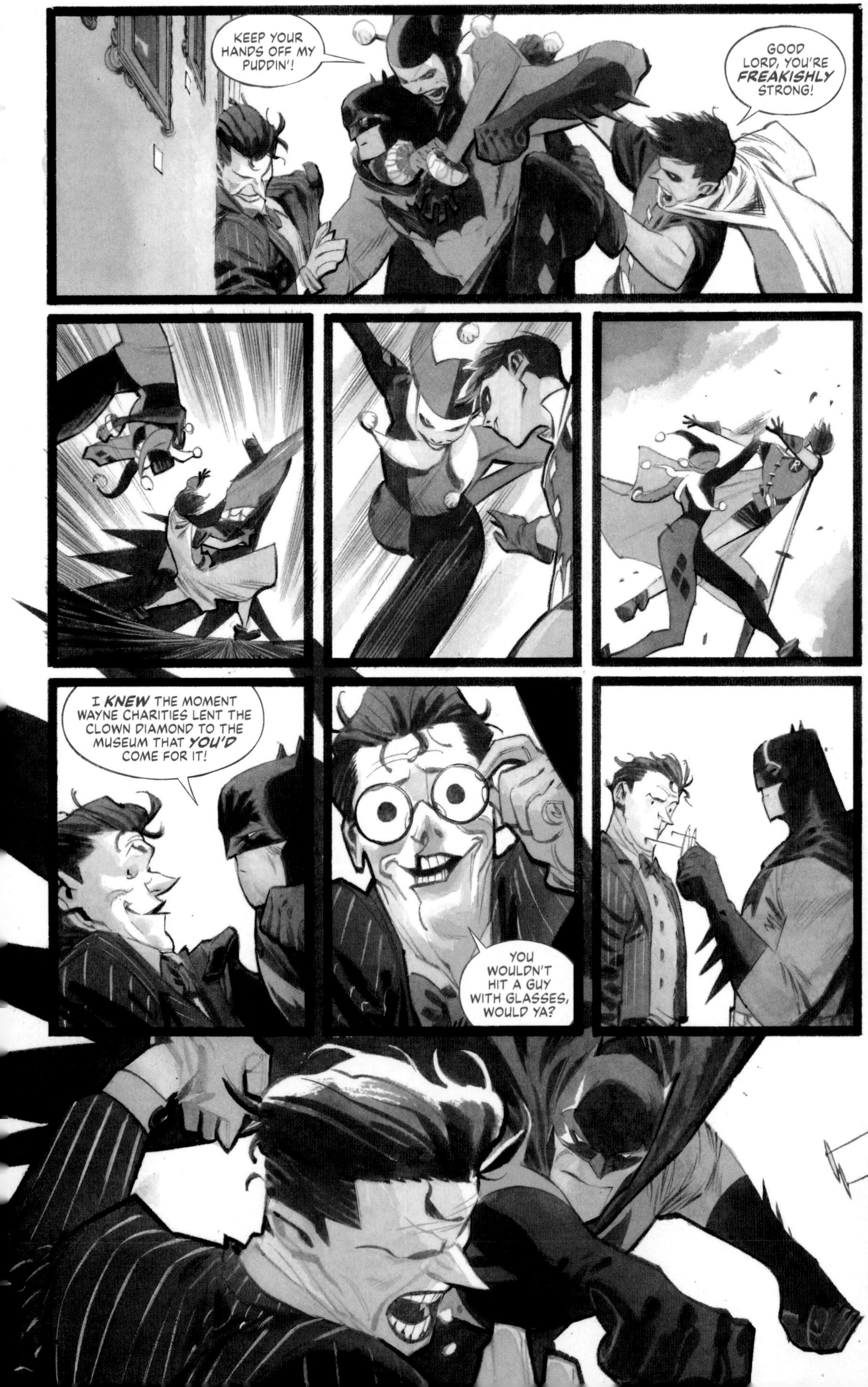
KEEP YOUR HANDS OFF MY PUDDIN'!
GOOD LORD, YOU'RE FREAKISHLY STRONG!
I KNEW THE MOMENT WAYNE CHARITIES LENT THE CLOWN DIAMOND TO THE MUSEUM THAT YOU'D COME FOR IT!
YOU WOULDN'T HIT A GUY WITH GLASSES, WOULD YA?

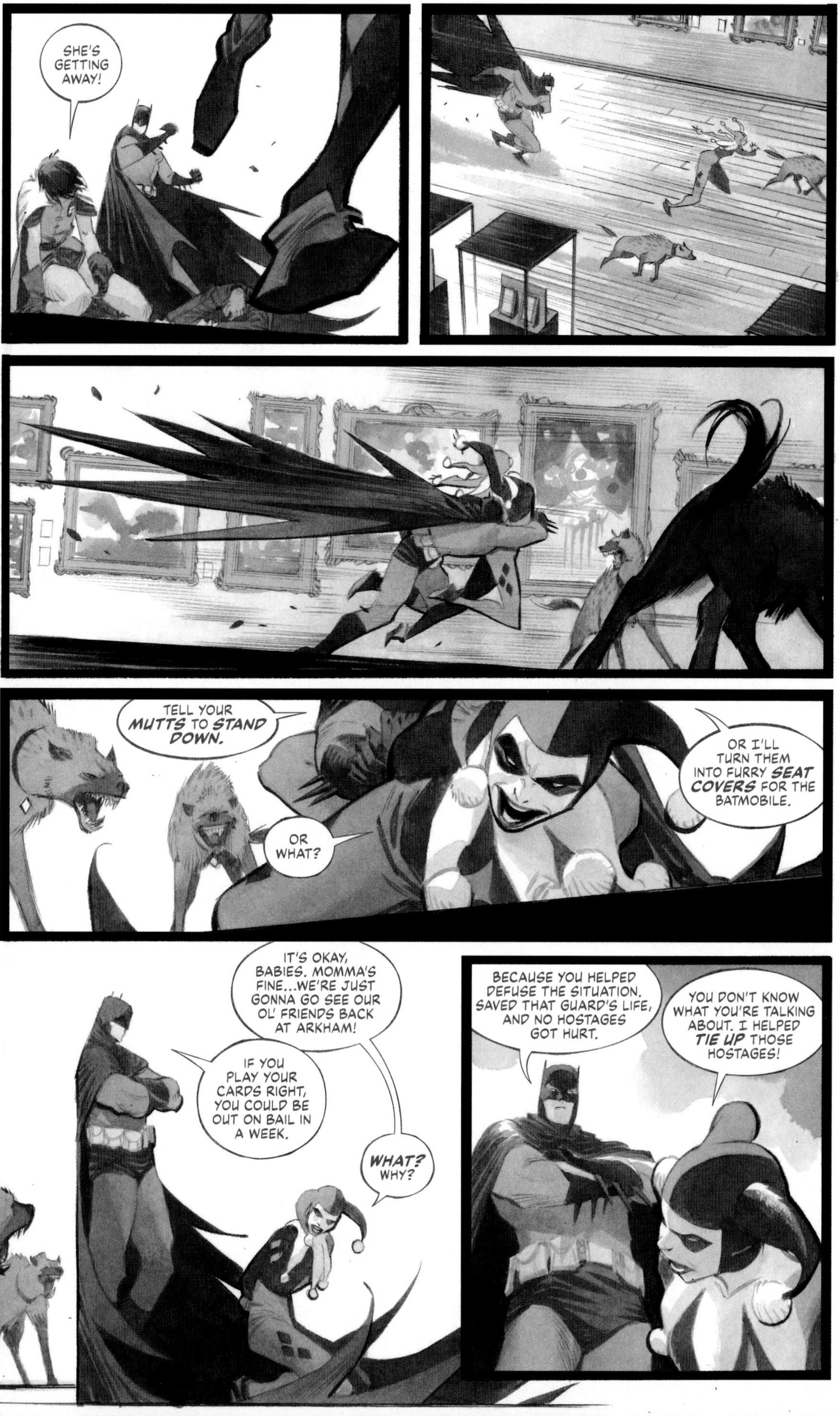
SHE'S GETTING AWAY!
TELL YOUR MUTTS TO STAND DOWN.
OR WHAT?
OR I'LL TURN THEM INTO FURRY SEAT COVERS FOR THE BATMOBILE.
IT'S OKAY, BABIES. MOMMA'S FINE...WE'RE JUST GONNA GO SEE OUR OL' FRIENDS BACK AT ARKHAM!
IF YOU PLAY YOUR CARDS RIGHT, YOU COULD BE OUT ON BAIL IN A WEEK.
WHAT? WHY?
BECAUSE YOU HELPED DEFUSE THE SITUATION. SAVED THAT GUARD'S LIFE, AND NO HOSTAGES GOT HURT.
YOU DON'T KNOW WHAT YOU'RE TALKING ABOUT. I HELPED TIE UP THOSE HOSTAGES!

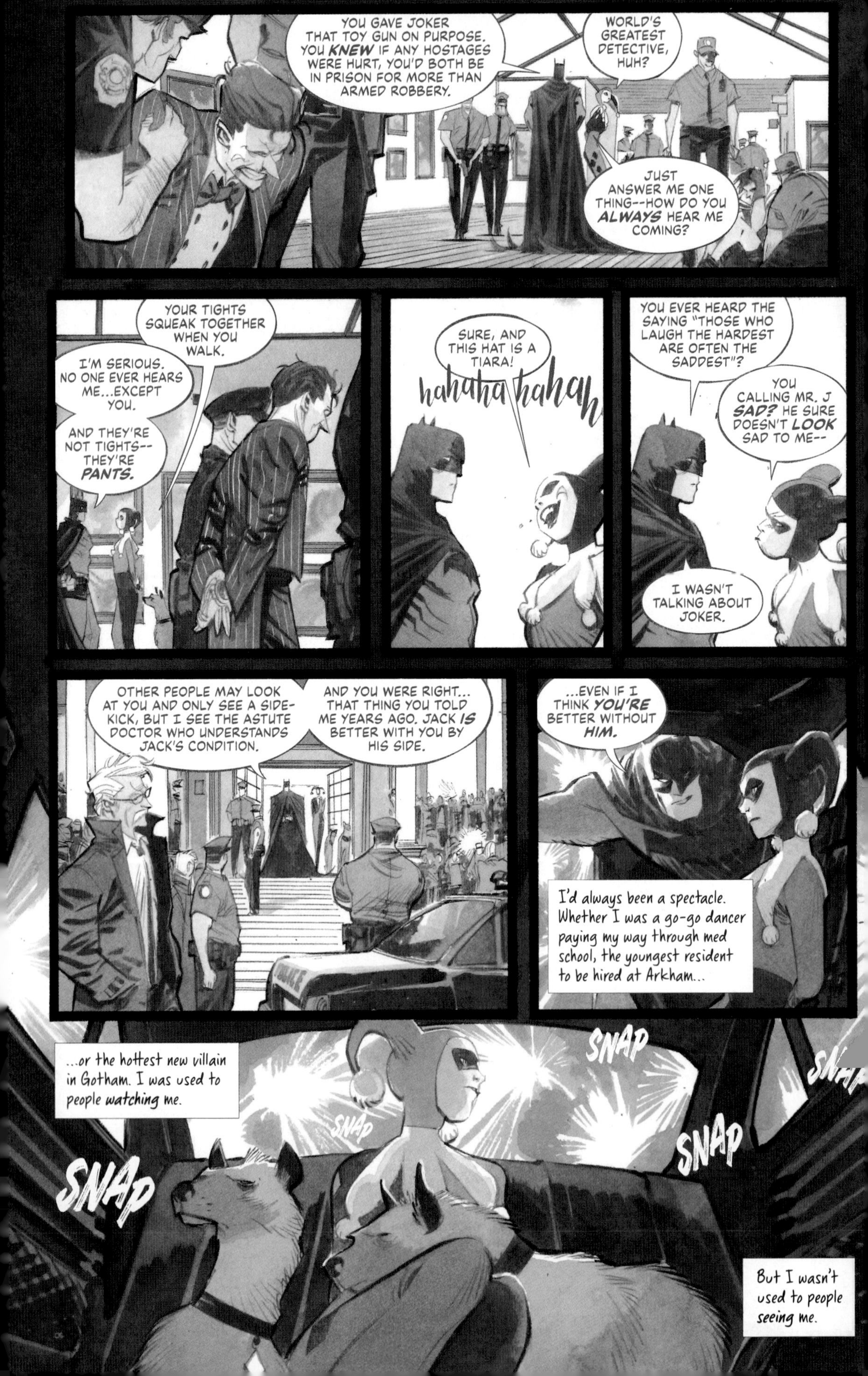
YOU GAVE JOKER THAT TOY GUN ON PURPOSE. YOU KNEW IF ANY HOSTAGES WERE HURT, YOU'D BOTH BE IN PRISON FOR MORE THAN ARMED ROBBERY.
WORLD'S GREATEST DETECTIVE, HUH?
JUST ANSWER ME ONE THING--HOW DO YOU ALWAYS HEAR ME COMING?
YOUR TIGHTS SQUEAK TOGETHER WHEN YOU WALK.
I'M SERIOUS. NO ONE EVER HEARS ME...EXCEPT YOU.
AND THEY'RE NOT TIGHTS--THEY'RE PANTS.
SURE, AND THIS HAT IS A TIARA!
hahaha hahah
YOU EVER HEARD THE SAYING "THOSE WHO LAUGH THE HARDEST ARE OFTEN THE SADDEST"?
YOU CALLING MR. J SAD? HE SURE DOESN'T LOOK SAD TO ME--
I WASN'T TALKING ABOUT JOKER.
OTHER PEOPLE MAY LOOK AT YOU AND ONLY SEE A SIDE-KICK, BUT I SEE THE ASTUTE DOCTOR WHO UNDERSTANDS JACK'S CONDITION.
AND YOU WERE RIGHT... THAT THING YOU TOLD ME YEARS AGO. JACK IS BETTER WITH YOU BY HIS SIDE.
...EVEN IF I THINK YOU'RE BETTER WITHOUT HIM.
I'd always been a spectacle. Whether I was a go-go dancer paying my way through med school, the youngest resident to be hired at Arkham...
...or the hottest new villain in Gotham. I was used to people watching me.
SNAP
SNAP
SNAP
SNAP
SNAP
But I wasn't used to people seeing me.

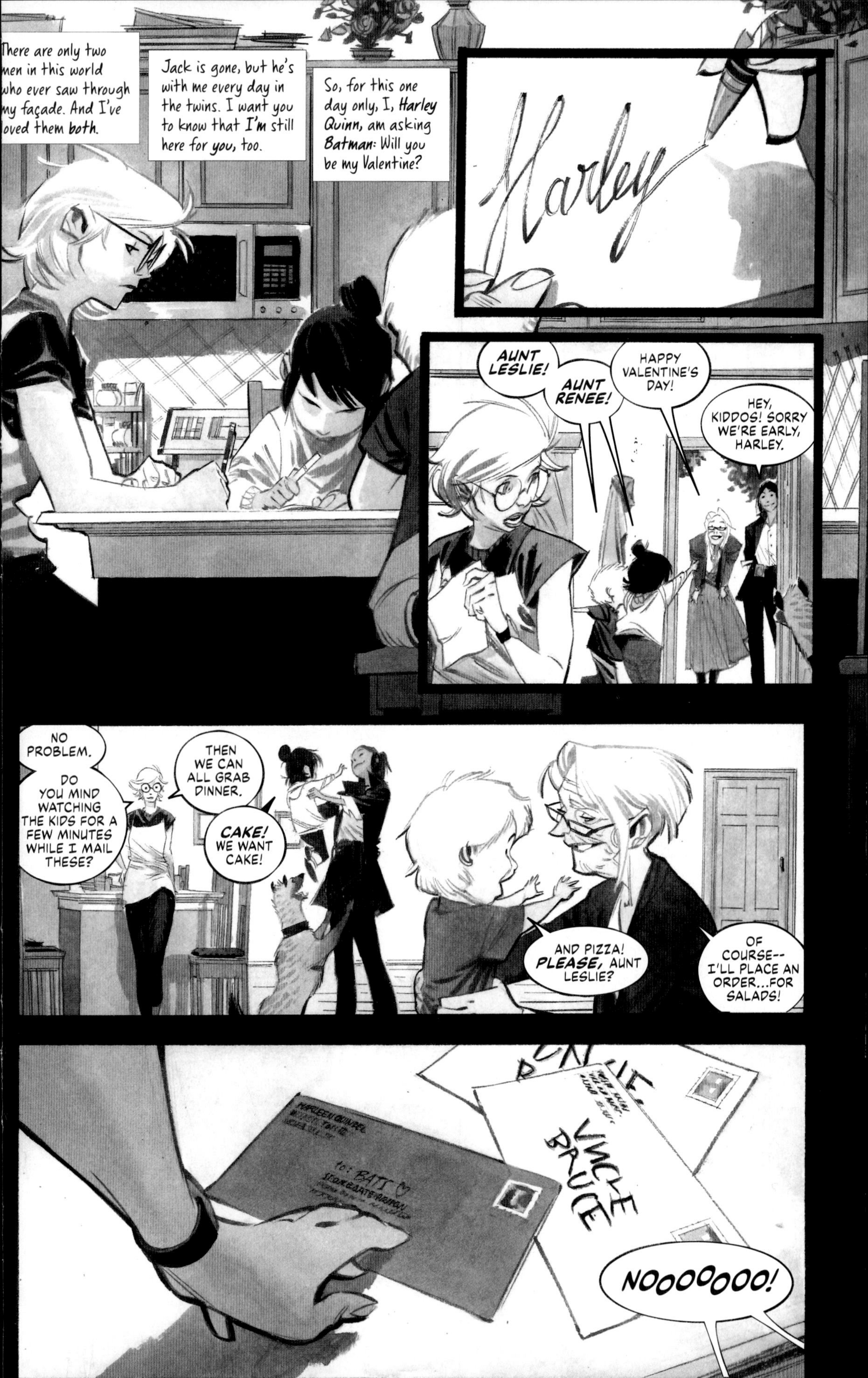
There are only two men in this world who ever saw through my façade. And I've loved them both.
Jack is gone, but he's with me every day in the twins. I want you to know that I'm still here for you, too.
So, for this one day only, I, Harley Quinn, am asking Batman: Will you be my Valentine?
Harley
AUNT LESLIE!
AUNT RENEE!
HAPPY VALENTINE'S DAY!
HEY, KIDDOS! SORRY WE'RE EARLY, HARLEY.
NO PROBLEM.
DO YOU MIND WATCHING THE KIDS FOR A FEW MINUTES WHILE I MAIL THESE?
THEN WE CAN ALL GRAB DINNER.
CAKE! WE WANT CAKE!
AND PIZZA! PLEASE, AUNT LESLIE?
OF COURSE-- I'LL PLACE AN ORDER...FOR SALADS!
to: BATT ♡
UNCLE BRUCE
NOOOOOOO!

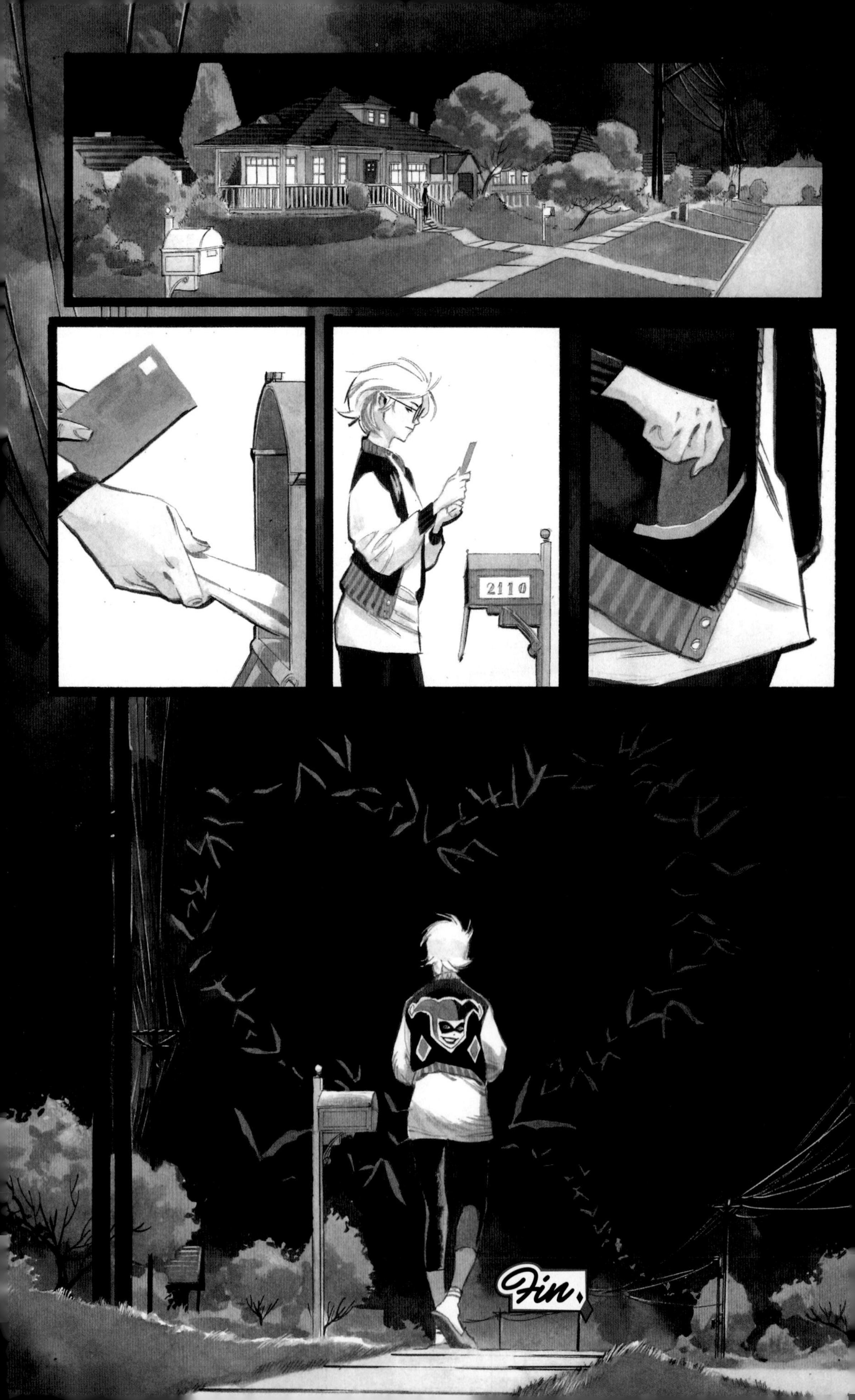
2110
Fin.

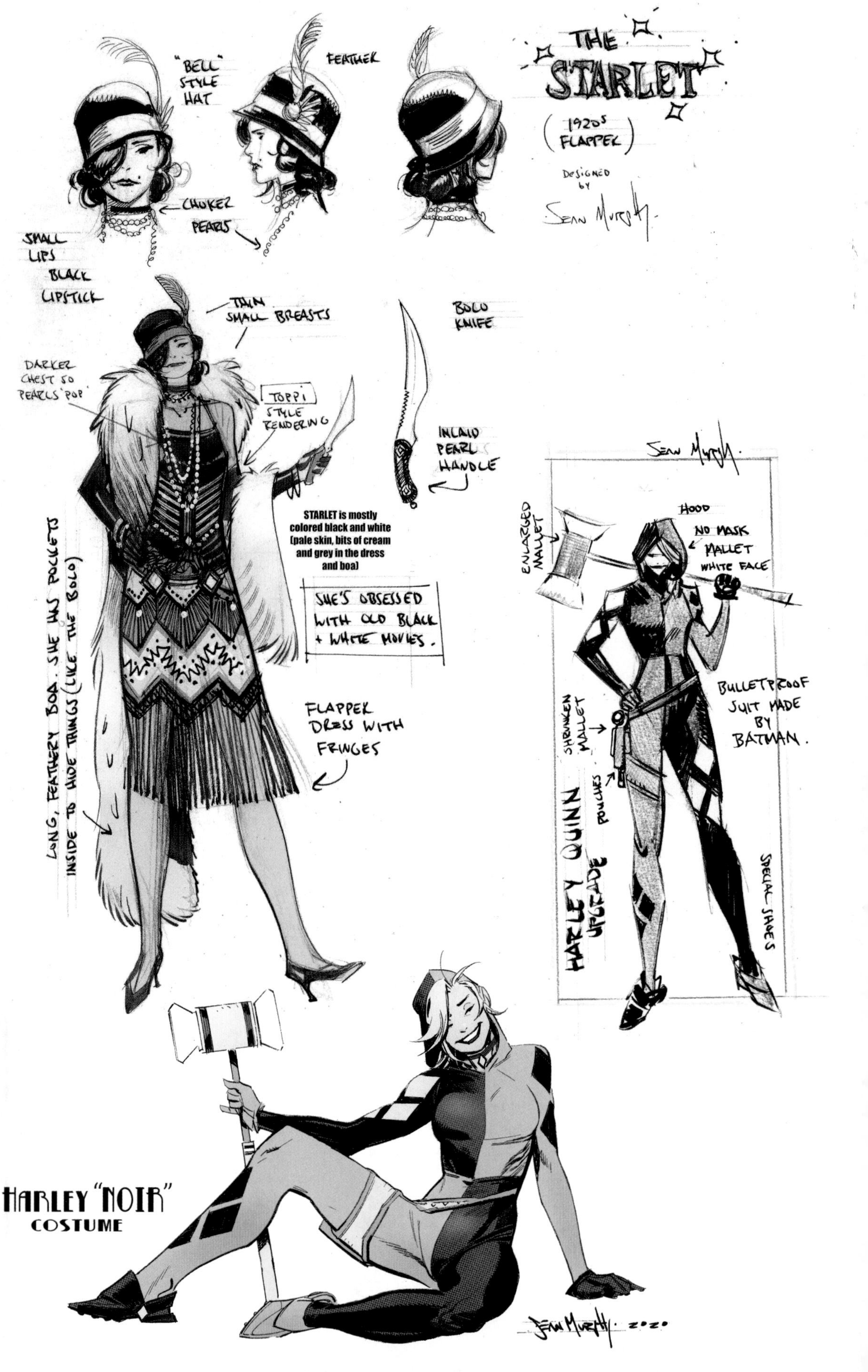

THE STARLET
(1920s FLAPPER)
DESIGNED BY
SEAN MURPHY.
"BELL" STYLE HAT
FEATHER
CHOKER
PEARLS
SMALL LIPS
BLACK LIPSTICK
THIN SMALL BREASTS
BOLO KNIFE
DARKER CHEST SO PEARLS 'POP'
TOPPI STYLE RENDERING
INLAID PEARL HANDLE
STARLET is mostly colored black and white (pale skin, bits of cream and grey in the dress and boa)
SHE'S OBSESSED WITH OLD BLACK + WHITE MOVIES.
FLAPPER DRESS WITH FRINGES
LONG, FEATHERY BOA. SHE HAS POCKETS INSIDE TO HIDE THINGS (LIKE THE BOLO)
SEAN MURPHY.
HOOD
NO MASK
MALLET
WHITE FACE
ENLARGED MALLET
BULLETPROOF SUIT MADE BY BATMAN.
SHRUNKEN MALLET
POUCHES
HARLEY QUINN UPGRADE
SPECIAL SHOES
HARLEY "NOIR" COSTUME
SEAN MURPHY. 2020

Preliminary character designs for
Sofia Valentine, the Producer, and Hector Quimby
by **Matteo Scalera**

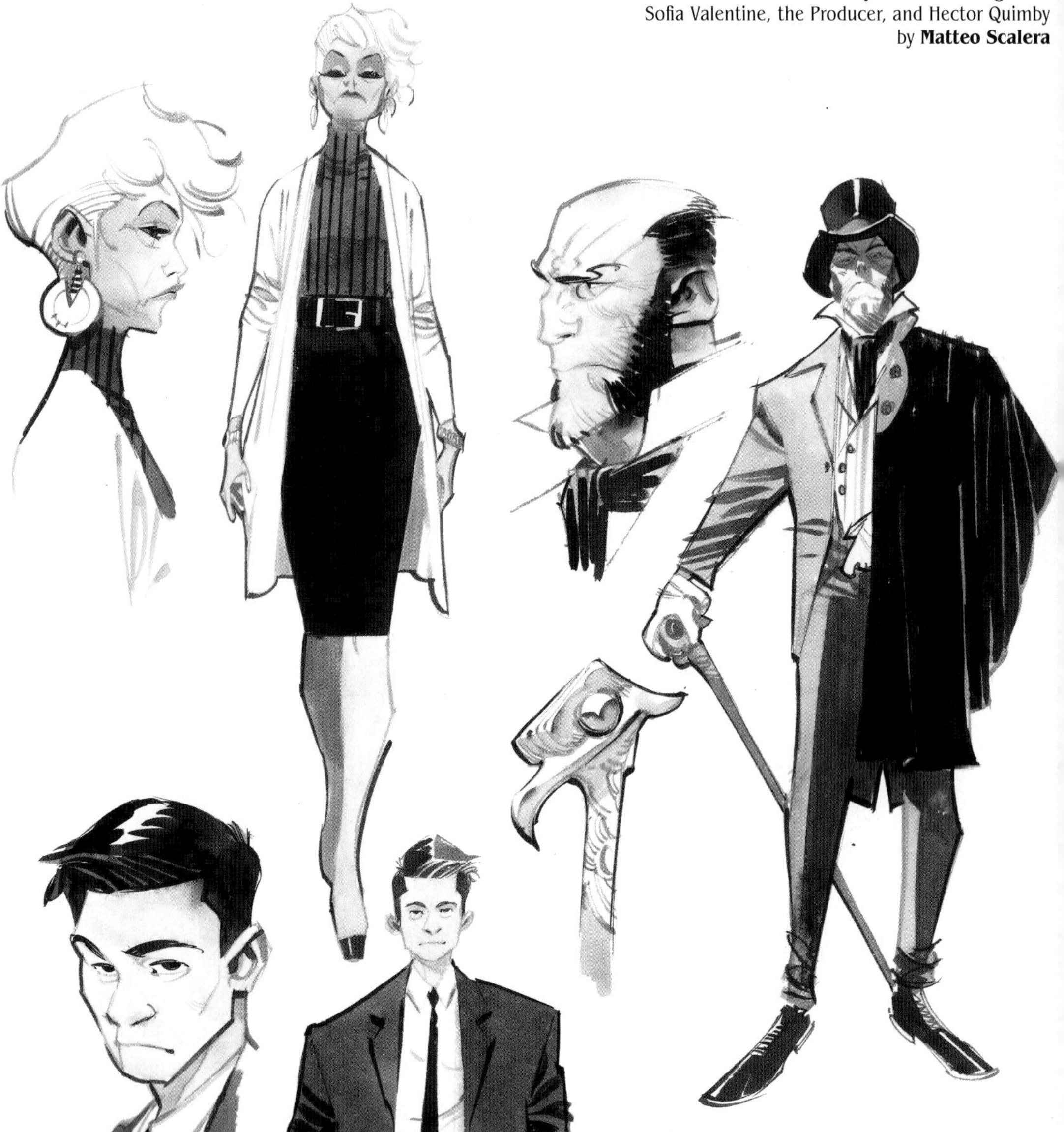

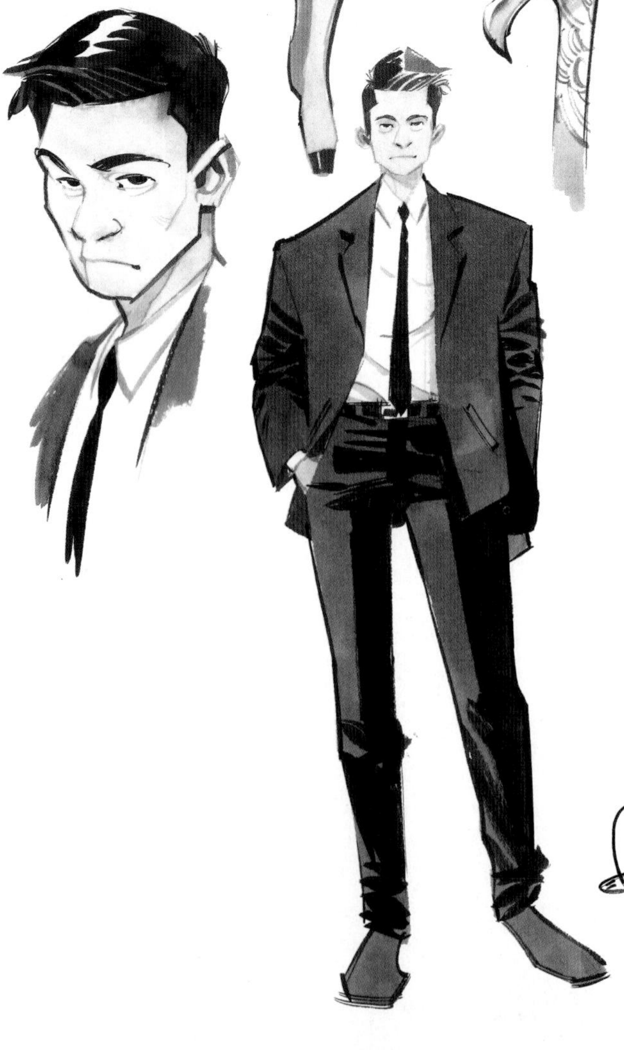

...and a note from **Katana Collins**:

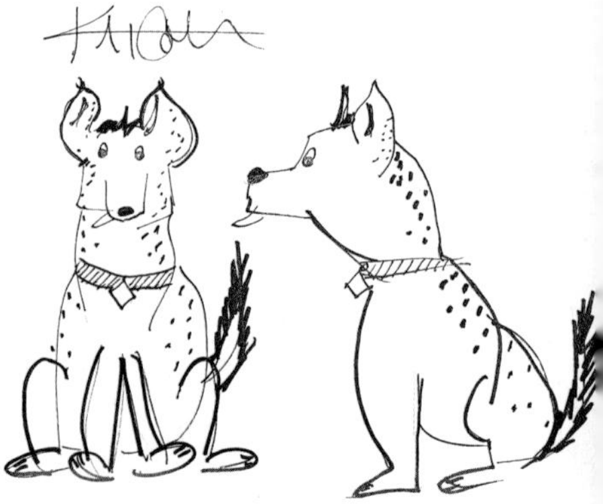

"So...Sean insisted I try to draw a doodle of the hyenas. Here it is—and now you all know why he's the artist and not me."